A Handicapping Guide To Playing The

Bet To Win!!

Bobby Zen

Outskirts Press, Inc.
Denver, Colorado

Bet To Win !!

Outskirts Press, Inc.
http://www.outskirtspress.com

ISBN: 978-1-4327-0895-5

Outskirts Press and the "OP" logo are trademarks belonging to Outskirts Press, Inc.

PRINTED IN THE UNITED STATES OF AMERICA

Acknowledgements

All of the charts, past performances and race results listed in this book are courtesy of TSNHorse.com. Reprinted with permission from the copyright owner. All references to TSN refer to TSNHorse.com. TsnBET™ is a trademark of TSN. SuperTote™ is a trademark of TSN. TSN uses data supplied by Equibase Company. Cover photo courtesy of Dave Wells.

I would like to thank my better half, Lisa, for her support, as I wrote this book while recovering from surgery.

I also want to thank my brother, Rick, for his help and input as I put many years of experience, agony of claims of foul, and photo finishes to print.

I fondly remember my Dad, going to the track 3 hours before post with a pocket full of cigars, to study that form and get ready for the double. We miss you.

Preface

There is plenty of excitement at the track. You may even enjoy the fun at an OTB or casino, which are both rapidly gaining popularity. The crowd can be very raucous at live racing; including drinking, smoking and plenty of conversation about how you should have had that last one, or about the big one you just hit.

You have been studying the program, racing form, tip sheet, or whatever you use to pick your horses all morning. You have it all figured out. But, then.....

You may want to take a look at the horses in the paddock, maybe catch the trainer giving the jockey for the 1 instructions (inside info?). Then you hear the bugler playing the call to post and the jockeys mount up. Watch the horses begin to warm up (doesn't the 4 look ready?). That guy with the cowboy hat you were just talking with said 'the word' was out on the 7.

Your buddy likes the 9 because he won his last out by 5 lengths. Your wife adores the 6 because the silks on the jockey are to die for. The guy next to you says the 3 is a lock because he is the only speed.

You can probably see where this is going; or perhaps you have been there already. Everybody likes at least one horse in the race for their particular reason. Hey, that is some of what makes this a fun game.

Now the horses are loading in the gate. Suddenly, you second guess your bet and run back to the window for some more action. Win, place, show, exacta, trifecta, pick 3, pick 6, superfecta, grand slam.... Man, I gotta have that.

Now they are barreling down the stretch, hooves pounding the dirt, the crowd is yelling, as you are, and it's a photo finish! You have to wait out a gut-wrenching 3 or 4 minutes as they sort out the final order. Finally, the results are posted:

Win 2
Place 4
Show 9

The 7 rounds out the super and you begin to go through your tickets. Didn't you have that trifecta box? Weren't you going to put the 2 in that pick 3? Turns out that you bet $42 in that race and did not cash a ticket.

Guess what? The same thing happens every day at every track all day long. There are a hundred reasons why you don't come out ahead at the track, but there are a few ways to win *consistently* at the track.

There are plenty of services, systems and books that tell you how you are going to figure the entire card in 15 minutes and hit 70% of your bets. This isn't one of them. I will share with you a solid way to identify live horses, and how to make money with those choices.

Table of Contents

Chapter 1: Tools 1

Example A 6

Example 1A 8

Chapter 2: Prime Power 9

Example 1 13

Chapter 3: Conditions 15

Example 2 22

Chapter 4: Speed Ratings 23

Example 3 27

Chapter 5: The Specialists 29

Example 4 33

Chapter 6: Trainers 35

Example 5 39

Chapter 7: Jockeys 41

Chapter 8: Class 47

Example 6 53

Chapter 9: Track Bias 55

Chapter 10: Claim to Fame 61
Example 7 65
Chapter 11: How About Some Time Off? 67
Chapter 12: Money Management 101 73
Example B 77
Chapter 13: Go Figure! 79
Chapter 14: Odds And Ends 85
Order Form 89
Appendix 91

Chapter 1
Tools

There is good news for you right out of the box. The tools I am talking about are not hammers, screwdrivers and wrenches. These tools are what we are going to use to find those live horses.

There are many good sources available for past performances, statistics, breeding and other types of information. The Daily Racing Form (drf.com) is available online and at most betting facilities and some newsstands. The Thoroughbred Sports Network (tsnhorse.com) is a very good source online. Equibase Company (equibase.com) is also a good source online.

I must mention the NTRA and their website NTRA.com, which is very informative about the industry and latest news. It is user-friendly and worth a look every day. There is much to be found there, including information about most tracks in the country.

You are faced with the first of many decisions as we journey through the land of picking winners at the track. If you are familiar with the various choices, you may have a favorite information source and that should be fine. You just need to be able to get the information that we are going to cover in this book. You may buy the Daily Racing Form at the track, a tried and true for many years. Several tracks publish their program with past performances in them (I don't care for those as much because most of the statistics we want are not in them). I use tsnhorse.com for several reasons.

- They have several choices on past performances
- In-depth daily newsletter
- Selection sheets
- Statistic sheets
- Early programs
- Full results
- Charts
- Several other handy services

Tsnhorse also offers online wagering through TsnBET.com ™. This service is not available in all states; you need to check availability in your area. There is a great tracking system for your bets here. We will talk about this more, but you need to track your results, so you know what is working and what is not.

I have developed a worksheet that I use for compiling information and statistics on a race card for the day. It is called the Contender Checklist (example 1A). There is no magic or anything real special about it; it's just a good tool for getting the information down on our contenders.

I will clarify now that this book is a handicapping method, and not a system. A system usually requires every piece of information to be handled exactly the same way each time. We will talk about each step of the handicapping process, and the various ways to handle each one.

Most of the information that I gather as I am preparing for race day, goes onto this sheet. I have devised numerous abbreviations for statistics, trends and other information that we use on our search for winners. Please refer to examples as we work our way through the information. I probably get a bit esoteric about how I track the information, but it is a good way to reach conclusions as I handicap.

You will see a Handicapping Checklist that contains the format for sorting out contenders from the rest of the field (too corny to call them pretenders). See example A at the end of this chapter.

So, we have gathered our tools for handicapping a race card. We will spend a section discussing how you decide what track (or tracks) you will play today.
The tools are:

- Past performances
- Handicapping Checklist
- Contender Checklist
- Red and black pens
- Calculator

It is time for our first discussion on statistics. I am a 'numbers' guy. "What does that mean?" – you might ask. I will explain to you as we also delve into the subject of whether handicapping the horses is an art or a science.

Being a numbers guy means I want as much statistical information as I can get. In the horse racing business, that means percentages of winners, money won, speed ratings, class ratings, etc., from various angles (and there are a lot of angles). Such as:

- Trainer win %
- Trainer with sprint to route win %
- Trainer with turf to dirt win %
- Trainer with certain jockey %
- Jockey with early speed horse %
- Jockey with sprint horse %

There are dozens of these bits of information. This takes us back to where you get your information and you need this type of statistics. They will be used on the Contender Checklist.

There are many other statistics that come into play, also. These include the horses win percentage, in-the-money percentage, win percent at this track, win percent at this distance, average money won per start; this list goes on.

OK, if you are not a 'numbers' guy (or gal, to be politically correct), then you are getting pretty concerned right now about all these statistics, right?

Not to worry, that's why you have me (my book, that is).

So, let's get into the overview on how we use the tools, the statistics will take care of themselves. You just have to record the notes and numbers in black or red. The one statistic I want you to remember and understand is this:

The average field size is 9 horses. So, if all things were equal, each horse has an 11% chance of winning (1 chance out of 9). When we are recording notes and numbers on the Contender Checklist, we use a black pen for statistics 11% or better. We use a red pen for statistics 10% or worse. I'm a simple guy with a simple system; black marks are good and red marks are bad. The same goes for any notes you make as you go, good comments in black and bad comments in red.

Now, let's talk about whether handicapping is a science or an art. How you think about this affects how you handicap (if you don't really care, please go on to the next chapter).

You guys (gals) that are in a hurry, are still going to need to cover everything else in the book to use this format for picking winners.

The science part is gathering and recording all the various pieces of information. The tools available today make tons of info easier to get than it used to be. Yes, I go back to the old days of waiting at the newsstand to get the form for today's races. I go back even farther to my Dad taking me to the track and learning to read the form with him.

If he could hit the Double, he was in heaven. I envision him hitting the double every day now, may he rest in peace.

Therefore, the science is doing your homework; finding out all you can find out about the horse, trainer, jockey, owner, track, etc.

The art part of this equation is understanding when the 'class' of the race is more important than the jockey. Or, the early speed is more important than post position. Or, the recent claim is more important than the last place finish last out. Or, the switch to a hot jockey is more important than the horse never winning at this distance.

The art part is harder to apply because there are no solid substitutes for experience. Trust me in saying that there is no 'one size fits all', there is no 'magic bullet', there is no 'lock', or any other promise or guarantee in this game.

Stay humble. Watch, listen and learn.

Example A

Handicapping Checklist

(Use black pen and red pen – red for 'bad')

1. PRIME POWER –
   - TSN rank (3=39%, 6=46%, 10=55%) [Top 4]
2. RUN STYLE –
   - E, EP, P, S with early speed number [E5]
3. CONDITIONS –
   - List race conditions, look for the horse *most* qualified [Q]
4. LAST 3 SPEED RATINGS –
   - Pattern up or down? [↑ ↓]
5. LAST 3 –
   - Double or triple advantage? [DA – TA]
6. RACING SPEED AVERAGE –
   - 5 Point advantage [RSA]
7. TRACK SPECIALIST –
   - Won here (- 0-6), (1-10), (11% up) [-T] [T] [T]
8. DISTANCE SPECIALIST –
   - (-0-6), (1-10), (11% up) [-D] [D] [D]
9. TRAINER ANGLE –
   - List the 'most applicable' angle [-3%] [25%]
10. JOCKEY ABILITY –
    - Look for the 'most applicable' style [-J] [J]

USE Top 10 Qualifier list for contenders

11. CLASS RANK –
    - Lowest level, past winning level, avg $ won, TSN Class [$]
12. TRACK BIAS –
    - Past week, today's notes [speed/closers/post]

13. POST POSITION –
    - Compare to run style, distance, and/or last few races [pp]
14. WON LAST –
    - Or number of wins in a row [w]
15. CLAIM –
    - Last out or recent or multiple [C]
16. HEAD TO HEAD –
    - Faced other runners/advantage [HH]
17. TIME OFF -
    - Layoff, time between races, etc [-265]
18. WORKOUTS –
    - List as needed (Layoff, Maidens, etc) [w *]
19. WIN PERCENT –
    - List as needed (Divide wins by starts) [25%]
20. TSN Top 5 Profit Line Rank –
    - From SuperTote™ [1,2,3]

'Run' the race beforehand; who has advantages?
What should happen?

Make notes during or after; what DID happen.

Handicap *Yourself*. What is working, what tracks do you win at, what type races work better, what surface. Play your strengths. Track your performance and document monthly.

Work hard. Stay focused. Apply discipline.

It's one long game, it's a marathon – not a sprint.

Have a positive, winning attitude. You are in it to ***win***.

Contender Checklist

Results	Race#	Conditions	Dis	Prime 1	Prime 2	Prime 3	Prime 4
	1						
	2						
	3						
	4						
	5						
	6						
	7						
	8						
	9						
	10						
	11						
	12						
	13						
	14						
Bankroll							
Action Bets						Track Bias	
Win/place							

Chapter 2
Prime Power

This is as close as I get to endorsing a supplier of information. I suggested several earlier, and I will tell you that I use TSN for several reasons. It is very convenient being on-line; I look at early programs for all tracks running every day. I make a decision on each race card as to who has the most races I like for the day. One of the things that we need to do, is know what tracks, races, trainers, etc. are the ones we win with. So, I look for the track that has the most races that I think I can hit, and that is my choice to handicap for the day.

Over the years, I have used several of TSN's options. I used the Key-Stats for a long time, and the Selection Sheet is a handy one-pager that I have used. Most of the time I use the Ultimate Past Performance with comments. It offers the past performances with several extras included. For the balance of this book, I will be referring to information from this source.

My Contender Checklist is designed to list the top 4 Prime Power horses in ranking order. This is the beginning of the contender process and is typically what I build my information around. I will run the disclaimer now that I do not always play their top choice, but this is a starting point. You may have a different 'first cut' look at the field. Some guys use class rankings first, some use speed ratings first, some use jockeys first.

The checklist will work for you however you want to apply your top 4 contenders.

Here is the reason I build around the Prime Power rankings. The research has been done on thousands of races, and the statistics are very strong. Here are the rankings:

	Wins
Top horse	31%
3 points +	39%
6 points +	46%
10 points +	55%

When my Dad was teaching me how to read the form, we had nothing like that! If we did, I would have said, 'Hey Dad, why don't we just look for *those* horses?' He would be smoking and chewing that cigar, and then heading for that old Daily Double window.

By now you know what I think about statistics – 'Numbers don't lie!'

So, we list the top 4 Prime Power ranks on the Contender Checklist in the respective boxes. As mentioned, we list the advantage if there is one. An example would be the top ranked horse has a 7 point advantage; we would list the 46% in black next to his number. (See example 1)

Let's go on to the next step. We now list the run-styles with early speed numbers. There are four run-styles and they are:

E for early speed

E/P for on or near the early lead
P for off the pace
S for deep closers

There is possibly a number listed after the run-style; this represents early speed points. This is a basic number system with the higher the better (basically representing gate speed). So, an E7 horse is going to get out of the gate and be on the lead faster than anyone with a lower rank, providing no bad racing luck happens (like hit the gate or something). This information comes into play as we try to decide how the race is going to be run. This is one of our instructions near the bottom of our Handicapping Checklist.

List the run-styles and early speed numbers next to the horse number for your top 4 choices.

Let's discuss these run-styles and some of the things we want to look for. There can be dozens of scenarios. One might be that there is only one early speed horse; if you find no reason to think another will beat him, he is probably a good bet (odds permitting).

An opposite to that is 7 speed horses and one good deep closer. Now the closer may have the best chance.

The reality of it is these scenarios are not too common, when they are, they are sometimes bet down so low, they become a risky bet (more on this in 'Betting is a Business').

As you are listing run-styles, you should begin to get a feel for how the race should run. Is there a lot of early speed horses? Are there a lot of deep closers? Does a certain run-style look like it will have an advantage? Maybe there are 12 horses in the race, and you like the 12, but it's a 5 furlong race with a short run to the turn; can he make the lead? These are the things you look for when listing the run-styles. (See example 1)

After we gather all our information on the Contender Checklist, we are going to 'run' the race beforehand, to try and figure where the advantages are.

It's time to note that I run through all 20 points on the Handicapping Checklist one race at a time. In other words, I don't take one step at a time going through the card, I walk all the way through each race before doing the next. With experience, it should take 1 to 2 hours to handicap an entire card. After each race runs, I review what happened to see if I was on track, and make notes accordingly.

OK, we have our top 4 contenders listed with run-styles and early speed points; let's take a look at the conditions.

Example 1: Contender Checklist

Results	Race#	River/Thistle Conditions	Dis	5/11/2007 Prime 1		Example 1 Prime 2	Contender Checklist Prime 3	Prime 4
	1			4 E5		5 P2	6 E6	7 E5
	2			2 EP2	39%	5 P4	1 EP3	4 EP2
	3			6 E8	39%	2 S2	3 P2	7 EP1
	4			8 E8		2 P3	5 EP3	7 EP1
	5			7 E6	39%	3 EP3	1 E5	8 S2
	6			6 EP6	39%	2 EP8	1 EP5	7 P4
	7			4 EP7		8 EP4	6 EP5	3 EP3
	8			10 EP6		3 P2	2 EP5	6 EP6
	9			7 E5		3 P2	6 EP5	5 P1
	10			1 EP4		2 S3	7 EP5	6 E5
	11			6 EP6		7 EP7	1 S	2 S
	12			3 EP7	46%	2 EP7	7 EP6	8 EP4
	13			8 E6		4 P3	3 E1	1A S
	14			10 E8	46%	1 S2	9 P2	4 EP5
Bankroll								
Action							Bias	
Win/place								

Chapter 3
Conditions

The next thing to look at as we continue to handicap this race card, are the race conditions. This is a very important part of the process, and lots of folks skip it completely. We want to get a leg up on them right now. The conditions are the rules that govern whether a horse is allowed to run in a particular race.

There are basic conditions that are pretty straight-forward. They are maidens, claiming, allowance and stakes races. But, like most things in this game, it's not that simple. Let's break them down and get a better understanding.

Maiden races are for horses that have not won a race in their life. They can be maiden claiming or maiden special weight. Claimers are considered next, and special weights are a type of allowance race.

Claiming races mean that the horse can be claimed from the owner at the stated price. Claiming price $10,000 means a licensed trainer and/or owner can put in a claim before the race runs, and he is the new owner after the race is over and he pays the $10,000. He does not collect the purse, if any, the prior owner gets that.

Trainers typically move their horses up and down in the claiming ranks according to how they are performing. A sharp performing horse might move up through the ranks from a $5000 tag to a $6250 tag to a $10,000 tag. Here is where the 'art' part of handicapping comes into play. Can the horse handle the move up the ladder? It is typically tougher competition the further up the ladder you go. Does the trainer have a plan in mind? Is he looking for a soft spot? Is he looking to get rid of the horse by dropping the claiming price?

The science part is looking at the statistics. Using an example from TSN's Unlimited Past Performances; looking at horse #7, we might see 'down 2 classes' 27%, meaning the trainer wins with this move 27% of the time. We mark 27% in black on our Contender Checklist in #7 box. This is how we compile useful statistics (more on how we fill out the Contender Checklist shortly). Looking at #5, we might see '31-90 days away' 2%, meaning the trainer wins 2% of the time with horses that have not raced in 31-90 days. This is bad. We mark 2% in red on our Contender Checklist in #5 box.

Along with the various claiming prices, there are other conditions. We might see NW2L, which means non-winners of 2 races in their life. A good example of a horse well qualified for this condition might have broke his maiden (won his first ever) in his last race, while his speed ratings have been going up. This would mean he's been running faster each race, and he learned how to win last time. We would also look for him to only have a few lifetime races. An example of a horse NOT well qualified for this condition might be 1 for 31 races lifetime, and ran last in his last 3 races.

Other conditions are NW3L, NW4L and various times since a win. Such as non-winners of a race in 6 months, non-winners of 2 in 9 months, etc. These possibilities go on and on.

There are maiden claiming races which are non-winners racing for a claiming price. There are MSW (maiden special weight), which are maidens that cannot be claimed (similar to allowance races), which we will talk about next.

Allowance races are races where the horse cannot be claimed, and the allowances are in weight concessions made for various conditions of age, races at certain distances, etc. Again, the main conditions will be NW2L, NW3L, non-winners of a race other than maiden, claiming or starter, etc.

Stakes races and/or handicap races are typically larger purses and possibly even Graded Stakes (G1, G2, G3), which are graded by the NTRA. Weight concessions are typically given for similar reasons; such as, age, gender, past wins, etc.

I am coming to a point in the race conditions. I am not going to list them all, I think that becomes counter-productive (and boring) after a while. Here is our lesson about conditions:

- Make sure that you read and understand them fully. You may find that the trainers do not use them properly on a frequent basis. This is good for us and I'll tell you why.
- The horse that is the *most* qualified statistically has a better chance of winning the race. Let's say that the race is for NW3L (non-winners of 3 lifetime) and we compare all 9 entrants.

	Races	Win	Place	Show
#1	15	1	1	2
#2	13	2	3	2
#3	9	2	4	2
#4	26	2	1	5
#5	12	1	2	1
#6	32	2	8	3
#7	15	2	5	4
#8	8	2	1	0
#9	21	2	3	2

What do you think about this field? Do you see any that jump out from a statistical view? The 3 and 8 are our best choices from a comparison on conditions. Let me stress that point about conditions. This is just one aspect of the handicap process. It is not the be-all to end-all, but it is one factor in the process of identifying contenders.

So, for our Contender Checklist, we mark in black a Q by the 3 and the 8, because they have won 2 out of 8 or 9 tries for a 25% win.

Some horses here that have probably learned how to lose are the 4 and the 6, as they have had a lot of races and not done much.

The 1 and the 5 will be ranked lower because they qualify for a NW2L race; why are they in this race? So, we might put a red Q to mark them as under-qualified.

There are conditions for allowance races, optional claiming races, starter allowance races and others that may have many qualifiers written in the conditions. You must make sure you understand the conditions, so you can look at each horse's record to see how well he qualifies for the race.

I don't know how many times I have looked at a horse in a race and said:

'What the heck is he doing in this race? What is the trainer thinking?'

Sometimes there is a reason, so make sure you are looking at everything to answer that question. The reality of it is that many times the horse does not belong in the race, maybe he just 'needs a race', maybe the owner wants to see him run that day, who knows?

There is another major factor written in the conditions; it is the purse of the race. That is, the money to be won and split up accordingly to the top 4 or 5 finishers. The winner takes the lion's share, typically about 60%, and the rest drops off quickly for 2nd, 3rd, 4th, etc.

How important do you think the purse is? For the most part, I would say it's pretty important; it is how most of the folks in the business get paid. It also creates another statistic that we can use in the money won part of the past performance. You will find it in the upper right corner and gives money won in several formats such as:

- life
- this year
- last year
- distance
- track

Once again, another way to separate a 'pro' from a non-contender. We will talk about the money won in detail when we talk about class. One thing to be wary of is when he won the money. Some horses may have had a great year as a 3 year old, or won one big race, or some similar circumstance that may have been a long time ago; and it does not necessarily make him a contender today.

For the handicapping part, the purse is a great guideline on comparing allowance and stakes races. It is helpful on shipper's (horses moving from one track to another). A $5000 claimer running for a purse of $4500 moves to a track where the $5000 claimers run for a purse of $12,000, will probably find stiffer competition.

We are now getting into more notes we will make on our Contender Checklist. Feel free to copy the example from the book; if you don't have copy capability or just want to get forms from me, that's fine, too. I will give you some options on getting forms, templates, etc. in the back of the book. Either way, you need a blank one to record our information for each day's race card.

I will suggest that you save these for reference at the end of the day; to go back and see how you did, what worked, and as mentioned earlier, to track your own performance.

There is another important bit of information in the conditions. It is the distance and surface for today's race. This is critical information for several reasons, and we will cover the distance and surface factor later on. For now, you will record today's distance and surface on the Contender Checklist in the appropriate spot. I arbitrarily assume dirt surface, so I just mark 'turf' if it is not on dirt.

Having done all our homework on the conditions, we record for the first race from Thistledown (see example 2):

C 4000   6
1/17

This means it is a claiming race for $4000, and the entrants have not won a race in 17 months, and the distance is 6 furlongs. A good qualifier won 16 months ago, and has some recent good tries (2nd by a neck, 3rd by a head). Even better would be good tries at stiffer levels, $6500 claimers, $5000 claimers. Make sense? Again, there are a hundred examples, but we are looking for the *most* qualified entrants.

Race 2 from River Downs looks like this:
C 5000   6
F NW2

Claiming race for $5000, fillies and mares, that have not won 2 races in their life, at 6 furlongs. A good qualifier here would only have a few lifetime races, show improving speed ratings, and won within the last couple of races.

Race 8 has more than one condition to consider; it is for non-winners of 3 in 17 months *or* non-winners of four lifetime. So, a horse need only meet one of these qualifications to race here. A good qualifier here might have won 3 races lifetime out of 12, and the last race finished 2nd by a nose in stronger company (C $6250). Another good qualifier might have 9 wins lifetime, won 2 in 16 months, and his last 2 were very close to a win.

You will notice in this example race card (which is an actual race day from Ohio 7 & 7) that I have listed the maiden races with a minus sign. That is a personal preference, because I do not care for maiden races very much. I do look at them and handicap them, I just don't make any serious wagers on them. I am leery of first-time starters, and I dislike horses that have not been able to win yet. It's nothing personal, I know they have to start somewhere; it does not mean I have to bet on them.

Let me clarify something on the examples and notes. I talk about writing the negatives in red, but as I went to print, I was informed I could print in two colors – black and white. So, I have changed my examples to a (-) minus sign, I still want you to make your marks in red.

I have entered the rest of the information for all 14 races from this day. See example 2.

Let's review what we have so far:

Contender Checklist with race conditions and distance listed in the appropriate spots. Take the time now to jot down the date and track at the top, just to keep things in order. Also, you may be playing more than one track.

You should have a copy of the Handicapping Checklist to refer to for guidance on the order in which we handicap (and for symbols to use).

Recap the 'conditions' lesson:

Read and understand the conditions. Look for the horse(s) that is most qualified. Discount the ones that are least qualified. Mark the list accordingly. Black for good, red for bad. Pretty simple, so far, right?

Read on, my friend.

Example 2: Contender Checklist

		River/Thistle		5/11/2007		Example 2		Contender Checklist			
Results	Race#	Conditions	Dis	Prime 1		Prime 2		Prime 3		Prime 4	
	1	C 4000 1/17	1M	4 E5		5 P2		6 E6		7 E5	
	2	C 5000 F NW2	6	2 EP2	39%	5 P4		1 EP3		4 EP2	
	3	C 4000 NW2	5 1/2	6 E8	39%	2 S2		3 P2		7 EP1	
	4	STR ALW 8300 (5000)	5 1/2	8 E8		2 P3		5 EP3		7 EP1	
	5	C 6250 NW3	6	7 E6	39%	3 EP3		1 E5		8 S2	
	6	C 4000 2/17	1M	6 EP6	39%	2 EP8		1 EP5		7 P4	
	7	C 6250 open	5 1/2	4 EP7		8 EP4		6 EP5		3 EP3	
	8	C 4000 3/17 or NW4	6	10 EP6		3 P2	-Q	2 EP5		6 EP6	
	9	MC 4000 (-)	6	7 E5		3 P2		6 EP5		5 P1	
	10	C 4000 open	6	1 EP4		2 S3		7 EP5		6 E5	-Q
	11	C 4000 F NW4	5 1/2	6 EP6		7 EP7		1 S		2 S	
	12	ALW 13,600	6	3 EP7	46%	2 EP7		7 EP6		8 EP4	
	13	MSW (-)	6	6 E6		4 P3		3 E1		1A S	
	14	MC 5000 (-)	1M	10 E8	46%	1 S2		9 P2		4 EP5	
Bankroll											
Action								Bias			
Win/place											

Chapter 4
Speed Ratings

Speed ratings are great for a numbers guy, but everyone that plays the horses had better know something about them. The good news about speed ratings are that it's another area that has seen a lot of improvement over the years. If you don't know it, we owe a great deal to a terrific handicapper by the name of Andrew Beyer. He was on the cutting edge of speed ratings in the mid 1970's. He devised a speed rating system that worked very well, and he wrote a book called Picking Winners. I remember it well, because I loved it. Beyer has written several books since then, and I recommend all of them. The rest of the story, of course, is that it's his system speed ratings you see in the Daily Racing Form that we know as Beyers.

Now, most of the information suppliers have good speed rating systems, including TSN. We use the speed ratings from the Ultimate Past Performances in several ways. Look at the race summary section, and you will see the last 4 final speed numbers for all runners in the race. The last 3 races are Sp1, Sp2, and Sp3 (with Sp1 being the most recent).

If the numbers are trending up like this: 82 78 74, this is a positive pattern. Give him a black arrow pointing up (for improving speed). If the numbers are trending down like this: 62 68 74, this is a negative pattern. Give him a red arrow pointing down (for declining speed).

Looking at the same group of speed ratings, look for a Double Advantage; a horses last 2 speed ratings are higher than ALL other's last 2 ratings. Give him a black DA for the double advantage.

Use the same concept for a Triple Advantage on the last 3 speed ratings. This one is very powerful, and you don't see it very often. Give him a black TA for the triple advantage.

Look to the right of the Final Speed category and you will see the Racing Speed Average (Rcg Spd Avg). This category is just 'helping' you with the numbers, so if you see an average that is 5 points (or more) higher than all the rest, list this in black as RSA. This represents a distinct speed rating advantage over the field.

Down near the bottom left corner of the Summary is a category called Back Speed. This is another piece of our speed rating analysis, and it represents the best speed the horse has ever hit at this distance and surface. What we want to see is a horse with improving speed ratings (from above) and an even higher back speed listed here. We know he can likely race back to a prior speed rating if his speed ratings are improving.

There is one more angle to look for that involves speed ratings (and class), so let's cover it now. When we see a horse with improving speed ratings *and* a drop in class, it is a very positive move. The example would be 3 improving speed ratings like the 82 78 74 listed above, and a drop in claiming price from $10,000 to $4000. This is a significant angle and we list it with a black arrow up, and a black arrow down next to it. (see example 3, race 9, horse 7). By the way, even though I don't like maiden races, he won that race. We will cover class in depth in an upcoming chapter.

I want to talk about pace while we are in the speed rating discussion. The pace is what happens during the running of the race. Who makes the early lead, who lays just off the early speed, and who comes from way back, etc? This is important because what happens early in the race typically has a huge effect on how the race finishes out. Two of the most common scenarios are:

1. One horse breaks out quickly, makes a big early lead, settles into stride, and then leads all the way around, with no one getting near him. This is called wiring the field, because he went wire to wire.
2. Several horses break quickly and battle for the lead for the first half of the race, and wear each other down, and the off-pace (or closers) win the race. There is also an illusion that the closers are flying at the end, but usually it's the speed horses running out of gas.

There are dozens of ways that the pace can play out in a race, and this is one of the reason's that we list the horses running style on the Contender Checklist. As we walk through the handicapping steps of the race, we need to be aware of the various run-styles to start to get a feel for how we think the race is going to run. There will be more discussion about this when we cover track bias.

We should talk about turf races here, because speed ratings and pace figure effects are quite different on turf races. Remember I said I did not care for turf races, and this is the main reason. I use speed figures and pace ratings as a very big part of the handicapping process. The vast majority of turf races are won by come-from-behind horses, many times with the entire field in contention for the final 1/16 of the race. I just think there are way too many bad things that can happen to change the outcome with everyone making their run at the end. So, the rule of thumb on pace in turf races is to look for the big late pace number in the Ultimate Past Performances.

It may seem rather odd that we do not record the speed ratings, but we will have plenty of numbers and symbols by the time we finish. What we record are trends up and down with arrows, double or triple advantages, and 'racing speed average' advantage. Look at example 3 to see our notes on speed ratings.

The recap for this chapter is:

- Checking the last 3 speed ratings for trends up or down (arrows)
- Checking the last 3 speed ratings for double or triple advantage
- Checking racing speed average for a 5 point advantage
- Checking back speed to know what speed a contender might run today
- Look for the lone early speed horse
- Look for late pace numbers in turf races

Example 3 Contender Checklist

Results	Race#	Conditions	Dis	Prime 1	Prime 2	Prime 3	Prime 4
		River/Thistle		5/11/2007	Example 3	Contender Checklist	
	1	C 4000 1/17	1M	4 E5 ↓	5 P2 RSA	6 E6	7 E5 -↓
	2	C 5000 F NW2	6	2 EP2 39% DA	5 P4	1 EP3 -↓	4 EP2 -↓
	3	C 4000 NW2	5 1/2	6 E8 -↓ 39%	2 S2	3 P2	7 EP1 -↓
	4	STR ALW 8300 (5000)	5 1/2	8 E8	2 P3	5 EP3	7 EP1
	5	C 6250 NW3	6	7 E6 ↑ 39%	3 EP3 ↑	1 E5	8 S2
	6	C 4000 2/17	1M	6 EP6 -↓ 39%	2 EP6 ↑	1 EP5	7 P4
	7	C 6250 open	5 1/2	4 EP7	8 EP4	6 EP5	3 EP3
	8	C 4000 3/17 or NW4	6	10 EP6 -↓	3 P2 -Q	2 EP5 -↓	6 EP6
	9	MC 4000 (-)	6	7 E5 ↑ ↓	3 P2	6 EP5 DA	5 P1
	10	C 4000 open	6	1 EP4 ↑	2 S3	7 EP5	6 E5 -Q
	11	C 4000 F NW4	5 1/2	6 EP6	7 EP7	1 S	2 S
	12	ALW 13,600	6	3 EP7 46% RSA	2 EP7	7 EP6	8 EP4
	13	MSW (-)	6	8 E6 ↑ DA	4 P3 ↑	3 E1	1A S
	14	MC 5000 (-)	1M	10 E8 46% DA	1 S2	9 P2	4 EP5 -↓
Bankroll							
Action						Bias	
Win/place							

Chapter 5
The Specialists

We are now going to look at two aspects of handicapping that make up another area that many folks don't even bother with. The ability of a horse on a certain track, or at a certain distance. If they do talk about it, they say that the trainer handles all that and he knows what he's doing. Well, guess what, sometimes, *some* of the trainers know what they are doing. From my end, from the statistical end, I'm sure that a lot of the times, the trainer does not know what he's doing.

I can be pretty blunt, so let's not take that out of context (I hope some trainers are reading this book). I know there are plenty of times there is a good reason to mix it up; from dirt to turf, from sprint to route, from 6 furlongs to 1 1/16 miles to 4 furlongs. I understand the reasons and we are going to use statistics to our advantage for this concept. What we ultimately will look for, are the high percentage moves.

These two points are fairly easy to run down, once you know what to look for. Let me explain the qualifiers, and then we are going to talk about several examples. Look at a full past performance in the upper right hand corner of any horse. (Remember me knocking some of the track program past performances; many of them do not have this information). You will see several lines of info, two of which are this horse's performance at this track, and his performance at this distance.

As listed on the Handicapping Checklist; if he has raced here at this track 6 times or more with no wins, give him a red T. If he has won at least 1 out of 10 here, give him a black T. If he has won 11% or more here (use calculator if needed {# of wins divided by # of starts here}), give him a black and underlined <u>T.</u>

OK, it's not as bad as it sounds, and once you get used to it, it's pretty simple.

We handle the distance in exactly the same way. Same statistics and format. If he has raced 6 or more times at this distance with no wins, red D. If he has 1 win out of 10 at this distance, black D. If he has won 11% or more at this distance, give him a black underlined <u>D</u>.

I am going to list several of these and separate the good from the bad (you thought I was going to say good, bad and ugly, didn't you?).

Race 1	Horse 5	Tdn 14 races	5 wins gets a <u>T</u> (35%)	Dis 8 races	2 wins gets a D
Race 2	Horse 4	RD 10 races	0 wins gets a –T	Dis 14 races	1 win gets a - D
Race 7	Horse 6	Tdn 16 races	4 wins gets a T	Dis 9 races	0 wins gets a - D
Race 11	Horse 6	Tdn 6 races	1 win gets a T	Dis 13 races	3 wins gets a D
Race 13	Horse 4	Tdn 1 race	0 wins (no mark)	Dis 8 races	1 win gets a D

The last example leads into some other scenarios. He has raced here only once, and did not win, so it's not good or bad; just not enough information, so, no mark at all. One of the things we are establishing in this chapter on track and distance, is what we know about a horse in a certain circumstance. He likes the track, he wins here often, he is a 'horse for the course'. Or, he seldom (or never) wins here, he does not like the track.

He loves 5 furlongs, wins 4 of 5 at this distance; but, he's 0 for 11 at 1 1/16 miles. Think he's finally going to stretch out today? Possible, but I am literally not betting on it.

So, here is what we are looking for:

The track Specialist (wins a high percentage of races here).
The distance Specialist (wins a lot at this distance).

Here are some things to take a hard look at, some things that you might think fit:

He likes 5 furlongs; he should do just as well at 6.
He likes 7 furlongs; then a mile should be good, too.
He's got early speed at 1 1/8; he should kill 'em at 7 furlongs.
He was closing in his last 2 at 6 furlongs; he'll get them all at 1 mile.

All of these things *might* happen, but I'm looking for statistics that tell me they **did** happen before. That's what we are trying to find. Back to the trainer concept, we are going to study the trainer statistics soon. Now, if you tell me it's a Scott Lake horse that goes from route to sprint and wins 32% of the time, I'm going to listen. If it's Brand X trainer that is 0 for 32 with sprint to route, what do you think I'm going to do?

There are other surfaces to discuss; turf races and the newcomer which is the 'All Weather ', artificial surface. There is also a 'turf to dirt' angle, and a 'dirt to turf' angle that used to be incredibly hard to detect. Now, you just have to check the trainer stats, again, coming right up.

Turf races for me are another type I don't care for. I know, a lot of folks love them, and I think that's great. I simply don't do well with them and it's something I still need to work on. For our purposes here, the turf specialist is found the same way. With the same statistics and the same format, the concept is still good.

The all-weather surface (listed as AW) presents a different challenge. Many of the tracks with this surface have only recently installed it. We are going to have to watch them, and compile statistics to make decisions. We will cover that more in the track bias section.

Recap the specialists.

Wins a lot at this track T and/or distance D, we like them.
Loses a lot at this track -T and/or distance -D, we don't like them.
Wins a lot on turf gets TF, loses a lot on turf gets -TF.
See example 4.

Got it?

Example 4: Contender Checklist

		River/Thistle		5/11/2007		Example 4		Contender Checklist			
Results	Race#	Conditions	Dis	Prime 1		Prime 2		Prime 3		Prime 4	
	1	C 4000 1/17	1M	4 E5 -T -D	↓	5 P2 T D	RSA	6 E6	T D	7 E5 D	-↓
	2	C 5000 F NW2	6	2 EP2 DA	39% -T -D	5 P4 D	-T	1 EP3 D	-↓	4 EP2 -T -D	-↓
	3	C 4000 NW2	5 1/2	6 E8 -↓	39%	2 S2		3 P2	-T -D	7 EP1-↓	
	4	STR ALW 8300 (5000)	5 1/2	8 E8	T D	2 P3		5 EP3	D	7 EP1	T D
	5	C 6250 NW3	6	7 E6 ↑	39% T	3 EP3 ↑	 T	1 E5	T D	8 S2	T D
	6	C 4000 2/17	1M	6 EP6-↓	39% -D	2 EP8 ↑	D -T	1 EP5	T D	7 P4	-T -D
	7	C 6250 open	5 1/2	4 EP7	T D	8 EP4	T D	6 EP5	T -D	3 EP3	T D
	8	C 4000 3/17 or NW4	6	10 EP6-↓	D	3 P2	D -T -Q	2 EP5 -↓	T	6 EP6	T D
	9	MC 4000 (-)	6	7 E5 ↑ ↓		3 P2	-D	6 EP5	DA	5 P1	
	10	C 4000 open	6	1 EP4 ↑	T D	2 S3	T D	7 EP5	T D	6 E5	T D -Q
	11	C 4000 F NW4	5 1/2	6 EP6	T D	7 EP7	-T -D	1 S	T D	2 S	T
	12	ALW 13,600	6	3 EP7	46% T D RSA	2 EP7	-T -D	7 EP6	T D	8 EP4	-T -D
	13	MSW (-)	6	8 E6 ↑	 DA	4 P3 ↑	D	3 E1	-T -D	1A S	
	14	MC 5000 (-)	1M	10 E8 DA	46%	1 S2		9 P2	-T -D	4 EP5 -↓	
Bankroll											
Action								Bias			
Win/place											

Chapter 6
Trainers

We are going to cover one of the human factors on how horses perform at the track. These guys/gals (I want to remind you occasionally that I'm politically correct) can have a tremendous effect on a horse's performance. I do not pretend to know exactly what it looks like in the barns, stalls, and backstretch area; but I am very sure there is a lot of hard work and long hours. I do have a great respect for hard work, and for what I'm sure is frequently *not* very rewarding.

From a statistical view, there can be several angles to consider on each horse in a given race. Remember my rule about statistics; we are looking for high percentage plays, 11% is an average number in an average situation. So, numbers better than 11% will be in black, numbers less than 11% will be in red. There are also going to be a lot of stats to look at, as many as 4 or 5 per horse in a race.

Here comes the art of handicapping again. We are not going to list all those numbers, as that can be too confusing. Therefore, we are going to have to figure out which one applies best. You're thinking this sounds like a lot of work, but that's some of the fun in figuring out who's going to win the race.

By now, I'm assuming you are using a good information source; they will have this trainer info. I will refer to the card from River/Thistle that I've been using from the beginning. Let's look at some of these:

Race 1	Horse 4	Claiming 13%; Down 2 classes 22% We list 22%, easy choice
	Horse 6	No class change -7%
Race 3	Horse 6	Shipper 21%; 1st start w/trnr 25% We list 25%
Race 5	Horse 7	No class chg 13%; Wnr last race 18% We list 18%
	Horse 8	Up 1 class - 9%; Btn favorite 22% We list -9%, looks like tough move up
Race 7	Horse 4	Btn favorite 27%; Claimimg 21% We list 27%, with a class drop
	Horse 6	Claiming 22%

One thing to consider on statistics about trainers (all statistics, for that matter), we would like to see a good 'sampling'. A good sampling means a large enough number to allow for patterns to develop. Let's say that a horse has won one of two races lifetime. The stat says 50% wins; yes, it's 50%, but it's still just one win. Now, when he has 14 races and he has won 7, that is 50% wins worth talking about. Do we have to use what we have? Yes, if he only has 2 races he only has 2 races. We just don't put as much value on it from a statistical standpoint. Aaah, the art of handicapping; ain't it great?

More statistics on trainers? You bet! We get his starts, wins, places, shows and win percentage at this meet. We get his starts for the calendar year, win percentage, ITM (in the money) percentage, and

ROI (return on investment). We get all those numerous angles; Sprnt-Sprnt-Rte 20%, No class chg 7%, Mdn win L/R 12%, there are dozens of them.

The track's website or program will also generally give you some basic trainer stats; number of win, place, show, etc. If you follow a certain track, or have a 'home' track, you will want to be closer to the day to day stuff. Who is on a win streak, who comes out of the gate quick and early in the season, who is good with shippers from certain other tracks, etc.

OK, I see you starting to get that glazed-over look; so, stop with the statistics for a while, right? The reality of the scenario on the trainers is that you must make a decision on how much of the information on the trainers you want to apply, and how you want to use it. What we are trying to figure out is:

What do we think he is trying to do with this horse in this race? Most horses follow what we call a 'form' cycle. It is common for them to be improving or declining in their performance on a cycling basis. A good cycle might look like a race every 10 to 14 days, at a level where he is competitive, and his speed ratings are improving each time out. Or, he races every 3 or 4 weeks, and he wins each time, and the trainer moves him up a notch in the claiming ranks.

We are trying to draw conclusions on the trainer's intentions to improve that form cycle. Or, to get him back on a winning cycle, if he's not currently racing well. That's where we look for patterns like 'down 2 classes' 33% wins. Winner last race 27%. Sprint-sprint-route 25%.

The other end of the spectrum showing declining form on a horse might be that he finished last in his last 3 races. The trainer stat shows 'claiming 4%'. He's probably not going to 'wake up' and win if there are other horses in the race showing signs of life. Remember, we are always comparing the field in a race to one another, trying to decide the eventual winner.

The statistics part of the trainer analysis is a key piece of info, and it is an area with a varying scope of importance, depending on who is handicapping. I put a lot of emphasis on any horse with a trainer angle that is 22% or higher. If he wins with this angle twice as often as the norm, it's worth considering. Conversely, if he only wins 3-4% of the time with a particular move, I down grade that horse's chance in this race.

Many trainers win off a claim, and many win off workouts. Those two pieces will be covered with their own discussion later.

Remember our basic rules as we consider the trainer; good numbers get written in black, bad numbers get written in red. If all the angles are overwhelming to you, the least I would do is list his win percentage for the year. The numbers to record on the Contender Checklist are the ones you think are significant as you look at each of your top 4 contenders in a race. If a horse has a new trainer with poor statistics, I would list him with a red -T. (See example 5).

There is an angle about trainers combined with certain jockeys to be considered which we will cover with the jockey segment. Let's talk about the colorful pilots of our horses next.

Example 5: Contender Checklist

Results	Race#	Conditions	Dis	Prime 1		Prime 2		Prime 3		Prime 4	
		River/Thistle		5/11/2007		Example 5		Contender Checklist			
				4 E5	↓	5 P2	RSA	6 E6	T D	7 E5	-↓
	1	C 4000	1M	-T -D		T D		-7%		D	
		1/17		22%							
				2 EP2	39%	5 P4	-T	1 EP3	-↓	4 EP2	-↓
	2	C 5000	6	DA	-T -D	D		D		-T -D	
		F NW2			+J	-4%		27%	-J	-6%	
				6 E6 -↓	39%	2 S2		3 P2	-T -D	7 EP1-↓	
	3	C 4000	5 1/2		T/J						
		NW2		25%		-10%					
				8 E8	T D	2 P3	-9%	5 EP3	D	7 EP1	T D
	4	STR ALW	5 1/2	20%					+J	19%	
		8300									-J
		(5000)		7 E6 ↑	39%	3 EP3 ↑		1 E5	T D	8 S2	T D
	5	C 6250	6		T		T				
		NW3		18%		28%	T/J	-10%		-9%	
				6 EP6-↓	39%	2 EP8 ↑	D	1 EP5	T D	7 P4	-T -D
	6	C 4000	1M		-D		-T				
		2/17		-9%	+J	13%		-3%			-J
				4 EP7	T	8 EP4	T D	6 EP5	T	3 EP3	T
	7	C 6250	5 1/2		D			T/J	-D		D
		open		27%	T/J	17%	-J	22%		24%	
				10 EP6-↓	D	3 P2	D	2 EP5 -↓	T	6 EP6	T D
	8	C 4000	6		15%	11%	-T			-9%	
		3/17 or					-Q				
		NW4		7 E5 ↑ ↓		3 P2	-D	6 EP5	DA	5 P1	
	9	MC 4000	6		22%		23%				
		(-)					+J		-J -T		
				1 EP4 ↑	T D	2 S3	T D	7 EP5	T	6 E5	T
	10	C 4000	6		29%		19%		D		D
		open							21%	-Q	-10%
				6 EP6	T	7 EP7	-T -D	1 S	T D	2 S	T
	11	C 4000	5 1/2		D						
		F NW4		-J	14%						-6%
				3 EP7	46%	2 EP7	-T -D	7 EP8	T D	8 EP4	-T -D
	12	ALW 13,600			T D						13%
			6	28%	RSA						
				8 E6 ↑		4 P3 ↑	D	3 E1	-T -D	1A S	
	13	MSW	6		DA		-2%		19%		
		(-)									
				10 E8	46%	1 S2		9 P2	-T -D	4 EP5 -↓	
	14	MC 5000	1M	DA			9%				21%
		(-)			+J						
Bankroll											
Action								Bias			
Win/place											

Chapter 7
Jockeys

This section comprises part 2 of the human factor on our horse racing analysis. The little guys (and gals) that ride the horses are tremendous athletes. We may not think of them like that very often, but handling an animal that weighs ten times as much as you do, is no easy task. Most of these folks work very hard, and once again, there are a lot of them that do not make a lot of money.

We all see the much publicized and network broadcast on the Kentucky Derby, Preakness, Belmont and Breeder's Cup races. It all looks glamorous and exciting; and it is, make no mistake, but, there are about 345 other days in the year that are not quite as dramatic. There are plenty of jockeys that ride for small amounts of money, many of whom ride a day card at one track, and then a night card somewhere else. You think you have a long day?

Now let's talk about how the jockeys influence our betting decisions. We are able to get a lot of information on the jockeys, similar to the trainer's information. The main stats we get on Ultimate Past Performances are:

- Win, place, show and win% for this meet
- Win%, ITM%, and ROI for the year
- Win%, ITM% and ROI for *this horses* run style
- Win%, ITM% and ROI with this trainer in the last 60 days
- Win%, ITM% and ROI at Sprint/Route (whichever this race is)

You want to talk about some powerful information, this is good stuff. As I said earlier, I have a lot of admiration for what they (jockeys) do. But, the fact remains, there are many categories where some of them are excellent, and some areas where they are not so good. That is where we look for advantages to use in our favor.

By now you know the statistical outlook, positive percentages will be better than 11%, less than that will be posted in red. There are some obvious situations to look for like a rider with high win percentage on early speed horses gets a mount on an early speed horse. A rider that wins a lot on closer type runners, gets a mount on a closer. Let me point out, the jockey is just one part. These moves do not make some runner a lock. You might be surprised how often a local favorite jockey gets a mount, and he gets bet down to 3-5 without any indication the horse can win. That's OK, it's good for us.

There are 'streaks' to talk about with jockeys. They sometimes get hot and win 40%-50% of their races for a while. This can be perpetuated by smart trainers; as they see the hot streak, they try to put him on the best horse. What you want to do is go along for that ride when that happens. There is a comment section in the Ultimate Past performances with Comments that will alert you to this very situation (along with dozens of others that we will talk about). It says just that, 'hot jockey last 7 days 20 7-3-3'.

We know we want to look for these positive moves, and most of the time, they are right there in the statistics. Something a little less obvious is the move from a low percentage jockey to a high percentage rider, or, the move from a poor rider on early speed horses to a sharp speed rider. Any time you see a jockey change, look at the statistics and try to decide if it's a positive or a negative move. You must also be aware of the jockey w/this trainer stat; many trainers have a favorite jockey they use to win. It happens quite often, and it hurts to catch it *after* the race is over. Look at race 3 at Thistledown, horse 6 Hunterpunter, and you will see Hot Tnr/Jky combo in last 14 days (18 5-4-2); which means their last 18 races together have scored 5 wins, 4 places, 2 shows for a 61% ITM. These kind of stats get my attention.

We can look at the jockey switch on the #10, Laterornever, in the 14th race at River Downs; which was to a high % jockey, and realize it is icing on the cake for this one.

The opposite side of this angle is the switch from a jockey that seems like he has the right skills, to one that seldom wins on this type horse. Don't ask me why that happens, I'm sure at least some of the time, there are reasons. Once again, I'm not betting on those types of moves. I can say I have plenty of loss experiences to tell, where I thought the jockey just had to 'hang on'. That is seldom the case. Unfortunately, the jockey with a 3% win percentage probably isn't going to suddenly get better on the horse you like.

I look specifically for some change in the jockey situation. Going from the high percentage jockey to a low percentage would get a red –J. Going from a low percentage jockey to a high would get a +J. One other combination to look for is hot trainer and jockey combination (comments); this would be listed as T/J on the Contender Checklist.

Some examples of a high percentage jockey would be:

- Jockey w/E types 23% (getting on an E type runner)
- Jockey w/Trn L60 19%
- Jockey w/Sprints 25% (in a sprint race)
- Jockey w/S types 18% (on an S type runner)

These examples show up on a regular basis; sometimes the betting public is on it, sometimes they are not. You may be surprised how often you find a great combination like one of the examples above that is not getting played. We will cover the betting and overlays in depth later.

A less obvious advantage may show up in the past perfomances when a jockey rides a certain horse, the horse improves performance. These are subtle differences that are a little harder to catch, but you watch for them to hook up and you look for improvement. There is frequently 'chemistry' between jockey and horse, and you want to know where that exists, because it's one more advantage you may have in a race.

We may as well talk about the weight factor now, and some of you are not going to like my outlook. It flies in the face of the opinions of a lot of race fans and handicappers. Remember when I talked about the horse weighing ten times the jockey? My thoughts about the weight factor of the jockey are this; I do not think there is much effect at all on the horse. Let's say the horse weighs 1100 pounds, and the jockey weighs 115. Now we add 3 pounds to the jockey, what is the percentage of difference? You know I have the answer; it's .0027, which is less than 3 one-hundredths. I make it equivalent to putting 3 quarters in your pocket and saying that would slow you down. I don't buy it.

As a matter of fact, the whole discussion about weight seems to come up less and less in the press and television coverage. You are certainly entitled to your opinion, but you won't see any discussion about weight in my Checklist. I just don't consider it.

Now let's consider what the trainers might be thinking. They might seek out a 'bug boy', who is an apprentice jockey that get's up to 10 pounds off the required weight on the horse. These apprentices sometimes get on hot streaks, just as most good jockeys do, and they get better mounts. Again, I don't think it's the weight factor. Many aspects of this business are cyclical; that is there are many 'streaks'.

Winning, and losing, runs in cycles depending on several factors. My point here is that the jockeys run in those cycles, too. So, catch them when they are hot, and ride (win) with them.

We've had a good discussion about the jockeys. To recap:

We are looking for positive and/or negative moves with jockeys. Positive moves as listed above get a black +J. Negative moves get a red –J. (example 5)

Let's move on to the wild, wonderful, wacky world of the discussion about class.

Chapter 8
Class

If there is one area of handicapping that draws more discussion, has more opinions, and challenges our concept of art versus science, this is it. There are numerous ways to measure class as we know it, and we are going to cover some of them.

Here are some, certainly not all, ways to measure class:

- Original sales price of horse
- Stud fee when bred
- Sire & Dam's sire various statistics
- Last claiming price
- Average claiming price
- Claiming price in which he won
- Allowance purse at which he won
- Any purse where he was competitive
- Average money won by horse – this year
- Average money won by horse – lifetime

- Numerous class ratings at TSNHorse, Daily Racing Form, and most of the other information suppliers

You will hear discussions about the 'class of the race', 'back class', 'classy horse'; this list also goes on. Okay, now I have you worried about the class factor. It is not an easy one, nor is it the 'heavyweight' in the handicapping business that it was once considered. Make no mistake, it is an important factor in picking the live horses, and it might be the most important factor in any given race, but it must be figured with all the other aspects we talk about.

The way I handle the class factor is systematic; it's not just statistics here. As I mentioned, there are several class ratings at the services, and I am not 100% sold on any of these. The one I pay most attention to is TSN's Average Class Last 3. I hold the most value on any horse's last 3 or 4 races. Remember the review about form cycles, the last 3 or 4 races are a good snapshot of where he is on that cycle, and whether he is improving or declining.

We know we typically get the last ten races of a horse in the past performances. That is usually enough information for me to make a class determination. I am looking for a level that he has been able to compete well in. My definition of competing well means he won or was very close to winning (2nd or 3rd, within a length or two). So, if it's a $7500 claiming race, I need to know if he is competitive at this level. He's won at this level, or been close. Now is a good time to remember our 'conditions' lesson: Non-winners of 2 lifetime $7500 is a much lower level than an 'open' $7500 claimer, with open meaning no restrictions.

There is another solid way to look at class, and that is the value of the purse (listed in the conditions) he is competing for versus purse value in the last few. You are going to have to do some research by understanding the purse structures for the track you are playing, and the tracks they may ship from. I use this format for allowance and stakes races; the claiming races usually are easier to figure because the claiming price is a good guideline.

Following that logic will lead you to average money won for this year. This is fairly current information and easy to get, in the upper right hand box on a horses past performance, with the current year being on top. If it is early in the year (January, February, March), I usually use the prior year. Yes, we are talking about some work again, and there are some simpler options that we review at the end of this chapter.

There is another factor to consider in the class discussion. What about horses moving up in class? He wins for $5000 claiming; can he win at $7500? Or $31,000 allowance purse moving up to $40,000? Or Allowance winner moving up to stakes level? There are numerous moves like this, and just as many moves down the ladder. From $10,000 claimer to $5000; from allowance $21,000 to claimer $15,000, from G2 stakes to state-bred stakes.

I'm not going to give you an answer for each of these scenarios, because there is no one size fits all. What we are looking for is evidence that this horse can compete with this field in today's race. The three main tools for me in this category are:

- Ultimate Past Performance Summary Average Class Last 3
- Claiming price in which he was competitive
- Average money won in high price allowance and stake races

There are some things that are less obvious and have value. The first time a horse drops from allowance races into claiming races; the same for Maiden Special Weight to claiming. They should show some signs of life to be considered; if they ran dead last 5 times in a row, I probably would not look twice.

They have been running in G1, G2, or G3 races and beating half the field, and today is a softer allowance race.

They ran well for $10,000 claiming, then ran for $20,000 a couple of times and beat half the field, and today back for $10,000.

There is another tool that works very well in TSN Ultimate Past Performances w/comments. In the body of each horses past performances, there is an information box. I think of it as a watchdog. The set-up on it is very good, in that the positive comments are on the left side of the box. Those comments might say:

* Drops in class today
* Ran second vs tougher in last race
These positive comments are denoted by a star.

The comment section on the right side of the box is for negative type comments, which are listed with a bullet point. Some of these might be:

- Moves up in class from last start
- Beaten by weaker in last start

This comment section is not only for pointing out positive or negative class moves, it may list any positive or negative move; I just want to introduce that piece of information here. We will discuss these comments in depth later.

As we have been working through the different aspects of handicapping my way, we have been making entries on the Contender Checklist. What we have when we finish figuring a race, is the top 4 contenders with various entries in their box on the sheet. Most likely, some are black and some are red. What we want in *our* top contender is all black notations, meaning they are all positive.

My point in this discussion is that there are many times as we are handicapping each horse, there may be no note at all for a certain aspect (like class), because he has no outstanding statistic. In other words, the default on any handicapping point is no mark at all. Nothing better than the rest, and nothing worse. That's OK. In fact, it is some of the beauty of this method of handicapping. If there is nothing outstanding, there may not even be a reason to bet.

So, if he is running in a $10,000 claimer, and that's where he's been running, there is no notation on class for this horse. A Maiden Special Weight running in a similar MSW race, gets no notation on class. Allowance race with a purse of $25,000 getting a runner that's been competing for $26,000 purses, probably no note (not significant).

Now, we take that competitive runner from the $10,000 claimer, and he drops to a $5000 claimer, we give him a black $ for a positive class move. We see that competitive filly dropping from MSW (purse $18,000) down to Maiden Claiming $7500, we give her a black $ for a positive class move. A substantial drop in claiming price (or purse price) for a competitive horse, is a positive move.

The other side of the coin is the horse moving up in class (claiming price or purse value). If he won or ran strong in his last race, he is a likely candidate to move up the ladder. How much of a move up can he make? Well, that's the $64 question, isn't it? There are a couple of solid ways to answer that question. One is to check your trainer statistics (recall our lesson on trainers) and look for a high (15% or more) success rate with moving up in class. Another way is to scan those past 10 races in the past performances and see if he has been able to do it before.

We want to look at his recent form; a sharp horse may move up the class ladder several times in a row. If he has been winning with authority, or strongly contending in his last few races, he is a prime candidate to move up. This is especially true in younger horses; 2 year olds, 3 year olds, and 4 year olds in the early part of the year. For record keeping purposes, all horses' birthdays are January 1. This means on January 1 of each year they all turn a year older, which in turn means they are still maturing or 'growing up' until well into their 4th year. So, a young horse showing signs of improvement has probably not realized his potential yet. I know I said I didn't care for maidens too much (especially Old Maids), but I love to see a young horse on the improve. I'm sorry, I could not resist the 'Old Maid' joke.

In our sample race day, we have the #4 in the 7th race dropping from a competitive Allowance $11,400 to an open claimer @ $6250. He gets a $. In the 9th race, we have a competitive MC$10,000 dropping to a MC$4000, he gets a $. The other contenders with the $ are the top ranks from Average Class Last 3 races. Our Contender Checklist for this race day now has our notes about class (example 6).

Some of you may be wondering about the 'less than top grade' runners at Thistledown and River Downs, and I don't mind telling you that I love these type of races. But, this method of handicapping works just as well with the runners at Churchill Downs, Santa Anita, Woodbine, Aqueduct, and any other thoroughbred track. You are doing your research and comparing statistics and compiling notes the same way, no matter what track you want to play.

Let's recap the class discussion, and what to look for. We looked at several ways to measure class, and it really depends how much time you want to spend on this aspect. When we refer to the Handicapping Checklist, we are reminded to notate a positive class move with a black $. We need to mark a negative class move with a red -$. Your default on class (if you don't want to do the research) can be the Average Class Last 3 from the Ultimate Past performances. Give the highest rated horse the black $.

We are ready to talk about the track bias and how it may affect our runners today.

Example 6: Contender Checklist

		River/Thistle		5/11/2007		Example 6		Contender Checklist			
Results	Race#	Conditions	Dis	Prime 1		Prime 2		Prime 3		Prime 4	
				4 E5	↓	5 P2	RSA	6 E6	T D	7 E5	-↓
	1	C 4000	1M	-T -D		T D	$	-7%		D	
		1/17		22%							
				2 EP2	39%	5 P4	-T	1 EP3	-↓	4 EP2	-↓
	2	C 5000	6	DA	-T -D	D	$	D		-T -D	
		F NW2			+J	-4%		27%	-J	-6%	
				6 E6 -↓	39%	2 S2		3 P2	-T -D	7 EP1- ↓	
	3	C 4000	5 1/2		T/J						
		NW2		25%	$	-10%					
				8 E8	T D	2 P3	-9%	5 EP3	D	7 EP1	T D
	4	STR ALW	5 1/2	20%				$	+J	19%	
		8300									-J
		(5000)		7 E6 ↑	39%	3 EP3 ↑		1 E5	T D	8 S2	T D
	5	C 6250	6		T		T				
		NW3		18%	$	28%	T/J	-10%		-9%	
				6 EP6- ↓	39%	2 EP8 ↑	D	1 EP5	T D	7 P4	-T -D
	6	C 4000	1M		-D		-T				
		2/17		$ -9%	+J	13%		-3%			-J
				4 EP7	T	8 EP4	T D	6 EP5	T	3 EP3	T
	7	C 6250	5 1/2	$	D			T/J	-D		D
		open		27%	T/J	17%	-J	22%		24%	
				10 EP6- ↓	D	3 P2	D	2 EP5 -↓	T	6 EP6	T D
	8	C 4000	6		15%	11%	-T		$	-9%	
		3/17 or					-Q				
		NW4		7 E5 ↑ ↓		3 P2	-D	6 EP5	DA	5 P1	
	9	MC 4000	6		22%		23%				
		(-)		$			+J		-J -T		
				1 EP4 ↑	T D	2 S3	T D	7 EP5	T	6 E5	T
	10	C 4000	6		29%		19%	$	D		D
		open							21%	-Q	-10%
				6 EP6	T	7 EP7	-T -D	1 S	T D	2 S	T
	11	C 4000	5 1/2		D					$	
		F NW4		-J	14%						-6%
				3 EP7	46%	2 EP7	-T -D	7 EP6	T D	8 EP4	-T -D
	12	ALW 13,600		$	T D						13%
			6	28%	RSA						
				8 E6 ↑		4 P3 ↑	D	3 E1	-T -D	1A S	
	13	MSW	6		DA		-2%		19%		$
		(-)									
				10 E8	46%	1 S2		9 P2	-T -D	4 EP5 -↓	
	14	MC 5000	1M	DA	$		9%				21%
		(-)			+J						
Bankroll											
Action								Bias			
Win/place											

Chapter 9
Track Bias

A track bias by definition is a condition in or on the racing surface that will have a positive or negative effect on a horses run style. Some of the most obvious conditions are the weather and the track maintenance crew. The soil, sand, dirt, and now 'Artificial Surface', are seldom the same at any two tracks. The turf courses are all different also; different types of grass, different length of grass, rails moved in or out at will to change the course.

The track layout itself can be very different from one facility to another. We have some 'bull ring' (5 or 6 furlong) tracks, many tracks at one mile, and some up to a mile and a half long. Some have a short stretch of a few hundred feet and some are over 1000 feet to the finish line.

There is a silver lining to the cloud I just put over you with all the track variables. Remember our lesson about Track Specialists? This is some of why there are horses for courses, they like the surface or the turns or whatever it is. I don't want to take anything away from that; that is a stand alone statistic.

On any given day, some factor may exist that is going to have a pronounced effect on how horses run today. First, we need to know if there is a typical bias. Does this track normally favor early speed horses? Is the track normally faster (better) on the rail? Is the #1 post better in a 5 furlong race?

One of the best ways to answer these questions is to be a 'regular' at the track, meaning you go there often, or follow them on one of the racing channels on TV, or one of the video streaming networks on the internet. If you want to follow a track or circuit, you have some good choices (I will give references at the back of the book). It's the old-fashioned handicapper in me (Thanks again, Dad) that says if you follow a circuit, you actually get to know (about) the jockeys, trainers, track bias, and so on.

Having said that, it is not necessary to do those things; we can get all we need to pick winners from our information sources. When we look at the Ultimate Past Performances, there is a section called Track Bias Stats and it has a load of information about our subject of choice right now. It has the Meet totals (for this race distance) which contains the speed bias % (races won by early speed), the % of races won by each of our runstyles, the post position win % by rail 1-3, 4-7, and 8+. There is also another cool 'watchdog' which puts a + by a favorable condition, and a ++ by the best run style for this track/distance.

All the same statistics are duplicated for the week we are in so you can compare what has been happening for the meet to this week, to help identify a current track bias. Now, all you have to do is watch today's races and decipher if all that is still holding true today.

Man, every time I think I've got a simple explanation, it starts to look scary. It's not. This is more of the fun stuff, because sometimes there is a big payday attached.

So, let's figure out how we look for the track bias. We talked about 'running the race' beforehand; we are going to do that now. Let's look at the 3rd race from Thistledown on May 11. It's a 5 ½ furlong for c4000 NW2L. Our top Power Rating (39%) is #6 Hunterpunter, with an E8 runstyle, our second rated is #2 Command The Best with an S2 runstyle, the third is #3 Great Charisma with a P2, and fourth is #7 What Now Wynn with an E/P1.

Our snapshot (Contender Checklist) shows the 6 with 39%, $, and dropping speed ratings (not good), hot trainer/jockey combination, off 47 days (not good) but a 25% trainer with 31-90 days off. The 2 has been way out of it in his last several races. The 3 is 1 for 41 lifetime and does not like the track or the distance. The 7 is 1 for 30 lifetime and has not contended in several races.

We excuse the 6 for his last two races, because he showed good early speed in races over his head (c$7500), took a six week rest, came to a hot trainer, and should wire this field. He does. This confirms a speed bias for now as expected. The crowd was on him, too, as he only paid $5 to win, but he was the first leg in an easy Pick 3 that paid $165.

We are going to 'run' some more of these races after we have all our info. For now, we have confirmed the track to favor speed as expected. The steps are:

- To have a good idea what to expect from the track by understanding the recent Track Bias Stats
- To have an expectation of how the race should run (pace factors)
- Understand the reasons the race does not play out like expected

Maybe someone got left at the gate, or bumped hard coming out of the gate and lost 5 lengths.

Maybe the jockey got him in trouble, running into a wall of horses, or swinging him 6 wide on the turn.

Maybe he washed out early (sweaty and nervous), and just couldn't run his race. Or maybe there *is* a track bias today, which you definitely need to know about. Here are some things to watch for:

- Early speed horses go much farther than past performance indicates
- Early speed horses quit sooner than normal
- Closers are making up a lot more ground than normal
- Closers can't get out of the back of the pack
- Post 1 is always on the lead
- Post 10 is on the early lead
- Most winners are in the middle of the track in the stretch
- Most winners are on the rail in the stretch

Make your observations as you watch each race. If you are going to remember these observations, great! If you are like me (and do *not* have the memory of an elephant), make notes. I make my notes on the Contender Checklist as the day goes on, and keep referring back to see about bias (and jockeys, trainers, etc). This is one of the 'art' parts of handicapping; you have to get a feel for what's going on and why. Some of the better high percentage jockey's will get that feel for the track and the bias, if there is one. Watch what they do, where they steer to on the track, and if they are winning while they do it.

This part requires some quick checking between races, because if there is a track bias today, you may need to re-think how the race is going to run. If there is a speed bias, you want to look again at the early speed horses. Conversely, if there is a bias against speed, that front runner you liked, may not look so good now. You get the picture.

Now we need to talk about post positions, the effect they may have on the horses, and the effect they may have on the running of the race. We consider the post position at the same time as track bias, because they are closely related. Our 'base' information on post position comes from our Track Bias stats in the Ultimate PP's, as listed earlier, including the watchdog that gives a + to the favorable post position. One piece of this information is a little harder to figure; the 'rail' position can be assumed by any horse with the early speed (and sharp jockey) that can get there.

We also want to look at the horse's post in his last few races, and decide whether he has been helped, or hurt, or no effect by post. An example might be an E/P run style horse has been in post 9 or 10 his last few races, with several other early speed runners inside him, forcing him wide to a first turn: Did it push him out of contention? Does he get post 1 today which has a + and the 2 and 3 post are both slow on the break? Do we look at his last 10 races and see that he always performs badly from post 7, 8, or 9?

I am reluctant to make assumptions and draw conclusions on this part of the handicapping process until I see a few races on the day. So, I typically do not mark anything regarding post or bias ahead of time. I will have expectations based on what I have read in the Track Bias Stats and the Race Summary. I record notes as I go after each race is run, and make adjustments to my picks if I see a bias is present today. I will mention another handy tool on TsnBET.com: after each race in the results dropdown menu is an instant chart function. I will go back and read this as soon as possible after each race to help decide if there is a track bias, or anything else I may have missed.

Another great thing that happens if you do catch a track/post bias, the horses that ran against it may improve next time out. The horses that had it their way, may not be so good next time out. That is of great value to those that follow a regular circuit. Keep notes, or keep your Contender Checklist with notes; there's money to be won!

Chapter 10
Claim to Fame

There is not really anything famous in this chapter (yet), but I do like the cliché. We are going to cover some various other things that we see in the Past Performances that are worth talking about.

We reviewed claiming races earlier, and I just want to remind you that a claim is for real money. The horse we talked about claiming for $10,000 is purchased for 10,000 real dollars; a check is written for that amount so the new owner can take the horse with him. I belabor the point because when that happens, we need to pay attention. The new owner and/or trainer usually have high expectations from that horse, and we might want to do the same. There are many trainers that win with a high percentage of first or second time out after a claim, and we want to know when that might happen. We also want to watch for horses that have been claimed multiple times; if so many people want him, there must be a reason. A quick scan of each horses past performances will point out the –c, and who he was claimed from. One of our best clues on recent claim angle is contained in the body of the Ultimate Past Performances w/Comments, in the trainer statistics that we covered earlier.

What we are looking for is a high win percentage of 1st after a claim, or 2nd after a claim. That is our flag to take a good look at this horse, and may jump him up to a contender (even without a good Power Rating) if there is anything else to support that. There happens to be an example of what we do *not* want to see, in this race card example. Look at race 7, horse #2, Mr. Simon To You, claimed last out for $3500. The look at the trainer stats show +1st after claim 33%, and we think we are on to something. But wait, the 33% is only 1 of 3, and he has only won 6% of his races this year. And he has been off for 194 days, with just a couple of slow workouts. And he has jumped up to c6250, while his past 10 races show he cannot run with those types. So, he remains a throw-out, and we are right as he runs 4th in a field of 7.

We would like to see a recent claim that comes right back to the races, in less than 30 days, and is spotted in a class that he has been able to compete. Or, we have a trainer's statistic that shows a high % win after 1st claim (and it's more than one win), and possibly up one class with a statistic that show's a good win % up one class. There are numerous examples of this type of move; look for the good % to show that the trainer knows how to place the horse competitively after a claim. Identify a recent claim on the Contender Checklist with a black c, and record the win % with it. If it is a high %, that's great, it puts our contender a little further up. If it is a low %, record it in red, and it downgrades our contender.

Our next 'fame' tip is to look for horses that won their last race; or more than 1 race in a row. There are many good horses and/or good trainers that can put together win streaks, and it can be as good for us as it is for them. One of the best ways to catch this angle is in the comment section of the Ultimate Past Performances, in the trainer statistics. You can also see it in the last 10 races of the past performances, and can check the number of wins in the information box of the horse (though you cannot identify streaks there).

Take a look at the 10th race on our card, the #6 Wazoo City. He won his last race, and at first glance, it does not look that impressive. The trainer stat is not great, either. But, he won his only race at this track; he is 2 for 5 at this distance; he has raced well in higher (c12,500) company; the jockey has won one race today, and ran second in another. Now, the win last race looks good, especially at 9/2 odds. The jockey stays hot and wins and completes another very playable pick 3 worth $615.60.

If the horse could win last time, he's worth a look *this* time. Mark down the previous winners on your Contender Checklist with a W, and if he won more than one in a row, put the number next to the W3 (for 3 in a row). See example 7.

Famous tip #3 is to look for horses that have raced each other in the past, and note who won that race. This one is not easy to find, and you only get it with old fashioned homework. You must look at race dates in each horse's past performance, and see if the date and race number match another in today's race. It is common for similar class ranks to run against each other, so it is worth looking for. Sometimes horses go against each other frequently, and they trade beating each other. This isn't worth a lot, but it is if the same horse wins most or all of the time.

I must bring up one of the best examples of this that I can think of, possibly some of the greatest head-to-head battles ever. The duels between Affirmed and Alydar are classic, not to mention that Affirmed is our last (to date) Triple Crown winner, gaining the crown in 1978. The main story is the Triple Crown races that year; these two went at each other in all 3 races. I'm sure you know that Affirmed won all 3, thus being a great example of the head-to-head tip. The story behind the story is that they raced each other 10 times during their careers, all great races, with Affirmed winning 8 of them, although he was disqualified in the last one. If you can't tell, Affirmed remains one of my all-time favorites.

We have a couple of examples of our head-to-head tip from our 7 & 7 race day in Ohio (see example 7). The first one is the 11th race, and

the #6 holds a head-to-head over the #7 and the #4. The angle does not pay off as the #4 turns the tables and wins, and we do not have him. You know I'm going to say it;
"You can't win 'em all!".

However, the 12th race has a head-to-head with the #3 over the #8, and he wins. I must note that the #3 held just about every advantage in the race, and everyone had him at $3.20 to win. It's still better than a sharp stick in the eye, right?

Let's talk about one more tidbit that I use occasionally, and that is the win percentage of a horse. It's a fairly simple statistic to run (easy for me to say, right?), and it's another one that we need the calculator for. I'll run the disclaimer on this one now; I do not use it all the time, it's kind of a backup for a tiebreaker type thing. Say there is two or three contenders I can't split, and I want one for a pick 3 or something, I might use this. We simply take the number of wins for a period of time; this year, this year and last year, or lifetime; and divide it by the number of starts. An example would be 10 wins divided by 25 starts = 40%. Tiebreaker goes to the horse with the highest win percent.

Let's press on to the layoff factor.

Example 7: Contender Checklist

Results	Race#	Conditions	Dis	Prime 1		Prime 2		Prime 3		Prime 4	
		River/Thistle		5/11/2007		Example 7		Contender Checklist			
				4 E5	↓	5 P2	RSA	6 E6	T D	7 E5	↓
	1	C 4000	1M	-T -D		T D	$	-7%		D	
		1/17		22%			-333				-175
				2 EP2	39%	5 P4	-T	1 EP3	↓	4 EP2	↓
	2	C 5000	6	DA	-T -D	D	$	D	W	-T -D	
		F NW2			+J	-4%	-166	27%	-J	-6%	
				6 E8 ↓	39%	2 S2		3 P2	-T -D	7 EP1 ↓	
	3	C 4000	5 1/2		T/J						
		NW2		25%	$	-10%	2oL				
				8 E8	T D	2 P3	-9%	5 EP3	D	7 EP1	T D
	4	STR ALW	5 1/2	20%	W			$	+J	19%	
		8300							C	-196	-J
		(5000)		7 E6 ↑	39%	3 EP3 ↑		1 E5	T D	6 S2	T D
	5	C 6250	6	W	T	W	T				
		NW3		18%	$	28%	T/J	-10%	2oL	-9%	
				6 EP6 ↓	39%	2 EP8 ↑	D	1 EP5	T D	7 P4	-T -D
	6	C 4000	1M		-D		-T				
		2/17		$ -9%	+J	13%		-3%	3oL		-J
				4 EP7	T	8 EP4	T D	6 EP5	T	3 EP3	T
	7	C 6250	5 1/2	$	D			T/J	-D		D
		open		27%	T/J	17%	-J	22%	2oL	24%	W2
				10 EP6 ↓	D	3 P2	D	2 EP5 ↓	T	6 EP6	T D
	8	C 4000	6		15%	11%	-T		$	-9%	
		3/17 or					-Q				
		NW4		7 E5 ↑ ↓		3 P2	-D	6 EP5	DA	5 P1	
	9	MC 4000	6		22%		23%				-261
		(-)		$			+J		-J -T		
				1 EP4 ↑	T D	2 S3	T D	7 EP5	T	6 E5	T
	10	C 4000	6		29%		19%	$	D	W	D
		open		W2		W		W2	21%	-Q	-10%
				6 EP6	T	7 EP7	-T -D	1 S	T D	2 S	T
	11	C 4000	5 1/2	HH	D	-HH				$	-175
		F NW4		-J	14%						-6%
				3 EP7	46%	2 EP7	-T -D	7 EP6	T D	8 EP4	-T -D
	12	ALW 13,600		HH $	T D				-262	-HH	13%
			6	28%	RSA						
				8 E6 ↑		4 P3 ↑	D	3 E1	-T -D	1A S	
	13	MSW	6		DA		-2%		19%		$
		(-)			2oL						
				10 E6	46%	1 S2		9 P2	-T -D	4 EP5 ↓	
	14	MC 5000	1M	DA	$		9%				21%
		(-)			+J						
Bankroll											
Action								Bias			
Win/place											

Chapter 11
How About Some Time Off?

The subject of time off between races is covered by a wide variety of opinions. I love the weeks before the Kentucky Derby every year, because everyone becomes an expert on horseracing (recognize my sarcasm yet?). It's like they reinvent every aspect of handicapping from what happened in last year's Derby, including time between races. This year, 2007, was no different.

Barbaro, bless his soul, had set a new standard in 2006. He came off a 5 week layoff and had only 2 starts in 4 months, and he won the Derby. Not to take anything away from him, the Derby win was a beauty, but he did not survive the effort. We all know what happened in the Preakness, and I'm the last person to place blame over something like that. But, it does *not* seem like a path to follow, does it?

Here are some of the comments before this year's Derby:

"He's been off 6 weeks and he's ready."

"He's been rested 8 weeks and he is ready to run."

Several trainers were quoted in saying they had only raced twice this year. One says he's ready after being off 8 weeks; another is challenged whether he is fit after being off 8 weeks.

What gives?

The fact of the matter is, time off between races is different from horse to horse; it is different from trainer to trainer. There is no one size fits all (have I said this before?). If there was a 'cookie-cutter' answer to the question, wouldn't all horses follow the same pattern? There are hundreds of questions to ask after every racehorse finishes a race; there are dozens of questions before they run their first race!

Let's try to break down the mystery of how much time off between races there should be. In the old days (I can say that because I belong to AARP), the rule of thumb was don't bet a horse that's been off more than 30 days. Now, there is no hard and fast rule, but we need a guideline to help us figure the layoff factor. I use the 30 day rule with qualifiers.

First; we need to know how long he's been off, and we get that at a glance in the Ultimate Past Performance Summary – Days Since L/R – the number is listed. If he has been off more than 30 days, I write the number in red on the Contender Checklist. Then, I look at the Trainer Stat's (31-90daysAway) and see if he is good at this angle. You know the drill; 11% or lower gets listed in red, 12% and higher gets listed in black (the higher the better). I would also look for 1 or more workouts, and we will talk about that shortly. I will say the 30 day rule is more applicable to low and middle class claimers. It is more common for good allowance and stakes class horses to be off longer without losing form (fitness).

Having said that, I still take a hard look at any runner off more than 30 days. Our clues are the trainer's stats, and the horses past performance. Look at his last 10 races; has he had a layoff before, and how did he perform after the layoff? Is there a pattern, like off 45 days and 2 workouts and then a strong race? What does his last 2 years performance box tell us? Does he race 15-20 times per year? Does he race 4 times per year?

OK, don't want to look that deep? Mark down over 30 days off in red, and check the trainer stats (see example 7).

Many horses benefit from the time off, or layoff, very much like us taking a vacation. One of the big differences with racehorses, is they frequently need to 'race' back into shape. This brings up another 'watchdog' from the Comment Section, which will read 'Eligible to improve in 2nd start since layoff', or 'Eligible to improve in 3rd start since layoff'. That is our clue to look harder at his last 10 races and see if he's been in this situation before, and how he responded. We are looking for breaks in action, or time off, and how many races it took for him to compete again. Some horses are ready right out of the gate after a layoff, but most need a race or two. We mark this on our Contender Checklist as 2oL (2nd off layoff), or 3oL (3rd off layoff) in black, because we expect improvement.

So how do workouts fit into the picture? This is another one that rests squarely on the trainer, and you have to do your own homework on how the trainer of this horse uses workouts. If the horse has been off a while, and has no workouts, I am quite leery of his chances. If he has one or two slow workouts, I'm still suspicious. If he has a few solid workouts, I feel better. If he has a bullet, even better a recent bullet, I'll give him a good chance.

This entire function still just indicates he might run back to something he's done in the past (remember the back speed category?). Workouts alone will not typically make a horse faster than he has been.

How do we know what a good workout is? It does depend on the track, but here are some guidelines.

- 3 furlongs 35-37 seconds

- 4 furlongs 47-49 seconds
- 5 furlongs 59-1:01
- 6 furlongs 1:13-1:15
- 7 furlongs 1:27-1:29

You should get the drift; anything around 12/12.5 seconds per furlong is pretty good. I usually look for consistency in number of works; and I consider workouts of 5 furlongs or longer as more serious workouts. There is another great way to gauge a workout; if it is the fastest work of the day, it will be listed with a bullet point, just like the ones above.

I do not typically put a lot of weight on the value of workouts, though this is an area that some guys build their entire handicapping process around. I get what I am looking for from the Ultimate Past Performances as I listed above. There is a Clocker's Report at TSN, and the Daily Racing Form typically has good detailed information, if you want to do more with workouts.

The other big application for workouts is with first-time starters and maidens. You know how I feel at this point about maidens, but we are going to cover them. (See, I take the good with the bad.) I said I don't make big win bets on them, but they are frequently involved in the pick 3, which is one of my favorite exotic bets.

The format is basically the same with maidens; I would like to see several works, getting better as they go, and maybe a recent bullet work. I would check the trainer's stats with maidens; you know what to look for. This leads into the application of medications that frequently begins with maidens, and even first time starters.

There are two main medications used with thoroughbreds, lasix and bute. The technical name for lasix is Furosemide, and it is used for 'bleeders', horses with exercise-induced pulmonary hemorrhage (EIPH). Lasix has been used for over 30 years now, and the question as a handicapper is: what will it do for the horse? I think the only time to talk about it is after the first or second use, because if it is going to help, it will happen right away. It will be marked with a bold capital L in the past performances on the first application, and it may help the horse with breathing, which might help him go faster and/or farther. I have seen horses 'wake up' on the first race after receiving it, so look for it and use your own judgment.

Bute is short for Butazolidin, which is an NSAID (non-steroidal anti-inflammatory drug). It fights pain, inflammation and fever; we would compare it to aspirin. These medications can be controversial, and I do have my thoughts on that, but I am not going to get into that discussion here. Some states/countries do not allow these medications, so, be advised as a horse goes off and on treatment.

One other point to be made about maiden races, which is one of the reasons I do not particularly like them, is that there is a high percentage of odds-on favorites in these contests that win for reasons I can't fathom. I refuse to believe in conspiracy theories, but this one does test me.

There is another good bit of information available for all horses, but probably more important for first-time starters, in the right-middle side of a horses past performance. It is the sire and dam's (horse's parents) average winning distance (AWD), the win % of offspring, and the Sire Production Index (spi). The scoop on the spi is the higher the better; by the way, breeding is another area that a lot of folks spend a lot of time on; I'm not one of them. But, it's another area you can do a lot of work and research on, and TSN has the products; in fact, they have entire books on Maiden Stats and Sire Stats. If you become an expert, please get back to me on that one. Seriously.

Chapter 12
Money Management 101

Oh boy, here comes the fun stuff, right? Well, kind of. Here is the first rule in money management at the track: Discipline. Here is the second rule in money management: More discipline.

Here is why I talk so much about discipline. We are going to earmark a certain amount of money as a bankroll, and we are going to apply percentages to that to decide how much any certain bet is going to be. Our job is to grow that bankroll, and we do that by making solid bets when we have a good chance of winning. Seems simple enough, doesn't it?

Remember where we were when we started this book? At the track, making that last minute bet, because we got caught up in the excitement, the rush that comes with cashing the ticket on the winner! Here is where the discipline comes in; you cannot and should not be placing another bet as they are loading in the gate. You plan ahead, you have your wagers figured out, and time your arrival at the window to catch a last look at the odds, to make sure you get the value you decided you need before you place that bet.

Let's look at how we get that value. Refer to Example B; Betting is a Business, one of your basic tools. Please don't get too worked up over the 'morning line' you are told to set. You must have a good idea as to what chance your horse has of winning the race; that is what this is referring to. Let's say there is an 8 horse field, so each horse has a 12.5% chance of winning, if all things were equal. Now, say we've thrown out 4 of them with almost no chance of winning. Now our 4 contenders have at least a 20% -25% chance each. Now we have 1 of those that has several good points (black marks and high percentages on the Contender Checklist), so we think he has a 50% chance of winning. This equals 1/1 odds on our chart, so we need 3/2 or better to make him a win bet.

I know it's not an easy concept, but the point is to establish your horse or multiple horses chances of winning, match that to the chart for approximate odds, then look to the right for the odds you need to get to make it an overlay. Once you get familiar with that chart, it is simple. Technically, the proper way is to establish odds for the entire field, but that takes a lot of time; and I want that time for handicapping. So, I set odds on my top choice, and one or two others if I think they have a good chance.

Before we place any bets, we must establish the bankroll amount. For me, that is a real number which consists of the amount in my betting account at TsnBET.com ™, and cash I have earmarked for wagering at the track.

Let's assume that amount is $1000 for sake of discussion. Our format calls for us to bet up to 4% of our bankroll on win and/or place, which would be $40. The win bet is simple, and may be all you want to do. You just need the good odds (which are overlay odds) when you place your bet. As cautioned earlier, don't wait until the last second to make that bet. The odds may change again; there is nothing you can do about that.

I like to watch the place pool percentages for overlays, also, but that requires a quick statistical analysis of the percentages. If my choice has less than 20% of the pool bet on him to place, I will make that bet. For the above scenario, I would split my bet, $20 to win and $20 to place. I watch the odds board and prepare to place my bets about 5 minutes prior to post.

Let me run the disclaimer now about the money that makes up your bankroll. The rule of thumb is that you do not play with money that you cannot afford to lose. That is not to say we plan on losing, you just need to know there is that risk. I stand by that, and I always have. Never bet money that you need for bills, groceries, family and all the other things that should be important to you. Playing the horses is fun, and I have enjoyed it for some 40 years (Geez, how old am I?). Keep it in perspective; apply discipline as it says on the Handicapping Checklist.

Back to that bankroll of $1000; we take 5% of it ($50), and that is what we have to play exotics. These can be doubles, pick 3, pick 4, exacta, trifecta, and superfecta; depending on your track, there are a lot of choices. For me, the bread and butter bets are win, place, doubles and pick 3's. That is why I have the qualifier on the pick 3 and pick 4; if you are going to play them, the best bet is to have a 'single' somewhere in there. That's a horse you feel has a solid chance of winning, and you build a ticket around him. My money won on these type bets went up dramatically when I began to use the qualifier. Write down your bankroll, action and win/place amounts at the bottom of your Contender Checklist.

Obviously, you can massage the money management and bet choices to meet your personal preferences, but it is imperative that you track your performance on a regular basis. You must know what is working and what is not, and make adjustments as needed. That is how I came up with my qualifier on the pick 3.

We talked about Andy Beyer in chapter 4, when we reviewed speed ratings. Now I would like to bring up another great handicapper/writer, Steven Davidowitz, who wrote "Betting Thoroughbreds". This book was first published in 1977, and has been revised twice. There is a wealth of information in that book, including excellent suggestions on wagering. Davidowitz and Beyer were instrumental in my training with their books in the 70's, and I highly recommend Steven's books as well as Andy's. I applaud them, and their research that was much more difficult then than it is now. They continue to work hard in the racing business, and I owe them many thanks.

I want to talk about some more functions available at TsnBET.com™. One of them is #20 on your Handicapping Checklist, the TSN Top 5 Profit Line Rank. I use it when I am playing a track there, and it's user friendly. They have established a 'profit line' much like what we should have, so it's a cool comparison tool to see how our choices stack up to theirs. If it happens to be way different than my line, I go back and see if I missed something. It just kind of keeps me on my toes. You just click on (Tools) from the live odds board and then click on 'Top 5 Profit Line Rank', and it will list them in order of rank.

I have talked about tracking your bets, and there are plenty of ways to do that, including the old pen and legal pad. I also mentioned early in the book about a choice at TsnBET.com™, and it is the one I use. From the web site, you can click 'Manage Your Account', and then click 'Detailed Account History Report', and from there you can pick dates, tracks, types of bets, and sort the information any way you want. More importantly, you can get your win percentages just like Bobby Zen has been telling you to do.

Put your wallet away for now, and read on.

Example B
Betting is a Business

Bet *only* when you have an edge.
Manage your money; maximize your advantage.

Odds Chart

Odds to Chance of Winning	%	Approximate Odds	Bet Win
> 50-50	50+	< 1-1	7/5
50-50	50%	1/1	3/2
1-3	33%	2/1	3/1
1-4	25%	3/1	9/2
1-5	20%	4/1	6/1
1-6	18%	5/1	7/1
1-7	15%	6/1	8/1
1-8	12.5%	7/1	9/1
1-10	10%	9/1	11/1
< 1-10	9%	10/1	13/1

Set your own 'morning line', or chance of winning for all (at least contenders); this is your approximate odds. Be honest. Remember to handle your emotions.

- Evaluate your bankroll before the day begins.
- WIN/PLACE bets are up to 4% of bankroll. Watch pools for place bets.
- ACTION (exotics) are 5% of bankroll *per day.*
- Pic 3 or Pic 4 qualifier: Must have at least one leg @ 39% or better win chance.
- Play the overlay, avoid the underlay. (Easier said than done)
- Check BobbyZen.com for racing information and supplies.

Chapter 13

Go Figure!

We have looked at several angles from various races on our sample day from the Ohio 7 & 7 program; now, let's go through some more of those and come up with some betting choices. We should have our Contender Checklist with our various black and red notes from the Handicapping Checklist, and any other notes you have made along the way, our past performances to refer to, and Betting is a Business. We start with a bankroll of $600; win/place bets will be up to $24, and we have $30 in the exotic pool.

Looking at race 1, the top 4 contenders all have some red comments, and none are impressive. The 5 is a track and distance specialist, and he holds an RSA over this group, but he has been off almost a year. There is nothing to indicate he is ready to win off that layoff, so we pass the race. We are right as the 8 wins the race at 3-1, with no reason to support him at the window.

Now is the time for me to tell you I am a conservative bettor; I pass a lot of races. Not only do I need strong reasons to bet, I want to see how the track is running. That is not to say I never bet the first or second race, but I seldom take a flyer early.

We look at our figures for race 2, and see a lot of red like race 1 had. The 2 holds a 39% Prime Power advantage, and a double advantage on the speed rating. But, he does not like the track, or the distance, and he is 1 for 25 lifetime. The 5 is even money and has been off 166 days, with a 4% trainer win rate off the layoff. We pass again and the 5 wins, but is an underlay at $4.40 for the win.

We go to race 3 and we are not anxious at all, because we know it's one long game; there are always more races (where do you think the 'Zen' comes from?). We ran this race in chapter 9; our bet here is a $2 pick 3; 6 with 5,7,8 with 3,7. This is a $12 bet that singles the 6 in this race (he meets our pick 3 qualifier at 39%). The 6 wires the field as we expected, and we are on our way.

Race 4 has several contenders, with the 5 looking like the strongest; because he is a recent claim, he likes the distance, his last several races are good, and he ships from the all-weather tracks which do not typically favor early speed horses (though we have nothing on the trainer). We are alive in the pick 3 and we bet the 5 to win at 5/2 odds, for $20. The mystery trainer on the 5 turns out wrong, as he does not fire and runs 5th, but our other choices in the pick 3 run 1st and 2nd. This was a starter allowance race, which is kind of a funny animal, and there are some horses that put together good long runs at these types of races. The 7 is one of those; we can see he won at least 6 of these in a row last year, and his trainer is a 19% winner off the layoff. The 8 was an obvious choice from his last win and top Prime Power rating.

We go to race 5 with 2 live runners in the pick 3; the 3 and the 7. We like the 7 to win; he is a 39% Prime Power, won his last here easily, the trainer and jockey are hot now, and he looks like a nicely improving 3 year old. It looks like the 3 may go with him for the early lead, and he is our 2nd choice. The race plays out exactly as planned (which makes it all a lot of fun), they battle all the way around, and the 7 takes command and draws clear at the finish. We did not bet to win because we know the pick 3 will pay over $150.00 if the 7 or 8 wins, but we did start another $2 pick 3, which is 7 with 1,2, and 6 with 4 and 6. We collect $165 for our winning pick 3.

Race 6 has the 6 with a 39% Prime Power, but does not like the distance, and the trainer is only a 9% winner this year (and that is only one win); therefore, no win bet. The 1 likes the track and the distance, but the trainer is a 3% winner. The 2 has improving speed and likes the distance, but does not like the track. There is no additional bet, we are conservative (insert laugh here, I do not know that *you* are conservative), I do not like anyone enough to bet win. My brother, Rick, who was instrumental in helping me write this book, is not quite so conservative. I love my brother, but he never met a race he didn't like; you know what I mean? Anyway, we are right, because the 4 pounds them all at 10/1 odds, and we are out of the pick 3.

We go to race 7 (the 8 is scratched) and we have a solid choice in the 4, we give him a 33% chance of winning, so we want 3/1 or better for a win bet. Valid Victory (4) likes the track, loves the distance, has a hot trainer/jockey combo, and gets a class drop. We bet $20 to win (final odds are 5/2), and the 6 beats him by a neck. I still feel good about the race; we were competitive and we are up $100 for the day.

Our review of race 8 is not exciting at first, because there are no standouts. But, we have a strong pick in the 9th race that we can build a pick 3 around. And, our top choice in the 10th (1) is scratched. Nobody said this was easy. Let's talk about the 9th and look at the reasoning in this decision. This race is a MC 4000, which is not typically my kind of race. The 7 is a standout because he has the great angle of improving speed ratings and down in class, a 22% trainer angle, looks like the early speed of the field on a 'speed day' at Thistledown, and the rest of the field looks pretty awful.

So, our pick 3 bet (there is no win bet) will be our top 4 picks in the 8th race; 2,3,6 & 10 with 7 with 2,6 &7 in the 10th race. This is 12

bets (4 x 1 x 3), so we will bet the $1 pick 3 to make it a $12 bet. The 2 and 6 duel to the half, and the 2 takes over and wins easy.
We know the 7 wins the 9th race (we have talked about this one a few times), and there is no win bet at even money, but we have the first two legs of the pick 3.

Let's see how we made our choices in the 10th race. Our top choice, the 1, scratched out, so let's digress for a moment. If there is a late scratch, or a change in surface (from turf to dirt), that affects my top choice, I frequently pass the race. I'm kind of a stick in the mud, I don't like to scramble at the 11th hour to make changes, and I usually don't risk money on those scenarios. Having said that, we knew about the 1 at the beginning of the day, so we planned accordingly. We don't like the remaining contenders enough to bet win, but we use all 3 in the 3rd leg of this pick 3 (began in 8th race). The 2 does not fire, and the 4,6,7 & 8 are all in it to the stretch. We talked about the 6 in chapter 10, and he strikes the front with one of the better jockeys here, winning by daylight over the 7. The $2 pick 3 pays $615.60; we have a $1 ticket that collects half at $307.80. What a great parlay this turns out to be; consider the winners odds at 3-1, 7-5, and 9-2, no long shots. Wow!

Now I want to talk about what can happen with a good score like this. If you are not careful, you can suddenly make bad choices. Things like betting much heavier thinking you can't do anything wrong, you are on a hot streak, go like crazy. By the way, you can also 'get stupid' after several losses in a row (which will happen), and make similar bad decisions. That is when the discipline must kick in, it's why I have the reminders on the Handicapping Checklist and Betting is a Business. That's why we use percentages (loosely designed after the 'Kelly Criterion') of our bankroll for bets. When you are winning, the bet amounts will go up. When you are losing, the amounts go down. Remember we said our job is to grow the bankroll; this maximizes those win streaks and minimizes the losses.

We go to the 11th race and we like the 6 for several reasons. She is a distance specialist, she likes the track, she gets a class drop, and she holds a head-to-head over the 7. The rest of the contenders have little to talk about and a lot of red marks. We want to overlook the 0 for 30 on the jockey, but it comes back to haunt us as she has the clear lead at the top of the stretch, and gets beat by the 4 and the 5. Our $25 win bet goes in the pocket of someone that had a reason to play the 4, and we quickly realize we are not invincible.

We have another standout in the 12th race; the 3 is a 46% Prime Power and she likes the track and the distance. We give her a 50% chance of winning, and will take 7/5 or better with an aggressive win bet. We are not going to get the price, as she goes off at 60 cents on the dollar, and we can never bet win at those odds. There is a simple $2 pick 3 that is the 3 with 4 and 8 with 10; cost is $4. We are right about the 3 in this race, as she wins easily. The pick 3 was our last bet, as races 13 and 14 are maidens.

We played the 8 in the 13th off of a double advantage in speed, improving speed ratings, 2nd race off a layoff, and ran 2nd last time out. We played the 4 off improving speed ratings and ran 2nd here (TD) last out, even though the trainer stats are not too good. The 4 takes control at the top of the stretch and wins it by a length.

The 10 was our only choice in race 14, as he was a 46% Prime Power, held a double advantage on speed, and got an upgrade on the jockey. The 4 has a 5 length lead after 6 furlongs, but the 10 patiently runs him down to win by a solid length, and it caps off a good day for us at the Ohio 7 & 7 program. The pick 3 pays out $23.80, our smallest score of the day, and we gladly cash in.

We bet $105 for the day and collect $496.60 which is a very strong day. I don't want to sound like a commercial (like all those diets we see), but these results are not typical every day. My form of handicapping occasionally puts us on the favorite; that is why you must be disciplined about money management. I usually wager about 6-12% of my bankroll in a day, and hit about 35%-40% of my wagers. I talked about the qualifier on pick 3's earlier, and that was a huge turning point in my game. I used to play dozens of combinations, with a lower hit rate, and the pick 3 was a consistent money loser for me.

I still look for a solid win bet at good odds for a large part of my winnings. The pick 3 or pick 4 is more of an action bet that is a good way to use a horse I really like, but odds are too low to bet win. I also like the daily double; it is another good parlay, and you can check the payoffs on them ahead of time. Some tracks offer a rolling double all day long, another of my choices when looking for a race card to play.

I'm sure some of you are wondering about all those other exotic bets I talked about; I am sorry, but I seldom play any bets other than what we have covered. Remember I said to understand and play your strengths; these are mine. You can easily apply Betting is a Business to your strengths, as well.

We have a few more things to cover in the next chapter. Relax, you will be at the track before you know it!

Chapter 14
Odds and Ends

We are ready to put it all together and go to the races. In our wonderful age of technology, you have several ways that you can do that. The first and probably still the most exciting is to go to the live races. If you are geographically close enough to a track, that is the best choice. Make sure you arrive early enough to follow our format.

The next choice is to play and watch the races on the internet. TsnBET.com™ is my first choice, and there are several others you can find with a search engine on the web.

There are a few racing channels on some cable networks and satellite providers, where you can watch races on television. The main channels are TVG and HRTV, and Dish Network is your best choice to get both channels. Each of these networks carries various tracks and has links to several racing services. Tell them Bobby Zen sent you, and they should treat you right.

There are also several betting choices by telephone; again, TSN has this service as do many others.

I must run the disclaimer now that there are different regulations by state; so, depending on where you live, these services may or may not be available to you. I will refer you back to NTRA.com as your guide to racing in North America.

I typically play on the internet, simply for the convenience factor. I love to go to live races, and do so when I can. But, from the internet I can pick from all the tracks offered on a given day, and choose the one I think offers the best betting opportunities, based on my strengths and preferences. I seldom play more than one track at a time, as I want to watch the races, make notes, and try to understand what adjustments I may need to make.

Let's talk about some of the things that come up on race day and during the card. One of the biggest factors can be the weather. Rain and storms will typically move turf races to the dirt, and will make the track sloppy, muddy, good, wet-fast, and other types of "off" conditions. When track conditions change, I want to go back and look at past performances for horse's history on the off going. Then I am going to watch some races and see whether the track is playing fair; you can sometimes catch a bias in these conditions. You must revisit your handicapping when the track conditions change.

Scratches are common at the track, where a horse is removed from the race card by the trainer or the track veterinarian. Early scratches are easy enough; they are announced well before the first race. If it is one of your choices, revisit your remaining contenders and see how it changes what you thought would happen in the race, and adjust according to our procedures. Late scratches are tougher, and if my top choice is a late scratch, I probably pass the race (remember, I don't like that 11th hour stuff).

It is fairly common to have jockey changes; make sure to get those changes and revisit the stats on the new jockey. You might get a nice pick-up from this, if a high percentage jockey gets moved to your horse of choice. The track will announce overweights on jockeys for the day; you know my thoughts on the weight factor, unless a jock is 20 pounds overweight (he may have gone berserk at the buffet).

Now you need to be prepared for what we call ‘racing luck’. There are many things that can happen to challenge your predicted outcome (to put it nicely). Your horse might get left at the gate, he might get bumped, pinched, or the jockey could fall off, or any number of bad things. Here is what you need to know about this: It all evens out in the end. For every DQ you lose, you will win one. For every bad break at the gate, you will get a good break when *another* horse is left at the gate. I stress this point because there is nothing you can do about these things, and it is important that you don’t get discouraged and make bad decisions, thinking you are ‘snakebit’.

The one point to make about racing luck is to look at comments in horses past performances; if there are repeated comments like: left at gate, reared at start, trouble loading, and similar trouble lines telling you the horse has problems, he should not be your choice, anyway. I’ll say the same thing about bad rides; if a jockey shows a 1% or 2% win rate in a certain type race, what do you think you are going to get this time?

Remember, there are winning and losing streaks in every sport; this sport of kings is no different. My advice at the end of chapter one was to stay humble, watch, listen and learn. That advice is good until the end of time.

Order Form

Laminate Placard	Handicapping Checklist	$3.00
Laminate Placard	Betting is a Business	$3.00
Pack of 25	Contender Checklist	$5.00

TO ORDER PRODUCTS OR SERVICES:
Drop me a note and a check in the mail and tell me what you need.

Send via mail to:
Bobby Zen Enterprises
975 Ivy Drive
Zanesville, Ohio 43701

Email: BobbyZen@gmail.com

Or visit me on the web at: www.BobbyZen.com

Or simply call toll free: 866-907-4531

All orders processed within 24 hours.

Appendix

Ultimate PP's w/ Quick Play Comments **River Downs** Clm 4000NW1Y+ 1 Mile. 4up Friday, May 11, 2007 **Race 1 (TDN - #1)** **tsnhorse.com**

#	Speed Last Race		#	Prime Power		#	Class Rating		#	Best Speed at Dist	
5	Slews Resurrection	66	4	Cinematic	103.8	5	Slews Resurrection	108.2	7	Bandana	88
8	Mountain Top	63	5	Slews Resurrection	103.7	6	Proud American	105.4	3	Perfect Cali	85
6	Proud American	57	6	Proud American	96.2	7	Bandana	105.2	5	Slews Resurrection	84

1

Exacta / Trifecta / Superfecta (Ten Cent Minimum)
Daily Double
Pick 3 (Races 1-2-3)

	E1	E2/LATE	SPEED
PARS:	76	68/ 71	68

Simulcast of Thistledown race number 1

1 Mile. Clm 4000NW1Y+ Purse $6,600. FOR FOUR YEAR OLDS AND UPWARD WHICH HAVE NOT WON A RACE IN 2006-2007. Weight, 120 lbs. Claiming Price $4,000 (Ohio Registered Foals Preferred).
Post Time: (1:05)/12:05/11:05/10:05

1 European Defense (P 5)

6/1 — Own: Mark Yagour; Inc. — Black red my; red braces
MUNAYLLA FILMER (44 3-9-7 7%)

$4,000 B. g. 10
Sire: Defense Witness (Skip Trial)
Dam: European Lady (Lord Rebeau)
Brdr: Mark Yagour Inc. (OH)
Trnr: Schuster Robin (29 1-2-3 3%)

Power Rating: 92.1 (8th) — L 120

Life:	84 11-12-9	$126,722	88	Fst	65 10-8-7	$97,698	88
2007	1 0-0-0	$186	55	Off	17 1-4-2	$28,650	85
2006	17 0-1-2	$3,335	70	Dis	4 1-0-2	$12,110	81
Tdn	47 6-7-5	$58,978	81	Trf	2 0-0-0	$374	68
				AW	0 0-0-0	$0	

2007	45	7%	42%	+2.15
JKYw/ P types	63	14%	29%	+1.72
JKYw/ Trn L60	4	0%	50%	-2.00
JKYw/ Routes	6	17%	33%	+17.80

2007	33	3%	21%	-0.82
Sprint to Rte	37	14%	24%	-0.38
No class chg	261	6%	25%	-1.33
Claiming	343	5%	24%	-1.40

Sire Stats: AWD 6.3f 14%Mud 77MudSts 0.50spi
Dam'sSire: AWD 7.0f 10%Mud 526MudSts 1.04spi

★ Eligible to improve in 2nd start since layoff
● Always far back in last start ● Poor Jockey win% ● Poor Trainer win%

DATE TRK	DIST						RR	RACETYPE	CR	E1	E2/	LP	1c	2c	SPD	PP	ST	1C	2C	Str	FIN	JOCKEY	ODDS	Top Finishers	Comment	
20Apr07Tdn10	5½ ft	:23	:464	:591	1:053	3↑	104	Clm4000n19m	103	79	72/	62	-8	-5	55	7	2	43	45	58½	511	Munaylla F122	Lb 23.40	CpNAmnc3OlLord2½SickIVgs½	Wide early; weakened	7
27Nov06Tdn7	6f ft	:224	:47	:593	1:124	3↑	103	Clm3500n3y+	104	74	65/	84	-4	-7	61	3	7	99½	108¾	98½	87¼	MunayllaF117	Lb 60.40	Exposer½Inca Prince1½MonoRidge½	Failed to menace	12
12Nov06Tdn8	5f gd	:223	:473		1:003	3↑	104	Clm3500n1Y	104		73/	68			57	5	8	87½	89½	74½	45½	Felix JE123	Lb 15.80	Pesyngs3½RoylCly1ChcknSopKd1	Passed tiring rivals	8
04Nov06Tdn10	170 ft	:232	:48	1:141	1:453	3↑	104	Clm3500n2y+	102	65	54/	65	-6	-6	55	2	3½	43	55	68	612¾	MunayllaF116	Lb 14.60	RglDsclsmkSctSctStrnkMslyFr4½	Good position; tired	8
16Oct06Tdn8	170 ft	:234	:481	1:134	1:462	3↑	105	Clm3500n19m	103	70	67/	53	-4	+4	55	1	42	42½	55	69½	619	FelicianoR122	Lb 19.70	TrcknOhdWhxsChrb3½Whtsthat1	Saved ground; no rally	8
01Oct06Tdn5	6f gd	:231	:471	1:001	1:131	3↑	104	Clm3500n19m	104	81	71/	78	-7	-7	61	6	2	41	54	64½	67	MunayllaF123	Lb 11.80	BlazinDr½ExpectedComndPGloMonteks½	Even effort	9
17Sep06Tdn8	6f ft	:222	:463	1:001	1:132	3↑	104	Clm3500n19m	105	80	83/	73	+2	0	67	12	4	68½	52½	2½	53½	MunayllaF122	Lb 17.80	BgLrdNF½BlzDr½ExpctdCndhd	Wide; needed more late	12
31Aug06Tdn5	5½ ft	:222	:462	1:001	1:07	3↑	104	Clm3500n19m	106	81	80/	63	+4	+6	65	1	8	75½	57	56	34½	MunayllaF122	Lb 12.30	AlwysTkCsh4WireLdr½EuropnDfns1	Mild bid; inside	10
13Aug06Tdn4	6f ft	:224	:464	1:00	1:14	3↑	103	Clm3500n19m	106	78	76/	74	0	+1	61	11	3	55	54¼	34½	33	MunayllaF122	Lb 36.20	GryForum½OurMoment2½EuropenDefensenk	Wide trip	12
05Aug06Tdn5	5½ ft	:222	:462	:594	1:064	3↑	103	Clm3500n19m	103	76	77/	63	+4	+6	61	6	1	78½	77½	99½	64	Banda S122	Lb 60.10	ZelousCpothdAmznRvr½OrMomntnk	Mild bid; no threat	11

04Apr Tdn 4f ft :493 B 3/10 29Mar Tdn 3f ft :381 B 6/13 23Mar Tdn 3f gd :392 B 3/6 13Jan'06 Mnr 3f gd :404 B 18/20 04Nov'05 Tdn 3f ft :374 B 4/6 06Sep'04 Tdn 3f ft :373 B 9/25
18Jan'04 Mnr 4f ft :491 B 2/24 11Nov'03 Mnr (d) 4f my :533 B 17/22 04Nov'03 Mnr 4f ft :54 B 26/29 25Feb'03 Mnr 4f ft :503 B 6/20 30May'01 Tdn 3f ft :364 B 4/15 02May'01 Tdn 4f ft :50 B 11/15

2 Sober Moment (S 0)

12/1 — Own: Tracy L. Newman — Dark green; yellow diamonds
DAILEY ANTHONY (35 1-5-3 3%)

$4,000 Dkbbr m. 7
Sire: Judge T C (Judge Smells)
Dam: Last Moon (Lear Fan)
Brdr: Upson Downs Farm (KY)
Trnr: Newman Tracy L. (4 0-2-0 0%)

Power Rating: 86.7 (7th) — L 115

Life:	64 2-7-2	$44,900	72	Fst	47 2-5-2	$33,537	68
2007	3 0-0-0	$354	55	Off	17 0-2-0	$11,263	72
2006	19 0-3-1	$7,134	66	Dis	31 2-3-0	$24,168	72
Tdn	32 1-3-1	$12,499	62	Trf	0 0-0-0	$0	
				AW	0 0-0-0	$0	

2007	120	7%	27%	-0.39
JKYw/ S types	125	3%	22%	-1.72
JKYw/ Trn L60	3	0%	67%	-2.00
JKYw/ Routes	30	3%	27%	-1.63

2007	11	0%	27%	-2.00
No class chg	137	5%	15%	-1.07
Claiming	197	4%	15%	-1.31

Sire Stats: AWD 7.0f 13%Mud 805MudSts 0.93spi
Dam'sSire: AWD 8.4f 12%Mud 634MudSts 2.68spi

● Always far back in last start ● Poor Speed Figures ● Only 2 wins in 64 career starts ● Poor Trainer win%
● Switches to a Low% jockey ● Poor record at this track

DATE TRK	DIST						RR	RACETYPE	CR	E1	E2/	LP	1c	2c	SPD	PP	ST	1C	2C	Str	FIN	JOCKEY	ODDS	Top Finishers	Comment	
28Apr07Tdn12	1m gd	:23	:472	1:142	1:424	4↑	104	ⒻC4000n2y+	103	60	64/	47	+13	+7	47	4	815	714	79½	69	519½	Barrera F114	L 23.40	WhisperingBls3½Capucine6½LeviBid½	Failed to menace	8
07Apr07Mnr3	170 ft	:241	:492	1:16	1:492	3↑	103	ⒻC5000n1Y	96	53	48/	57	-9	0	47	7	69½	69	610	714	719	Oro E121	L 15.80	DonasTrl2½Frtythrdys2½VlysAlynk	Slow;asked;no factor	7
21Jan07Mnr2	170 gd	:241	:482	1:134	1:451	3↑	105	ⒻC5000n1Y	103	47	39/	80	-14	-8	56	10	108½	78	712	813	813½	QuinonesLM121	L 16.20	IvGotToWin1½DonasTrl1½ThisMBoy½	Failed to respond	10
28Nov06Mnr2	170 ft	:241	:491	1:161	1:503	3↑	103	ⒻC5000n2Y	107	57	55/	83	-1	+3	66	7	99½	89½	57½	43½	2hd	PereiraOM119	L 29.30	TwtMySthhdSbrMmnt3½SOlArch½	Swung7w; surged late	10
20Nov06Tdn7	170 sy	:234	:492	1:16	1:48	3↑	104	ⒻC3500n2Y	105	58	54/	76	-9	-8	61	8	77½	74½	53	34	25½	Pilares CP116	L 19.60	ChpgnTst5½SbrMmnt2½MsnyLdy1½	Rallied; second best	8
14Nov06Mnr5	1m ft	:251	:50	1:162	1:442	3↑	104	ⒻC5000n1Y	103	53	54/	69	-7	-3	54	9	88½	69½	48½	512	518	Davila JM121	L 13.50	SaphireHl4½DonasTrl6InFocusnk	Mild bid1/4;level off	9
30Oct06Tdn5	1m ft	:243	:492	1:152	1:433	3↑	102	ⒻC3500n2y+	104	67	56/	78	-3	+2	62	4	57½	51½	54½	51½	2½	Pilares CP116	L 7.60	MryMstr½SobrMmnt1½TwtMySthhd	Rallied; gaining late	7
15Oct06Tdn7	170 ft	:232	:493	1:154	1:474	3↑	102	ⒻC3500n2y+	103	55	46/	75	-13	-8	56	4	67	42	53½	52½	36	Pilares CP116	L 25.80	TpMchn3½DncrsDfnsnkSbrMnt½	Never far back; evenly	7
05Oct06Tdn4	170 ft	:233	:482	1:142	1:472	3↑	104	ⒻC3500n19m	100	49	40/	39	-2	+4	31	8	89	811	814	817	828½	DeveauxSR122	L112.80	Fxpel1NnisPrincs2½ProdAmrcn6½	Showed little; trailed	8
29Sep06Tdn8	170 sy	:232	:482	1:154	1:49	3↑	102	ⒻC3500n3L	100	51	42/	51	+4	+1	40	8	91210	1013	911	914	918	DeveauxSR117	L 53.70	Whataventure4½Level Bidhd Brackenberry3½	No factor	10

12Feb Mnr 5f ft 1:053 B 6/6 29Apr'06 Tdn 4f ft :493 B 3/20 11Nov'05 Tdn 3f ft :384 B 2/3 19Feb'04 Mnr 4f ft :521 B 15/15 03Feb'04 Mnr (d) 4f my :502 B 12/29 06Dec'03 Mnr 3f ft :391 B 2/2
24Nov'03 Mnr 5f ft 1:053 B 2/9 13Oct'03 Tdn 4f ft :503 B 8/15 27Jly'03 CD 4f ft :50 B 47/67 18Jly'03 CD 4f ft :511 B 20/24 06Jun'03 CD 6f ft 1:181 B 2/2 25May'03 CD 5f ft 1:042 B 32/33

tsnhorse.com

Ultimate PP's w/ Quick Play Comments

River Downs Clm 4000NW1Y+ 1 Mile. 4up Friday, May 11, 2007 Race 1 (TDN - #1)

E1 76 | E2/LATE 68/ 71 | SPD 68

---

6 Proud American (E 6)

5/2 — Own: Elmer C. Cowan — Green; yellow sash; yellow sleeves
PILARES CHRISTIAN P. (58 5-12-8 9%)

$4,000 Ch. m. 7 OBSOCT 2000 $46k
Sire: Proud And True (Mr. Prospector)
Dam: Affpuerto (Theatrical (Ire))
Brdr: Donald R. Dizney (FL)
Trnr: Cowan Gary (16 2-2-0 13%)

Power Rating: 96.2 (3rd) — L 115

Life:	53 4-10-9	$77,191	76	Fst	31 1-5-8	$26,271	72
2007	3 0 3-0	$2,796	66	Off	9 2-4-0	$24,513	70
2006	9 0-1-3	$3,717	69	Dis	8 1-3 1	$8,256	69
Tdn	15 2-4-4	$16,167	72	Trf	13 1-1-1	$26,407	76
				AW	0 0-0-0	$0	

2007	80	10%	41%	-1.02
JKYw/ E types	153	12%	34%	-0.34
JKYw/ Trn L60	8	0%	12%	-2.00
JKYw/ Routes	18	11%	39%	-0.48

2007	16	12%	25%	-0.91
No class chg	195	8%	33%	-1.03
Btn favorite	10	0%	60%	-2.00
Claiming	244	7%	33%	-1.14

Sire Stats: AWD 7.1f 11%Mud 319MudSts 0.76spi
Dam'sSire:AWD 9.2f 16%Mud 376MudSts 3.87spi

★ Ran 2nd vs similar in last race

DATE TRK	DIST						RR RACETYPE	CR	E1	E2/	LP	1c	2c	SPD	PP	ST	1C	2C	Str	FIN	JOCKEY		ODDS	Top Finishers	Comment	
03May07Tdn9	1m ft	:243	:491	1:15	1:422	3↑	103 Clm4000n1y+	104	60	56/	71	-8	-3	57	2	42	52¾	32	23	24¾	Pilares CP117	L	*2.00	Lods4¾Proud American1¾Sunder Bay¾	Second best	9
07Feb07Beu6	1m ft	:242	:481	1:142	1:393	3↑	102 ⒻC3500C	106	73	62/	79	-3	-6	66	4	31½	2hd	1½	1½	21¼	Paucar E124	L	*1.90	Dixigal1¼ProdAmrcn3Quilmydr1½	Bid; dueled; willingly	9
24Jan07Beu4	170 gd	:242	:494	1:17	1:491	3↑	103 ⒻC3500C	106	62	55/	71	-9	-5	58	6	23	31	21½	22½	23	Paucar E124	L	*2.10	ArcicJlc3PrdAmrcn5¾Dxigal2½	Chased;inside;2nd best	8
10Nov06Tdn2	170 ft	:232	:492	1:153	1:47	3↑	106 ⒻC3500n2Y	106	57	51/	73	-15	-11	58	4	23	31½	22	22½	3¾	Pilares CP116	L	5.70	Gldscld4Faxapel2¾ProudAmrcn1¾	Flattened out; stretch	7
26Oct06Tdn6	170 ft	:241	:484	1:15	1:471	3↑	105 ⒻC3500n29m	106	62	63/	66	-7	-3	61	3	52¼	33½	31½	34½	3¾	Pilares CP116	L	2.90	Misvly2Faxpel4¾PrdAmrcnnk	Contended; needed more	10
05Oct06Tdn4	170 ft	:233	:482	1:142	1:472	3↑	104 ⒻC3500n19m	106	68	65/	64	-2	+4	61	1	32	32	22	21	3¾	Pilares CP122	L	*1.90	Faxapel1NnisPrinces2¾ProudAmricn6¼	Rallied; bid;hung	8
22Sep06Tdn2	1m ft	:241	:482	1:143	1:424	3↑	103 ⒻC3500n19m	107	72	70/	76	+3	+6	69	8	22	24	23	21	2¾	SkerrettJ122	L	3.60	Misvley¾ProdAmrcn3¾NnisPrncs2¾	Led between calls	9
27Jly06Tdn13	140 sy	:23	:481	1:151	1:462	3↑	104 ⒻC3500n16m	102	74	53/	51	0	-1	45	9	1hd	2hd	56	91210	15½ SkerreJ122	L	5.70	HnldRvr1Lckynnot5¾RdRslyn1¾	Dueled; dropped back	10
29Jun06Tdn1	170 ft	:224	:473	1:143	1:471	3↑	103 ⒻC3500n16m	102	70	56/	56	+4	0	51	4	32	33½	43½	57½	610½	SkerretJ122	L	8.30	BadBdBrend1¾BidMsy1WhirStorm3½	Well placed; tired	9
27May06Tdn5	170 ft	:234	:49	1:151	1:462	3↑	106 ⒻC5000n16m	103	63	55/	58	-11	-11	52	2	1hd	21	31½	89	813¾	ClnngrJrWT122	L	12.70	HinsomGl6¾BdBdBrnd1BidMy¾	Dueled; used up; tired	9

29Apr Tdn 4f ft :53 B 17/21 13Apr Tdn 5f ft 1:054 B 5/5 12Jan Beu (d) 5f my 1:052 B 5/6 26Nov'06 Tdn 4f ft :513 B 3/2 08Nov'06 Tdn 3f gd :393 B 6/6 15Sep'06 Tdn 5f ft 1:031 B 2/4
16Jly'06 Tdn 4f ft :531 B 7/7 09Apr'06 Tdn 4f ft :51 B 11/16 ●01Apr'06 Tdn 4f ft :484 B 1/13 07Nov'05 Tdn 4f ft :502 B 1/3 ●12Sep'05 FE 3f ft :353 H 1/8 26Jly'05 FE 2f ft :23 H 1/3

---

7 Bandana (E 5)

8/1 — Own: Bookman Racing Stable Llc — Yellow, black stripes
MAGRELL JANE M. (27 0-6-4 0%)

$4,000 Dkbbr. g. 10
Sire: Academy Award (Secretariat)
Dam: If At First (Relaunch)
Brdr: R. K. Lucas (KY)
Trnr: Huffman Candace M. (2 0-1-0 0%)

Power Rating: 95.9 (4th) — L 120

Life:	89 16-16-10	$275,772	92	Fst	57 13-6-6	$197,521	92
2006	9 0-1-1	$4,879	75	Off	14 2-2-3	$49,811	86
2005	19 5-3-1	$53,020	92	Dis	20 5-3-4	$97,856	88
Tdn	0 0 0-0	$0		Trf	9 1-2-1	$29,240	85
				AW	0 0-0-0	$0	

2007	30	0%	37%	-2.00
JKYw/ E types	119	5%	19%	-1.43
JKYw/ Routes	6	0%	33%	-2.00

2007	2	0%	50%	-2.00
+90+ days away	5	20%	40%	-1.00
+1st strt wtrn	3	33%	67%	-0.33

Sire Stats: AWD 7.2f 9%Mud 718MudSts 0.77spi
Dam'sSire:AWD 7.0f 19%Mud 1212MudSts 3.21spi

★ Highest Speed Figure at Today's Distance ★ Best Dirt Speed is fastest among today's starters ● Has not raced for more than 5 months ● Poor Jockey win%
★ Drops in Class today

DATE TRK	DIST						RR RACETYPE	CR	E1	E2/	LP	1c	2c	SPD	PP	ST	1C	2C	Str	FIN	JOCKEY		ODDS	Top Finishers	Comment	
Previously trained by BOOKMAN CLARK A.																										
17Nov06Mnr10	1 1/16 ft	:243	:49	1:152	1:521	3↑	105 Clm5000n1Y	103	70	61/	32	+6	+11	41	9	32	44	35	99	1016¼	Magrell JM121	Lb	6.30	ThrbnRbn¾FlyByPr2¾OnMorWn4½	Tracked pace; wilted	10
24Oct06Mnr10	170 ft	:231	:472	1:133	1:454	3↑	105 Clm5000n1Y	106	73	67/	61	-5	-2	60	4	2½	2hd	31	45	49¼	MagrellJM121	Lb	4.60	AlxdsBd2Bortz1¾MactwBy6	Pressed pace; weakened	10
24Sep06Mnr2	1m ft	:233	:471	1:141	1:421	3↑	106 Clm5000n2Y	107	89	75/	66	+11	+3	66	3	1hd	1hd	1½	2hd	44¾	MagrellJM115	Lb	7.20	Brtbicky1¼EpcActnkWyTTrst3	No breathers; weakened	9
Previously trained by KING GARY M.																										
19Jly06Del8	1m ft	:231	:47	1:13	1:391	3↑	108 Clm5000n16mx	107	89	81/	56	+6	-2	63	5	2hd	2½	2hd	47	816	Umana J123	Lbf	41.80	Wild Paul6¾Brass Arrow3American Princenk	Used up	10
25Jun06Del6	170 sy	:232	:481	1:15	1:452	3↑	108 Clm5000n16mx	108	82	70/	53	-1	-10	57	9	31½	3hd	2½	59	720¼	MadrigalJrR123	Lbf	10.60	MmboMn4¾Alnsky6¼RcknAgn¾	Pressed pace; faltered	9
29May06Del10	1 1/16 ft	:243	:484	1:14	1:48	3↑	106 Clm5000n16mx	108	78	76/	69	-3	-1	71	6	1½	11	11	1½	25¼	MadrigalJrR123	Lbf	6.20	LcnsToTor5¾StrcrosdNtiv6¾Bandn6¼	Faded to share 2nd Dead heat	7
08May06Del1	1 1/16 ft	:232	:473	1:14	1:472	3↑	107 Clm5000	104	89	77/	28	+8	-3	47	3	2hd	1hd	2½	59¾	529¼	Elliott S119	Lbf	3.40	CrossKeys2¾Elgloesmio5¾YoyoJbo7	Tired; being eased	7
21Jan06Tam11	1 1/16 ft	:241	:482	1:132	1:454	4↑	109 Clm6250	110	77	75/	77	-8	-5	75	5	12	1hd	21	32	49½	Vli-gomezH118	Lb	3.50	SoctySm¾Sibrino4¾CmOnSmky1	Gradually weakened	9
10Jan06Tam4	1 1/16 ft	:234	:474	1:133	1:462	4↑	108 Clm6250	110	70	66/	73	0	-7	68	3	33	34½	3½	2½	35	Vli-gomezH118	Lb	3.80	DreminOfGrn4¾ColonlLol¾Bandn2	Bid 1/4p; wknd late	10
30Dec05Tam6	1 1/16 ft	:233	:472	1:121	1:461	3↑	109 Clm8500	110	83	80/	63	+2	+5	70	4	2½	2hd	21	32½	49½	Vli-gomezH118	Lb	5.80	Adhm3Goldnrun2ColonlLol¾	Pressed 3/4; weakened	10

20Apr Tdn 4f ft :503 B 20/29 12Apr Tdn 4f my :521 B 15/19 18Sep'06 Tdn 3f ft :372 B 3/11 30Apr'06 Del 4f ft :511 B 13/16 06Dec'05 Tam 4f ft :501 B 20/44 28Jly'05 AP 4f ft :512 B 72/86
07Jly'05 AP 4f ft :54 B 42/46 21Mar'05 Haw 4f ft :50 B 5/19 21Feb'05 Haw 4f gd :492 B 5/20 08Jun'04 Mnr 3f ft :373 B 3/16 17Apr'04 Haw 5f gd 1:023 B 9/17 13Mar'04 Haw 5f ft 1:023 B 20/28

---

8 Mountain Top (E/P 4)

12/1 — Own: Miguel Coll — White; blue bars; yellow sun
URIETA-MORAN VICTOR (63 6-9-9 13%)

$4,000 B. g. 6
Sire: Zafonic (Gone West)
Dam: Monroe (Sir Ivor)
Brdr: Juddmonte Farms (GB)
Trnr: Morales Nabu (8 0-0-1 0%)

Power Rating: 95.9 (5th) — L 120

Life:	45 3-5-3	$63,086	83	Fst	27 1-4-2	$37,289	83
2007	2 0-0-0	$124	63	Off	7 2-0-1	$17,984	77
2006	15 0-0-2	$5,041	78	Dis	4 0-1-1	$5,228	78
Tdn	7 0-0-1	$1,323	67	Trf	11 0-1-0	$8,613	77
				AW	0 0-0-0	$0	

2007	72	14%	44%	-1.23
JKYw/EP types	112	15%	42%	-0.26
JKYw/ Trn L60	3	0%	0%	-2.00
JKYw/ Routes	12	17%	50%	-0.53

2007	8	0%	13%	-2.00
Sprnt-Sprnt-Rte	9	11%	11%	+3.84
Sprint to Rte	18	11%	28%	+1.58
No class chg	44	7%	18%	+0.17

Sire Stats: AWD 8.0f 17%Mud 59MudSts 3.17spi
Dam'sSire:AWD 8.0f 15%Mud 511MudSts 3.26spi

★ Eligible to improve in 3rd start since layoff ● Only 3 wins in 45 career starts ● Poor Trainer win% ● Poor record at this track

DATE TRK	DIST						RR RACETYPE	CR	E1	E2/	LP	1c	2c	SPD	PP	ST	1C	2C	Str	FIN	JOCKEY		ODDS	Top Finishers	Comment	
29Apr07Tdn13	5½ ft	:23	:47	1:001	1:071	4↑	106 Clm4000n1y+	106	74	70/	68	-1	+2	63	4	7	107¼	1110	77¼	63½	Munayila F122	Lbf	13.70	Clever JimmyC¾Tiger On Tour1Res Nullius¾	Late gain	12
15Apr07Tdn7	5f gd	:223	:462		:584	4↑	106 Clm4000n13m	108		70/	76			60	6	7	77¾	79	69½	55	MunayllaF122	Lbf	34.10	CptnBing1¼RdmptnSng1CmpChin1¾	Failed to menace Dead heat	9
17Sep06Tdn8	6f ft	:222	:463	1:001	1:132	3↑	104 Clm3500n19m	103	73	71/	76	+2	0	58	10	2	99¾	98¼	119	108½	Oro E122	Lb	11.60	BigLordNlson2¾BlazinDr¾ExpectedComndhd	No factor	12
08Sep06Tdn2	6f ft	:23	:472	1:001	1:131	3↑	104 Clm3500n19m	105	81	70/	87	-5	-8	67	5	5	47	54½	33½	33½	Oro E122	Lb	9.10	ChckSttion2¾BgLordNlsn¾MontnTop2	Mild bid; inside	9
24Aug06Tdn8	5f ft	:223	:47		1:001	3↑	101 Clm3500n16m	102		78/	69			60	3	7	84¾	64¼	67¾	56	Oro E122	Lb	6.50	SonOfMrlh3¼Gibustr¾LilGent¾	Saved ground; evenly	10
17Aug06Tdn13	170 ft	:234	:483	1:152	1:47	3↑	105 Clm3500n4L	105	63	59/	65	-8	-6	58	7	69½	54½	43	36	411½	Banda S118	Lb	4.20	Galero1¾Truckin On6¾My Texas Tim¾	Evenly late	11
29Jly06Tdn11	170 ft	:23	:472	1:132	1:443	3↑	108 Clm5000n16m	107	64	67/	72	-2	-3	66	7	57¼	77¾	75	45½	511	Oro E122	Lbf	8.80	ClaimForm2¾IrishEmblm2¾Red I Am5¾	Failed to menace	8
Previously trained by GUTIERREZ ANGEL																										
05Jly06Del3	1 1/16 sy	:241	:484	1:134	1:472	3↑	108 Clm5000n16mx	107	69	64/	76	-4	-2	68	5	33½	34½	39½	39½	310½	Jurado EM123	Lb	11.50	Allensky7¾AmericaPrince3¾MountinTop4	Failed to gain	5
25Jun06Del8	170 sy	:232	:481	1:15	1:452	3↑	108 Clm5000n16mx	108	82	71/	61	-1	-10	62	4	21	2hd	1½	36	616	Bella AO123	Lb	10.10	Mambo Moon4¾Allensky6¾RockinAgain¾	Dueled; empty	9
07Jun06Del5	6f wf	:223	:462	:581	1:122	3↑	108 Clm5000n16mx	107	84	83/	67	-4	-8	62	5	4	32½	33	47½	414	Bella AO123	Lb	12.50	SctRn7¾TxsPion2WdsrDcks4¾	Well placed; gave way	7

●18Feb'06 Tam 6f ft 1:163 B 1/4 27Nov'05 Tam 4f ft :51 B 18/22 30Mar'05 Bow 4f ft :511 B 12/14 19Feb'05 Evt 4f ft :511 Bg21/43 10Dec'04 FG 5f ft 1:024 B 16/61 18Nov'04 FG 4f ft :513 B 34/47
10Nov'04 Kee 4f ft :521 B 8/8 30Oct'04 Kee 4f wf :532 B 9/11 01Oct'04 Sar tr.t 4f ft :51 B 7/16 26Aug'04 Bel tr.t 5f ft 1:013 B 3/16 14Aug'04 Bel tr.t 5f ft 1:04 B 14/17 08Aug'04 Bel 4f ft :52 B 33/34

tsnhorse.com

Ultimate PP's w/ Quick Play Comments — **River Downs** Clm 4000NW1Y+ 1 Mile. 4up Friday, May 11, 2007 **Race 1 (TDN - #1)**

E1	E2/LATE	SPD
76	68/ 71	68

Last 3 Years

		RACETYPE STATS:	# Races	Win%	FAVORITES Itm%	$2ROI	Average Field Size	Median $2 Win Payoff	% Winners < 5/1	% Winners >= 5/1 < 10/1	% Winners >= 10/1
TDN	3up	CLM 3500 - 5000 N365 Dirt 8f - 8.5f	43	19%	60%	-1.11	8.7	$8.20	65%	14%	21%

Track Bias Stats

	* MEET Totals *					* WEEK Totals *			
DIRT 8.0f	Speed Bias: 74%		WnrAvgBL		DIRT 8.0f	Speed Bias: 89%		WnrAvgBL	
# Races: 23	04/12 - 05/06		1stCall: 2.4		# Races: 9	05/03 - 05/06		1stCall: 2.2	
%Wire: 13%			2ndCall: 0.8		%Wire: 11%			2ndCall: 1.0	
	Early	Speed	Late	Speed		Early	Speed	Late	Speed
Runstyle:	E	E/P	P	S	Runstyle:	E	E/P	P	S
	+	++				+	++		
Impact Values	1.47	1.49	0.91	0.13	Impact Values	1.72	1.71	0.57	0.00
%Races Won	26%	48%	22%	4%	%Races Won	22%	67%	11%	0%
Post Bias:	RAIL	1-3	4-7	8+	Post Bias	RAIL	1-3	4-7	8+
			+			+		+	
Impact Values	0.94	0.52	1.43	0.87	Impact Values	1.74	0.87	1.17	0.77
Avg Win %	13%	7%	24%	6%	Avg Win %	22%	11%	19%	5%

Race Summary

#	HorseName	ML Odds	Med Eqp	Days Since L/R	Run Style	PTS	Avg Dist/Surf PACE-SPEED E1	E2/Late	Spd	Avg Race Rtng	Best Pace E1	E2/Late	Final Speed Sp1	Sp2	Sp3	Sp4	ACL	Rcg Spd Avg	R1	R2	R3	Mud Spd	Pedigree Stats Mud Sts	Mud % Mud	Sire AWD	Dam Sire's AWD
5	Slews Resurrection	3/1	L	333	P	2	65	72/ 81	(75)	109	65	69/ 85	66	76.	69	69.	106.3	70	108	108	106	69	92	12	7.3	6.5
8	Mountain Top	12/1	L	12..	++E/P	4	65	66/ 71	(66)	107	69	72/ 77	63	60	58	67	105.6	60	106	106	104	68	59	17	8.0	8.0
6	Proud American	5/2	L	8.	+E	6	68	59/ 75	* 63*	103	73	70/ 79	57.	66.	59.	58.	103.6	61	103	102	103	45	319	11	7.1	9.2
7	Bandana	8/1	L	175	+E	5	84	74/ 61	(63)	107	89	81/ 69	41.	60.	66.	63.	105.9	56	105	105	106	57	718	9	7.2	7.0
1	European Defense	6/1	L	21.	P	5	68	61/ 59	(55)	105	70	67/ 65	55	61	57	55.		58	104	105	104		77	14	6.3	7.0
2	Sober Moment	12/1	L	13..	S		54	52/ 64	* 51*	105	67	64/ 84	47.	47.	55.	66.	103.6	50	104	103	105	61	805	13	7.0	8.4
3	Perfect Call	10/1	L	77..	S	4	58	56/ 58	(50)	105	76	70/ 67	46.	48	55	48.		50	103	103	106	70	158	15	6.5	7.8
4	Cinematic	4/1	L	13	+E	5	89	75/ 35	47	109	89	82/ 77	47.	48	56	79.		50	108	106	109	48	162	19	6.4	6.9

Speed Last Race	Back Speed	Current Class	Average Class Last 3	Power Rating	Early Pace Last Race	Late Pace Last Race
66 Slews Resurrection	79 Cinematic	106.0 Proud American	108.2 Slews Resurrection	103.8 Cinematic	89 Cinematic	71 Proud American
63 Mountain Top	76 Slews Resurrection	103.2 Cinematic	105.4 Proud American	103.7 Slews Resurrection	73 Slews Resurrection	68 Mountain Top
57 Proud American	73 Mountain Top	102.9 Sober Moment	105.2 Bandana	96.2 Proud American	72 European Defense	65 Slews Resurrection
55 European Defense	71 Bandana	98.9 Perfect Call	104.9 Mountain Top	95.9 Bandana	70 Bandana	64 Perfect Call
47 Sober Moment	69 Proud American	NA Slews Resurrection	104.6 Cinematic	95.9 Mountain Top	70 Mountain Top	62 European Defense
47 Cinematic	66 Sober Moment	NA Mountain Top	103.4 European Defense	92.1 European Defense	60 Proud American	47 Sober Moment
46 Perfect Call	57 Perfect Call	NA Bandana	101.7 Sober Moment	86.7 Sober Moment	60 Sober Moment	35 Cinematic
41 Bandana	55 European Defense	NA European Defense	101.2 Perfect Call	83.8 Perfect Call	55 Perfect Call	32 Bandana

#	Speed Last Race		#	Prime Power		#	Class Rating		#	Best Speed at Dist	
2	Julie's Rib	56	2	Julie's Rib	91.3	5	Slybecca	103.1	2	Julie's Rib	60
5	Slybecca	56	5	Slybecca	87.9	2	Julie's Rib	102.5	5	Slybecca	56
1	Careful Carol	50	1	Careful Carol	86.6	4	Morning Moon	100.4	3	Chestnut Anna	55

2

Exacta / Trifecta / Superfecta (Ten Cent Minimum) / Pick 3 (Races 2-3-4)

	E1	E2/LATE	SPEED
PARS:	86	78/ 68	58

6 Furlongs. ⓕⓢClm 5000 Purse $6,800. SIMULCAST FROM RIVER DOWNS. FOR REGISTERED OHIO BRED FILLIES AND MARES THREE YEARS OLD AND UPWARD WHICH HAVE NEVER WON TWO RACES. Three Year Olds, 116 lbs., Older, 124 lbs. Non-winners of a race since April 11 Allowed 2 lbs. A race since March 11 Allowed 4 lbs. Claiming Price $5,00 0 .

Post Time: (1:25)/12:25/11:25/10:25

1 Careful Carol (E/P 3)

Own: M. Y. Stables: Inc.
5/1 Yellow, green my
ADAM MATHIEU G. (17 2-4-2 12%)

$5,000 Ch. f. 3
Sire: Mahogany Hall (Woodman)
Dam: Slight At Night (Executive Order)
Brdr: South River Ranch Inc. (OH)
Trnr: Nance Michael W. (7 1-2-1 14%)

Power Rating: 86.6 (3rd) 114

Life:	7 1 - 1 - 0	$5,255	55	Fst	3 0 - 0 - 0	$797	51
2007	6 1 - 1 - 0	$4,795	55	Off	4 1 - 1 - 0	$4,458	55
2006	1 0 - 0 - 0	$460	25	Dis	3 1 - 0 - 0	$3,705	51
RD	0 0 - 0 - 0	$0		Trf	0 0 - 0 - 0	$0	
				AW	0 0 - 0 - 0	$0	

2007	69	10%	33%	-0.77
JKYw/EP types	75	7%	21%	-1.06
JKYw/ Sprints	30	13%	33%	-0.47

+2007	105	23%	61%	-0.60
+31-90daysAway	253	18%	44%	-0.44
+Mdn wnr L/R	52	27%	48%	-0.40
Claiming	569	17%	46%	+0.06

Sire Stats: AWD 7.0f 10%Mud 233MudSts 0.65spi
Dam'sSire: AWD 6.8f 15%Mud 968MudSts 0.79spi

★ Won last race (BEU 03/24 6f Dirt sloppy fsMd 5000)

● Moves up in class from last start ● Has not raced in 48 days
● Best Speed rating is well below the Avg Winning Speed

DATE TRK	DIST						RR	RACETYPE	CR	E1	E2/	LP	1c	2c	SPD	PP	ST	1C	2C	Str	FIN	JOCKEY		ODDS	Top Finishers	Comment	
24Mar07Beu^{4}	6f sy^{6}	:23^{2}	:48	1:01	1:14^{2}	3↑	96	ⓕⓢMC5000	99	80	73/	62	-3	0	50	3	4	2½	1^{1}	1^{1}	1^{nk}	Paucar E^{116}	b	*0.80	CrefulCrol^{nk}FrenchBbe^{5}¾RdCruisr^{2}	Just lasted; driving	7
07Mar07Beu^{2}	6f ft	:22^{2}	:46^{3}	:59^{1}	1:11	3↑	97	ⓕⓢMC5000	97	68	62/	75	-1	-4	51	1	6	6^{10}	6^{10}	4^{8}	4^{12}¾	Paucar E^{116}	b	1.80	ScotshMis^{4}¾SuprmBird^{4}SunSprt^{4}½	Passed tiring rivals	7
23Feb07Beu^{1}	5½ gd	:22^{4}	:47^{2}	1:00	1:07	3↑	97	ⓕⓢMC5000	100	80	73/	64	+2	+4	55	6	2	5^{3}½	4^{5}	3^{4}	2¾	Paucar E^{116}	b	*1.90	PlnOfThDy¾CrefulCrol^{1}½SuprmBird^{2}¾	Late rally; gaining	7
09Feb07Beu^{2}	5½ ft	:22^{4}	:46^{1}		1:06^{2}	3↑	99	ⓕⓢMdn 9.2k	98	74	74/	42	+1	+12	41	1	7	6^{5}½	7^{6}¾	7^{6}¾	6^{7}¾	Stokes LA^{116}	b	*0.50e	Baby Back Rib^{1}¾Chucks Legacy^{1}½Half Shell^{2}½	No factor	9
22Jan07Beu^{1}	6f gd	:24	:50^{1}	1:03^{4}	1:17	3↑	99	ⓕⓢMdn 9.2k	98	80	69/	60	-2	-6	43	8	4	5^{7}	3^{7}	3^{7}	4^{9}½	Paucar E^{116}	b	3.70	Forest Mil^{7}Imation^{1}½Kona Sunset^{1}	3 wide; tired	8
06Jan07Beu^{1}	5f sy^{5}	:23^{4}	:48^{4}		1:01^{3}		103	ⓕMdn 6.7k	98		64/	25			1	6	6	6^{8}¾	7^{15}	8^{18}	9^{34}½	Stokes J^{120}		2.60e	TimlessJewel^{4}¾SwetGretings^{2}PharawyEyes^{3}½	Outrun	9
01Dec06Beu^{1}	5½ ft	:23	:48^{1}	1:00^{3}	1:07^{4}		103	ⓕⓢMdn 9.2k	101	67	47/	33	+2	+1	25	5	4	5^{10}	5^{12}	4^{18}	4^{18}½	CamaqueC^{120}		14.10	Chissmountin^{8}½HighHopsGP¾SnSprt^{4}	5 wide; no factor	6

30Dec'06 Beu 4f ft :49^{2} B *3/25* 21Dec'06 Beu 4f ft :51^{2} B *15/20* 29Nov'06 Beu (d) 3f ft :38 B *5/10* 08Nov'06 Beu 3f ft :39^{2} Hg *6/8* 23Jly'06 RD 4f ft :50 Bg *3/15* 02Jly'06 RD 3f ft :40 B *5/6*

2 Julie's Rib (E/P 2)

Own: Mary Ann Thomas
4/1 White, black horsehead
OUZTS PERRY WAYNE (142 18-25-20 13%)

$5,000 Dkbbr. m. 5
Sire: Alladin Rib (Da' White Judge)
Dam: Double Your Honey (Honey Jay)
Brdr: Win Row Farm; Ltd. & Ronald F. Bates (OH)
Trnr: Thomas Mary Ann (0 0-0-0 0%)

Power Rating: 91.3 (1st) L 120

Life:	25 1 - 3 - 3	$8,402	60	Fst	16 1 - 2 - 0	$6,471	56
2007	3 0 - 1 - 0	$1,230	60	Off	9 0 - 1 - 1	$1,931	60
2006	15 1 - 2 - 1	$6,447	58	Dis	15 1 - 1 - 0	$5,187	60
RD	9 0 - 0 - 0	$1,151	44	Trf	0 0 - 0 - 0	$0	
				AW	0 0 - 0 - 0	$0	

2007	501	10%	34%	-0.79
JKYw/EP types	137	9%	27%	-1.10
JKYw/ Sprints	277	9%	34%	-0.94

+2007	10	40%	60%	+5.50
+Up one class	1	100%	100%	+25.60

Sire Stats: AWD 6.7f 16%Mud 148MudSts 0.70spi
Dam'sSire: AWD 6.7f 10%Mud 1544MudSts 1.08spi

★ Highest Last Race Speed Rating (tie) ★ Highest Speed Figure at Today's Distance
★ Best Dirt Speed is fastest among today's starters (tie) ★ May improve while returning to a sprint
★ Ran 2nd in last race

● Only 1 win in 25 career starts ● Poor record at this track ● Poor record at this distance

DATE TRK	DIST						RR	RACETYPE	CR	E1	E2/	LP	1c	2c	SPD	PP	ST	1C	2C	Str	FIN	JOCKEY		ODDS	Top Finishers	Comment	
21Apr07Beu^{2}	1m ft	:25^{1}	:50^{2}	1:16^{2}	1:43^{3}	3↑	103	ⓕC3500n2y+	104	63	58/	66	8	0	56	5	1½	1^{hd}	1½	1½	2^{1}	Ortiz W^{120}	Lb	2.90	Doxolgst^{1}JuliesRib½Quite ADish^{nk}	Dueled; held place	6
14Apr07Beu^{3}	6f gd^{6}	:22^{3}	:46^{4}	:59^{3}	1:12^{4}	3↑	103	ⓕC3500n2y+	103	86	77/	71	+1	+6	60	2	4	4^{1}½	6^{5}	6^{5}½	4^{2}½	De LA^{120}	Lb	8.50	ThyAwnd¾MJExprs^{nk}MsRuDLc^{1}½	Angled out; mild rally	7
02Apr07Beu^{9}	5f ft	:23^{2}	:48^{1}		1:01^{2}	3↑	100	ⓕC3500n2L	100		74/	59			43	1	6	7^{4}¾	7^{8}¾	5^{5}½	4^{4}½	De LA^{120}	Lb	7.10	DominntCrkstr^{1}BnkThDo^{2}PrvtTricks^{1}½	Saved ground	8
13Dec06Beu^{1}	1^{70} gd	:24^{2}	:49^{2}	1:16^{3}	1:48^{4}	3↑	101	ⓕC3500C	105	67	60/	64	-4	+1	58	2	2^{hd}	1^{hd}	2^{hd}	2^{1}	2½	Stokes LA^{124}	Lb	10.30	PerfectHrt½JulisRib^{3}RecordTost^{4}½	Long duel; hard try	9
29Nov06Beu^{2}	1m ft	:24^{3}	:49	1:15^{1}	1:42^{3}	3↑	100	ⓕC3500C	101	66	53/	55	+1	+5	46	5	5^{8}½	3^{2}½	2^{4}	2^{7}	4^{8}	Endres J^{124}	Lbf	18.60	IukSlew^{4}¾GltrCpy¾CrcsPrksTco^{2}½	Chased; weakened	10
14Nov06Beu^{2}	6f ft	:22^{4}			1:13^{2}	3↑	103	ⓕC3500n2y+	101	72	66/	82	+3	+5	43	1	7	7^{9}½	6^{11}	5^{10}	5^{14}	CamaqueC^{120}	Lbf	17.70	SndAdFght^{3}½BoulBol½TkeMOn^{nk}	Showed little; inside	8
28Oct06Beu^{7}	5½ sy^{6}	:23^{4}	:49^{3}	1:02^{2}	1:09^{3}	3↑	101	ⓕC3500n2y+	102	66	57/	60	-6	-8	41	11	10	11^{7}½	9^{4}½	6^{7}½	5^{9}	Calo JL^{120}	Lb	31.80	AgisHidwy^{4}½CrtsMyoS^{nk}MsRuDLc^{3}	Passed tiring rivals	12
Previously trained by BATES C. LOUIS																											
03Sep06RD^{8}	6f ft	:23	:46^{1}	1:00^{2}	1:14^{2}	3↑	96	ⓕⓢClm5000n2L	99	73	68/	60	-1	+4	44	11	11	10^{6}	9^{7}½	8^{6}¾	7^{9}½	SolomonN^{120}	Lb	36.70	BudpestStr^{5}Gunagelchgod^{nk}BurstOfApluse^{no}	No factor	12
06Aug06RD^{5}	6f ft	:23^{1}	:47^{1}	1:01^{1}	1:16	3↑	94	ⓕⓢClm5000n2L	97	74	63/	66	+1	+4	43	7	8	9^{6}½	10^{8}½	9^{6}½	7^{6}¾	SolomonN^{120}	Lb	34.20	GreyGlnt^{no}PblcEny¾Gongtchgod^{1}½	Improved position	11
11Jun06RD^{4}	1^{70} sy^{6}	:24	:50^{1}	1:16^{3}	1:48^{2}	3↑	100	ⓕⓢClm5000n2L	98	59	35/	51	-7	-11	36	2	3^{4}½	4^{2}½	5^{7}	4^{12}	4^{20}½	SchaeferGA^{120}	Lb	36.20	Noprop^{1}¾MeanDriene^{nk}Canvas Lady^{12}¾	Failed to respond	8

24Mar Beu (d) 3f sy :40^{2} H *6/8* 24Oct'06 Beu 3f ft :37^{1} B *5/6* 13Oct'06 Beu 3f ft :38^{1} B *4/19* ●19Sep'05 RD 3f ft :37^{2} B *1/5* ●02Sep'05 RD 3f ft :36 B *1/4* ●29Jun'04 RD 5f ft 1:03 B *1/5*
21Jun'04 RD 4f ft :51 Bg *2/3* 08Jun'04 RD 5f ft 1:05^{3} Bg *9/11* 23May'04 RD 5f ft 1:06 B *1/2* 11May'04 RD 4f ft :52 B *8/13* 17Apr'04 RD 4f ft :51^{3} B *12/23* 10Apr'04 RD 3f ft :39^{3} B *9/14*

Ultimate PP's w/ Quick Play Comments **River Downs** ⒻⓈ Clm 5000 6 Furlongs. 3upF&M Friday, May 11, 2007 **Race 2**

E1	E2/LATE	SPD
86	78/ 68	58

3 Chestnut Anna (E/P 5)

4/1 — Own: Greg Verderber — Red, white 'v' on black triangle — ENDRES JESSICA (8 1-0-0 13%)

$5,000 Ch. m. 6 — Sire: Latvia (Danzig Connection) — Dam: Candy Whistles (Far Out East) — Brdr: Dr. Greg R. Verderber (OH) — Trnr: Verderber Greg (2 1-0-0 50%)

Power Rating: 82.8 (5th) — 124

	Sts	W	P	S	Earn	SPD		Sts	W	P	S	Earn	SPD
Life:	17	1	2	1	$9,655	55	Fst	16	1	2	1	$9,555	55
2007	2	1	0	0	$4,068	45	Off	0	0	0	0	$0	
2006	4	0	0	0	$486	48	Dis	13	1	2	1	$8,915	55
RD	13	1	2	1	$8,961	55	Trf	1	0	0	0	$100	46
							AW	0	0	0	0	$0	

2007	173	5%	17%	-1.40
JKYw/EP types	168	7%	27%	-1.42
+JKYw/ Trn L60	2	50%	50%	+0.30
JKYw/ Sprints	132	6%	16%	-1.28

2007	4	25%	25%	-0.85
Mdn win L/R	2	0%	50%	-2.00
Claiming	14	7%	43%	-1.20

Sire Stats: AWD 6.7f 4%Mud 81MudSts 0.38spi
Dam'sSire:AWD 7.1f 14%Mud 1593MudSts 1.10spi

★ Won last race (RD 05/04 6f Dirt fast fsMd 5000) ★ Eligible to improve in 3rd start since layoff

● Moves up in class from last start ● Poor Speed Figures in each recent start ● Poor record at this track ● Only 1 win in 17 career starts ● Poor record at this distance

DATE TRK	DIST		RR	RACETYPE	CR	E1	E2/	LP	1c	2c	SPD	PP	ST	1C	2C	Str	FIN	JOCKEY	ODDS	Top Finishers	Comment	
04May07RD[1]	6f ft	:23[4] :48[3] 1:17[2] 3↑	97	ⒻⓈMC5000	100	79	64/	61	-2	-3	41	6	1	2[hd]	2[hd]	1[hd]	1[1]¼	Endres J[124]	*1.30	ChestnutAn[1]¼RdCruisr[nk]AlydnSpt[3]	Drew clear, driving	6
28Apr07Beu[8]	5½ ft	:23[4] :48[4] 1:01[1] 1:07[4] 3↑	100	ⒻⓈMdn 9.2k	99	81	64/	61	-3	-4	45	3	3	2[1]	4[4]	4[5]¼	4[7]¼	Endres J[124]	26.80	Chucks Legacy¾Meluvsrasins[no]Flirtini[4]¼	Gave way	7
16Jly06RD[3]	6f ft	:22[4] :46[3] 1:00 1:14[3] 3↑	100	ⒻⓈMdn 13k	98	78	59/	62	+1	+1	38	1	5	5[4]¼	8[9]	8[8]¼	7[10]¼	Endres J[124]	30.30	Slybecca[1]¾Classy Forest[nk]RachelInTransit[1]	No factor	10
06Jly06RD[11]	Ⓣ 1m fm	:23[3] :47[4] 1:13 1:38[1] 3↑	103	ⒻMdn 10k	101	72	47/	62	+1	-1	46	7	5[3]½	6[1]¼	8[8]¾	8[13]	8[17]	Endres J[124]	80.20	Diva[3]Hopewebreakeven[hd]Queen Bahri[1]¼	Gave way	11
16Jun06RD[11]	6f ft	:22[4] :46 :58[3] 1:13[4] 3↑	101	ⒻⓈA13600n2L	98	71	56/	58	-1	+3	32	1	7	8[8]¼	9[14]	9[15]	8[19]¼	Endres J[120]	25.80	SiMiBout[2]¾MotormothS¾MisPtch[5]	Failed to menace	9
08Jun06RD[5]	6f ft	:23 :46[4] 1:00[1] 1:15 3↑	101	ⒻⓈMdn 13k	100	81	69/	64	+1	+3	48	11	1	6[3]¼	7[7]¼	8[8]	8[9]¼	Endres J[124]	26.00	MotormouthSu[1]¾Donamour[no]RachelInTransit[1]¾	No rally	11
28Aug05RD[9]	6f ft	:22[3] :45[4] :59 1:11[3] 3↑	102	ⓈA12300n2L	100	77	71/	66	-7	-9	51	7	1	2[2]¼	3[2]	5[6]¼	4[10]¼	CamaqueC[114]	21.90	Yankee Win[3]¾WatchMeSweep[hd]Kais Reward[6]¾	Faltered	7
31Jly05RD[4]	6f ft	:22[2] :46 :58[3] 1:11[2] 3↑	101	ⒻⓈMdn 11k	99	85	74/	61	-4	-10	49	10	4	3[1]	6[3]¼	7[10]	7[17]¼	Paucar E[123]	19.50	Celestia[2]Whitewater Maze[6]¼Runnin Joy[2]	Brief speed	10
19Jly05RD[8]	6f ft	:22[4] :44[4] :58[4] 1:12[4] 3↑	99	ⒻⓈMdn 11k	101	74	74/	67	-4	+10	54	5	1	3[5]	3[8]	3[7]	2[6]¼	Paucar E[123]	19.90	AnotherAnie[6]¼ChestnutAna[3]¼FrenchBbe[no]	Second best	11
02Jly05RD[7]	6f ft	:23[1] :46[3] :59[1] 1:13[2] 3↑	97	ⒻⓈMC5000	101	74	69/	74	-6	-6	55	4	5	2[3]	2[7]¼	2[2]¼	2[2]¾	Ouzts PW[123]	2.90	CJsGoldRs[2]¾ChstnAn[1]¾Somwoulfx[7]¼	Chased winner	9

21Apr Beu 5f ft 1:05[1] B *6/7* 15Apr RD 3f my :40 B *2/3* 27May'06 RD 5f ft 1:05 B *5/6* 19May'06 RD 4f my :52[3] B *2/2* 05May'06 RD 3f ft :37[1] B *4/11* 21May'05 RD 5f ft 1:05[1] B *7/9*
14May'05 RD 4f my :51 Bg*2/5* 07May'05 RD 3f ft :40 B *3/4* 17Aug'04 RD 5f ft 1:06 B *7/12* 10Aug'04 RD 4f ft :51[3] Bg*4/9* 30Jly'04 RD 4f ft :54 Bg*22/24* 23Jly'04 RD (d) 3f ft :39[4] B *10/11*

4 Morning Moon (E/P 2)

10/1 — Own: Gregg Hoover — White: blue blocks; blue blocked 'h' — CALO JOSE LUIS (64 10-6-7 16%)

$5,000 B. f. 4 — Sire: Mercer Mill (Forty Niner) — Dam: Moon Bright (High Brite) — Brdr: Pine Ridge Farm (OH) — Trnr: Hoover Greg (1 0-0-0 0%)

Power Rating: 86.5 (4th) — L 120

	Sts	W	P	S	Earn	SPD		Sts	W	P	S	Earn	SPD
Life:	17	1	3	1	$9,475	53	Fst	14	1	3	0	$8,762	53
2007	1	0	0	0	$116	47	Off	3	0	0	1	$713	41
2006	14	1	3	1	$8,979	53	Dis	14	1	3	1	$9,154	53
RD	10	0	2	1	$3,694	53	Trf	0	0	0	0	$0	
							AW	0	0	0	0	$0	

2007	214	14%	40%	-0.52
JKYw/EP types	277	13%	40%	-0.72
JKYw/ Trn L60	1	0%	0%	-2.00
JKYw/ Sprints	158	13%	39%	-0.53

2007	9	11%	22%	+1.98
Claiming	48	6%	27%	-1.10

Sire Stats: AWD 6.2f 12%Mud 394MudSts 0.61spi
Dam'sSire:AWD 6.5f 15%Mud 1636MudSts 0.98spi

★ Drops in Class today ★ Eligible to improve in 2nd start since layoff

● Poor Speed Figures ● Only 1 win in 17 career starts ● Poor record at this track

DATE TRK	DIST		RR	RACETYPE	CR	E1	E2/	LP	1c	2c	SPD	PP	ST	1C	2C	Str	FIN	JOCKEY	ODDS	Top Finishers	Comment	
28Apr07RD[11]	6f ft	:22[4] :46[1] :59[2] 1:13[1] 3↑	102	ⒻⓈA13600n2L	101	81	76/	56	-2	-1	47	1	4	5[3]¼	5[8]	7[11]	7[15]¼	Calo JL[120]	Lb 30.60	DtySbrt[10]MotrmthS¾TomburDFms[7]¼	Through after half	8
25Nov06Beu[4]	6f ft	:23 :47[3] 1:00[3] 1:14 3↑	101	ⒻⓈClm5000n2L	100	78	66/	66	-2	-3	47	5	3	3[3]¼	5[8]	4[8]¼	5[9]¾	AndersonM[122]	Lb 7.80	RglsBigGrl[3]¾Myhyml[1]¼MrcysHp¾	Dropped back; inside	9
18Nov06Beu[7]	6f ft	:22[4] :47[1] :59[4] 1:13 3↑	102	ⒻⓈA10500n2L	101	73	56/	78	-3	-6	48	7	2	5[5]¼	7[9]¼	6[9]¼	6[8]¼	AndersonM[118]	Lb 29.70	Lady Spirit[1]¾Motormouth Sue[6]¾Era Bayou¾	No factor *Dead heat*	8
03Nov06Beu[2]	6f ft	:23[3] :49[3] 1:02[3] 1:15[4] 3↑	96	ⒻⓈMC5000	101	77	62/	76	-5	-12	51	8	1	3[1]	1[2]	1[2]	1[hd]	Stokes LA[122]	Lb *1.60	MrnngMn[hd]TomburDFms[9]¾Mystx[2]¾	Bore out late; lasted	8
25Oct06Beu[9]	6f ft	1:14 3↑	99	ⒻⓈMdn 9.2k	99	74	55/	60	-3	-8	33	3	2	5[5]¼	7[9]	5[10]	4[18]¾	Stokes LA[121]	Lb 8.70	Donamour[16]¼MercyHony[1]¼HedMistres¾	No rally; inside	11
07Oct06Beu[6]	6f ft	:23[1] :48 1:01[3] 1:15[2] 3↑	96	ⒻⓈMdn 9.2k	98	76	69/	65	-2	0	48	8	1	4[3]¼	4[3]	2[2]¼	2[4]	Stokes LA[121]	Lb 5.70	RchlInTrt[4]MrngM[1]¼TmbrDFms[3]¼	Stalked; second best	8
01Sep06RD[14]	5½ ft	:23[2] :48 1:01[2] 1:08[2] 3↑	99	ⒻMC5000	101	78	65/	68	-3	-5	46	5	2	5[1]¼	2[1]	2[2]	4[2]	Paucar E[120]	Lb 7.30	VictorG[1]AnAdMsc¾NtiveDughtr¾	Failed to sustain bid	10
18Aug06RD[3]	6f ft	:22[4] :47[1] 1:01[1] 1:16[1] 3↑	97	ⒻⓈMC5000	100	73	60/	77	+6	+5	50	5	5	4[8]¼	6[9]¼	4[4]¼	2[1]	Stokes LA[118]	Lb 9.70	CryForKps[1]MornngMn[hd]MrcyHony[1]¼	Best stride late	9
05Aug06RD[7]	6f ft	:24 :49[2] 1:02[4] 1:17 3↑	98	ⒻⓈMC5000	94	79	58/	28	-4	-12	8	6	1	4¾	5[2]¼	6[8]	6[28]¼	Stokes LA[118]	Lb 2.50	Billie Faye Rib[2]¼MercyHoney¾StickyTouch[6]	Gave way	8
Previously trained by NAPIER WILLIAM J.																						
14Jly06RD[1]	6f ft	:23 :46[4] 1:00[4] 1:15[1] 3↑	99	ⒻⓈMC5000	101	81	78/	62	+2	+3	53	2	2	2[3]¼	2[2]¼	2[2]¼	2[4]¼	Stokes LA[118]	Lb 6.10	BcksInThWds[4]¼MrnngM[3]BiliFyRib[4]	Chased; 2nd best	8

21Apr RD 5f ft 1:04 B *2/4* 07Apr RD 4f ft :50[2] B *2/11* 31Mar RD 3f ft :36[1] B *2/6* 12Mar'06 Npr 5f gd 1:05 Bg *11/13* 05Mar'06 Npr 5f gd :10[2] B *6/12* 18Nov'05 Tdn 4f ft :51[4] B *7/7*
22Oct'05 Tdn 5f gd 1:03[3] Bg *4/12* 14Oct'05 Tdn 5f ft 1:03[1] B *6/9* 07Oct'05 Tdn 4f my :51[4] Bg *6/10* 22Sep'05 Tdn 3f ft :38 B *5/7* 15Sep'05 Tdn 3f gd :37[4] B *3/9* 08Sep'05 Tdn 3f ft :40[4] B *7/7*

5 Slybecca (P 4)

2/1 — Own: Richard L. Alderson — Yellow, navy blue stars — FELIX JULIO E. (85 11-16-12 13%)

$5,000 Dkbbr. f. 4 — Sire: Flight Forty Nine (Forty Niner) — Dam: Sly Spitfire (Pleasant Tap) — Brdr: Dick Alderson (OH) — Trnr: Moore Dennis T. (14 3-3-2 21%)

Power Rating: 87.9 (2nd) — L 120

	Sts	W	P	S	Earn	SPD		Sts	W	P	S	Earn	SPD
Life:	11	1	2	3	$13,997	56	Fst	7	1	1	2	$10,190	56
2006	8	1	2	1	$11,975	56	Off	4	0	1	1	$3,717	56
2005	3	0	0	2	$1,932	41	Dis	9	1	2	2	$12,815	56
RD	5	0	2	0	$5,506	55	Trf	0	0	0	0	$0	
							AW	1	0	0	0	$75	56

2007	246	9%	37%	-0.23
JKYw/ P types	117	13%	34%	-0.35
JKYw/ Trn L60	16	6%	50%	-0.21
JKYw/ Sprints	160	8%	34%	-0.38

2007	61	16%	44%	-0.37
90+ days away	45	4%	20%	-1.02
Shipper	151	8%	30%	-1.27
Down one class	56	11%	41%	-0.76

Sire Stats: AWD 6.0f 9%Mud 301MudSts 0.50spi
Dam'sSire:AWD 8.2f 15%Mud 647MudSts 1.77spi

★ Highest Last Race Speed Rating (tie) ★ Best Dirt Speed is fastest among today's starters (tie) ★ Drops in Class today

● Has not raced for more than 5 months ● Poor '90+ days away' trainer record: 4% wins 45sts

DATE TRK	DIST		RR	RACETYPE	CR	E1	E2/	LP	1c	2c	SPD	PP	ST	1C	2C	Str	FIN	JOCKEY	ODDS	Top Finishers	Comment	
26Nov06TP[4]	Ⓐ 6f ft	:22[4] :46[2] :58[4] 1:11[1] 3↑	104	ⒻC7500n2L	104	78	67/	76	-8	-8	56	5	3	6[2]¼	7[5]	8[7]½	7[8]¼	MojicaJr R[118]	L 18.90	SnpThRbn[2]DncForDgh¾PwrOn[1]	3 wide; no menace	10
11Nov06Hoo[3]	5½ gd	:23[1] :48[1] 1:07[2] 1:07[2] 3↑	99	ⒻC5000n2L	102	74	67/	75	-10	-8	56	6	4	3[1]¼	4[2]¼	2[2]½	3[3]	Blake J[119]	L *2.70	LileRidge[1]¼Boundlesdtr[1]¾Slybec[6]	Drftd in;best of rest	10
25Oct06Hoo[6]	6f ft	:23[2] :48[4] 1:02[2] 1:16 3↑	98	ⒻMC5000	104	79	66/	75	-1	-7	54	7	2	4[2]	3[1]	1[hd]	1[3]¼	MojicaJr R[118]	L *1.70	Slybec[3]¼LdyWithAHrt[4]¾DncngWl[no]	5wide turn, driving	9
24Aug06RD[13]	6f ft	:22[4] :46[2] 1:00[4] 1:15[2] 3↑	98	ⒻⓈMdn 13k	100	75	72/	65	+5	+10	51	8	9	7[8]¼	7[10]	5[8]	4[9]	Paucar E[119]	L 5.30	EraByou[9]¼HeadMistres[2]¼RachelInTrnst[1]¾	Bobbled start	12
11Aug06RD[4]	6f gd[s]	:23[3] :47[1] 1:00[2] 1:14[2] 3↑	100	ⒻⓈMdn 13k	102	75	68/	75	-7	-5	55	8	2	6[3]¼	6[4]¼	5[9]¾	2[5]¼	Paucar E[119]	L 4.30	Miss Patch[5]¼Slybecca[1]¾Rachel In Transit[nk]	Late rally	11
29Jly06RD[2]	6f my[s]	:22[4] :46[3] 1:01 1:14[3] 3↑	100	ⒻⓈMdn 13k	101	79	73/	58	+1	+7	46	9	2	6[4]¼	6[3]¾	5[5]¼	5[7]¼	PrescottRA[118]	L 5.60	MsSothrnSnd[2]¾RchlInTrnst[2]¾Gngn¼	5 wide; no rally	11
16Jly06RD[3]	6f ft	:22[4] :46[3] 1:00 1:14[3] 3↑	100	ⒻⓈMdn 13k	103	81	74/	68	+1	+1	55	2	6	4[2]¾	3[1]¼	1[hd]	1[1]¾	PrescottRA[118]	L 16.20	Slybec[1]¾ClsyForest[nk]RchlnTrnst[1]	Bore in late stretch *(Placed 2nd through disqualification)*	10
Previously trained by NEMANN RYAN																						
22Jun06RD[5]	6f ft	:23 :47[3] 1:01[1] 1:15[2] 3↑	100	ⒻⓈMdn 13k	98	81	72/	52	+2	-2	41	10	7	5[3]	4[1]	7[5]¼	7[10]¼	Sanchez C[117]	L 23.10	MnRvrBby[no]RchlnTrst[2]¼BslClgry[3]	Failed to sustain bid	12
Previously trained by MOORE DENNIS T.																						
15Nov05Beu[1]	5½ sy[s]	:22[3] :47[3] 1:00[4] 1:07[3]	107	ⒻⓈMdn 9.2k	107	83	66/	55	0	+1	41	8	3	4¾	3[3]¼	5[5]	6[6]¼	CcmiqueMA[120]	5.20	ForSocks¾S.R.AlladinGrl[3]¾MotormouthSu[no]	Gave way	9
29Oct05Beu[4]	6f ft	:22[4] :48[3] 1:01[3] 1:14[4]	107	ⒻⓈMdn 9.2k	103	78	61/	61	+1	-9	38	4	7	4[3]¾	6[2]¼	3[5]¼	3[9]¼	Eads JR[121]	5.20	Mynymilie[5]¼Aladin Queen[3]¾Slybecca[1]	No rally	9

03May RD 4f ft :50[4] B *2/3* 28Apr RD 3f ft :38[2] B *7/9* 23Oct'06 TP 3f ft :38[3] B *1/1* 13Jun'06 RD 5f ft 1:03[1] Bg*8/15* 06Jun'06 RD 5f ft 1:04 B *3/9* 29May'06 RD 4f ft :50 B *4/4*
20May'06 RD 4f ft :51[4] B *10/15* 13May'06 RD 4f my :51 B *3/11* 06May'06 RD 3f ft :38[2] B *4/6* 07Oct'05 Hoo 5f ft 1:04[4] B *4/5* 28Sep'05 TP 5f ft 1:05[2] Bg*4/8* 22Sep'05 TP 4f ft :49[1] Bg*6/18*

tsnhorse.com

E1	E2/LATE	SPD
86	78/ 68	58

Ultimate PP's w/ Quick Play Comments

River Downs FS Clm 5000 6 Furlongs. 3upF&M Friday, May 11, 2007 Race 2

6 3/1 **French Babe (E 4)**
Own: Stanley Richards
Green; green 1 on white slat
ROJAS CHRISTIAN (49 7-7-3 14%)

$5,000 Ch. m. 4 OHSEP 2003 $1k
Sire: French Legionaire (Grey Legion)
Dam: Ships Babe (An Eldorado)
Brdr: Daniel C. Stearns Dvm. (OH)
Trnr: Richards Stanley (0 0-0-0 0%)

Power Rating: 80.9 (8th) 122

	Starts	W	P	S	Earnings	Spd		Starts	W	P	S	Earnings	Spd
Life:	29	1	1	7	$14,795	55	Fst	22	1	0	6	$11,428	55
2007	6	1	1	1	$5,593	49	Off	7	0	1	1	$3,367	49
2006	5	0	0	0	$435	42	Dis	19	0	1	6	$8,764	54
RD	7	0	0	3	$4,290	54	Trf	0	0	0	0	$0	
							AW	0	0	0	0	$0	

2007	153	9%	27%	+0.56
JKYw/ E types	164	13%	35%	-0.08
JKYw/ Sprints	83	8%	23%	+1.21

2007	15	7%	27%	-1.68
Claiming	42	0%	2%	-2.00

Sire Stats: AWD 6.4f 8%Mud 901MudSts 0.38spi
Dam'sSire: AWD 6.7f 11%Mud 533MudSts 0.56spi

★ Drops in Class today ★ Early Speed running style helps chances
★ Ran 3rd vs tougher in last race

● Poor Speed Figures ● Only 1 win in 29 career starts ● Poor Trainer win%

DATE TRK	DIST							RR	RACETYPE	CR	E1	E2/	LP	1c	2c	SPD	PP	ST	1C	2C	Str	FIN	JOCKEY	ODDS	Top Finishers	Comment	
16Apr07Beu8	6f	ft	:233	:49	1:014	1:143	3↑	100	FSA10500n2L	100	79	65/	68	-3	-8	48	4	8	41½	42	33	34½	HernandezL119	b 16.60	BbyBckRb2½TomburDFms1½FrnchBb2½	No rally; inside	6
04Apr07Beu4	1m	ft	:243	:502	1:18	1:452	3↑	95	FSMC5000	99	64	44/	65	-1	-3	47	5	1½	1½	12½	14	12½	FrazitaJrLJ124	b *1.40	FrenchBb2½RdCruisr4½YsMothr6	Dueled, clear, driving	7
24Mar07Beu4	6f	sy5	:232	:48	1:01	1:142	3↑	96	FSMC5000	99	81	71/	64	-3	0	49	6	2	1½	21	21	2nk	FrazitaJrLJ124	b 11.90	CarefulCrolnkFrenchBbe5½RdCruisr2	Finished willingly	7
07Mar07Beu2	6f	ft	:222	:463	:591	1:11	3↑	97	FSMC5000	95	74	68/	59	-1	-4	43	4	4	57½	47½	69½	617½	Stokes LA124	b 12.20	Scottish Miss4½SupremBird4Sun Spirit4½	Steadied start	7
23Feb07Beu1	5½	gd	:224	:472	1:00	1:07	3↑	97	FSMC5000	99	81	69/	56	+2	+4	48	3	5	43½	58	58½	45	FrazitaJrLJ124	b 14.50	PlanOfTheDy½CarefulCarol1½SupremeBird2½	No threat	7
15Jan07Beu4	5½	sy5	:231	:482	1:01	1:074	3↑	97	FSMC5000	97	71	59/	57	-1	-4	40	6	6	56½	47	48	48½	FrazitaJrLJ124	b 14.70	FillyforennkPlanOfTheDay4½SunSpirit3½	3 wide; no rally	8
20Dec06Beu10	6f	ft	:234	:493	1:024	1:161	3↑	98	FSMdn 9.2k	92	74	57/	33	-1	-3	12	6	3	84½	86½	917	923	FrazitaJrLJ124	b 41.50	Mercy Honey1½FillyforennoMystaire4	Outrun	9
04Mar06Beu4	6f	ft	:233	:484	1:022	1:163	3↑	100	FMdn 6.7k	96	72	66/	26	-2	+3	12	1	6	67½	711	613	1034½	Calo JL124	b 41.20	SpringDeelte½Diorama7½Bank TheDoe2	Showed little	10
15Feb06Beu6	6f	ft	:231	:483	1:02	1:153	3↑	100	FSMdn 9.2k	100	77	70/	55	-1	-7	41	4	8	24	33	43½	810½	AndersonM124	b 58.10	MchlsSstr3½CoxMHidi2½ClsyForst1½	Rushed early; tired	11
21Jan06Beu8	6f	ft	:23	:481	1:012	1:144	3↑	99	FSMdn 9.2k	99	72	61/	65	-2	-4	41	7	9	77	89½	58½	614½	Calo JL124	b 19.30	YankeeSummer1½CoxMeHeidi1My LilDevil1½	No factor	12

27Nov06 Beu 4f ft :50 B 8/12 17Nov06 Beu (d) 3f my :39 B 7/10 03Jan06 Beu (d) 3f my :424 B 16/16 ●18Nov05 Beu 3f ft :372 B 1/4 ●04Nov05 Beu 3f ft :36 B 1/11 ●20Oct05 Beu (d) 3f my :37 B 1/9
06May05 Beu 5f ft 1:041 B 10/11 29Mar05 Beu (d) 4f my :49 B 1/2 ●21Mar05 Beu (d) 4f my :511 B 1/6 14Mar05 Beu 3f ft :381 B 2/4 22Oct04 Beu 3f ft :374 B 5/9 02Oct04 Beu 4f wf :521 Bg 8/11

Last 3 Years RACETYPE STATS:	# Races	FAVORITES Win%	Itm%	$2ROI	Average Field Size	Median $2 Win Payoff	% Winners < 5/1	% Winners >= 5/1 < 10/1	% Winners >= 10/1
RD 3up S CLM 5000 N2L Dirt 6f	27	59%	81%	+1.16	8.7	$6.00	85%	11%	4%

Track Bias Stats

*** MEET Totals ***

DIRT 6.0f
\# Races: 64
%Wire: 47%

Speed Bias: 80%
04/06 - 05/08

WnrAvgBL
1stCall: 1.4
2ndCall: 1.0

	Early	Speed	Late	Speed
Runstyle:	E	E/P	P	S
	++	+		
Impact Values	1.66	1.29	0.72	0.33
%Races Won	52%	28%	11%	9%

Post Bias:	RAIL	1-3	4-7	8+
			+	
Impact Values	0.85	0.89	1.14	0.71
Avg Win %	12%	13%	19%	4%

*** WEEK Totals ***

DIRT 6.0f
\# Races: 14
%Wire: 64%

Speed Bias: 86%
05/03 - 05/08

WnrAvgBL
1stCall: 1.2
2ndCall: 0.8

	Early	Speed	Late	Speed
Runstyle:	E	E/P	P	S
	++			
Impact Values	1.98	1.09	0.94	0.00
%Races Won	64%	21%	14%	0%

Post Bias	RAIL	1-3	4-7	8+
	+		+	
Impact Values	1.91	0.80	1.29	0.00
Avg Win %	29%	12%	22%	0%

Race Summary

#	HorseName	ML Odds	Med Eqp	Days Since L/R	Run Style	P T S	Avg Dist/Surf PACE-SPEED E1	E2/Late	Spd	Avg Race Rtng	Best Pace E1	E2/Late	Final Speed Sp1	Sp2	Sp3	Sp4	ACL	Rcg Spd Avg	R1	R2	R3	Mud Spd	Pedigree Stats Mud Sts	Mud %	Sire AWD	Dam Sire's AWD
5	Slybecca	2/1	L	166	P	4	77	67/ 75	(55)	101	81	74/ 76	56.	56.	54.	51.	99.2	55	104	99	98	46	301	9	6.0	8.2
2	Julie's Rib	4/1	L	20	+E/P	2	86	76/ 65	' 52*	102	86	77/ 71	56	60.	43.	58		53	103	103	100	41	148	16	6.7	6.7
1	Careful Carol	5/1		48	+E/P	3	76	68/ 66	' 50*	98	80	74/ 75	50	51.	55.	41.	96.8	52	96	97	97	50	233	10	7.0	6.8
6	French Babe	3/1		25	++E	4	80	67/ 62	' 48*	99	81	69/ 68	48.	47	49	43.	98.6	48	100	95	96	49	901	8	6.4	6.7
4	Morning Moon	10/1	L	13.	+E/P	2	81	76/ 56	47	102	81	78/ 78	47.	47.	48.	51.	97.7	47	102	101	102	41	394	12	6.2	6.5
3	Chestnut Anna	4/1		7..	+E/P	5	80	64/ 61	' 43'	99	81	69/ 64	41.	45.	38.	46T	96.8	41	97	100	100		81	4	6.7	7.1

Speed Last Race	Back Speed	Current Class	Average Class Last 3	Power Rating	Early Pace Last Race	Late Pace Last Race
56 Slybecca	60 Julie's Rib	101.8 Julie's Rib	103.1 Slybecca	91.3 Julie's Rib	76 Morning Moon	76 Slybecca
56 Julie's Rib	56 Slybecca	100.5 Morning Moon	102.5 Julie's Rib	87.9 Slybecca	73 Careful Carol	68 French Babe
50 Careful Carol	55 Careful Carol	99.4 Chestnut Anna	100.4 Morning Moon	86.6 Careful Carol	67 Slybecca	66 Julie's Rib
48 French Babe	53 Morning Moon	99.1 Careful Carol	99.6 French Babe	86.5 Morning Moon	65 French Babe	62 Careful Carol
47 Morning Moon	48 French Babe	99.1 French Babe	98.8 Chestnut Anna	82.6 Chestnut Anna	64 Chestnut Anna	61 Chestnut Anna
41 Chestnut Anna	48 Chestnut Anna	NA Slybecca	98.7 Careful Carol	80.9 French Babe	63 Julie's Rib	56 Morning Moon

#	Speed Last Race	
4	Windcauseruckus	60
1	Hooves Of Thunder	59
5	Erotick Mountain	55

#	Prime Power	
6	Hunterpunter	94.0
2	Command The Best	90.9
3	Great Charisma	89.7

#	Class Rating	
6	Hunterpunter	104.2
7	What Now Wynn	102.2
3	Great Charisma	101.7

#	Best Speed at Dist	
7	What Now Wynn	67
6	Hunterpunter	66
4	Windcauseruckus	65

3

Exacta / Trifecta / Superfecta (Ten Cent Minimum) / Pick 3 (Races 3-4-5)

Simulcast of Thistledown race number 3

	E1	E2/LATE	SPEED
PARS:	89	86/ 74	70

5½ Furlongs. Clm 4000NW2L Purse $6,900. FOR THREE YEAR OLDS AND UPWARD WHICH HAVE NEVER WON TWO RACES. Three Year Olds, 120 lbs., Older, 122 lbs. Non-winners of a race since April 11 Allowed 2 lbs. A race since March 11 Allowed 4 lbs. Claiming Price $4,000 (Ohio Registered Foals Preferred) .

Post Time: (1:45)/12:45/11:45/10:45

5 1/2 FURLONGS

1 Hooves Of Thunder (P 1) $4,000

9/2
Own: Bruno Schickedanz
White; blue stripes
SKERRETT JEFFREY (76 16-3-11 23%)

Ch. g. 5 ONTDEC 2003 $2k
Sire: With Approval (Caro Bre))
Dam: Bibbie Boppie Boo (Prospect Bay)
Brdr: Box Arrow Farm; Kimberly Conn & Randyconn (ONT-C)
Trnr: Radosevich Jeffrey A. (62 15-12-6 29%)

Power Rating: 89.0 (5th) 122

Life:	7	1 - 0 - 1	$5,405	59	Fst	3	0 - 0 - 0	$363	51
2007	2	1 - 0 - 1	$4,550	59	Off	4	1 - 0 - 1	$5,042	59
2006	4	0 - 0 - 0	$745	56	Dis	2	1 - 0 - 0	$3,998	58
Tdn	2	1 - 0 - 1	$4,550	59	Trf	0	0 - 0 - 0	$0	
					AW	0	0 - 0 - 0	$0	

2007	71	23%	42%	-0.26
JKYw/ P types	88	8%	50%	-1.35
JKYw/ Trn L60	2	0%	50%	-2.00
+JKYw/ Sprints	54	22%	41%	-0.06

+2007	168	20%	52%	-0.32
+Mdn win L/R	56	27%	55%	+0.05
+Claiming	1654	22%	51%	-0.28

Sire Stats: AWD 7.7f 15%Mud 983MudSts 1.57spi
Dam'sSire:AWD 6.4f 14%Mud 351MudSts 1.01spi

★ Hot Jockey in last 7 days (20 5- 3- 3) ★ Switches to a high% Jockey ★ High % Trainer
★ Won last race (TDN 04/27 5.5f Dirt sloppy Md 4000) ★ Eligible to improve in 3rd start since layoff
● Moves up in class from last start ● Best Speed rating is well below the Avg Winning Speed

DATE TRK	DIST						RR	RACETYPE	CR	E1	E2/	LP	1c	2c	SPD	PP	ST	1C	2C	Str	FIN	JOCKEY		ODDS	Top Finishers	Comment
27Apr07Tdn[3]	5½ sy	:23[3]	:48[3]	1:02	1:08[3]	4↑	99	MC4000	101	77	70/	78	-3	-6	59	8	5	6[3]	3[2]½	2[1]	1[1]	Spieth S[122]	L	3.00	HvsOfThndr[1]HevnsBoy[2]½EsasCt[nk]	Left handed urging 8
12Apr07Tdn[12]	6f sy	:23[2]	:48[2]	1:01[4]	1:14[4]	4↑	99	MC4000	100	77	66/	76	-5	-9	55	9	3	4[3]	4[3]½	4[3]	3[5]¾	Dailey A[122]	L	6.00e	ShilohsCt[3]¾HevnsBoy[1]¾HovsOfThndr[6]	Best of the rest 10
Previously trained by FOURNIER MARK																										
29Oct06FE[2]	5f my[s]	:23[1]	:47[1]		1:00	3↑	102	MC5000	100		71/	73			56	3	6	8[6]½	8[9]¼	8[10]	8[7]¾	RobinsonEK[120]	L	27.70	GenerlDputy½Essa's Cal[1]¾DiefTheChll½	Showed little 9
10Oct06FE[10]	6f ft	:22[3]	:46[1]	:58[1]	1:12[4]	3↑	102	MC5000	101	77	57/	75	0	+3	46	10	8	8[4]½	11[12]	9[13]	8[9]	RobinsonK[120]	Lb	7.70	SmkNSnshn[1]EdieThSrg[2]¾RegalEs[nk]	Failed to menace 12
24Sep06FE[5]	6f gd	:23[1]	:47[4]	1:00[3]	1:14[1]	3↑	101	MC5000	103	74	60/	78	-2	-5	52	5	8	7[4]½	10[6]½	4[5]	4[3]½	RobinsonK[120]	Lb	12.80	JudithsTril[1]¼ImARobber[1]¾GenerlDputy[nk]	Going well late 11
Previously trained by WARRING JEFF																										
22Jan06Tam[5]	6f ft	:21[1]	:44[1]	:57[2]	1:11	3↑	104	Mdn 18k	100	66	52/	57	+10	+11	28	4	8	8[17]	10[23]	10[24]	10[30]½	ClementeA[123]	L	94.10	Windigo[4]¾King Bull[2]¾Calculating Man[1]¾	No threat 10
27Dec05Tam[1]	6f ft	:23	:46[2]	:58[4]	1:11[3]	3↑	104	MC25000	101	62	61/	77	-5	-7	51	7	11	11[12]	11[13]	10[13]	9[19]½	ClementeA[118]	L	23.60	YouAMyDstiny[no]SwetDevil[3]½JungITig½	Showed little 11

31Mar Tdn 4f ft :50[4] Bg 20/37 20Mar Tdn 4f ft :50[1] B 5/5 29Dec'06 Mnr 6f ft 1:19[1] Bg 1/2 23Dec'06 Mnr (d) 4f my :53[1] B 11/19 15Dec'06 Mnr 4f gd :53 B 4/14 18Sep'06 FE 4f ft :50[2] H 18/31
11Sep'06 FE 4f ft :50[2] H 9/9 05Sep'06 FE 5f ft 1:02 Hg 5/7 28Aug'06 FE (d) 4f my :50[2] H 3/8 ●21Aug'06 FE 3f ft :36[1] H 1/15 14Aug'06 FE 4f ft :51 Hg 6/17 07Aug'06 FE 4f ft :52[3] H 21/21

2 Command The Best (S 2) $4,000

10/1
Own: Dave Rapp And Burnt Clover Farm
White; green 'burnt clover farm'
URIETA-MORAN VICTOR (63 8-8-8 13%)

Dkbbr. h. 7 KEESEP 2001 $140k
Sire: Forest Wildcat (Storm Cat)
Dam: Sovereign Command (Sovereign Dancer)
Brdr: Dr. J. Fred Miller III (KY)
Trnr: Marino James G. (11 1-2-1 9%)

Power Rating: 90.9 (2nd) L 118

Life:	16	1 - 1 - 4	$20,427	75	Fst	11	1 - 1 - 3	$18,696	75
2007	1	0 - 0 - 0	$69	50	Off	5	0 - 0 - 1	$1,731	63
2005	4	0 - 0 - 1	$819	57	Dis	1	0 - 0 - 0	$69	50
Tdn	9	1 - 0 - 1	$8,047	65	Trf	0	0 - 0 - 0	$0	
					AW	0	0 - 0 - 0	$0	

2007	72	14%	44%	-1.23
JKYw/ S types	133	8%	29%	-0.68
JKYw/ Trn L60	7	14%	57%	-1.20
JKYw/ Sprints	60	13%	43%	-1.36

2007	11	9%	36%	-1.49
No class chg	156	10%	28%	-0.77
Claiming	182	10%	29%	-0.76

Sire Stats: AWD 6.3f 17%Mud 595MudSts 1.87spi
Dam'sSire:AWD 7.4f 14%Mud 1170MudSts 2.74spi

★ Best Dirt Speed is fastest among today's starters ★ Eligible to improve in 2nd start since layoff
● Finished far back in last start ● Only 1 win in 16 career starts

DATE TRK	DIST						RR	RACETYPE	CR	E1	E2/	LP	1c	2c	SPD	PP	ST	1C	2C	Str	FIN	JOCKEY		ODDS	Top Finishers	Comment
27Apr07Tdn[11]	5½ sy	:23[3]	:48[1]	1:00[4]	1:07[2]	4↑	102	Clm4000n2L	100	79	66/	62	-7	-7	50	7	1	5[1]½	4[4]½	4[6]½	6[11]	Urieta-moranV[118]	Lb	49.40	NoCrs[nk]ThieOfFm[4]¾HndslyWld[3]	Lacked late response 10
28Jly05Tdn[12]	6f ft	:22[4]	:47	:59[4]	1:13[1]	3↑	101	Clm3500n2L	102	75	70/	75	-2	-5	57	4	8	8[8]	7[4]½	4[5]½	3[6]¾	HannigardL[118]	Lb	34.00	OrShdow[4]CalMeGold[2]¾ComndTheBest¾	2w; late gain 10
16Jly05Tdn[12]	6f sy[s]	:22[3]	:47	1:00[2]	1:14	3↑	102	Clm3500n2L	99	68	57/	70	+1	0	43	3	7	10[10]	10[12]	10[12]	9[12]¾	GonzalezLA[116]	Lb	22.80	TrvALng[hd]ClMGold[1]CostngBrnz¾	Bumped start; trailed 10
20Jun05Tdn[4]	6f ft	:22[2]	:46[1]	:59[3]	1:13[2]	3↑	102	Clm3500n2L	99	72	63/	61	0	+3	40	3	7	10[7]½	10[11]	10[10]	8[15]	ClnngrJrWT[116]	Lb	37.70	MilitryPresence¾CoastingBrnz[2]HillbillyKing[2]	Trailed 10
06Jun05Tdn[6]	6f ft	:23	:47[1]	1:00[3]	1:13[4]	3↑	102	Clm3500n2L	100	67	60/	69	-3	-4	44	7	4	8[8]¾	9[8]¾	9[8]¼	7[12]	ClnngrJrWT[116]	Lbf	8.60	OtsTownshp[2]¼SlewCityExprs¾CandinEdition¾	Outrun 9
10Dec04Tdn[4]	1m gd	:23[2]	:47[2]	1:13[2]	1:41[3]	3↑	108	Clm10000n4L	106	71	66/	59	+10	+11	56	5	6[7]½	7[9]¾	7[10]	7[10]	5[15]½	DeveauxSR[118]	Lbf	33.30	AshtonsDreams[4]½SmartTale[1]Mr. Irish Love[6]¾	No factor 7
20Nov04Tdn[6]	6f sy	:22[2]	:46[1]	:58	1:12[2]	3↑	105	Alw12600n2L	104	84	84/	68	+2	+3	63	1	7	5[4]¾	5[6]¾	5[7]¼	6[10]¾	FelicianoR[117]	Lbf	20.80	Shwnly[3]¾LcGrpe[2]¾ThornRod[1]¼	Early speed; gave way 9
08Nov04Tdn[4]	6f ft	:22[2]	:46[3]	:59[3]	1:13	3↑	106	Alw12600n1x	104	71	71/	75	+2	0	58	7	9	9[10]	8[8]¾	8[15]	7[9]½	FelicianoR[120]	Lbf	26.80	Mr. Simon To You[2]Glitter Cat[1]¾Wooli Too[nk]	Outrun 9
16Sep04Tdn[1]	6f ft	:23	:47[1]	1:00[2]	1:13[3]	3↑	101	Mdn 11k	104	85	80/	74	3	-3	65	1	4	1[hd]	1[hd]	1[1]	1[1]¾	ClnngrJrWT[122]	Lbf	*0.20	CmndThBst[1]¾Clmnsdr¾ThKglsAlv[7]	Set pace; driving 5
Previously trained by GIGLIO HEATHER A.																										
02Sep04Mth[1]	6f ft	:22	:45[1]	:58[1]	1:12	3↑	103	MC10000	105	78	69/	86	+1	+5	66	1	10	9[5]¾	6[10]	5[6]½	3[2]	Rocco J[122]	Lb	5.90	Tmb[1]¾CntThWs[nk]CndThBst½	Angled out lane;closed 12

21Apr Tdn 4f ft :54[1] B 20/20 12Apr Tdn 3f my :38[3] Bg 5/11 31Mar Tdn 3f ft :39[3] B 18/22 24Mar Tdn 3f ft :44 B 17/17 04May'05 Tdn 4f ft :52 Bg 5/6 17Apr'05 Tdn 4f ft :53[1] B 18/21
09Apr'05 Tdn 3f ft :40[2] B 26/30 22Oct'04 Tdn 3f ft :38[1] B 2/6 13Aug'04 Mth 4f ft :51 B 29/41 19Jun'04 Mth 4f ft :49[3] B 17/59 13Jun'04 Mth 4f ft :50[1] Bg 24/41 22May'04 Nf 5f ft 1:03[1] B 2/5

Ultimate PP's w/ Quick Play Comments — **River Downs** Clm 4000NW2L 5½ Furlongs. 3up Friday, May 11, 2007 **Race 3 (TDN - #3)** E1 89 E2/LATE 86/74 SPD 70

3 Great Charisma (P 2) — $4,000

Own: Ashley And Ronald Behrens
6/1 Pink, purple circled 'b' roo
HERNANDEZ LUCIANO (11 1-0-0 9%)

Grro. g. 6
Sire: Charismatic (Summer Squall)
Dam: Elite Dancer (Northern Jove)
Brdr: Farnsworth Farms (KY)
Trnr: Behrens Ronald P. (12 2-2-1 17%)

Power Rating: 89.7 (3rd) — L 113^5

	Starts	W-P-S	Earnings	SPD	Surface	Starts	W-P-S	Earnings	SPD
Life:	41	1 - 7 - 6	$20,544	64	Fst	33	0 - 4 - 5	$12,169	64
2007	1	0 - 0 - 0	$69		Off	8	1 - 3 - 1	$8,375	60
2006	12	1 - 4 - 2	$10,898	60	Dis	4	0 - 1 - 1	$2,433	64
Tdn	13	1 - 4 - 2	$10,967	60	Trf	0	0 - 0 - 0	$0	
					AW	0	0 - 0 - 0	$0	

2007	222	9%	28%	-0.65
JKYw/ P types	52	10%	37%	-0.95
JKYw/ Trn L60	1	0%	0%	-2.00
JKYw/ Sprints	158	11%	32%	-0.46

2007	123	6%	36%	-1.58
No class chg	210	11%	29%	+0.40
Claiming	382	9%	29%	-0.23

Sire Stats: AWD 7.5f 14%Mud 309MudSts 1.21spi
Dam'sSire: AWD 6.7f 10%Mud 1358MudSts 1.55spi

★ Eligible to improve in 2nd start since layoff
● Never threatened the leaders in last start ● Poor Speed Figures ● Only 1 win in 41 career starts

DATE TRK	DIST	Fractions	Final	Age	RR RACETYPE		E1	E2/	LP	1c	2c	SPD	PP	ST	1C	2C	Str	FIN	JOCKEY		ODDS	Top Finishers	Comment	
27Apr07Tdn^11	5½ sy	:23^3 :48^1 1:00^4	1:07^2	4↑	102 Clm4000n2L								9	9				-	Banda S^116	Lb	16.90	NoCrsTbleOffmHndslyWld	Swerved; lost jockey	10
11Nov06Tdn^7	6f sy	:23^4 :48 1:01^2	1:15^1	3↑	101 Clm3500n2L	102	74	70/	72	-8	-4	54	4	5	5^2¾	4^3	3^5	4^4¾	FelicianoR^120	Lb	3.70	AllThrYl½WhlNwWy^3½NvlComndrnk	Well placed; evenly	9
29Oct06Tdn^8	6f gd	:23^2 :48 1:01^4	1:15^3	3↑	101 Clm3500n2L	102	77	71/	70	-2	-1	53	7	3	3^3	3^3	4^2	2^3	Banda S^123	Lb	7.10	Epwnt^3GrtChrshdTksnlknwn¾	Rallied; up for second	8
13Oct06Tdn^5	5f ft	:23^2 :48^1	1:00^4	3↑	102 Clm3500n2L	101		67/	70			50	9	9	9^6¾	9^9¼	9^8¼	7^9¼	HernandezO^123	Lb	18.90	PacrlesMgc^1¼SirShrk^3¼WarswWrior^2¼	Off slowly; wide	9
02Oct06Tdn^6	6f gd	:22^3 :47^1 1:01	1:14^3	3↑	98 MC3500	103	77	70/	75	+3	0	57	8	4	8^5¾	5^4	2^hd	1½	HernandezO^123	Lb	4.80	GrtChrism½DmscsDncr^2½FrEch^3½	Split horses; driving	12
18Sep06Tdn^7	6f ft	:23^1 :48^1 1:02	1:15^3	3↑	97 MC3500	102	74	70/	71	0	-8	54	4	9	8^8¼	3^1	1½	2^1	HernandezO^122	Lb	2.60	BlYOw^1GrtChrsm^3½DscsDncr^1½	Rallied; second best	11
02Sep06Tdn^8	6f sy	:22^4 :47 1:00^2	1:14^1	3↑	98 MC3500	100	81	81/	68	-1	0	60	11	5	4^2	3^hd	2^hd	3^1¾	HernandezO^122	Lb	3.20	Nrsin^1¾BulYoOvrnkGrtChrism^1¼	Drew even; outfinished	11
20Aug06Tdn^8	6f gd	:22^4 :47^1 1:00^2	1:14^4	3↑	98 MC3500	101	74	67/	75	+1	+1	54	6	8	8^8¼	6^5¼	4^2¾	2½	HernandezO^122	Lb	4.80	FvHorns½GreatChrismnkJudgAgin½	Rallied; just missed	12
06Aug06Tdn^12	6f ft	:23 :47^2 1:00^4	1:14^1	3↑	98 MC3500	98	77	66/	65	-3	-5	46	10	7	6^2¾	6^4¼	5^5	4^8	HernandezO^122	Lb	11.00	BdnOflhSd^2½Crdnz^4¾NlnTmhd	Middle of pack; evenly (Placed 3rd through disqualification)	10
20Jly06Tdn^7	1m ft	:25^2 :50^3 1:18^4	1:43	3↑	99 MC7500	98	56	44/	52	-18	-16	38	2	4^4	2½	4^3	6^8¼	6^22¼	RosendoJ^122	Lb	4.60	EuroWins^7¼MilitryBrs^2TopCrlndr^2¼	Contended; faltered	6

24Apr Tdn 3f ft :36^1 B 2/9 29May'06 Tdn 5f ft 1:03^3 B 6/7 ●26May'06 Tdn 4f my :50^1 B 1/5 ●17Aug'05 Sud 3f ft :35 H 1/19 14Aug'05 Sud 3f ft :37^4 B 2/2 30Dec'04 Tam 3f ft :36^3 B 5/24
12Nov'04 Crc 3f ft :37^1 Bg 4/11 31Oct'04 Crc 3f ft :37 B 3/10 01Oct'04 Crc 3f ft :36^3 B 3/12 10Sep'04 Crc 4f ft :51 B 25/42 02Sep'04 Crc 5f ft 1:06^3 B 12/12 21Aug'04 Crc 3f ft :36^3 B 4/31

4 Windcauseruckus (E 5) — $4,000

Own: Josh Faulkner
5/1 Black, white 'f', white lightening bolt
MARTINEZ, JR. LUIS J. (44 7-7-7 16%)

Ch. g. 4
Sire: Perigee Moon (Hennessy)
Dam: Crowning Beauty (Beau Genius)
Brdr: James T. Babisson (ONT-C)
Trnr: Faulkner Joe C. (26 6-2-3 19%)

Power Rating: 87.9 (7th) — L 118

	Starts	W-P-S	Earnings	SPD	Surface	Starts	W-P-S	Earnings	SPD
Life:	22	1 - 1 - 2	$17,898	65	Fst	15	0 - 1 - 2	$10,155	65
2007	3	1 - 0 - 0	$5,831	60	Off	7	1 - 0 - 0	$7,743	61
2006	15	0 - 0 - 1	$3,001	61	Dis	13	1 - 1 - 2	$16,301	65
Tdn	3	0 - 0 - 0	$197	60	Trf	0	0 - 0 - 0	$0	
					AW	0	0 - 0 - 0	$0	

2007	111	12%	40%	-0.68
+JKYw/ E types	190	19%	38%	-0.01
+JKYw/ Trn L60	4	25%	50%	-0.65
JKYw/ Sprints	79	10%	39%	-1.05

2007	26	19%	38%	+4.09
+2nd strt wltrn	43	23%	44%	+3.38
+Down one class	131	28%	50%	+0.77
+Claiming	1036	19%	43%	+0.27

Sire Stats: AWD 6.3f 13%Mud 39MudSts 1.15spi
Dam'sSire: AWD 6.9f 14%Mud 1512MudSts 1.13spi

★ Highest Last Race Speed Rating ★ Drops in Class today ★ High % Trainer
★ Early Speed running style helps chances
● Only 1 win in 22 career starts ● Poor record at this track ● Poor record at this distance

DATE TRK	DIST	Fractions	Final	Age	RR RACETYPE	CR	E1	E2/	LP	1c	2c	SPD	PP	ST	1C	2C	Str	FIN	JOCKEY		ODDS	Top Finishers	Comment	
20Apr07Tdn^12	5½ ft	:22^2 :46^1 :59	1:05^3	3↑	104 Clm6250n2L	103	90	86/	62	0	0	60	3	3	1½	2½	2^2	6^8¾	Skerrett J^118	Lb	44.70	MdyPdnHom^2¼SprPrior^4DncThMmb¾	Dueled; faded	7
Previously trained by ROMBIS DEBRA E.																								
10Mar07Mnr^2	5f gd	:22^3 :47^2	1:01^3	3↑	102 Clm5000n2L	97		76/	42			27	1	2	5^4½	8^12	10^13	10^20¾	PereiraOM^121	Lb	34.60	Invstngkd^2KisTheFlme¾Nzgul^1½	Gave way on the turn	10
18Feb07Mnr^1	5f gd	:23^4 :49^1	1:03	3↑	99 MC5000	102		83/	56			48	2	1	1^1½	1^hd	1^2	1^nk	PereiraOM^121	Lb	4.30	WndcusrucksnkThicx¾WldRng^2	Alert;3path;just held	10
Previously trained by NEWELL MICHAEL																								
11Nov06Tdn^8	6f sy	:23^4 :48^1 1:02	1:15^4	3↑	99 MC3500	96	72	54/	54	-6	-3	27	7	3	3^4	6^10	9^16	8^18¼	FelicianoR^121	Lb	18.30	DmscusDncr¾HevnsBoy^3HighHatMk^1½	Brief foot; tired	11
28Oct06Tdn^14	6f sy	:23^3 :49 1:02^3	1:16^1	3↑	98 MC3500	90	76	42/	13	-1	-7	-18	11	10	7^4¾	11^15	11^23	10^47¾	FelicianoR^121	L	4.50	IcStrBls^2½DscsDncr^1¾BlvYorLvr^1	Showed little; outrun	11
Previously trained by ROMBIS DEBRA E.																								
08Oct06FE^9	5f ft	:22^3 :46	:58^2	3↑	107 MC5000	102		83/	65			58	11	1	4^1¼	5^2¼	7^7¼	7^8¼	Quong MD^118	L	54.90	Glendw^2¾GodToBAliv^1¼Rghtndhbd¾	Factor otsd tired	11
26Sep06FE^5	5f ft	:22^3 :46^2	:59^2	3↑	103 MC5000	102		72/	72			57	9	9	10^7¼	8^9¾	8^12	8^4¼	Quong MD^118	L	45.15	Sthnhsphr¾Glndw^1¾ChggThTrnk	Wide trip no menace	12
17Sep06FE^8	5f ft	:22^3 :47	1:00^3	3↑	102 MC5000	103		89/	60			59	3	3	3^1	4^1¼	5^3¼	5^2¼	Piques DA^118	L	35.65	IqalutnkZorro D'oro^1Bon Affairnk	Evened out late	10
05Sep06FE^10	5f ft	:22^2 :46	:58^3	3↑	101 MC5000	102		75/	69			57	7	8	9^5¾	9^6¾	5^8	4^5¾	Piques DA^118	L	18.35	GlntGiltr^1¾Sthnhsphr^1¼PortApich^2¾	Belated inside run	10
22Aug06FE^10	6f ft	:23 :47^2 1:01	1:14^2	3↑	101 MC5000	106	70	53/	77	0	-1	45	3	6	11^8¼	12^13	11^10	10^10	Quong MD^118	L	7.80	RAbsoltMgc^2¼BlondCommndrhdDngJn¾	Bumped break	12

12Apr Tdn 4f my :50^2 B 8/19 27Mar Tdn 4f ft :50^3 B 1/1 30Jan Mnr 3f ft :37^2 B 6/18 11Jan Mnr 5f ft 1:04^2 B 4/7 08Dec'06 WO 3f ft :40^4 H 2/2 26May'06 FE 5f ft 1:03^4 B 10/10
22Apr'06 FE 3f ft :38 H 20/34 12Apr'06 FE 4f ft :51^4 H 24/25 27Mar'06 FE 3f ft :35^4 H 2/5 22Mar'06 WO tr.t 4f gd :50^4 H 16/32 06Mar'06 WO tr.t 3f ft :38^1 H 44/57 27Nov'05 WO tr.t 3f ft :40 H 10/10

5 Erotick Mountain (E/P 7) — $4,000

Own: Eleanor B. Lehman
6/1 Blue; gold 'l'; gold diamonds, gold sleeves
GONZALEZ LUIS ANTONIO (8 0-0-0 0%)

B. g. 5 OBSJUN 2003 $4k
Sire: Holy Mountain (Devil's Bag)
Dam: Erotick Tea (Once Wild)
Brdr: Michelle Severson (FL)
Trnr: Lehman Thomas D. (2 0-0-0 0%)

Power Rating: 88.8 (6th) — L 118

	Starts	W-P-S	Earnings	SPD	Surface	Starts	W-P-S	Earnings	SPD
Life:	20	1 - 3 - 5	$16,521	72	Fst	11	1 - 1 - 4	$11,125	72
2007	5	0 - 0 - 3	$1,635	58	Off	9	0 - 2 - 1	$5,396	72
2006	8	0 - 1 - 2	$3,720	72	Dis	12	0 - 1 - 4	$5,560	62
Tdn	0	0 - 0 - 0	$0		Trf	0	0 - 0 - 0	$0	
					AW	0	0 - 0 - 0	$0	

2007	526	15%	43%	-0.40
JKYw/EP types	350	17%	47%	-0.30
JKYw/ Sprints	282	16%	45%	0.30

2007	33	0%	15%	-2.00
No class chg	244	7%	26%	-1.06
Claiming	318	8%	25%	-0.91

Sire Stats: AWD 6.3f 15%Mud 154MudSts 0.53spi
Dam'sSire: AWD 6.4f 11%Mud 563MudSts 0.88spi

★ Best Dirt Speed is faster than the Avg Winning Speed ★ Early Speed running style helps chances
★ Ran 3rd vs similar in last race
● Poor Speed Figures in each recent start ● Only 1 win in 20 career starts ● Poor Trainer win%

DATE TRK	DIST	Fractions	Final	Age	RR RACETYPE	CR	E1	E2/	LP	1c	2c	SPD	PP	ST	1C	2C	Str	FIN	JOCKEY		ODDS	Top Finishers	Comment	
21Apr07Beu^4	5f ft	:23 :47^2	1:00^1	3↑	100 Clm3500n2L	101		83/	62			55	6	3	2^1½	2^2	3^4	3^3¾	Magera C^120	Lf	7.50	MgtyMd^1DmacsDncr^2¾ErtckMntn^2	Chased; weakened	7
03Apr07Beu^7	5f ft	:22^4 :47	1:00	3↑	99 Clm3500n2L	100		88/	58			54	1	2	2^hd	3^2	3^4	3^4¼	DeonauthKP^120	Lf	2.80	NpoloJ^2¼FrstWdr^2ErckMntn^2¼	Inside duel; weakened	6
26Mar07Beu^2	5f my	:22^3 :46^1	:58^4	3↑	100 Clm3500n2L	101		83/	58			50	3	2	2^1½	4^3¼	4^4½	4^3¾	DeonauthKP^120	Lf	6.60	ChstrThPstr^2¾WrOfAc^1¾FrstWdr^1¾	Drifted out into lane	7
23Feb07Beu^8	5f gd	:23 :47	:59^4	3↑	101 Clm3500n2L	100		79/	61			53	4	7	6^4½	5^3	5^8¼	4^6¾	DeonauthKP^120	Lf	4.50	HighlandJn^1¾MightyMids^2SalemsCl^3	3 wide; no rally	9
16Feb07Beu^3	5f ft	:22^7 :46^7	:58^7	3↑	100 Clm3500n2L	101		75/	69			58	6	9	6^7	6^7	5^4½	3^6¼	DeonauthKP^120	Lf	15.60	PrcOfLv^6FrtaMndrnkErckMntnnk	Broke slow; steadied	10
15Dec06Beu^4	5f ft	:23^3 :47^4	1:01	3↑	100 Clm3500n2L	102		85/	70			62	5	3	1^hd	2^3	2^8	3^3	Stokes J^120	Lf	2.30	GoldnAdvntr^1OckHmbr^2ErotckMntn¾	Finished evenly	12
29Nov06Beu^9	5f ft	:22^7 :46^7	:59^4	3↑	100 Clm3500n2L	102		89/	57			55	4	3	2^hd	3^hd	2^3	4^1¼	Endres J^120	Lf	4.20	ForstFlyr¾LittebitolvlynkScondrt¾	Dueled; outfinished	10
Previously trained by PATRICK R. GARY																								
18Nov06Hoo^5	6f my	:22^3 :47^7 1:00^4	1:14^2	3↑	102 Clm5000n2L	100	86	80/	48	+2	-3	43	10	1	3^2	4¾	7^4¾	9^14¼	PrescottRA^118	Lf	5.10	WindyBch^3¾KoperTrkQuePas^2¼	Brief speed; retreated	10
08Nov06Hoo^1	5½ my	:22 :46^3	1:06^1	3↑	103 Clm5000n2L	102	88	83/	59	-1	0	56	8	4	3^hd	4¾	5^2½	6^8¾	Valdes RA^118	Lf	2.70	Dr. Keith^2¾WazscrulyBoy^2¼LittleBul^1	5wide turn; faded	8
22Oct06Hoo^8	6f gd	:23 :47^4 1:00^3	1:14^1	3↑	102 Clm5000n2L	106	88	81/	81	-2	-6	72	9	2	1^1	1^1	1^1½	2^nk	Valdes RA^118	Lf	20.80	SgnngBsnkErckMntn^1¼HrsThyFlhr^3¾	Pace; caught wire	10

25Aug'06 Hoo 5f ft 1:01^3 B 6/12 ●16Aug'06 Hoo 5f ft 1:02 B 1/5 17Apr'06 Ind 3f ft :37 B 10/23 30Aug'05 Hoo 4f ft :51^1 Bg 5/11 26Aug'05 Hoo 3f ft :36 Bg 6/27

Ultimate PP's w/ Quick Play Comments

River Downs

Clm 4000NW2L 5½ Furlongs. 3up Friday, May 11, 2007 **Race 3 (TDN - #3)** E1 89 E2/LATE 86/74 SPD 70

6 Hunterpunter (E 8)

3/1 Own: Pamela Halter Orange: white 'p' on blue bal
SPIETH SCOTT (84 11-10-7 17%)

$4,000 B. g. 3
Sire: Albert The Great (Go For Gin)
Dam: Expect Anne (Valid Expectations)
Brdr: Kevin Halter (KY)
Trnr: Radosevich Jeffrey A. (62 15-12-5 29%)

Power Rating: 84.0 (1st) L 116

Life:	13 1 - 1 - 0	$5,705	66	Fst	11 1 - 1 - 0	$5,705	66
2007	5 1 - 0 - 0	$3,900	66	Off	2 0 - 0 - 0	$0	54
2006	8 0 - 1 - 0	$1,805	62	Dis	7 1 - 0 - 0	$4,245	66
Tdn	0 0 - 0 - 0	$0		Trf	0 0 - 0 - 0	$0	
				AW	0 0 - 0 - 0	$0	

+2007	278	16%	43%	-0.67	+2007	168	20%	52%	-0.32
+JKYw/ E types	413	23%	53%	-0.24	+1st start w/trn	159	25%	52%	+0.08
JKYw/ Trn L60	89	17%	48%	-0.83	+31-90daysAway	367	25%	54%	-0.04
JKYw/ Sprints	196	17%	45%	-0.58	+Shipper	341	21%	48%	-0.46

Sire Stats: AWD 7.4 18%Mud 85MudSts 1.37spi
Dam'sSire:AWD 6.2 15%Mud 527MudSts 1.27spi

★ Hot Trn/Jky combo in last 14 days (18 5- 4- 2) ★ Drops in Class today
★ Switches to a high% Trainer ★ Early Speed running style helps chances
● Poor Speed Figures in last 2 starts ● Has not raced in 47 days

Previously trained by LOCKE JOHN G.

DATE TRK	DIST					RR RACETYPE	CR	E1	E2/	LP	1c	2c	SPD	PP	ST	1C	2C	Str	FIN	JOCKEY		ODDS	Top Finishers	Comment
25Mar07Hou1	6f ft	:21 4	:45 3	:58 4	1:12 4	106 Clm7500n2L	101	92	85/	33	+4	+4	35	1	5	2hd	2 2½	5 3½	6 21½	Eramia RE 116	Lb	4.20	GrndPchr 1½PcRn½TpGcAvgr 6½	Dueled inside; stopped 6
10Mar07Hou7	5½ ft	:22 1	:45 3		1:05 2	107 Clm7500n2L	104	88	81/	56	0	+1	51	8	1	2hd	2½	5 4½	8 10½	Eramia RE 122	Lb	3.80e	StryUpsng nolovstbck 3ByHro½	Dueled outside;stopped 8
10Feb07Hou6	5½ ft	:22 3	:46 2		1:06 2	104 MC15000	107	86	83/	75	-2	0	66	1	2	1 1½	1 1	1 1	1½	Eramia RE 122	Lb	11.40	Huntrpntr½AlohHnk¾Totalwo½	Long drive; held sway 11
26Jan07Hou5	5½ gd	:22	:46 1		1:06 1	104 MC10000	103	90	82/	61	+2	0	54	2	2	1 1½	1 2	3 1	6 7½	Eramia RE 122	Lb	11.40	FlsTakTk nkSncStrl½ExctgAft 3½	Headed 3/16;gave way 10
19Jan07Hou4	5½ my	:22 2	:46 4		1:07	104 MC10000	104	87	73/	57	0	-2	49	8	3	3½	3 1½	4 3½	6 9	Eramia RE 122	Lb	3.60	Invstbck nkBlicScrt 3½Alngcmbl 1½	Dueled;3w turn;faded 12
09Dec06Hou10	6f ft	:22 1	:46 2	1:00 1	1:14 1	105 MC10000	108	90	85/	58	+2	+3	56	1	8	1½	1½	1 2½	2 4½	HamiltonO 122	Lb	4.70	JonesTune 4½Huntrpntr 4ShawneCl 1	Pace; clear; tired 12
21Nov06RP8	6f ft	:21 4	:44 3	:57 3	1:11 1	107 MC15000	107	93	94/	45	+2	+8	53	2	6	1hd	2 1	4 8	5 14½	Eramia RE 120	Lb	79.40	AhlyVctry 8½ZpRTTtWr 2EbnyEvg 3½	Hustled; gave way 12
30Oct06RP6	6½ ft	:22 1	:46	1:12 2	1:19 2	106 MC15000	105	83	76/	47	0	-2	43	11	1	3 2½	4 3	7 8½	8 15	Eramia RE 120	Lb	6.70	PrncnPrspcts 5ClicSmino AlThBrk½	Vied; drftd stretch 11
06Oct06RP3	1m ft	:23 2	:47 4	1:14	1:41 4	107 MC20000	107	79	69/	28	+8	+8	39	2	1 2	1½	1½	5 7	6 19½	Eramia RE 120	Lb	6.30	Rare Wood 8½Measurement 6½At The Brink 3	Pace; faded 8
02Sep06RP2	6f ft	:22	:45 4	:59 1	1:13 1	108 MC30000/25	105	90	82/	35	+4	+8	34	10	4	4½	5 2½	9 18	10 17½	Eramia RE 117	Lb	7.70	Allon Jet 1Storm Shadow½Fifth Dale½	Steady retreat 12

24Feb Hou 5f my 1:06 2 H 12/13 12Jan Hou 5f ft 1:06 4 B 17/17 28Dec'06 Hou 5f ft 1:04 2 H 29/32 10Nov'06 RP 5f ft 1:06 B 18/19 23Oct'06 RP 5f ft 1:03 3 H 20/27 26Sep'06 RP 5f ft 1:06 H 22/24
12Aug'06 RP 5f ft 1:04 1 H 29/34 05Aug'06 RP 5f ft 1:04 4 H 32/38 28Jly'06 RP 4f ft :55 H 35/36 17Jun'06 LS 5f gd 1:03 4 B 15/23 10Jun'06 LS 4f ft :49 2 Bg 20/75 03Jun'06 LS 5f ft 1:03 2 B 28/38

7 What Now Wynn (E/P 1)

10/1 Own: R And P Racing Stables; Inc. Red and blue halves; white r and s
CLONINGER; JR. WELDON T. (41 16-7-2 37%)

$4,000 Dkbbr. g. 5
Sire: Halo's Image (Halo)
Dam: Whatnowmylove (Wavering Monarch)
Brdr: T. Wynn Jolley & Harry Hoglander (FL)
Trnr: Faulkner Rodney C. (60 6-6-2 10%)

Power Rating: 89.0 (4th) L 118

Life:	30 1 - 5 - 5	$18,882	71	Fst	29 1 - 3 - 5	$13,478	71
2007	4 0 - 0 - 0	$866	57	Off	10 0 - 2 - 0	$5,404	70
2006	13 0 - 2 - 3	$6,237	64	Dis	13 0 - 3 - 2	$8,035	67
Tdn	11 0 - 2 - 3	$5,725	64	Trf	0 0 - 0 - 0	$0	
				AW	0 0 - 0 - 0	$0	

+2007	44	34%	59%	+1.03	2007	251	16%	37%	+0.27
+JKYw/EP types	57	21%	40%	+0.04	No class chg	1430	15%	43%	-0.37
+JKYw/ Trn L60	8	38%	88%	+0.45	Claiming	2189	15%	43%	-0.29
+JKYw/ Sprints	33	33%	55%	+0.79					

Sire Stats: AWD 6.7 13%Mud 466MudSts 1.67spi
Dam'sSire:AWD 6.8 13%Mud 1399MudSts 1.25spi

★ Hot Jockey in last 7 days (20 7- 4- 1) ★ Hot Trn/Jky combo in last 14 days (8 3- 3- 1)
★ Highest Speed Figure at Today's Distance ★ High % Jockey
★ Best Dirt Speed is faster than the Avg Winning Speed
● Never threatened the leaders in last start ● Only 1 win in 30 career starts

DATE TRK	DIST						RR RACETYPE	CR	E1	E2/	LP	1c	2c	SPD	PP	ST	1C	2C	Str	FIN	JOCKEY		ODDS	Top Finishers	Comment
27Apr07Tdn11	5½ sy	:23 3	:48 1	1:00 4	1:07 2	4↑	102 Clm4000n2L								8	3				-	Stokes LA 119	Lb	17.90	NoCrsTbleOfFmetHndsmlyWld	Clipped heels; fell 10
13Apr07Tdn13	6f ft	:22 3	:47 2	1:00 2	1:13 2	4↑	102 Clm4000n2L	102	71	67/	71	0	-8	51	8	11	8 9½	7 7½	7 5½	7 13½	MagrellJM 118	Lb	14.10	ArBornElbur 5½ScrtyMTrk 2½ColorMFr½	Failed to menace 12
27Mar07Mnr2	5½ ft	:22 4	:47 2	1:00 3	1:07 2	3↑	103 Clm5000n2L	103	78	72/	59	0	-1	57	1	8	8 6½	8 7½	4 8	4 10	Oro E 116	Lbf	24.50	RockBostr 2MjorStrikr noEchngRdg 6	Rallied past others 10
05Mar07Mnr2	5½ gd	:23 1	:48 2	1:02	1:09 1	3↑	103 Clm5000n2L	102	75	75/	53	+2	+2	55	9	8	9 8½	8 12	8 6½	6 12½	Oro E 116	Lb	10.30	RcngStrp 1½StllyClk 6GnOnAHch nk	Slow early; no factor 10
24Nov06Tdn10	5f ft	:22 1	:46 3		1:00	3↑	102 Clm3500n2L	103		74/	71			59	4	8	7 8	7 8½	6 7	2 3	MagrellJM 117	Lb	4.30	WldTmtn noWhtNwWyn 2½DmacusDncr 1	Rallied; inside 9
11Nov06Tdn7	6f sy	:23 4	:48	1:01 2	1:15 1	3↑	101 Clm3500n2L	105	78	76/	73	-8	-4	60	9	2	2½	1hd	1 1	2½	SkerrettJJ 117	Lb	3.50	AlThrYl½WhtNwWy 3½NvlComnd nk	Dueled; led; caught 9
29Oct06Tdn8	6f gd	:23 2	:48	1:01 4	1:15 3	3↑	101 Clm3500n2L	102	83	77/	62	-2	-1	52	2	5	2hd	1hd	2hd	4 4	MagrellJM 117	Lb	1.80	Empwrnt 3GrtChrsm hdTksonknwn½	Dueled; weakened 8
15Oct06Tdn7	6f ft	:22 4	:46 4	1:00	1:13 4	3↑	102 Clm3500n2L	105	86	83/	68	-2	+1	62	5	3	1½	1 1	1 1½	3 1	MagrellJM 117	Lb	6.90	Lob½Highlyconfidnt nkWhatNowWyn 2½	Led; caught late 11
01Oct06Tdn3	6f gd	:22 3	:47	1:00 2	1:13 3	3↑	102 Clm3500n2L	103	76	73/	72	0	-3	57	6	9	10 8½	7 4½	5 3½	4 8	MagrellJM 117	Lb	4.70	Slew's Temper 3½Magical Halo 1½OuteANight½	Late rally 11
28Aug06Tdn4	6f gd	:22 2	:45 4	:58 4	1:13 1	3↑	102 Clm3500n2L	102	87	87/	58	+1	+7	58	2	5	2 1½	2 3	3 5½	4 7½	MagrellJM 118	Lb	2.30	Kbone 2MagicalHlo 4½SlewsTmpr½	Chased; weakened 8

24Feb Beu 4f ft :49 Bg 6/11 02Feb Beu 3f ft :39 2 B 9/10 24Sep'06 Tdn 4f ft :49 B 2/7 ●29Apr'06 FE 4f ft :48 H 1/23 21Apr'06 FE 4f ft :48 H 3/22 13Apr'06 FE 3f ft :36 H 5/14
29Oct'05 FL 3f ft :37 4 B 12/25 18Sep'05 FE 3f gd :38 4 B 8/10 02Jly'05 FE 3f ft :38 B 9/13 25Jun'05 FE 3f ft :37 2 H 8/12 19May'05 FE 3f ft :36 2 H 4/11 10May'05 FL 5f ft 1:01 3 D 9/22

8 Society Fox (E/P 1)

10/1 Own: James Eafford White, green blocks
MAILHOT PIERRE (21 0-0-2 0%)

$4,000 Dkbbr. g. 4
Sire: Fortrail (Heading Back Home)
Dam: Wings Of Society (Imp Society)
Brdr: Andy Stronach & Dean Brice (ONT-C)
Trnr: Eafford James (7 0-1-1 0%)

Power Rating: 82.3 (9th) L 118

Life:	17 1 - 1 - 1	$7,471	64	Fst	9 0 - 0 - 1	$1,437	48
2006	11 1 - 1 - 1	$6,789	64	Off	8 1 - 1 - 0	$6,034	64
2005	6 0 - 0 - 0	$682	31	Dis	1 0 - 0 - 0	$163	20
Tdn	14 1 - 1 - 1	$7,066	64	Trf	0 0 - 0 - 0	$0	
				AW	0 0 - 0 - 0	$0	

2007	21	0%	10%	-2.00	2007	10	0%	20%	-2.00
JKYw/EP types	77	9%	29%	-0.79	90+ days away	30	0%	10%	-2.00
JKYw/ Trn L60	1	0%	0%	-2.00	No class chg	163	1%	10%	-1.90
JKYw/ Sprints	17	0%	12%	-2.00	Claiming	197	2%	11%	-1.81

Sire Stats: AWD 6.1 13%Mud 222MudSts 1.01spi
Dam'sSire:AWD 7.2 13%Mud 506MudSts 1.04spi

● Finished far back in last start ● Has not raced for more than 5 months ● Only 1 win in 17 career starts
● Best Speed rating is well below the Avg Winning Speed ● Poor Jockey win% ● Poor Trainer win%
● Poor record at this track

DATE TRK	DIST						RR RACETYPE	CR	E1	E2/	LP	1c	2c	SPD	PP	ST	1C	2C	Str	FIN	JOCKEY		ODDS	Top Finishers	Comment
20Nov06Tdn8	1 70 sy	:23 2	:48 4	1:16	1:49	3↑	107 Clm3500n2L	101	68	51/	60	0	-1	50	8	4 2	4 2	7 4½	7 8	8 10½	Mailhot P 120	Lb	18.80	ThndrOnc 7½BstGmbl 1½CkVctry½	Wide early; weakened 10
29Oct06Tdn3	1 70 gd	:23 1	:49 4	1:17 1	1:49	3↑	99 MC3500	103	65	52/	82	-9	-12	64	1	1 3	1 1½	1hd	1½	1 3½	Mailhot P 120	Lb	2.50	SoctyFox 3½BuckyCountry 3½FrEcho hd	Re-rallied driving 7
12Oct06Tdn6	1 70 gd	:23 2	:49 1	1:15 4	1:48 2	3↑	99 MC3500	100	68	54/	72	-5	-4	59	8	6 3½	2hd	3 3	3 3	4 4½	Mailhot P 120	Lb	3.20	MercisScrt hdBrbiesAlKn 4½BckyContry hd	Middle move 10
30Sep06Tdn4	1 70 gd	:23 3	:48 3	1:16 2	1:49 2	3↑	99 MC3500	102	70	50/	72	+1	-4	57	1	3 1	3 1	4 2	3 1½	2½	Mailhot P 118	Lb	6.20	BilBaby½SocietyFox 4½BuckeyCountry 3½	Rallied; gaining 8
15Sep06Tdn8	1 70 ft	:23 2	:48 4	1:15 2	1:48 1	3↑	100 MC3500	100	54	41/	68	-2	0	49	5	9 6½	9 8	9 12	5 14	6 13½	Mailhot P 118	Lb	26.00	PaidLove 7½FrEcho nkBarbiesAlKne 2½	Failed to menace 12
01Sep06Tdn3	1 70 ft	:24	:49 3	1:16 3	1:49 2	3↑	99 MC3500	100	54	40/	59	-9	-7	44	7	3 1½	3 2	5 2¼	4 5	3 6	Mailhot P 118	Lb	31.60	FutrKngs½FrEcho 5½SoctyFox 7½	Never far back; evenly 9
19Aug06Tdn7	1 70 sy	:23 3	:50 1	1:16 4	1:48 2	3↑	100 MC3500	99	57	52/	59	-16	-12	50	3	4 1½	3 1½	5 2½	5 6½	4 10	Mailhot P 117	Lb	37.40	Speedy Pioneer 5½Future Kings 5½Far Echo 5	No rally 8
06Aug06Tdn12	6f ft	:23	:47 2	1:00 4	1:14 1	3↑	98 MC3500	97	73	57/	70	-3	-5	42	6	6	7 4½	8 6½	8 9½	7 10	Magera C 120	Lb	69.50	BdounOfthSnd 3½Cordonz 4½NotInTem hd	Failed to menace 10
22Jly06Tdn8	6f sy	:23	:47 1	1:00 1	1:13 1	3↑	99 MC3500	97	70	63/	62	-4	-8	41	8	5	9 7½	8 8	8 13	8 18½	Magera C 115	Lb	79.90	Pair Of Queens 3½My Man Matt 3½Far Echo 3	No factor 11
01Jun06Tdn13	6f ft	:22 4	:47	1:00 1	1:14	3↑	99 MC3500	95	62	50/	61	-2	-3	29	5	10	12 11	12 14	12 20½	12 19½	Bracho JA 117	Lb	53.50	Vacation Fun 6½Cordonazo½Strange Fruit½	Trailed 12

02May Tdn 4f ft :50 2 B 6/8 16Apr Tdn 3f ft :38 1 B 15/20 31Mar Tdn 4f ft :53 1 B 30/37 10Jly'06 Tdn 5f ft 1:06 B 6/6 03Jly'06 Tdn 5f ft 1:03 4 B 3/7 24Jun'06 Tdn 5f ft 1:04 4 B 6/6
09Jun'06 Tdn 4f ft :50 4 B 7/10 11May'06 Tdn 4f my :51 3 B 5/5 26Apr'06 Tdn 4f ft :49 2 B 6/17 21Apr'06 Tdn 4f ft :50 4 B 12/22 14Dec'05 Tdn 4f ft :52 4 B 1/1 12Nov'05 Tdn 4f ft :51 3 B 10/18

tsnhorse.com

Ultimate PP's w/ Quick Play Comments **River Downs** Clm 4000NW2L 5½ Furlongs. 3up Friday, May 11, 2007 **Race 3 (TDN - #3)** E1 89 E2/LATE 86/ 74 SPD 70

9 **Go Ryan Go (S 0)** $4,000 Ch. g. 4
8/1 Own: Peruvian Glass And More; Inc.
Blue
ORO ERNESTO (53 4-4-10 8%)

Sire: Comeonmom (Jolie's Halo)
Dam: Flying Cormorant (Cormorant)
Brdr: David Ranney (NY)
Trnr: Morales Ricardo (10 2-0-3 20%)

Power Rating: 84.4 (8th) L 118

Life:	16	1 - 2 - 0	$7,812	62	Fst	12	1 - 1 - 0	$6,283	62
2007	2	0 - 0 - 0	$142	58	Off	4	0 - 1 - 0	$1,529	54
2006	14	1 - 2 - 0	$7,670	62	Dis	2	1 - 0 - 0	$4,084	54
Tdn	16	1 - 2 - 0	$7,812	62	Trf	0	0 - 0 - 0	$0	
					AW	0	0 - 0 - 0	$0	

2007	216	9%	30%	+0.41	2007	16	12%	31%	+4.60
JKYw/ S types	290	11%	38%	+0.56	1-5 days away	61	13%	41%	-0.11
+JKYw/ Trn L60	10	20%	50%	+8.56	Down one class	59	3%	19%	-1.23
JKYw/ Sprints	134	8%	26%	+0.19	Claiming	411	8%	25%	-0.40

Sire Stats: AWD 7.7f 16%Mud 19MudSts 1.04spi
Dam'sSire:AWD 7.4f 15%Mud 1365MudSts 2.39spi

★ Drops in Class today ★ Eligible to improve in 3rd start since layoff

● Only 1 win in 16 career starts ● Best Speed rating is well below the Avg Winning Speed
● Poor record at this track ● Poor 'Down one class' trainer record: 3%wins 59sts

DATE TRK	DIST						RR RACETYPE	CR	E1	E2/	LP	1c	2c	SPD	PP	ST	1C	2C	Str	FIN	JOCKEY		ODDS	Top Finishers	Comment
06May07Tdn^{12}	6f ft	:22^2	:46	:59	1:12^2	3↑	^{102}Clm6250n2L	100	68	58/	75	-2	0	**48**	4	10	10^{9}¼	10^{12}	9^{12}	8^{11}	Oro E^{118}	Lb	32.40	Goldstream^{no}Grey Picture^{4}Table OfFame^2	No factor 10
13Apr07Tdn^{13}	6f ft	:22^3	:47^2	1:00^2	1:13^2	4↑	^{102}Clm4000n2L	103	71	65/	81	0	-8	**58**	3	9	10^{9}¾	8^{8}¼	6^{5}½	5^{9}¾	Oro E^{118}	Lb	23.40	AirBorneEltbuer^{6}½ScrutyMcTrk^{2}½ColorMeFre½	No threat 12
11Nov06Tdn^7	6f sy	:23^4	:48	1:01^2	1:15^1	3↑	^{101}Clm3500n2L	100	60	56/	73	-8	-4	**43**	1	9	8^{9}¾	8^{10}	7^{11}	6^{10}¾	Oro E^{118}	Lb	10.60	AmIThrYt½WhtNwWy^{3}½NvlComnd^{nk}	Failed to menace 9
27Oct06Tdn^7	5f ft	:22^1	:46^3		:59^3	3↑	^{101}Clm3500n2L	100		74/	64			**54**	7	8	8^{9}¼	8^{9}¾	7^{9}¾	7^{11}½	Oro E^{121}	Lb	14.90	BigBbLop^{7}WldTrntion^{hd}SirShrk^{1}¼	Showed little; outrun 8
16Oct06Tdn^3	6f ft	:22^4	:46^4	:59^4	1:13	3↑	^{101}Clm5000n2L	99	73	68/	64	-3	-3	**46**	2	5	5^6	4^7	4^7	6^{14}½	MurrayBaF^{121}	Lb	7.50	Swelbabo^{2}½AmIThereYt^{6}½Presdforcsh^{4}½	Dropped back 7
09Oct06Tdn^6	5½f ft	:23	:48	1:02	1:08^4	3↑	^{99}MC7500	101	71	67/	67	+2	+2	**53**	1	7	7^{8}½	7^{8}½	4^2	1½	Oro E^{121}	Lb	*2.40	GRynG½cStormBts^{1}½RnByThDvl½	Closed fast; up late 10
29Sep06Tdn^9	6f sy	:23	:47^3	1:00^3	1:14^1	3↑	^{99}MC7500	101	69	64/	78	-2	-4	**54**	10	6	7^9	5^{8}½	4^{7}¼	2^{8}½	Oro E^{120}	Lb	5.00	NoLmtins^{8}½GRynG^{1}½DntRgsWnr^1	No match for winner 10
16Sep06Tdn^4	6f ft	:22^2	:46^4	1:00^2	1:14^1	3↑	^{99}MC7500	102	66	65/	86	+3	+3	**62**	8	7	6^{12}	4^{8}½	3^{4}½	2^1	Oro E^{120}	Lb	10.50	JolisJwl^{1}GoRynG^{3}¾RnByThDvl^{1}½	Closed fast; gaining 8
02Sep06Tdn^6	6f sy	:22^4	:47	1:00^2	1:14^1	3↑	^{99}MC3500	97	73	66/	72	-1	0	**51**	5	8	8^6	8^{7}¼	7^{6}¾	8^{7}½	Oro E^{120}	Lb	43.50	Nuristan^{1}½Bat You Over^{nk}Great Charisma^{1}½	No threat 11
20Aug06Tdn^8	6f gd	:22^4	:47^1	1:00^2	1:14^4	3↑	^{99}MC3500	99	77	65/	56	+1	+1	**37**	5	7	6^{4}¾	7^{6}½	9^{9}½	11^{11}	Uriel-mornV^{119}	Lb	16.30	FivHorns½GreatCharisma^{nk}JudgeAgn½	Dropped back 12

29Apr Tdn 4f ft :51^3 B *11/21* 22Apr Tdn 3f ft :37 B *3/12* 11Apr Tdn 3f ft :36^2 Bg *2/14* 06Apr Tdn 4f ft :49^4 B *2/11* 31Mar Tdn 3f ft :38^3 B *14/22* 08Sep'06 Tdn 3f ft :37^3 B *7/10*
30Aug'06 Tdn 3f ft :36^3 B *4/6* 31Jly'06 Tdn 3f ft :36^1 B *2/15* 28May'06 Tdn 5f ft 1:02^4 B *5/8* 12May'06 LS 3f ft :36^4 Bg *7/23* 30Apr'06 LS 3f ft :36 H *11/37* 23Apr'06 LS 3f ft :37^2 B *14/24*

tsnhorse.com

Ultimate PP's w/ Quick Play Comments **River Downs** Clm 4000NW2L 5½ Furlongs. 3up Friday, May 11, 2007 **Race 3 (TDN - #3)**

E1	E2/LATE	SPD
89	86/ 74	70

Last 3 Years		RACETYPE STATS:	# Races	FAVORITES Win%	Itm%	$2ROI	Average Field Size	Median $2 Win Payoff	% Winners < 5/1	% Winners >= 5/1 < 10/1	% Winners >= 10/1
TDN	3up	CLM 3500 - 5000 N2L Dirt 5.5f - 6f	101	38%	70%	-0.23	9.4	$6.20	68%	16%	16%

Track Bias Stats

DIRT 5.5f	* MEET Totals *		WnrAvgBL	
# Races: 34	Speed Bias: 74%		1stCall: 1.7	
%Wire: 26%	04/12 - 05/06		2ndCall: 1.1	
	Early	Speed	Late	Speed
Runstyle:	E	E/P	P	S
	++	+		
Impact Values	1.82	1.20	0.52	0.45
%Races Won	44%	29%	9%	18%
Post Bias:	RAIL	1-3	4-7	8+
			+	
Impact Values	0.47	0.71	1.25	0.96
Avg Win %	6%	9%	20%	6%

DIRT 5.5f	* WEEK Totals *		WnrAvgBL	
# Races: 12	Speed Bias: 67%		1stCall: 1.9	
%Wire: 25%	05/03 - 05/06		2ndCall: 1.3	
	Early	Speed	Late	Speed
Runstyle:	E	E/P	P	S
	++			
Impact Values	2.08	0.92	0.46	0.54
%Races Won	42%	25%	8%	25%
Post Bias	RAIL	1-3	4-7	8+
	+	+		
Impact Values	1.49	1.24	1.11	0.39
Avg Win %	17%	14%	17%	3%

Race Summary

#	HorseName	ML Odds	Med Eqp	Days Since L/R	Run Style	PTS	Avg Dist/Surf PACE-SPEED E1	E2/Late	Spd	Avg Race Rtng	Best Pace E1	E2/Late	Final Speed Sp1	Sp2	Sp3	Sp4	ACL	Rcg Spd Avg	R1	R2	R3	Mud Spd	Pedigree Stats Mud Sts	Mud %	Sire AWD	Dam Sire's AWD
6	Hunterpunter	3/1	L	47	++E	8	88	82/ 64	* 57*	106	93	94/ 75	35.	51.	66.	54.	104.7	51	106	107	104	49	85	18	7.4	6.2
5	Erotick Mountain	6/1	L	20	+E/P	7		82/ 63	* 56*	100	88	89/ 81	55.	54.	50	53.	99.9	53	100	99	100	56	154	15	6.3	6.4
7	What Now Wynn	10/1	L	14	+E/P	1	77	74/ 56	* 56*	104	88	87/ 75		51.	57.	55.	101.7		102	102	103	60	466	13	6.7	6.8
3	Great Charisma	6/1	L	14.	P	2	76	70/ 72	(55)	99	77	71/ 75		54	53.	50.	100.8		102	101	101	60	309	14	7.5	6.7
4	Windcauseruckus	5/1	L	21	++E	5	90	85/ 59	* 54*	102	90	89/ 77	60.	27.	48.	27	99.6	45	104	102	99	57	39	13	6.3	6.9
9	Go Ryan Go	8/1	L	5..	S		70	62/ 78	* 53*	103	83	74/ 86	48.	58.	43	54.	99.3	50	102	102	101	54	19	16	7.7	7.4
1	Hooves Of Thunder	9/2	L	14..	P	1	71	59/ 77	(50)	103	77	60/ 78	59	55	56	46.	98.7	57	99	98	102	59	983	15	7.7	6.4
2	Command The Best	10/1	L	14.	S	2	79	66/	(50)	102			50	57.	43	40.		50	102	101	102	50	595	17	6.3	7.4
8	Society Fox	10/1	L	172	+E/P	1	71	56/ 61	(34)	101	73	57/ 70	50	64	59	57		58	102	99	98	50	222	13	6.1	7.2

Speed Last Race	Back Speed	Current Class	Average Class Last 3	Power Rating	Early Pace Last Race	Late Pace Last Race
60 Windcauseruckus	72 Erotick Mountain	104.9 Hunterpunter	104.2 Hunterpunter	94.0 Hunterpunter	86 Windcauseruckus	78 Hooves Of Thunder
59 Hooves Of Thunder	66 Hunterpunter	102.5 What Now Wynn	102.2 What Now Wynn	90.9 Command The Best	85 Hunterpunter	75 Go Ryan Go
55 Erotick Mountain	64 What Now Wynn	102.1 Windcauseruckus	101.7 Great Charisma	89.7 Great Charisma	70 Hooves Of Thunder	62 Windcauseruckus
50 Command The Best	62 Go Ryan Go	101.6 Go Ryan Go	101.6 Society Fox	89.0 What Now Wynn	68 Society Fox	62 Command The Best
50 Society Fox	60 Windcauseruckus	100.8 Erotick Mountain	100.9 Go Ryan Go	89.0 Hooves Of Thunder	66 Command The Best	62 Erotick Mountain
48 Go Ryan Go	57 Great Charisma	NA Great Charisma	100.7 Erotick Mountain	88.8 Erotick Mountain	58 Go Ryan Go	60 Society Fox
35 Hunterpunter	52 Hooves Of Thunder	NA Hooves Of Thunder	100.5 Hooves Of Thunder	87.9 Windcauseruckus	NA Great Charisma	33 Hunterpunter
NA What Now Wynn	42 Society Fox	NA Society Fox	100.4 Windcauseruckus	84.4 Go Ryan Go	NA What Now Wynn	NA Great Charisma
NA Great Charisma	NA Command The Best	NA Command The Best	100.4 Command The Best	82.3 Society Fox	NA Erotick Mountain	NA What Now Wynn

#	Speed Last Race	
8	Swissle Stick	81
5	Step To The Music	78
2	Steelyeyed	76

#	Prime Power	
8	Swissle Stick	114.6
2	Steelyeyed	111.9
5	Step To The Music	111.6

#	Class Rating	
5	Step To The Music	110.6
2	Steelyeyed	110.0
7	City Rapid	109.1

#	Best Speed at Dist	
7	City Rapid	93
8	Swissle Stick	88
2	Steelyeyed	86

4

Exacta / Trifecta / Superfecta (Ten Cent Minimum) / Pick 3 (Races 4-5-6)

	E1	E2/LATE	SPEED
PARS:	92	93/ 80	81

5½ Furlongs. Str Alw8300 Purse $8,300. SIMULCAST FROM RIVER DOWNS. FOR THREE YEAR OLDS AND UPWARD WHICH HAVE STARTED FOR A CLAIMING PRICE OF $5,000 OR LESS IN 2006-2007. Three Year Olds, 116 lbs., Older, 124 lbs. Non-winners Of A Race Since April 11 Allowed 2 lbs. A Race Since March 11 Allowed 4 lbs. (Races Where Entered For $4,000 Or Less Not Considered In Allowances) .

Post Time: (2:05)/ 1:05/12:05/11:05

1 Rarify (E/P 4)

Own: David Atkins
8/1 Blue: silver star
VITEK JUSTIN J. (91 12-12-11 13%)

B. g. 4
Sire: Pembroke (Gone West)
Dam: Clarion Call (Wild Again)
Brdr: David Wayne Atkins (KY)
Trnr: Atkins David (2 1-0-0 50%)

Power Rating: 107.4 (5th)
Blnkr Off
L 120

Life:	13 2 - 2 - 1	$14,433	76	Fst	7 1 - 1 - 0	$7,722	75
2007	1 0 - 0 - 0	$0	75	Off	4 1 - 1 - 0	$5,241	73
2006	12 2 - 2 - 1	$14,433	75	Dis	2 0 - 1 - 0	$2,026	70
RD	2 1 - 0 - 0	$3,226	73	Trf	2 0 - 0 - 1	$1,470	68
				AW	5 1 - 0 - 0	$4,922	75

2007	226	11%	36%	+0.10
JKYw/EP types	182	12%	38%	-0.34
JKYw/ Trn L60	6	17%	50%	-1.47
JKYw/ Sprints	126	10%	39%	+0.30

2007	12	8%	25%	-1.73
Blinkers off	1	0%	0%	-2.00
Shipper	14	14%	29%	-1.14

Sire Stats: AWD 6.0f 15%Mud 608MudSts 0.87spi
Dam'sSire: AWD 7.4f 16%Mud 1/69MudSts 2.63spi

★ Drops in Class today ★ Eligible to improve in 2nd start since layoff

DATE TRK	DIST						RR RACETYPE	CR	E1	E2/	LP	1c	2c	SPD	PP	ST	1C	2C	Str	FIN	JOCKEY	ODDS	Top Finishers	Comment	
22Apr07Kee1	Ⓢ 6f ft	:22 4	:46 2	:58 1	1:10 2	4↑	111 Alw8000s	110	89	91/	75	-7	-3	75	9	2	2 1	2hd	7 3	8 6	Lebron V 118	Lb 53.50	OkDozr RubDbDb StpToThMsc	Dueled;weakened	9
19Nov06CT7	4½ ft	:22 1	:45 4		:52	3↑	108 Clm15000n3L	104		80/	72			59	2	6	5 3¼		4 6¾	4 10	Crnoch Jr F 120	Lb 6.20	Wtchthbr Whtythnk VinSbtSchoP	Failed respond; rail	10
25Oct06Kee3	Ⓢ 6f ft	:23 2	:46 3	:58 2	1:10 2	3↑	110 Clm16000	109	80	76/	87	-8	-8	72	7	5	8 1½	8 3½	8 2	7 2¼	BourqueDL 111	Lb 48.80	Pngburn LordAlexndr CortonsQust	8w lane;no bid	10
29Sep06TP8	Ⓢ 6f ft	:22 1	:45 3	:57 3	1:09 3	3↑	109 Clm15000n3L	108	74	75/	91	-4	-10	75	2	6	9 7¼	8 4½	7 5	5 4¼	Paucar E 117	Lb 7.30	Pangburn MrAntagonizer Homely	Off inside; late bid	9
20Sep06TP7	Ⓢ 6f ft	:22 4	:46	:58 1	1:10 3	3↑	103 Clm7500n2L	107	78	76/	90	-7	-10	74	2	4	4 2	4 1½	1 2½	1 6¾	Paucar E 117	Lb *0.80	Rarify PaydayFrdy E ALockwood	Waited mid turn	7
13Sep06Hoo8	5½ my	:22 1	:46 3		1:06	3↑	104 Clm7500n2L	107	84	85/	77	-3	-2	70	5	3	4 1¼	3hd	3hd	2¼	PompellTL 114	Lb 3.80	Macs RobRoy Rarify Summer Gulch	Dueled; hung	9
24Aug06Elp8	Ⓣ 5½ fm	:22 2	:45 4	:57 1	1:03 1	3↑	109 Alw22000n1x	104	73	68/	69	-7	-9	63	4	4	5 6	6 6½	7 8¼	7 10¼	Troilo WD 118	L 27.10	Copertud AgentHnry MrCoch	Moved inside;tired	7
11Jly06Cnl8	Ⓣ 5f fm	:21 2	:44 3		:57	3↑	104 Clm12500n2L	108		88/	71			68	9	3	3 3	4 4½	5 6½	3 1	KaramnosH 118	L 5.80	Glenners Rough Day Rarify	Wide, late bid	12
20Jun06Ind7	6f ft	:22 2	:45 3	:58	1:11	3↑	104 Clm7500n2L	108	86	85/	72	-2	0	68	1	3	2 1	2hd	2½	2 1¼	ClementeA 118	LB 4.20	Whpcrckwy Rrfy ChinOfMrcls	Led late; outfinished	7
10Jun06Ind1	Ⓢ 1 70 sy	:25 3	:49 2	1:15 1	1:43	3↑	106 Clm15000n2L	105	66	66/	61	-3	-5	60	1	7 8	6 5¼	4 2	5 5¼	6 12½	ClementeA 118	LB 15.90	LRoj GetOnBord GintSwordsmn	Bid turn rail; tired	9

15Apr Vht 3f gd :38 1 B 1/3 ●07Apr Vht 4f gd :49 4 B 1/13 23Mar Vht 3f gd :39 2 B 1/1 16Jun'06 Vht 3f gd :38 4 B 4/4 29May'06 Vht 4f gd :52 1 B 2/5 21Apr'06 Vht 3f gd :39 4 B 2/2
●24Mar'06 Vht 4f gd :51 2 B 1/5 ●18Mar'06 Vht 4f gd :51 B 1/5 28Feb'06 Vht 3f gd :41 B 1/1 23Feb'06 TP 6f ft 1:20 1 Bg 2/3 17Feb'06 Vht 6f gd 1:25 Bg 1/1 04Feb'06 Vht 5f sy 1:07 4 B 1/1

2 Steelyeyed (P 3)

Own: Rebecca K. McGee
5/1 Orange; purple diamonds
FELIX JULIO E. (85 11-18-12 13%)

Ch. g. 7 KEESEP 2001 $166k
Sire: Crafty Prospector (Mr. Prospector)
Dam: Gerri N Jo Go (Top Command)
Brdr: Liberation Farm & Oratis Thoroughbreds (KY)
Trnr: McGee Rebecca K. (6 1-1-2 17%)

Power Rating: 111.9 (2nd)
L 120

Life:	44 8 - 9 - 6	$132,689	89	Fst	36 5 - 8 - 5	$96,048	86
2007	7 0 - 2 - 1	$6,194	83	Off	8 3 - 1 - 1	$36,641	89
2006	9 1 - 2 - 2	$11,450	86	Dis	4 0 - 2 - 0	$5,880	86
RD	1 0 - 1 - 0	$2,140	83	Trf	0 0 - 0 - 0	$0	
				AW	10 1 - 1 - 3	$10,984	80

2007	246	9%	37%	-0.23
JKYw/ P types	117	13%	34%	-0.35
JKYw/ Trn L60	3	0%	67%	-2.00
JKYw/ Sprints	160	8%	34%	-0.38

2007	23	9%	35%	-1.21

Sire Stats: AWD 6.7f 18%Mud 2418MudSts 2.01spi
Dam'sSire: AWD 6.9f 13%Mud 498MudSts 1.67spi

★ Ran 2nd in last race

DATE TRK	DIST						RR RACETYPE	CR	E1	E2/	LP	1c	2c	SPD	PP	ST	1C	2C	Str	FIN	JOCKEY	ODDS	Top Finishers	Comment	
27Apr07Ind8	6f ft	:21 2	:45	:58	1:10 3	3↑	108 Alw4000s	111	85	87/	80	+8	+6	76	2	8	4 6	4 6½	4nk	2 3¼	Felix JE 118	Lb 5.00	Chipotle Stelyeyed Mrkdown	Inside trip;outfinished	8
14Apr07RD8	5½ sy	:22 3	:45 3	:59	1:06	3↑	108 Clm15000	110	82	88/	74	+3	+7	83	6	5	4 7	4 3¼	2 1½	2 1¼	Felix JE 120	Lb 4.80	Favorite Fun Steelyeyed SwissleStick	5 wide rally	7
17Mar07TP8	Ⓢ 6½ ft	:23	:46 2	1:11 4	1:18 3	3↑	110 Clm12500	110	78	77/	79	-8	-8	69	3	7	3 2	3 2	3 2	5 3¼	Mojica O 120	Lb 7.80	Jaguar Joe Humble Earl Connywithay	Inside turn	8
07Mar07TP7	Ⓢ 1m ft	:25 1	:49	1:14 1	1:39 4	3↑	109 Clm16000	108	67	69/	72	-11	-7	66	3	1hd	2 2	2 1½	4 4	5 10¾	Mojica O 117	Lbf 5.30	Soringwithgls LiprsFork JagurJoe	Inside; gave way	8
17Feb07TP4	Ⓢ 6f ft	:22 4	:45 4	:57 4	1:10	3↑	110 Alw5000s	111	80	81/	90	-11	-11	79	5	4	3 2	4 3½	4 3½	3 7	Mojica O 120	Lb 9.20	Hoho Tow Funky Pirate Steelyeyed	Stumbled start	8
31Jan07TP7	Ⓢ 6½ ft	:23	:46	1:11 4	1:18 3	4↑	109 Alw5000s	110	82	84/	83	-5	0	77	8	3	5 2	5 6¼	4 5½	4 5¾	Mojica O 120	Lb 5.20	Count Rmi Hoho Tow GoldBrck	Lacked needed bid	8
14Jan07TP7	Ⓢ 6f ft	:21 4	:44 1	:56	1:08 2	4↑	109 Alw5000s	109	82	81/	91	-8	-4	80	10	3	8 3½	8 9½	7 13	5 8¾	Mojica O 120	Lb 6.20	Hoho Tow Dance Man RoaringCanyon	No menace	10
29Dec06TP2	Ⓢ 5½ ft	:22	:44 3	:56 4	1:03 1	3↑	110 Alw7500s	110	81	74/	76	+1	-5	74	10	6	6 6½	6 6	7 9½	6 8	Mojica O 120	Lb 10.30	JumpForJoyx FunkyPirte Pngburn	5 wide into turn	10
08Dec06TP3	Ⓢ 6f ft	:22 1	:45 1	:57 3	1:10	3↑	111 Alw7500s	113	76	86/	84	-2	-1	78	2	9	8 7½	7 4	4 7½	2 3½	Mojica O 120	Lb 13.90	CbsPowr Stelyeyd SBwtMmry	Rallied; not enough	9
03Nov06Mnr8	5½ ft	:22 4	:47 3	1:01	1:08 1	3↑	109 Alw5000s	110	83	98/	74	+6	+8	86	4	7	7 8½	6 8½	5 1½	4 3½	Ganpath R 115	Lb 8.60	PcAndJy ReintlsSimo OfOfThDy	Circled5w; bid hard	8

●31Mar TP 4f ft :47 4 B 1/28 ●11Jan TP 3f ft :36 B 1/8 ●25Nov'06 TP 4f ft :47 4 B 1/55 29Aug'06 TP 4f ft :50 3 B 11/17 10Aug'06 TP 4f ft :49 1 B 3/20 28Jly'06 TP 4f ft :50 2 B 4/10
14Jun'06 TP 5f ft 1:03 B 6/11 06Jun'06 TP 5f ft 1:02 4 B 6/13 31May'06 TP 5f ft 1:05 1 B 19/20 24May'06 TP 4f ft :51 2 B 14/22 27Apr'06 TP 4f ft :50 2 B 10/10 21Feb'06 TP 5f ft 1:04 1 B 7/12

Ultimate PP's w/ Quick Play Comments **River Downs** 5h Alw8300 5½ Furlongs. 3up Friday, May 11, 2007 **Race 4**

E1	E2/LATE	SPD
92	93/ 80	81

3 Warner Jazz Man (P 3)

15/1
Own: Davis Boys Stable
White, purple 'davis boys'
BUSH VERNON (65 11-11-10 17%)

Ch. g. 7
Sire: Warner Jones (Mr. Prospector)
Dam: Flame And Air (Powder Horn)
Brdr: Charles M. Massey (KY)
Trnr: Davis Melvin E. (1 1-0-0 100%)

Power Rating: 105.0 (6th) L 124

	Starts	W-P-S	Earnings	SPD		Starts	W-P-S	Earnings	SPD
Life:	19	3 - 2 - 1	$15,766	76	Fst	12	2 - 2 - 1	$10,674	70
2007	1	1 - 0 - 0	$3,600	76	Off	1	1 - 0 - 0	$4,110	76
2006	12	2 - 1 - 1	$8,928	70	Dis	7	2 - 1 - 0	$8,100	76
RD	1	1 - 0 - 0	$3,600	76	Trf	4	0 - 0 - 0	$1,584	69
					AW	3	0 - 1 - 0	$1,704	58

2007	347	10%	36%	-0.44
JKYw/ P types	173	14%	31%	-0.27
+JKYw/ Trn L60	1	100%	100%	+15.80
JKYw/ Sprints	202	9%	37%	-0.48

+2007	1	100%	100%	+15.80
+Win last race	2	50%	50%	+1.00

Sire Stats: AWD 6.4f 15%Mud 41MudSts 0.18spi
Dam'sSire:AWD 6.7f 10%Mud 226MudSts 0.66spi

★ Won last race (RD 04/26 5.5f Dirt muddy Clm 5000NW3L)
★ Eligible to improve in 2nd start since layoff
● Moves up in class from last start ● Best Speed rating is well below the Avg Winning Speed

DATE TRK	DIST		RR RACETYPE	CR	E1	E2/	LP	1c	2c	SPD	PP	ST	1C	2C	Str	FIN	JOCKEY	ODDS	Top Finishers	Comment	
26Apr07RD5	5½ my6	:231 :463 1:001 1:063 3↑	104 Clm5000n3L	108	87	88/	80	3	-1	76	7	1	2½	2½	2hd	1hd	Bush V120	Lb 7.90	WrnerJzMnhdKndsky4½LgsDmnd½	Prevailed; long drive	10
Previously trained by MATTINGLY JAMES E.																					
16Sep06KD7	Ⓣ 7f fm	:242 :474 1:113 1:24 3↑	108 Clm10000	104	80	78/	44	1	-4	47	5	10	84½	92¼	1113	1118¾	FaulknerG118	Lb 72.30	Tequila Party4¾Fancy Threat¾Old Scudder¾	Outrun	11
02Sep06Elp4	5½ ft	:231 :463 :584 1:051 3↑	105 Clm5000n3L	107	74	74/	84	-11	-8	68	2	3	52¼	41½	21	2no	FaulknerG120	Lb 21.40	FreLncClnoWrnrJzMn1½YodrLk½	Steady 1/2p;outgamed	8
19Aug06Elp7	6f ft	:231 :463 :582 1:104 3↑	106 Clm5000n3L	105	68	64/	88	-13	-12	63	4	7	64½	64¾	53½	47¾	Lanerie CJ120	Lbl 14.20	TallyWald4½FreLanceCal3CityStalkernk	Dft in bmp start	8
05Aug06Elp8	6½ ft	:221 :452 1:103 1:172 3↑	104 Clm5000n3L	107	78	80/	72	-6	-7	66	7	4	42½	32½	23	34¼	FaulknerG120	Lbl 23.90	BigChil4CitySlturnkWrnerJzMn4¾	3 wide bid; weakened	8
22Jly06Elp11	5½ ft	:222 :46 :581 1:043 3↑	104 Clm5000n3L	104	73	70/	67	3	-5	60	7	8	87¼	87¾	78½	68	FaulknerG120	Lbl 22.20	StuartG1½YodelerLk2½FreLanceCl1½	Improved position	10
Previously trained by BALL JERRY																					
23Jun06Fml9	6½ gd	:224 :464 1:181 3↑	106 Clm6500	106	71	68/	82	-12	-8	64	4	7	83¾	53½	45	45¾	Dunn P124	Lb 34.90	Gamblin¾Olue Thunder2½Riva's Image2½	No factor	9
14May06Wrd9	5½ ft	:22 :453 1:047 3↑	104 Clm15000n3L	107	80	66/	57	0	-7	48	6	8	88	88	97¼	89¾	Bishop MJ125	Lb 27.70	Regal ObenkBadiola1Loves Bonusnk	Showed little	9
14Apr06Wrd9	5f ft	:213 :44 :561 4↑	107 Clm10000	103		77/	65			56	2	6	10	107¼	1014	1014¾	Bishop MJ124	LBb 21.10	ShanBnk¾MagdelenMy1ProntoDashhd	Always outrun	10
02Apr06Wrd9	5½ gd	:221 :462 :581 1:081 3↑	106 Alw16000n1x	105	84	80/	54	+5	+4	52	7	8	74¾	52¼	63¾	63¾	Young SE123	LBb 4.60	Derby Opportunity2½Jettin AffirmednoAbbott¾	No factor	8

13Apr RD 3f ft :383 B 8/16 13Jun'06 Bsd 3f ft :381 B 3/8 05Dec'05 Jdm 3f gd :41 B 3/5 ●21Nov'05 Jdm 5f gd 1:05 B 1/5 29Aug'05 Jdm 4f hy :52 B 1/1 18Jly'05 Jdm 3f gd :39 B 1/3
●09Jly'05 Elp 4f ft :484 Hg 1/29 10Jun'05 Jdm 4f gd :51 B 4/6 ●26May'05 Jdm 4f gd :52 B 1/4 ●13May'05 Jdm 4f gd :52 B 1/9 03May'05 Jdm 4f gd :51 B 1/3 ●25Apr'05 Jdm 3f gd :381 B 1/5

4 Choice Union (S 0)

10/1
Own: Hilary J. Boone And Thomas E. Nugent
Orange, black sash, black bars on sleeves
SARVIS DEAN A. (99 23-11-17 23%)

Dkbbr. h. 6 EVDMAR 2004 $32k
Sire: Precocity (Afleet)
Dam: Blissful Union (John's Choice)
Brdr: John Franks (FL)
Trnr: Nugent Thomas E. (8 2-2-0 25%)

Power Rating: 97.1 (8th) L 120

	Starts	W-P-S	Earnings	SPD		Starts	W-P-S	Earnings	SPD
Life:	36	6 - 3 - 3	$77,357	83	Fst	20	3 - 3 - 2	$44,096	83
2007	4	2 - 0 - 0	$6,351	66	Off	14	2 - 0 - 1	$22,201	79
2006	17	1 - 1 - 0	$5,463	71	Dis	8	2 - 1 - 0	$17,590	79
RD	6	3 - 1 - 0	$10,504	71	Trf	2	1 - 0 - 0	$11,060	82
					AW	0	0 - 0 - 0	$689	58

2007	216	16%	38%	-0.22
JKYw/ S types	142	11%	37%	-0.20
+JKYw/ Trn L60	3	67%	100%	+37.53
JKYw/ Sprints	114	11%	30%	-0.36

2007	27	19%	44%	+3.73
+Win last race	6	33%	50%	+1.00

Sire Stats: AWD 7.0f 10%Mud 154MudSts 1.04spi
Dam'sSire:AWD 6.1f 10%Mud 105MudSts 0.57spi

★ Won last race (RD 04/27 5.5f Dirt good Clm 4000C)
● Moves up in class from last start ● Poor Speed Figures

DATE TRK	DIST		RR RACETYPE	CR	E1	E2/	LP	1c	2c	SPD	PP	ST	1C	2C	Str	FIN	JOCKEY	ODDS	Top Finishers	Comment	
27Apr07RD8	5½ gd6	:23 :463 1:007 1:074 3↑	104 Clm4000C	107	73	73/	67	+1	+6	61	5	7	77¾	78¼	54¼	1½	Sarvis DA124	L 6.50	ChcUnn½ThPrtyChrn¾OnEydGbb2	Closed with a rush	7
10Apr07RD6	6f ft	:233 :474 1:012 1:151 3↑	106 Clm4000n13m	109	67	66/	89	-4	-5	66	4	9	88½	75¾	31	1nk	Sarvis DA124	L 50.80	ChocUnionnkMnchito¾PotLmt¾	Saved ground; rallied	10
02Feb07TP8	Ⓐ 6½ ft	:232 :473 1:132 1:201 3↑	108 Clm5000n2Y	103	68	67/	64	-7	-6	50	1	6	77¾	77	612	716¾	Vitek JJ120	L 42.10	Pirate's Bid2¾Jarrett1½Desert Sword4½	Outrun	7
12Jan07Beu8	6f gd6	:222 :463 :593 1:124 3↑	106 Clm3500C	104	79	82/	61	+4	+6	56	12	3	67½	58	910	1111	Endres J120	L 25.10	CltCont1GnrlJosh1½SlwsTmpr2¼	3 wide; dropped back	12
13Dec06Beu8	6f gd	:221 :46 :59 1:12 3↑	105 Clm3500n2Y	109	76	78/	73	+4	+10	61	4	12	1111	1112	98¼	911½	CamaqueC120	L 14.30	Junket4Uncle Brother4Re Luhulnk	Broke slowly	12
17Nov06Beu8	6f sy6	:221 :461 :591 1:122 3↑	104 Clm3500n2Y	108	73	75/	84	+7	+8	68	7	10	911	810	85½	41½	CamaqueC120	L 29.90	KissOfTruthnkCRusselRun¾AirForms½	9 wide into lane	12
18Oct06Hoo8	5½ gd	:213 :45 1:033 3↑	108 Clm4000n29m	104	79	83/	48	-4	-1	59	9	8	98½	96¼	910	920¼	MojicaJr R120	L 30.40	Stealth Flier10¾Jenny's Gold3½Shagtime Paisly1¾	Trailed	9
23Sep06TP8	Ⓐ 6½ ft	:223 :453 1:111 1:174 3↑	105 Clm5000n29m	103	77	72/	68	-3	-1	57	5	6	54½	56¼	56	88¼	Paucar E120	L 11.80	PopCorky1¾HousOfSnston2½StormTl1½	Off inside; faded	9
17Sep06TP1	Ⓐ 1m ft	:244 :501 1:151 1:404 3↑	104 Clm5000n29m	103	60	59/	69	-14	-9	58	5	6	65½	57¾	67¾	79¾	712½ Paucar E124	6.00	DorosDonJuan2¾FinishLin6WldChrgernk	3 wide; faded	8
02Sep06RD12	6f ft	:231 :463 1:003 1:134 3↑	102 Clm4000n1y+	109	76	71/	83	-5	-3	65	3	6	63¾	54½	1hd	1½	Paucar E124	*1.60	ChcUnn¾MetFlwZ2JmysMgbcksno	Prevailed; driving	10

03Apr Tlc 5f ft 1:044 Bg 2/5 22Mar Tlc 5f ft 1:052 Bg 4/5 30Jan Tlc 3f ft :381 B 1/1 03Oct'06 Tlc 3f ft :373 B 4/9 19Jly'06 Tlc 5f ft 1:043 B 5/8 06Jly'06 Tlc 4f my :503 B 5/11
21Jan'06 Tlc 3f ft :374 B 4/9 13Jan'06 Tlc 3f gd :364 B 3/18 ●22Dec'05 Tlc 5f ft 1:014 B 1/7 25Nov'05 Tlc 3f ft :39 B 2/3 ●26Oct'04 Kee 5f ft 1:021 B 1/4 10Oct'04 Kee 5f ft 1:02 B 4/9

5 Step To The Music (E/P 3)

6/1
Own: Jennifer B. Tilley
White, green cross sashes
OUZTS PERRY WAYNE (142 18-25-20 13%)

Dkbbr. g. 4
Sire: Catienus (Storm Cat)
Dam: Clairvoyance (Siphon (Brz))
Brdr: Kenneth L Ramsey & Sarah K Ramsey (KY)
Trnr: Murphy Carolyn S. (1 0-0-0 0%)

Power Rating: 111.6 (3rd) L 122

	Starts	W-P-S	Earnings	SPD		Starts	W-P-S	Earnings	SPD
Life:	21	5 - 5 - 4	$48,798	78	Fst	20	5 - 4 - 4	$44,780	78
2007	7	3 - 2 - 2	$19,778	78	Off	1	0 - 1 - 0	$5,000	66
2006	9	2 - 0 - 2	$14,930	77	Dis	8	3 - 3 - 0	$29,660	78
RD	0	0 - 0 - 0	$0		Trf	0	0 - 0 - 0	$0	
					AW	12	5 - 3 - 4	$35,750	78

2007	501	10%	34%	-0.79
JKYw/EP types	137	9%	27%	-1.10
JKYw/ Trn L60	1	0%	0%	-2.00
JKYw/ Sprints	277	9%	34%	-0.94

2007	2	0%	50%	-2.00

Sire Stats: AWD 7.0f 17%Mud 219MudSts 1.27spi
Dam'sSire:AWD 6.6f 8%Mud 358MudSts 1.23spi

★ Recent Speed Ratings make him a threat ★ Drops in Class today
★ Ran 3rd vs tougher in last race

DATE TRK	DIST		RR RACETYPE	CR	E1	E2/	LP	1c	2c	SPD	PP	ST	1C	2C	Str	FIN	JOCKEY	ODDS	Top Finishers	Comment	
22Apr07Kee3	Ⓐ 6f ft	:224 :462 :581 1:102 4↑	111 Alw8000s	111	83	87/	82	-7	3	78	2	6	63¾	51¾	52	32	Troilo WD118	Lbl 22.50	OldDozrnoRubDbDb2StpToThMscno	5w trip;mild gain	9
Claimed from Hammond Everett Hammond Kim Trainer																					
05Apr07TP7	Ⓐ 6½ ft	:224 :462 1:122 1:19 3↑	110 Clm8000-c	117	86	90/	78	-4	2	78	8	1	41	3hd	1hd	21¼	Troilo WD120	Lbl 6.90	Pnecisln1¼StpToThMsc1¼GoldSmls1¼	4w; outfinished	8
15Mar07TP8	Ⓐ 6f ft	:221 :453 :582 1:113 3↑	107 Clm5000n39m	108	80	84/	84	-1	+1	76	3	3	25	23½	11½	1½	PrescottRA124	Lbl *2.40	StpToThMsc½FlyngChnc1¾MrPopeyno	Off inside; lasted	7
25Feb07TP4	Ⓐ 5½ ft	:222 :462 :591 1:054 3↑	107 Clm5000C	116	88	87/	85	-3	4	78	1	4	3hd	11	14	12¼	PrescottRA124	Lbl 5.90	StepToThMusic2¼Svimn1BstProspct1	Inside; driving	8
02Feb07TP6	Ⓐ 6f ft	:23 :47 :594 1:131 3↑	107 Clm7500n3L	108	87	87/	81	-4	3	76	4	2	1hd	11	12	1nk	PrescottRA120	Lbl *2.00	StpToThMscnkCornonKd1¼Rvncl¾	Jumped object 5/8 pl	7
18Jan07TP2	Ⓐ 5½ ft	:223 :462 :591 1:053 4↑	104 Clm5000n3L	106	88	80/	73	0	+1	65	9	1	4nk	31	27	2½	Mena M120	Lf *0.70	OrnlForst½StpToThMusic1½PistonT¾	4 wide into turn	10
11Jan07TP2	Ⓐ 6½ ft	:222 :452 1:102 1:171 4↑	106 Clm7500n3L	107	85	87/	72	-1	2	71	6	1	32½	21½	24	35	LeparouxJR120	L *1.90	PirtesBid4½EscpTctics½StpToThMusic2¾	4 wide 1/4 pl	7
21Dec06TP12	Ⓐ 6f ft	:213 :443 :57 1:10 3↑	107 Clm7500n3L	108	88	94/	74	+4	+4	76	9	1	43½	3½	21½	31½	Butler DP118	L 18.70	CCRydr1¾Ahndnk StpToThMscno	4 wide; bid, weakened	11
30Sep06Haw3	6f ft	:224 :471 1:00 1:13 3↑	106 Clm5000n3L	104	77	70/	73	-7	-16	56	7	5	53	64¾	78¼	711	CampbellJM118	Lf 4.70	BloThWds3¾WrgtchcvdnoCptnHs¾	3 wide; gave way	8
16Sep06Hoo1	6f ft	:221 :46 :581 1:132 3↑	105 Clm5000n3L	106	87	89/	65	+4	+7	65	6	7	43	47¼	44	47¾	MaciasJrG115	Lf 4.10	KingsPecenoFraznkDsordinthccurt2½	4 wide turn; empty	10

31Mar TP 3f ft :361 B 3/6 10Mar TP 4f ft :52 B 25/26 04Jan TP 4f ft :47 B 2/18 17Dec'06 TP 3f ft :38 B 6/7 08Dec'06 TP 5f ft 1:001 B 2/5 02Dec'06 TP 4f ft :492 B 32/57
26Nov'06 TP 3f ft :364 B 3/10 25Aug'06 Elp 5f ft 1:023 B 2/6 19Aug'06 Elp 4f ft :501 B 13/17 13Aug'06 Elp 3f ft :37 B 3/16 15Apr'06 Ind 4f ft :491 B 17/24 06Apr'06 TP 5f ft 1:06 B 13/13

tsnhorse.com

Ultimate PP's w/ Quick Play Comments **River Downs** Str Alw8300 5½ Furlongs 3up Friday May 11, 2007 **Race 4** E1 E2/LATE SPD 92 93/ 80 81

6 Look At This Cat (E/P 7)

12/1 Own: Hulon L. Womack
Purple, silver stars
SOLOMON NATHAN (4) 10-5-4 23%)

Dkbbr. c. 4 OHIOCT 2004 $1k
Sire: Noble Cat (Storm Cat)
Dam: Strict Miss (Honey Jay)
Brdr: Jeffrey L. Whitesell (OH)
Trnr: Womack Hulon Leslie (7 0-1-1 0%)

Power Rating: 103.3 (7th) L 120

Life:	22 3 - 3 - 2	$34,375	71	Fst	16 2 - 3 - 1	$21,387	71
2007	7 1 - 2 - 1	$8,300	71	Off	4 1 - 0 - 1	$12,876	69
2006	15 1 - 1 - 1	$16,130	71	Dis	3 1 - 0 - 0	$8,175	71
RD	12 2 - 2 - 2	$25,006	71	Trf	2 0 - 0 - 0	$112	71
				AW	9 1 - 1 - 0	$6,927	71

2007	69	17%	43%	+2.78
JKYw/EP types	85	9%	25%	-0.94
+JKYw/ Sprints	47	21%	51%	+4.43

+2007	18	6%	39%	1.07
+Sprnt-Rte Sprnt	7	29%	71%	+1.06
+Rte to Sprnt	13	23%	62%	+0.42

Sire Stats: AWD 6.6f 14%Mud 143MudSts 0.65spi
Dam'sSire:AWD 6.7f 10%Mud 1544MudSts 1.08spi

★ Hot Jockey in last 7 days (9 3 0 1) ★ Drops in Class today ★ High % Jockey
★ May improve at the shorter distance ★ Ran 3rd vs tougher in last race
★ 29% trainer: Sprnt Rte-Sprnt

● Poor Speed Figures ● Best Speed rating is well below the Avg Winning Speed ● Poor Trainer win%

DATE TRK	DIST		RR RACETYPE	CR	E1	E2/	LP	1c	2c	SPD	PP	ST	1C	2C	Str	FIN	JOCKEY		ODDS	Top Finishers	Comment	
26Apr07RD11	1m my6	:24¹ :48¹ 1:13² 1:40² 3↑	108 OC[illegible]	108	75	80/	65	8	1	68	1	1¹	1hd	2½	2⁴	3¹¹¾	Paucar E120	Lbl	12.30	Crypteeze Chad's Hero Look AtThisCat	Weakened	7
17Apr07RD8	6f ft	:22⁴ :46¹ :59 1:13¹ 3↑	106 Clm4000n2m	108	88	85/	73	1	-1	68	5	3	1hd	1¹	2hd	2¹¾	Paucar E120	Lbl	4.00	Series LokAtThisCat RaidTheParde	Bobbled start	7
31Mar07TP3	Ⓢ 6f ft	:22⁴ :46³ :58 1:12¹ 3↑	106 Clm5000n2m	107	82	78/	82	7	8	70	5	3	2hd	1hd	2hd	2nk	Lebron V122	Lbl	6.30	Treat LookAtThisCat BoldMov	Off inside; outfinshd	7
17Mar07TP4	Ⓢ 6f ft	:23¹ :47² :59³ 1:11⁴ 3↑	106 Clm5000n2m	106	75	67/	88	-11	-18	66	1	4	3²	3²	4²	5⁴½	Lebron V122	Lbl	3.80	Jarrett Estedad Mesque's Boy	Lost action 7/16 pl	8
07Mar07TP9	Ⓢ 6f ft	:23 :47 :59² 1:12¹ 3↑	106 Clm5000C	108	86	79/	81	-8	-9	68	2	5	3¹½	3¹	4²½	6⁴½	Lebron V122	Lbl	5.20	Storm Kingdom Suleiman Preston T	Inside; tired	9
07Feb07TP9	Ⓢ 6f ft	:23 :47³ 1:00⁴ 1:14¹ 3↑	106 Clm5000n3L	109	85	79/	83	-2	-5	71	2	6	5½	4¹½	3½	1¹½	Lebron V120	Lbl	7.40	LkAtThsCt MstrHools WslTrr	Wore down leaders	6
06Jan07TP7	Ⓢ 1m ft	:24¹ :47³ 1:13² 1:38³ 4↑	107 Clm5000C	109	80	68/	63	0	-8	60	4	1½	1hd	2½	6⁶	8¹²½	Lebron V120	Lbl	10.80	DesertMonrch ShipsCaptin LarryB	Inside;gave way	8
31Dec06TP7	Ⓢ 6f ft	:21³ :44⁴ :57⁴ 1:11¹ 3↑	105 Clm5000C	100	71	70/	81	+4	+8	63	1	7	7¹¹	6¹¹	4⁶½	4⁵½	Lebron V119	Lbl	9.20	ClaytonsPrty Fitruck Hslobgod	Inside; evenly late	11
Claimed from Napier Sherry Napier William J. Trainer																						
27Oct06Beu12	6f sy6	:22⁷ :46¹ :58³ 1:11⁴ 3↑	107 ⓈCS000n3L-c	101	85	78/	66	-3	-2	57	3	4	3½	3²	5⁷	7⁸½	Paucar E117	Lbl	*0.60	WhatOvl UnwngFight RockinEd	Weakened; inside	9
23Sep06TP3	Ⓢ 6½ ft	:23 :46¹ 1:11¹ 1:17² 3↑	106 Clm7500n3L	109	80	76/	85	-7	-7	57	9	3	3¹½	3²	5⁸	6⁹½	Troilo WD117	Lbl	4.90	Athendothdy ActThePt AcsToThCity	3 path; tired	9

20Jan TP 5f ft 1:03² B 15/22 23Dec'06 TP 6f ft 1:14² B 1/3 15Dec'06 TP 5f ft 1:00³ B 4/14 06Dec'06 TP 4f ft :48¹ Bg 6/27 21Oct'06 TP 5f ft 1:03 B 15/20 09Sep'06 TP 5f ft 1:01² B 6/16
12Aug'06 RD 5f ft 1:02² B 2/8 ●29Jly'06 RD 5f my 1:01 H 1/8 26Mar'06 Npr 5f gd 1:03 Bg 2/6 12Mar'06 Npr 5f gd 1:04 Bg 6/13 05Mar'06 Npr 5f gd :10² B 4/12 10Sep'05 TP 5f ft 1:04⁴ B 8/10

7 City Rapid (E/P 1)

5/2 Own: Charles Lawson
Red, white bars on sleeves
ROSARIO, JR. HECTOR L. (3 1-0-0 33%)

Ch. h. 8 KEEAPR 2001 $8k
Sire: Carson City (Mr. Prospector)
Dam: Zil (Zilzal)
Brdr: Cranford Stud (KY)
Trnr: Lawson Charles (8 1-0-3 13%)

Power Rating: 110.4 (4th) L 120

Life:	36 12 - 8 - 2	$173,726	93	Fst	28 11 - 6 - 1	$163,186	93
2006	13 7 - 0 - 1	$36,835	93	Off	5 1 - 0 - 1	$10,330	93
2005	6 1 - 2 - 0	$15,231	81	Dis	10 4 - 1 - 2	$32,448	93
RD	5 3 - 0 - 0	$16,454	93	Trf	1 0 - 0 - 0	$200	80
				AW	3 0 - 0 - 0	$232	78

2007	167	10%	31%	-0.74
JKYw/EP types	264	13%	36%	-0.62
JKYw/ Sprints	83	7%	25%	-1.19

2007	88	22%	53%	-0.52
+90+ days away	47	19%	43%	-0.43
+Btn favorite	114	21%	54%	-0.72

Sire Stats: AWD 6.4f 21%Mud 1329MudSts 2.19spi
Dam'sSire:AWD 8.0f 16%Mud 49MudSts 2.60spi

★ Highest Speed Figure at Today's Distance ★ Best Dirt Speed is fastest among today's starters

● Beaten by weaker in last start ● Has not raced for more than 6 months

DATE TRK	DIST		RR RACETYPE	CR	E1	E2/	LP	1c	2c	SPD	PP	ST	1C	2C	Str	FIN	JOCKEY		ODDS	Top Finishers	Comment	
27Oct06Beu10	5½ sy5	:21³ :45³ :57⁷ 1:03⁴ 3↑	109 Alw5000s	109	88	89/	71	0	-4	71	3	3	4²½	3²	5¹½	4⁴½	Paucar E120	L	*1.40	RglmRqust BrsBdBy IdyErgy	Close up; weakened	7
29Sep06TP4	Ⓢ 5f ft	:21⁴ :44⁴ :57¹ 3↑	109 Alw5000s	107		85/	68			64	5	5	5³½	5⁵½	7⁷½	8⁹	Paucar E120	L	4.40	Skpthgdprt DnceMn WwCngstdr	Inside turn; tired	10
Previously trained by DAVIS JOSEPH D.																						
01Sep06Mnr8	5½ ft	:21⁴ :45² :58⁴ 1:06¹ 3↑	110 Alw5000s	111	84	91/	64	+6	+13	77	4	6	6⁷½	6¹¹	4⁶	3³	Felix JE118	L	6.40	JmpFrJyz FlmOfJstc CtyRp	Angled upper;bid late	7
Previously trained by LAWSON CHARLES																						
06Aug06RD1	6f ft	:22¹ :45 :58¹ 1:12 3↑	107 Alw5000s	107	90	86/	72	+2	+5	68	1	3	4²½	3⁵½	4⁵½	4⁵	Minnock B117	L	*0.50	MyAsct RglmRqust RckCnty	Checked backstretch	7
02Jly06RD3	5½ ft	:22² :45² :58² 1:05⁷ 3↑	110 Alw5000s	112	94	100/	80	+2	+4	85	4	3	3½	2hd	1²	1⁴	Minnock B117	L	*0.40	CityRpid GoldBrick MississpiRiver	Drew off; driving	5
12May06RD11	5½ my5	:23 :45² :58⁴ 1:05⁷ 3↑	108 Alw5000s	115	92	106/	82	-3	+6	93	8	2	2hd	1²	1⁶	1⁸½	Paucar E124	L	*0.50	CityRpid Scolnwithddvl HohoTw	E wide; ridden out	9
06May06Beu6	6f ft	:22³ :46² :58² 1:10¹ 3↑	106 Alw5000s	113	86	88/	98	0	+12	92	7	2	2hd	1hd	1⁴	1⁵½	Paucar E124	L	*0.20	CityRpid CaptinJoob FotOnThFlor	Drew off; driving	9
25Apr06RD3	6f ft	:22¹ :45² :58¹ 1:11⁴ 3↑	108 Alw5000s	113	95	95/	83	+2	-1	85	1	1	1²	1¹½	1⁴	1⁸	Paucar E122	L	*0.20	CityRapid GoldSneker Storm Tale	Drew off; driving	5
18Mar06Beu8	5½ ft	:22³ :46⁴ :59 1:05³ 3↑	110 Alw5000s	113	93	96/	86	-1	-2	88	3	1	2hd	2½	1¹	1³½	Paucar E124	Ll	1.50	CityRpid DashOffme ExpctdFlt	Drew off; driving	6
07Mar06Beu3	5½ ft	:23 :48³ 1:01¹ 1:08 3↑	108 Alw5000s	113	93	91/	86	0	-3	83	3	2	2hd	1hd	1½	1⁵½	Paucar E124	Ll	*1.30	CityRpd ThreLdsMnr ThRjctdSton	Drew off; driving	5

30Apr Beu 4f ft :49⁴ B 5/6 19Mar Beu 3f ft :39¹ B 9/12 25Nov'06 Beu 3f ft :39⁴ B 12/14 20Sep'05 Sky 3f ft :39 B 1/1 04Aug'05 Sky 4f ft :49¹ B 1/1 19Jly'05 CD 4f ft :52⁴ B 55/56
26Jun'05 CD 4f ft :47³ B 3/47 26Apr'04 CD 3f ft :35 B 3/32 18Feb'04 Cdl 4f ft :50² B 6/17 07Jly'03 CD 4f ft :47³ B 2/41 16Apr'03 CD 3f ft :36² B 2/9 ●04Mar'03 Cdl 3f ft :36 Hg 1/12

8 Swissle Stick (E 8)

9/5 Own: Robert D. Nash
Orange, blue 'n'
PRESCOTT RODNEY A. (96 18-20-13 19%)

Ch. h. 5 BESMAR 2004 $600k
Sire: Swiss Yodeler (Eastern Echo)
Dam: Miss Soft Sell (Siyah Kalem)
Brdr: Mary N. Caldwell (CA)
Trnr: Flint Bernard S. (7 2-0-1 29%)

Power Rating: 114.6 (1st) L 124

Life:	35 3 - 4 - 4	$101,205	90	Fst	16 1 - 2 - 1	$65,718	88
2007	2 1 - 0 - 1	$6,526	81	Off	4 0 - 1 - 1	$7,670	74
2006	12 1 - 0 - 1	$22,247	90	Dis	9 1 - 0 - 1	$12,676	88
RD	2 1 - 0 - 1	$6,526	81	Trf	15 0 - 1 - 2	$25,125	90
				AW	0 0 0 0	$0	

2007	466	14%	46%	-0.27
JKYw/ E types	521	17%	43%	-0.33
+JKYw/ Trn L60	4	50%	75%	+0.75
JKYw/ Sprints	292	14%	48%	-0.17

2007	123	17%	38%	-0.61
+Wnr last race	303	20%	50%	-0.24

Sire Stats: AWD 6.0f 16%Mud 328MudSts 1.27spi
Dam'sSire:AWD 6.4f 12%Mud 451MudSts 0.71spi

★ Hot Trainer in last 14 days (3 2- 0- 0) ★ Highest Last Race Speed Rating
★ Early Speed running style helps chances ★ Won last race (RD 04/28 5f Dirt fast Alw 8000s)

DATE TRK	DIST		RR RACETYPE	CR	E1	E2/	LP	1c	2c	SPD	PP	ST	1C	2C	Str	FIN	JOCKEY		ODDS	Top Finishers	Comment	
28Apr07RD8	5f ft	:22¹ :45 :59² 3↑	108 Alw8000s	111		98/	75			81	2	3	1hd	1¹	1½	1½	PrescottRA120	Lbl	*1.00	SwslStck ChfOrmnd AfrInThAir	Inside; battled; held	5
14Apr07RD6	5½ sy5	:22³ :45³ :59 1:06 3↑	108 Clm15000	107	96	100/	61	+3	+7	72	5	1	1²½	1hd	3¹½	3⁴½	Diego I120	Lbl	4.40	FvoritFun Stelyeyd SwisiStick	Rapid pace; faltered	7
14Oct06Mnr2	6f ft	:22 :45² :58¹ 1:12² 3↑	103 Clm5000n2L	108	91	92/	74	+1	+3	74	4	1	1⁴	1²	1²	1²½	WhitneyDG115	Lbl	*0.40	SwslSlck FrstWdr MntnSprgs	Leg weary; held safe	10
17Sep06Mnr9	5½ ft	:22 :45³ :57³ 1:03⁴ 3↑	110 Alw31500n3L	107	91	77/	54	-2	-5	61	8	4	3¹	3²	9¹⁴	9²⁰½	WhitneyDG115	Lb	5.60	Ghostpr CntOB TruCore	Chased to1/4;weakened	9
Previously trained by MILLER DANNY L.																						
23Aug06AP7	Ⓣ 5f fm	:21⁴ :44³ :57⁷ 3↑	110 Alw29000n1x	110		88/	73			71	7	4	2¹½	2¹½	2¹½	5¹½	Graham J118	Lb	*1.90	BchOfArts AlphFino PrchrBrwn	Off rail; gave way *Dead heat*	11
Claimed from D. Wayne Lukas Lukas D. Wayne Trainer																						
30Jly06AP4	Ⓣ 5f fm	:22 :45 :56³ 3↑	112 Clm35000/30-c	112		93/	74			77	6	1	2hd	1½	1hd	5⁶	Ferrer JC119	Lb	3.70	Quietly Quick Elle Captain Malory	Awkward start	7
04Jly06CT9	4½ ft	:21¹ :44 :50¹ 3↑	114 ClDashH 100k	112		88/	76			72	1	3	2³		2⁵	3⁹½	AlmodovarG118	Lb	3.60	Outcshem BlownAdl SwislStck	Lacked needed rally	3
16Jun06CD4	Ⓣ 5f fm	:21² :44¹ :56 3↑	112 Clm50000/45	112		96/	77			83	6	2	2¹½	2¹½	2¹½	5⁴½	Borel CH118	Lb	7.10	JmpFrJyz BtsArWlkg GoLnkG	Lean in hmp start;4w	8
03Jun06CD11	Ⓣ 5f fm	:22 :45¹ :56⁴ 3↑	115 TxGBlartH 70k	115		97/	94			90	8	4	1¹½	1²	1hd	6³½	Jacinto J108	Lb	40.30	Yucatn AlcusKristy MightyBeu	Sprinted clear;taker	9
20May06CD3	Ⓣ 5f fm	:21⁴ :44³ :56³ 3↑	113 Clm40000	114		94/	79			82	1	1	1¹½	1¹½	1½	5¹	Jacinto J120	Lbl	19.80	ThtsrNark BtsArWlkg HtgHbly	Pace;inside;weakened	12

24Apr TP 4f ft :48 B 1/3 09Apr TP 5f ft 1:00³ B 1/3 31Apr TP 5f ft 1:00 B 2/7 ●25Mar TP 5f ft 1:00 B 1/7 18Mar TP 4f ft :47 B 2/16 11Mar TP 4f ft :47 B 2/12
04Mar TP 3f ft :35⁴ B 2/7 08Sep'06 CD 5f ft 1:00 B 2/13 ●16Aug'06 CD 4f ft :47¹ B 1/39 14Jly'06 CD 4f ft :47 B 2/45 ●26Jun'06 CD 3f ft :34³ B 1/14 14May'06 CD 4f ft :48⁴ B 9/52

tsnhorse.com

Ultimate PP's w/ Quick Play Comments **River Downs** Str Alw8300 5½ Furlongs. 3up Friday, May 11, 2007 **Race 4**

E1	E2/LATE	SPD
92	93/ 80	81

Last 3 Years	RACETYPE STATS:	# Races	FAVORITES Win%	Itm%	$2ROI	Average Field Size	Median $2 Win Payoff	% Winners < 5/1	% Winners >= 5/1 < 10/1	% Winners >= 10/1
RD 3up	STRALW 6700 - 10000 Dirt 5.5f - 6f	32	41%	72%	-0.27	7.4	$6.60	81%	13%	6%

Track Bias Stats

DIRT 5.5f	' MEET Totals '		WnrAvgBL		DIRT 5.5f	' WEEK Totals '		WnrAvgBL	
# Races: 38	Speed Bias: 74%		1stCall: 1.8		# Races: 7	Speed Bias: 100%		1stCall: 0.0	
%Wire: 45%	04/06 - 05/08		2ndCall: 1.6		%Wire: 100%	05/03 - 05/08		2ndCall: 0.0	
	Early	Speed	Late	Speed		Early	Speed	Late	Speed
Runstyle:	E	E/P	P	S	Runstyle:	E	E/P	P	S
	++					++			
Impact Values	1.94	0.87	0.72	0.47	Impact Values	4.00	0.00	0.00	0.00
%Races Won	58%	16%	11%	16%	%Races Won	100%	0%	0%	0%
Post Bias:	RAIL	1-3	4-7	8+	Post Bias	RAIL	1-3	4-7	8+
				+				+	+
Impact Values	0.74	0.92	1.02	1.27	Impact Values	1.03	0.69	1.13	1.82
Avg Win %	11%	13%	17%	7%	Avg Win %	14%	10%	19%	10%

Race Summary

#	HorseName	ML Odds	Med Eqp	Days Since L/R	Run Style	PTS	Avg Dist/Surf PACE-SPEED E1	E2/Late	Spd	Avg Race Rtng	Best Pace E1	E2/Late	Final Speed Sp1	Sp2	Sp3	Sp4	ACL	Rcg Spd Avg	R1	R2	R3	Mud Spd	Pedigree Stats Mud Sts	Mud % Mud	Sire AWD	Dam Sire's AWD
8	Swissle Stick	9/5	L	13..	++E	8		98/ 75	81	108	91	98/ 76	81.	72	74.	61.	108.5	76	108	108	103	72	328	16	6.0	6.4
5	Step To The Music	6/1	L	19	E/P	3	86	88/ 82	` 78`	110	88	94/ 85	78.	78.	76.	78.	109.5	77	111	110	107		219	17	7.0	6.6
2	Steelyeyed	5/1	L	14	P	3	82	84/ 84	` 77`	110	85	98/ 91	76.	83	69.	66	108.9	76	109	108	110	83	2418	18	6.7	6.9
7	City Rapid	5/2	L	196	E/P	1	89	92/ 72	(77)	110	94	100/ 80	71	64.	77.	68.	109.8	71	109	109	110	93	1329	21	6.4	8.0
1	Rarify	8/1	L	19.	E/P	4	89	91/ 75	75	112	89	91/ 91	75.	59.	72.	75.	105.0	69	111	106	110	70	608	15	6.0	7.4
6	Look At This Cat	12/1	L	15	E/P	7	83	81/ 79	' 69'	106	90	89/ 88	68	68.	70.	66.	106.1	69	108	106	106	69	143	14	6.6	6.7
3	Warner Jazz Man	15/1	L	15.	P	3	73	73/ 81	(66)	105	80	80/ 88	76	47T	68.	63.	104.9	64	104	108	105	76	41	15	6.4	6.7
4	Choice Union	10/1	L	14..	S		73	74/ 72	' 61'	106	79	83/ 89	61.	66.	50.	56.	104.0	59	104	106	106	68	154	10	7.0	6.1

Speed Last Race	Back Speed	Current Class	Average Class Last 3	Power Rating	Early Pace Last Race	Late Pace Last Race
81 Swissle Stick	86 Steelyeyed	111.0 Step To The Music	110.6 Step To The Music	114.6 Swissle Stick	91 Rarify	82 Step To The Music
78 Step To The Music	85 City Rapid	110.9 Swissle Stick	110.0 Steelyeyed	111.9 Steelyeyed	89 City Rapid	80 Warner Jazz Man
76 Steelyeyed	81 Swissle Stick	110.6 Steelyeyed	109.1 City Rapid	111.6 Step To The Music	88 Warner Jazz Man	80 Steelyeyed
76 Warner Jazz Man	78 Step To The Music	110.2 Rarify	108.5 Rarify	110.4 City Rapid	87 Steelyeyed	75 Rarify
75 Rarify	75 Rarify	107.1 Look At This Cat	108.3 Swissle Stick	107.4 Rarify	87 Step To The Music	75 Swissle Stick
71 City Rapid	71 Look At This Cat	106.5 Choice Union	107.8 Look At This Cat	105.0 Warner Jazz Man	75 Look At This Cat	71 City Rapid
68 Look At This Cat	71 Choice Union	NA City Rapid	106.3 Warner Jazz Man	103.3 Look At This Cat	73 Choice Union	67 Choice Union
61 Choice Union	68 Warner Jazz Man	NA Warner Jazz Man	106.0 Choice Union	97.1 Choice Union	NA Swissle Stick	65 Look At This Cat

#	Speed Last Race		#	Prime Power		#	Class Rating		#	Best Speed at Dist	
7	Madly Paddin Home	75	7	Madly Paddin Home	109.5	7	Madly Paddin Home	107.9	6	Lookshoot Altitude	84
3	Air Borne Ethauer	74	3	Air Borne Ethauer	104.0	1	Sweetbaboo	106.1	8	Seeking Awards	75
1	Sweetbaboo	66	1	Sweetbaboo	103.5	5	Cardashi	105.8	3	Air Borne Ethauer	75

5

Exacta / Trifecta / Superfecta (Ten Cent Minimum) / Pick 3 (Races 5-6-7)

	E1	E2/LATE	SPEED
PARS:	91	90/ 78	76

Simulcast of Thistledown race number 5

6 Furlongs. Clm 6250NW3L Purse $7,500. FOR THREE YEAR OLDS AND UPWARD WHICH HAVE NEVER WON THREE RACES. Three Year Olds, 120 lbs., Older, 122 lbs. Non-winners Of Two Races Since April 11 Allowed 2 lbs. A Race Since Then Allowed 4 lbs. Claiming Price $6,250 (Ohio Registered Foals Preferred) .

Post Time: (2:25)/ 1:25/12:25/11:25

1 Sweetbaboo (E 5) $6,250

6/1
Own: Richard Zielinski And Nancy Garrison
Navy, silver stars
SKERRETT JEFFREY (70 16-3-11 23%)

B. g. 5
Sire: Sweetsouthernsaint (Saint Ballado)
Dam: Corporate Focus (Gilded Age)
Brdr: Four Horsemen's Ranch & Thomas J. Cooper (FL)
Trnr: Zielinski Richard (4 1-0-1 25%)

Power Rating: 103.5 (3rd) L 118

Life:	11 2 2 2	$14,831	70	Fst	8 1 1 2	$8,015	70
2007	1 0 0 1	$750	66	Off	3 1 1 0	$6,816	68
2006	7 2 2 0	$12,561	70	Dis	8 1 2 1	$8,301	70
Tdn	11 2 2 2	$14,831	70	Trf	0 0 0 0	$0	
				AW	0 0 0 0	$0	

2007	71	23%	42%	-0.26
JKYw/ E types	186	17%	44%	-0.20
+JKYw/ Trn L60	3	33%	67%	-1.07
+JKYw/ Sprints	54	22%	41%	-0.06

+2007	4	25%	50%	-1.30
No class chg	50	10%	18%	-1.18
Btn favorite	8	12%	62%	-1.58
Claiming	71	8%	20%	-1.34

Sire Stats: AWD 7.3f 18%Mud 130MudSts 1.52spi
Dam'sSire: AWD 7.6f 15%Mud 465MudSts 0.76spi

★ Hot Jockey in last 7 days (20 5-3-3) ★ High % Jockey ★ Ran 3rd vs similar in last race
★ Eligible to improve in 2nd start since layoff

DATE TRK	DIST						RR RACETYPE	CR	E1	E2/	LP	1c	2c	SPD	PP	ST	1C	2C	Str	FIN	JOCKEY		ODDS	Top Finishers	Comment	
21Apr07Tdn13	5½ ft	:22⁴	:47²	1:00¹	1:06³	4↑	104 Clm6250n3L	106	84	77/	79	-1	-7	65	2	4	2½	2½	2hd	3½	SkerrettJ118	Lb	*1.40	VclryVsn1½OnAprchhdSwtbbo2	Drew even; outfinished	7
25Nov06Tdn9	6f ft	:22¹	:45⁴	:58⁴	1:12¹	3↑	106 Clm3500n3L	107	85	85/	75	+1	+2	70	2	6	3²	3³	3⁴½	2³½	SkerrettJ117	Lb	2.80	PlumTre3½SwetbabonkMjesticPlonrnk	Rallied for second	10
12Nov06Tdn7	6f gd	:22²	:46⁴	1:00¹	1:13²	3↑	103 Clm3500n3L	106	85	86/	72	+1	-1	68	4	3	3³	2hd	1¹	2²½	SkerrettJ120	Lb	*1.30	Another Sunset2½Sweetbaboo4½Winlathd	Second best	9
16Oct06Tdn3	6f ft	:22⁴	:46⁴	:59⁴	1:13	3↑	101 Clm5000n2L	106	85	82/	78	-3	-3	70	4	1	2½	2hd	1²	1⁷½	SkerrettJ117	Lb	2.00	Swtbbo7½AmlThnYt5½Prsdtcsh4½	Dueled; clear; driving	7
13Sep06Tdn3	5½ ft	:22⁴	:47²	1:00²	1:07	3↑	104 Clm10000n2L	105	83	71/	71	0	-2	64	4	5	5³½	6⁷½	6⁶	4⁴½	SkerrettJ116	Lb	16.80	CbrrnkWidlyChrtc1½FvStrExpr2½	Never far back; evenly	9
03Sep06Tdn11	6f sy	:22³	:47	1:00	1:12⁴	3↑	104 Clm10000n2L	104	87	80/	68	2	-7	60	7	2	2¹	3¹½	4⁴	7¹⁰	SkerrettJ116	Lb	15.40	GoldMedWinr2½FvStrExprs2LbysFrlc½	Chased; tired	10
20May06Tdn10	6f ft	:22³	:47	1:00	1:13	3↑	106 Alw12500n1x	103	85	74/	55	-1	-7	44	5	3	4²½	6⁵½	7¹²	7²¹	MrtinezJrLJ122	Lb	10.30	GLckyG#WhSlwWh1½ToToCrfynk	Brief foot; gave way	7
22Apr06Tdn3	5f gd	:22⁴	:47¹		1:00²	3↑	104 MC15000	107		86/	73			68	1	1	2hd	1¹	1³	1⁹½	GonzalezLA122	Lb	5.30	Sweetbabo9½CodesLttlBit½Kadin'sCathd	Much the best	7
05Nov05Tdn1	6f ft	:23¹	:47³	1:00⁴	1:14	3↑	101 Mdn 9.5k	103	83	74/	72	3	-5	58	4	3	2hd	2¹	3¹	3²½	HanniganL121	Lb	2.90	WeTwo½Best PalLouie1½Sweetbabo2½	Pressed; evenly	7
06Oct05Tdn10	6f ft	:22³	:46³	:59²	1:12²	3↑	100 Mdn 9.5k	101	87	81/	64	-1	-6	57	3	2	2½	4nk	3³½	3⁹½	Unel-mornV120	Lb	4.40	DrbyT4½OnRoylAh3½Swtbbo2½	Bore out;pressed;faded (Placed 7th through disqualification)	7

●12Apr Tdn 5f my 1:00³ B 1/7 ●03Apr Tdn 4f ft :49³ B 1/9 17Aug'06 Tdn 4f ft :49² B 3/10 08May'06 Tdn 4f ft :48¹ B 2/28 18Apr'06 Tdn 5f ft 1:02³ B 3/8 11Apr'06 Tdn 4f ft :49 B 2/18
30Mar'06 Tdn 3f ft :41² B 11/11 28Oct'05 Tdn 4f gd :54 B 14/14 04Sep'05 Tdn 4f ft :50² Bg 6/10 19Aug'05 Tdn 3f ft :39³ B 10/10 08Aug'05 Tdn 4f ft :49³ B 4/20 30Jly'05 Tdn 4f ft :50² B 7/9

2 Synhawk (E 0) $6,250

12/1
Own: Randy Joe Faulkner
Blue, white 'S', blue 'S' on white sleeves
MARTINEZ, JR. LUIS J. (44 7-7-7 16%)

B. g. 6
Sire: Wild Syn (Wild Again)
Dam: Dissident Hawk (Stutz Blackhawk)
Brdr: Jack D. Fisher (KY)
Trnr: Faulkner Randy Joe (29 5-2-5 17%)

Power Rating: 89.8 (9th) L 118

Life:	31 2 3 0	$18,783	70	Fst	25 2 3 0	$17,976	70
2007	7 0 0 0	$663	63	Off	6 0 0 0	$807	62
2006	17 2 1 0	$14,255	70	Dis	14 1 2 0	$10,857	70
Tdn	3 0 0 0	$209	58	Trf	0 0 0 0	$0	
				AW	8 1 3 0	$7,873	69

2007	111	12%	40%	-0.68
+JKYw/ E types	190	19%	38%	-0.01
JKYw/ Trn L60	18	17%	39%	+1.00
JKYw/ Sprints	79	10%	39%	-1.05

+2007	53	11%	32%	-0.18
+1st strt w/trn	38	32%	50%	+2.35
Up one class	36	11%	42%	-0.61
+Claiming	312	21%	45%	+0.47

Sire Stats: AWD 6.9f 9%Mud 54MudSts 0.55spi
Dam'sSire: AWD 7.1f 15%Mud 1881MudSts 0.71spi

★ Hot Trn/Jky combo in last 14 days (10 2-0-2) ★ 32% trainer: 1st strt w/trn

● Beaten by weaker in last start ● Poor Speed Figures in each recent start ● Poor record at this track
● Only 2 wins in 31 career starts ● Poor record at this distance

DATE TRK	DIST						RR RACETYPE	CR	E1	E2/	LP	1c	2c	SPD	PP	ST	1C	2C	Str	FIN	JOCKEY		ODDS	Top Finishers	Comment	
14Apr07Beu7	6f gd⁵	:22⁴	:46⁴	:59³	1:12³	3↑	102 Clm5000n3L	102	83	81/	68	0	+3	61	2	7	7²½	8³½	7²½	6³½	Paucar E120	Lb	16.80	StPrspctrhdFvclkChny½SrtOfPrr½	Angled out into lane	8
30Mar07Beu7	6f ft	:22²	:46¹	:58³	1:11²	3↑	102 Clm4000n3L	103	83	80/	72	+1	+2	63	3	3	5⁴	5⁶	6⁴½	4⁶	Paucar E120	Lbf	16.70	Gridwin4½Padre1Watrals WildOzzie½	Evenly; no rally	8
17Mar07Beu7	1m gd	:25¹	:50²	1:16⁴	1:42	3↑	103 Clm4000n3L	101	61	52/	59	-13	-13	48	2	2hd	1½	1²	5⁴	6¹³½	Paucar E120	Lbf	11.00	FruitsopOfnk ShBrsh4MnrCounty1½	Dueled; clear; tired	7
03Mar07Beu5	1 70 gd	:23³	:49²	1:15	1:46	3↑	103 Clm5000n3L	102	69	58/	55	-5	-3	52	5	2²	2¹½	4⁴	4¹²	5¹⁹½	CcmqueMA120	Lbf	25.70	Wintal8Shoo Brush2Fancy Fashion1½	Chased; tired	8
10Feb07Beu7	1m ft	:25	:49³	1:14¹	1:40¹	3↑	103 Clm5000n3L	102	62	55/	67	-14	+1	54	7	6⁴	6⁴½	6⁸½	7¹⁰	8¹⁰½	CcmqueMA120	Lbf	34.70	Major Mark1½StrongAsSton½Cash Town4½	3-4 wide trip	10
24Jan07Beu10	1 70 gd	:23¹	:47³	1:14²	1:45³	3↑	103 Clm4000n3L	101	71	56/	35	+1	+1	38	4	4⁴	4⁶½	9¹³	9²⁶	9³⁵½	Paucar E120	Lbf	7.50	DeputySrvc14½WnNGr4OurLdngMn½	Through after half	10
10Jan07Beu8	6f ft	:22²	:46⁴	1:00	1:13¹	3↑	103 Clm4000n3L	102	75	78/	62	+4	+8	54	10	12	10⁹½	9⁸½	9⁷½	10⁹½	HernandezL115	Lbf	12.00	ToughCut3½PowerFme2ClamedUphd	4 wide, no factor	12
29Nov06Beu5	1 70 ft				1:45³	3↑	103 Clm4000n3L	103	72	64/	56	+1	+3	56	9	4⁴½	2½	1hd	2hd	6⁴½	MelanconP120	Lb	17.40	GovsAc½FruitsoupOfnkMrTimCounthd	4 wide first turn	12
14Nov06Beu8	1 70 ft	:23³	:48⁴	1:15⁴	1:48¹	3↑	103 Clm5000n3L	101	63	49/	49	1	+1	43	3	4⁴½	4³½	8⁵½	8⁸½	8¹³½	HernandezL115	Lb	4.50	Lerbo4½HrbourTid1½FruitsopOf½	Dropped back; inside	9
31Oct06Beu8	6f wf⁵	:22³	:47²	1:00	1:12³	3↑	103 Clm4000n3L	105	77	73/	79	-3	-6	62	4	3	6⁴½	5³	5³½	4⁶	HernandezL115	Lbf	3.60	ImperilStr½SlewsTempr2½JustDazling2½	3 wide; no rally	8

13Jly'06 FE 3f ft :40⁴ B 19/20 07Jun'06 FE 3f ft :38² H 13/14 06May'06 FE 3f ft :38⁴ B 12/18 26Nov'05 TP 5f ft 1:06⁴ B 14/15 19Nov'05 TP 4f ft :51⁴ B 25/31 12Nov'05 TP 3f ft :38⁴ B 18/35
05Nov'05 TP 4f ft :50⁴ B 22/28 22Oct'05 TP 4f ft :52 B 22/27 15Oct'05 TP 3f ft :39¹ B 14/18 11May'05 Kee 5f ft 1:05⁷ B 11/12 03May'05 Kee 5f ft 1:03³ B 10/13 18Apr'05 Cd 5f ft 1:03¹ B 9/9

Ultimate PP's w/ Quick Play Comments **River Downs** Clm 6250NW3L 6 Furlongs 3up Friday, May 11, 2007 **Race 5 (TDN - #5)** E1 91 E2/LATE 90/ 78 SPD 76

3 Air Borne Etbauer (E/P 3)

4/1 — Own: Jack L. Boggs — White, red cross sashes, red bar on sleeves
SPIETH SCOTT (84 11-10-7 17%)

$6,250 B. g. 4 — Sire: Etbauer (Silver Deputy) — Dam: Aerial Launch (Relaunch) — Brdr: Keeran Biggs & Hays Biggs (AR) — Trnr: Radosevich Jeffrey A. (62 15-12-6 29%)

Power Rating: 104.0 (2nd) L 120

Life:	17 2-5-3	$43,739	80	Fst	11 2-3-1	$27,514	80
2007	5 2-0-1	$12,235	80	Off	4 0-2-1	$13,980	70
2006	12 0-5-2	$31,504	75	Dis	9 1-4-1	$28,179	75
Tdn	1 1-0-0	$4,002	74	Trf	2 0-0-1	$2,245	65
				AW	0 0-0-0	$0	

+2007	270	16%	43%	-0.67	+2007	168	20%	52%	-0.32
+JKYw/EP types	421	22%	53%	-0.33	Up one class	150	17%	47%	-0.45
JKYw/ Trn L60	89	17%	48%	0.83	+Wnr last race	456	28%	57%	-0.13
JKYw/ Sprints	196	17%	45%	-0.58	+Claiming	1654	22%	51%	-0.28

Sire Stats: AWD 6.5f 15%Mud 41MudSts 0.74spi
Dam'sSire:AWD 7.0f 19%Mud 1212MudSts 3.21spi

★ Hot Trn/Jky combo in last 14 days (18 5-4-2) ★ Speed Rating last race labels him a threat
★ Best Dirt Speed is faster than the Avg Winning Speed ★ High % Trainer
★ Won last race (TDN 04/13 6f Dirt last Clm 4000NW2L)
● Moves up in class from last start

DATE TRK	DIST		RR RACETYPE	CR	E1	E2/	LP	1c	2c	SPD	PP	ST	1C	2C	Str	FIN	JOCKEY	ODDS	Top Finishers	Comment
13Apr07Tdn13	6f ft	:223 :472 1:002 1:132 4↑	102 Clm4000n2L	108	86	79/	86	0	-8	74	2	7	42	21	12	15¼	Spieth S118	Lb *2.30	ArBornEtbr5¼SrfyMTrx2½ColrMFr½	Drew off; ridden out 12
01Apr07Mnr3	5f my	:223 :47 :593 3↑	102 Clm5000n2L	103		82/	67			60	3	4	67½	32	33	36	Spieth S118	Lb 4.10	Tashd shmrcndr3¼ArBrnEtbr1¼	Stalk;bid5w;need more 9
24Mar07Mnr7	5½ my	:223 :471 1:004 1:071 3↑	106 Clm10000n2L	104	86	71/	53	+1	-2	48	5	8	81½	93½	98½	913	Spieth S118	Lb 4.80	SnRsr4OciFrestone1½SgnorHgi	Slow;asked,no factor 10
02Mar07Mnr9	5½ ft	:22 :46 :59 1:061 3↑	107 Clm3000/20n2L	104	87	83/	45	+4	+7	55	6	6	54½	35½	79½	715	Spieth S117	Lb 11.00	CorondosStrik2Fresdo6Medin2	Chased3w;gave way 7
12Feb07Mnr2	5f ft	:222 :451 :573 3↑	101 MC10000	108		97/	82			80	3	2	22	21	2hd	1½	Spieth S121	Lb 1.50	ArBornEtbr½Valcs8½SprngFr3½	Abreast full extension 9
09Dec06Mnr4	5½ ft	:224 :472 1:011 1:082 3↑	104 Mdn 24k	102	93	90/	53	+2	+8	59	7	5	1½	3½	74½	710	Spieth S118	Lb 3.40	RlySttion1¼MstBADrm½TxCrdt1¾	Used hard; wore out 9
24Nov06Mnr6	5½ ft	:224 :471 1:004 1:08	106 Mdn 24k	107	92	94/	68	+2	+8	70	6	3	1½	12	11	23½	Spieth S118	Lb 7.60	DbCty2¼ArBornEtbrnkTxCrdt1¾	Rated pace overpowered 8
04Nov06Mnr6	6f ft	:233 :481 1:014 1:154 3↑	103 Mdn 24k	105	89	92/	72	-4	-2	73	3	1	1½	12	1hd	35½	Spieth S118	Lb 4.50	PortSgr5¼DvnWdrhdArBrnEtbr2¼	Hooked btw; weakened 8
Previously trained by WREN STEVE																				
22Sep06LaD11	6f ft	:222 :454 :581 1:114 3↑	103 MC25000	105	91	92/	61	+1	+1	64	3	4	2hd	1hd	43	57½	QuinonezLS120	Lb 5.30	Pillage2½PowerJens1¼HighAchievr2¼	Weakened inside 9
10Aug06LaD9	(T) 5f fm	:222 :462 :573 3↑	102 MC20000	101		60/	77			57	4	8	611	67½	66	58	Meche L120	Lb *0.90	BoldRstsnkHighAchivrnkZomingBuhno	Improved position 8

10Feb Mnr 4f ft :513 B 12/20 15Sep'06 LaD 3f ft :384 B 13/15 20May'06 LaD 4f ft :487 H 5/54 ●14May'06 LaD 3f ft :343 H 1/33 03May'06 LaD 5f ft 1:032 B 9/20 23Mar'06 OP 3f gd :354 H 4/11
16Feb'06 OP 4f ft :503 B 25/58 08Feb'06 OP 6f ft 1:152 Hg5/10 29Jan'06 OP 4f my :491 Hg4/36 22Jan'06 OP 5f sy 1:04 B 21/37 15Jan'06 LaD 5f ft 1:032 B 29/53 08Jan'06 LaD 5f ft 1:032 Bg35/52

4 Pair Of Queens (E 5)

10/1 — Own: Crumley Racing Stable; Llc — Red
CLONINGER, JR. WELDON T. (41 15-7-7 37%)

$6,250 Dkbbr. g. 4 FTMMAY 2006 $15k — Sire: Meadow Monster (Meadowlake) — Dam: Queen Judith (Dee Lance) — Brdr: David Miller (MD) — Trnr: Crumley Jevon (28 9-6-4 32%)

Power Rating: 94.3 (7th) L 118

Life:	17 2-1-1	$13,342	72	Fst	13 1-0-1	$7,301	72
2007	6 0-0-1	$1,186	60	Off	4 1-1-0	$6,041	72
2006	9 2-1-0	$11,796	72	Dis	10 1-1-0	$6,616	72
Tdn	7 2-1-0	$10,752	72	Trf	0 0-0-0	$0	
				AW	4 0-0-1	$834	60

+2007	44	34%	59%	+1.03	+2007	34	26%	53%	-0.01
+JKYw/ E types	71	18%	45%	-0.70	1st strt wtrn	8	0%	50%	-2.00
+JKYw/ Trn L60	19	37%	58%	+0.58	Up one class	19	11%	26%	-1.57
+JKYw/ Sprints	33	33%	55%	+0.79	+Claiming	148	24%	49%	+2.00

Sire Stats: AWD 6.2f 21%Mud 257MudSts 0.96spi
Dam'sSire:AWD 5.8f 15%Mud 254MudSts 0.42spi

★ Hot Jockey in last 7 days (20 7-4-1) ★ Hot Trn/Jky combo in last 14 days (10 3-2-0)
★ Switches to a high% Jockey ★ Switches to a high% Trainer
★ Early Speed running style helps chances
● Poor Speed Figures ● Poor 'Up one class' trainer record: 11%wins 19sts

DATE TRK	DIST		RR RACETYPE	CR	E1	E2/	LP	1c	2c	SPD	PP	ST	1C	2C	Str	FIN	JOCKEY	ODDS	Top Finishers	Comment
Previously trained by BAKER, JR. LARRY W.																				
17Apr07RD3	6f ft	:224 :461 :58 1:131 3↑	106 Clm4000n29m	104	87	83/	56	-1	-1	52	4	1	2hd	21	69½	611	Zuniga E120	Lb 49.50	Series1¾LokAtThisCat2½RaidThePride1¼	Faltered; faded 7
07Apr07RD9	6f ft	:23 :462 :58 1:131 3↑	104 Clm5000n3L	103	88	84/	61	-3	-2	58	5	2	2½	33	37	413½	SchaeferGA120	Lb 62.50	RysRuls4¾Kndsky8½LedrOfThPck¾	Prompted; faltered 9
10Mar07TP4	(A) 5½ ft	:224 :464 :582 1:054 3↑	104 Clm5000n3L	101	81	63/	58	-3	-7	50	3	2	52½	87½	89½	813	Butler DP120	Lb 12.00	Bulzar1¾Kandinsky2¾Brookladdie5½	Through early 8
18Feb07TP6	(A) 5½ ft	:23 :464 :583 1:044 3↑	106 Clm5000n3L	102	82	69/	62	-4	-6	56	2	3	32½	36	38½	311½	Butler DP120	Lb 5.20	Preston T1¾InnocentDeception10Pair Of Queens3¾	Tired 4
14Jan07TP3	(A) 6f ft	:222 :453 :58 1:102 4↑	105 Clm5000n3L	103	80	76/	72	-8	-9	60	11	4	31	42½	108½	108½	CcmqueMA120	Lb 79.00	HidenGlter1¾WeselTim½FbulousTrino	3 wide; gave way 12
04Jan07TP9	(A) 1 1/16 ft	:232 :47 1:12 1:444 4↑	105 Clm5000n3L	103	82	74/	44	+5	+6	55	11	21½	31½	63¾	912	1017½	CcmqueMA120	Lb 98.40	Mr. Shu6¾RoyalPybck1TruthInLnding2¼	Faded final 1/4 11
19Nov06Tdn8	6f sy	:224 :47 1:001 1:14 3↑	104 Clm3500n3L	100	81	66/	61	-1	+1	43	4	7	73¾	910	1113	1216½	Meyers T117	Lb 15.80	AmIThereYet1JohnTheBnker½BigBabaLoop4	Outrun 12
04Nov06Tdn12	6f ft	:221 :464 :584 1:123 3↑	104 Clm3500n3L	102	78	69/	64	0	+3	48	4	5	45½	69	69	917½	Meyers T117	Lb 3.40	FreshWaterBy2¾Kabone3¾DCDonin¾	Failed to respond 11
26Oct06Tdn1	170 ft	:224 :472 1:147 1:464 3↑	106 Clm7500n3L	101	83	60/	33	+6	+7	39	4	2hd	2½	56½	513	526¾	Meyers T117	Lb 3.40	SickStep2¾MajorMrk2½SekingAwrds5	Dueled; gave way 5
01Oct06Mnr7	1 1/16 gd	:232 :471 1:124 1:453 3↑	106 Clm6000n3L	105	82	74/	44	+1	-4	55	6	2hd	1hd	1hd	58½	518¾	Meyers T117	Lb 4.40	GoClbG8¾WcoRu4¾RelyClosShv3¾	No breathers; folded 7

28Dec'06 Hpt 4f ft :501 B 1/3 ●17Jly'06 Tdn 3f ft :354 Bg 1/29 02Jly'06 Tdn 4f ft :512 B 7/8 26Jun'06 Tdn 3f ft :391 B 17/18 09Jan'06 Mid 5f ft 1:03 B 1/1 12Dec'05 CT 3f ft :384 B 2/5
31Oct'05 Fai 3f ft :392 Bg 1/2 24Oct'05 Fai 4f ft :52 Bg3/4 22Aug'05 CT 5f ft 1:042 B 8/2 02Aug'05 CT 4f ft :492 Bg2/4 30Jly'05 Tlc 2f ft :251 B 1/1 27Jly'05 CT 4f ft :502 B 10/13

5 Cardashi (P 2)

5/1 — Own: Yellow Bird Stable — Black; gold parrot
BARRERA FRANCISCO (35 7-4-4 20%)

$6,250 B. g. 8 — Sire: Kirdashi (Bold Ruckus) — Dam: Honor Card (Honor Grades) — Brdr: Audre Cappuccitti (ONT-C) — Trnr: Shuman Joseph P. (15 2-4-3 13%)

Power Rating: 96.6 (5th) L 113⁵

Life:	16 2-3-1	$19,746	74	Fst	13 2-1-0	$15,226	72
2006	7 0-3-1	$6,492	74	Off	3 0-2-1	$4,520	74
2005	9 2-0-0	$13,254	65	Dis	9 1-3-1	$10,591	74
Tdn	9 1-3-1	$10,493	74	Trf	0 0-0-0	$0	
				AW	0 0-0-0	$0	

+2007	35	20%	43%	-0.21	2007	18	11%	56%	-0.58
JKYw/ P types	6	17%	50%	-0.33	90+ days away	88	7%	40%	-0.65
+JKYw/ Trn L60	4	50%	75%	+4.40	1st strt wtrn	24	12%	33%	-0.58
+JKYw/ Sprints	25	24%	44%	+0.36	No class chg	311	14%	44%	-0.05

Sire Stats: AWD 6.6f 10%Mud 213MudSts 1.34spi
Dam'sSire:AWD 7.2f 14%Mud 766MudSts 1.58spi

★ Hot Jockey in last 7 days (11 4-0-2) ★ Switches to a high% Jockey
● Poor Speed Figures in each recent start ● Has not raced for more than 5 months
● Poor '90+ days away' trainer record: 7%wins 88sts

DATE TRK	DIST		RR RACETYPE	CR	E1	E2/	LP	1c	2c	SPD	PP	ST	1C	2C	Str	FIN	JOCKEY	ODDS	Top Finishers	Comment
Previously trained by BALLARD THOMAS																				
26Nov06Tdn2	6f ft	:224 :471 1:001 1:13 3↑	106 Clm7500n3L	106	82	77/	73	-4	-8	61	2	4	51½	1hd	2hd	64	GonzalezLA117	Lb *2.00	MorinsTClmbnoTTsCl¾MyRcktr1¼	Rallied; flattened out 8
03Nov06Tdn13	6f ft	:223 :462 :591 1:124 3↑	107 Alw11000n1x	105	81	77/	69	-2	0	58	9	5	63¼	65½	88¾	710	SkerrettJ117	Lb 7.50	WstrnDckt¾CptolPnc2¾NLmlins¾	Wide early; no threat 9
12Oct06Tdn4	6f gd	:23 :472 1:001 1:13 3↑	107 Alw11000n1x	109	75	75/	75	-5	-8	61	3	4	75¼	42¾	34½	38½	Spieth S117	Lb 7.80	Wildly Charismatic4¾Virgil O3¾Cardashi2½	Best of rest 7
23Sep06Tdn4	6f ft	:223 :463 :593 1:124 3↑	107 Alw11300n1x	106	83	79/	79	-2	3	69	3	6	67¾	63½	73¾	54¾	Pilares CP116	Lb 29.60	All For Love1¾Frolic Over1Ancient Ruler1½	Even effort 10
26May06Tdn10	6f sy	:224 :463 :592 1:122 3↑	105 Clm10000n3L	108	86	81/	85	-4	-6	74	1	1	3½	32	21	22½	Spieth S118	Lb 2.70	All For Love2¼Cardashi1¾Da Fonzhd	Second best 6
11May06Tdn5	6f sy	:221 :46 :59 1:123 3↑	103 Clm7500n3L	106	86	86/	79	+2	+3	73	7	2	54	35	23½	24½	GonzalezLA116	Lb 3.20	Magoo's Magic4¾Cardashi4¾Halo's Flyerhd	Second best 7
01May06Tdn3	6f ft	:222 :46 :584 1:121 3↑	104 Clm7500n3L	106	85	86/	78	-1	-1	72	7	2	32	21½	21½	21¼	GonzalezLA116	Lb 8.70	Too Too Crafty1¼Cardashi3¾Derby Time½	Second best 7
19Dec05Tdn8	6f ft	:231 :48 1:013 1:154 3↑	104 Clm5000n2L	107	84	90/	74	+2	0	65	1	7	42½	31½	21	1hd	GonzalezLA116	Lb 11.50	CrdshhdTnWthWls1¾BluBlodWrior1¾	Up in final strides 11
05Dec05Tdn7	1m ft	:242 :483 1:142 1:414 3↑	106 Clm10000n2L	103	71	69/	55	-3	0	55	4	42½	32	41½	63½	517½	Felix JE116	Lb 22.00	AmricnChdd3nkLcky¾ElGrndHk3¼	Speed 3/4; flattened 6
Previously trained by CAPPUCCITTI AUDRE																				
19Nov05WO4	6½ ft	:223 :45 1:103 1:172	106 Clm10000	104	89	96/	43	4	+1	55	1	10	1hd	2½	1110	1118	RamirezMR117	Lb 78.55	AKAOsmod¾ImAKipr3RndmChork	Speed to turn;tired 11

28Apr Tdn 5f ft 1:041 B 5/6 21Apr Tdn 5f ft 1:041 B 6/8 ●14Apr Tdn 4f ft :474 B 1/17 02Apr Tdn 3f ft :372 B 6/9 26Mar Tdn 3f ft :421 B 13/13 04Oct'06 Tdn 5f ft 1:021 B 1/3
16Sep'06 Tdn 5f ft 1:042 B 6/8 07Sep'06 Tdn 5f ft 1:034 B 3/6 30Aug'06 Tdn 4f ft :503 B 4/5 ●18Aug'06 Tdn 3f ft :36 B 1/10 09Jun'06 Tdn 3f ft :37 B 4/6 25Apr'06 Tdn 5f gd 1:034 B 2/7

tsnhorse.com

Ultimate PP's w/ Quick Play Comments — **River Downs** Clm 6250NW3L 6 Furlongs 3up Friday, May 11, 2007 — **Race 5 (TDN - #5)** — E1 91, E2/LATE 90/ 78, SPD 76

6 Lootshoot Attitude (E/P 3) — $6,250

8/1
Own: Katie O'Leary
Red and black horizontal halves
PILARES CHRISTIAN P. (58 5-12-6 9%)

B. g. 6 OBSJUN 2003 $7k — Power Rating: 82.5 (8th)
Sire: Demaloot Demashoot (Bold Ruckus)
Dam: Dancer's Attitude (Gate Dancer)
Brdr: Adena Springs (ONT-C)
Trnr: O'Leary Aaron A. (7 0-1-2 0%)
L 118

Life: 33 2- 6- 6	$42,856	84	Fst	25 1- 5- 5	$36,677	84
2007 8 1- 3- 2	$6,273	71	Off	8 1- 1- 1	$6,179	71
2006 11 0- 1- 1	$4,284	70	Dis	13 1- 2- 3	$23,482	84
Tdn 2 0- 0- 1	$785	55	Trf	0 0- 0- 0	$0	
			AW	0 0- 0- 0	$0	

2007	80	10%	41%	-1.02	2007	26	4%	35%	-1.82
JKYw/EP types	151	9%	44%	-1.00	+Up one class	2	50%	50%	+0.40
JKYw/ Sprints	62	10%	42%	-1.18	Sprnt-Rte-Sprnt	2	0%	50%	-2.00
					Rte to Sprnt	2	0%	50%	-2.00

Sire Stats: AWD 6.2f 16%Mud 557MudSts 0.77spi
Dam'sSire: AWD 7.3f 15%Mud 1220MudSts 1.22spi

★ Highest Speed Figure at Today's Distance ★ Best Dirt Speed is fastest among today's starters
★ May improve while returning to a sprint
● Always far back vs weaker in last race ● Poor Speed Figures in each recent start ● Poor Trainer win%
● Only 2 wins in 33 career starts

DATE TRK	DIST		RR	RACETYPE	CR	E1	E2/	LP	1c	2c	SPD	PP	ST	1C	2C	Str	FIN	JOCKEY	ODDS	Top Finishers	Comment	
28Apr07Tdn14	1m gd	:24 :49 1:153 1:43 4↑	104	Clm4000n3L	102	65	52/	68	-1	-5	53	9	87½	84½	95¼	98½	912	Skerrett J118	L 3.90	Wsucrd3½BrndsScrt½SpdyPow½	Wide early; no factor	9
14Apr07Tdn14	6f ft	1:134 4↑	102	Clm4000n3L	104	83	78/	64	+1	+8	55	5	5	42½	45½	32	35	SkerrettJ118	L 3.00	HiHoArch1½Wholeiotspirit3½LotshotAttitude1	Evenly late	9
27Mar07Beu6	5f ft	:23 :471 :591 3↑	102	Clm3500n3L	103		81/	68			58	2	5	21½	32½	32	22¾	Paucar E124	L *0.70	SrchFrASta2½LotshAttd½QckHbr3½	Gamely held place	6
10Mar07Beu6	5½ gd	:23 :46 :59 1:053 3↑	101	Clm5000n2L	106	87	95/	68	-2	+8	71	1	2	12½	12	12	13¼	Paucar E120	L *1.40	LotshtAttd3½SlsCl3½SlPrdGy1½	Unchallenged; driving	8
26Feb07Beu3	6f sy	:224 :472 1:001 1:133 3↑	101	Clm4000n2L	104	91	86/	65	+4	+5	63	1	6	1½	1½	13½	2no	CcmqueMA120	L *1.70	TryNbrnoLtshtAttd2½OdYSlAk1½	Rushed up; caught wire	8
12Feb07Beu8	6f ft	:22 :453 1:094 3↑	102	Clm5000n2L	102	78	80/	73	0	0	64	10	7	66¼	65½	45½	38¼	CcmqueMA120	L *3.00	HHArch3½WhOlAc3LotshotAttd1	Stumbled start; 3 wide	10
31Jan07Beu4	5½ ft	:223 :462 :582 1:044 3↑	100	Clm5000n2L	102	81	71/	76	-3	8	60	3	4	31½	42	42	2½	CcmqueMA120	L 9.30	QtANght½LotshotAttud1½Dvlish12	3 wide; finished well	7
20Jan07Beu4	5½ ft	:223 :47 :592 1:061 3↑	100	Clm5000n2L	100	79	67/	55	+1	+1	49	10	5	45	56½	58	610	CcmqueMA120	L 22.50	Lttlbtohly1PrncOfLov5½QtANght1¾	Within range; no bid	12
Previously trained by GORDON DORNA M.																						
21Oct06FE8	6½ my	:222 :46 1:12 1:184 3↑	104	Clm4000n2L	103	77	74/	69	+6	+3	59	9	5	89½	89½	811	610½	Dionne M119	L 50.30	Glendawe6½Go Blue2Judiths Trail½	No threat wide str	10
25Sep06FE1	6f ft	:231 :47 :594 1:132 3↑	105	Clm4000n2y+	104	72	61/	80	-6	-2	53	2	7	74½	77½	65	43	Dionne M118	L 1.45e	LuckyRmucknoRegalMister1½La FastCat1½	Belated run	7

16Dec'06 Beu 4f ft :53 B 8/8 05Aug'06 FE 4f ft :481 H 4/16 17Jly'06 FE 3f ft :372 H 10/18 03May'06 FE 3f ft :384 H 13/13 27Apr'06 FE 3f ft :394 H 20/20 07Jun'05 FE 4f ft :481 H 2/25
19May'05 FE 3f ft :36 H 3/11 ●03May'05 FE 3f ft :36 H 1/25 ●28Apr'05 FE 5f ft 1:022 H 1/6 22Apr'05 FE 4f ft :484 H 8/50 16Apr'05 FE 3f ft :38 B 22/50 29Oct'04 WO 4f ft :49 H 10/42

7 Madly Paddlin Home (E 6) — $6,250

9/2
Own: Bridget Sipp
Red & white quartered; red & white sleeves
SANGUINETTI ANNE (72 10-9-8 14%)

B. g. 3 BESNOV 2004 $2k — Power Rating: 108.5 (1st)
Sire: Robannier (Batonnier)
Dam: Oomiak (Petesid)
Brdr: Robert H Walter Family Trust (CA)
Trnr: Sipp Burton K. (56 10-6-6 18%)
118

Life: 5 2- 0- 0	$15,320	75	Fst	5 2- 0- 0	$15,320	75
2007 5 2- 0- 0	$15,320	75	Off	0 0- 0- 0	$0	
2006 0 0- 0- 0	$0		Dis	0 0- 0- 0	$0	
Tdn 1 1- 0- 0	$4,380	75	Trf	0 0- 0- 0	$0	
			AW	0 0- 0- 0	$0	

2007	156	12%	37%	-1.10	2007	137	13%	41%	-1.18
JKYw/ E types	228	14%	37%	-1.04	Wnr last race	209	18%	40%	-0.41
JKYw/ Trn L60	71	17%	39%	-0.97	No class chg	827	13%	38%	-0.75
JKYw/ Sprints	121	12%	40%	-1.09	Claiming	1278	13%	37%	-0.76

Sire Stats: AWD 7.5f 16%Mud 55MudSts 1.58spi
Dam'sSire: AWD 7.4f 9%Mud 489MudSts 1.17spi

★ Highest Last Race Speed Rating ★ Best Dirt Speed is close to the Avg Winning Speed
★ Early Speed running style helps chances
★ Won last race (TDN 04/20 5.5f Dirt fast Clm 6250NW2L)
● Moves up in class from last start

DATE TRK	DIST		RR	RACETYPE	CR	E1	E2/	LP	1c	2c	SPD	PP	ST	1C	2C	Str	FIN	JOCKEY	ODDS	Top Finishers	Comment	
20Apr07Tdn12	5½ ft	:222 :461 :59 1:053 3↑	104	Clm6250n2L	107	89	89/	79	0	0	75	4	2	2½	1½	12	12¼	SanguinettiA118	*0.80	MdlyPdlnH2½SprPtr4DncThMb½	Dueled; drew clear	7
30Mar07DeD10	7f ft	:224 :472 1:143 1:274	108	Clm10000n2L	109	82	89/	61	-1	-2	67	1	3	34	3hd	23	48	SanguinettiA122	7.00	MistrMlu5½RportrsDrmnkAlrtToG?	Contention; bid; hung	9
09Mar07DeD7	7f ft	:233 :49 1:14 1:28	109	Clm20000n2L	109	82	75/	74	-8	-17	66	9	3	11	1½	33	78¾	SanguinettiA122	19.40	Don't Jinx 82½PalomoMister Milu1½	Speed; clear; faded	10
22Feb07DeD5	5f ft	:23 :471 1:001	104	MC20000	108		85/	79			72	7	1	11	1½	12	14¼	SanguinettiA122	*2.80	MdlyPdlnHm4½FlxBlst1MrSxyChnk	Clear; finished well	7
10Feb07DeD5	5f ft	:222 :462 1:00	108	Mdn 23k	105		81/	71			62	5	7	63½	46	57	66¼	SanguinettiA122	25.30	Cigar SamnoHarbor Bill½Tyrish3½	In middle; no bid	9

31Jan DeD 5f wf 1:05 Bg 6/72 ●23Jan DeD 4f ft :484 Bg 1/10 16Jan DeD 4f wf :51 B 4/7 10Jan DeD 3f ft :37 B 3/23 03Jan DeD 3f ft :384 B 12/21 28Dec'06 DeD 3f ft :414 B 13/15
23Dec'06 DeD 3f ft :383 B 12/47 08Sep'06 BM 5f ft 1:012 H 5/17 01Sep'06 BM 5f ft 1:023 H 7/14 25Aug'06 BM 5f ft 1:011 Hg 6/15 18Aug'06 BM 4f ft :491 H 5/10 11Aug'06 BM 4f ft :493 H 16/22

8 Seeking Awards (S 2) — $6,250

6/1
Own: Skipper And Debbie Hamilton
White, red 'sad', red lightning bolts
GONZALEZ LUIS ANTONIO (9 0-0-0 0%)

Ch. g. 4 — Power Rating: 98.3 (4th)
Sire: Seeking A Home (Seeking The Gold)
Dam: Grand Award (Bunny's Halo)
Brdr: Rolling Oaks Farm (TX)
Trnr: Faulkner Rodney C. (56 5-8-2 10%)
L 118

Life: 17 2- 4- 2	$23,673	75	Fst	9 1- 2- 2	$14,341	71
2007 2 0- 1- 0	$2,231	71	Off	7 1- 2- 0	$9,332	75
2006 15 2- 3- 2	$21,442	75	Dis	6 2- 2- 0	$16,258	75
Tdn 9 2- 2- 1	$16,501	75	Trf	1 0- 0- 0	$0	59
			AW	0 0- 0- 0	$0	

2007	526	15%	43%	0.40	2007	251	16%	37%	+0.27
JKYw/ S types	248	18%	41%	-0.36	Up one class	265	9%	34%	-0.66
JKYw/ Sprints	282	16%	45%	-0.30	+Btn favorite	249	22%	52%	-0.61
					Claiming	2189	15%	43%	-0.29

Sire Stats: AWD 6.0f 7%Mud 14MudSts 1.37spi
Dam'sSire: AWD 7.3f 12%Mud 1715MudSts 1.18spi

★ Eligible to improve in 3rd start since layoff
● Beaten by weaker in last start ● Outside posts have poor win%

DATE TRK	DIST		RR	RACETYPE	CR	E1	E2/	LP	1c	2c	SPD	PP	ST	1C	2C	Str	FIN	JOCKEY	ODDS	Top Finishers	Comment	
14Apr07Tdn14	6f ft	1:134 4↑	102	Clm4000n3L	103	80	74/	63	+1	+6	51	3	6	64	67	57½	57¼	Spieth S118	Lb *1.60	Hi Ho Arch1½Wholeiotspirit3½LootshotAttitude1	No threat	9
30Mar07Mnr10	6f ft	:23 :473 1:011 1:143 3↑	104	Clm6000n3L	107	87	82/	79	-1	-2	71	4	4	41	31	2hd	2¾	Spieth S115	Lb 6.50	Sqnkm¾SkngAwrds1½FungShr2	Dueled mid lic; outbid	10
25Nov06Tdn8	6f ft	:221 :454 :584 1:121 3↑	109	Clm3500n3L	107	76	76/	83	+1	+2	68	3	10	107¾	67	53½	43¾	Spieth S116	Lb 3.00	PlumTre3½SwelbabonkMjesticPionernk	Steady advance	10
12Nov06Tdn3	6f gd	:224 :463 :593 1:131 3↑	107	Clm10000n3L	106	82	79/	71	-3	-1	62	6	2	62¾	43½	44	58¼	Spieth S116	Lb 5.10	RtlsnkPont3ErWins½BySlrtBb1½	Wide early; no threat	6
26Oct06Tdn1	170 ft	:224 :472 1:142 1:464 3↑	106	Clm7500n3L	107	75	72/	65	+8	+2	65	5	44½	44½	2½	22	34¾	Spieth S116	Lb *1.60	SlckStep2½MajorMrk2½SeikingAwrds5½	Rallied; bid; hung	5
12Oct06Tdn1	1m gd	:231 :483 1:151 1:43 3↑	105	Clm10000n3L	107	76	67/	80	+2	0	70	1	31½	41½	42	32	21¼	Spieth S114	Lb 3.60	GldMdWr1½SkgAwrdnkTrPltnm2½	Rallied; up for second	7
30Sep06Tdn1	170 gd	:234 :491 1:154 1:473 3↑	105	Clm7500n3L	107	63	59/	74	-10	-7	63	6	21	21½	21	22	34	Spieth S116	Lb 2.10	NorthrnScph2½TruPltnum1½SkngAwrds4	Bore in start	7
(Placed 5th through disqualification)																						
03Sep06Mnr9	6f gd	:221 :452 :58 1:114 3↑	107	Clm15000n3L	104	73		51	-2	+1	59	4		89½		819	814¾	Skerrett J117	Lb 14.30	Darma½SystemsStev½Jaredslemper2½	Fog;offered little	9
19Aug06Tdn12	6f sy	:231 :471 1:002 1:14 3↑	105	Clm10000n2L	106	81	85/	81	-3	-1	75	2	4	53½	31½	1hd	11½	Spieth S114	Lb *1.60	SekingAwards1½PairOfQuens½Cabrer½	3 wide; driving	8
31Jly06Tdn8	6f ft	:222 :464 1:00 1:133 3↑	106	Clm15000n2L	107	83	77/	78	+3	-2	66	2	6	64½	43	31½	21½	Spieth S114	Lb *1.90	Madame Lil1½SeekingAwards1½Caprock4½	Second best	8

04May Mnr 4f ft :494 B 2/7 21Mar Beu (d) 5f my 1:034 B 3/4 12Mar Beu 4f ft :521 B 8/8 28Feb Beu 4f ft :484 B 3/20 30Jun'06 Tdn 4f ft :493 B 2/6 20May'06 LS 5f ft 1:022 B 8/28
14Apr'06 LS 3f ft :381 B 12/15 02Apr'06 Hou 3f ft :371 Hg 9/26 30Mar'06 Hou 5f ft 1:034 H 4/5 ●23Mar'06 Hou 4f ft :50 Hg 1/4 21Mar'06 Hou 3f ft :374 H 3/7 05Mar'06 Hou 3f ft :391 B 54/66

tsnhorse.com

Ultimate PP's w/ Quick Play Comments **River Downs** Clm 6250NW3L 6 Furlongs. 3up Friday, May 11, 2007 **Race 5 (TDN - #5)**

E1	E2/LATE	SPD
91	90/ 78	76

9 **Three Mile Harbor (E/P 4)**
Own: Kenneth A. Morgan
6/1 White: lavender diamonds
URIETA-MORAN VICTOR (93 8-9-6 13%)

$6,250 Dkbbr. h. 5 FTMSEP 2002 $18k
Sire: Mazel Trick (Phone Trick)
Dam: Shuga Cane (Belek)
Brdr: McKathan Farms (FL)
Trnr: Morgan Kenneth A. (2 0-1-0 0%)

Power Rating: 96.3 (8th)

L 118

	Starts	W	P	S	Earnings	SPD		Starts	W	P	S	Earnings	SPD
Life:	29	2	4	4	$28,679	74	Fst	23	2	3	3	$23,297	74
2007	5	0	1	2	$2,352	63	Off	4	0	1	1	$4,632	70
2006	15	1	1	2	$12,517	70	Dis	10	0	2	1	$9,029	70
Tdn	0	0	0	0	$0		Trf	2	0	0	0	$750	63
							AW	0	0	0	0	$0	

2007	72	14%	44%	-1.23
JKYw/EP types	112	15%	42%	-0.26
JKYw/ Sprints	60	13%	43%	-1.36

+2007	42	24%	64%	-0.45
Up one class	99	10%	35%	-0.32
Claiming	541	12%	36%	-0.54

Sire Stats: AWD 6.3f 20%Mud 258MudSts 1.29spi
Dam'sSire:AWD 6.5f 14%Mud 449MudSts 0.87spi

★ Best Dirt Speed is close to the Avg Winning Speed

- ● Beaten by weaker in last start ● Poor Speed Figures in each recent start ● Poor record at this distance
- ● Only 2 wins in 29 career starts ● Outside posts have poor win%
- ● Poor 'Up one class' trainer record: 10%wins 99sts

DATE TRK	DIST							RR	RACETYPE	CR	E1	E2/	LP	1c	2c	SPD	PP	ST	1C	2C	Str	FIN	JOCKEY		ODDS	Top Finishers	Comment	
02May07Beu^6	6f ft	:23	:46^4	1:06	1:13^2	3↑	100	Clm4000n3L	104	86	87/	64	+1	+9	**62**	1	5	3^1	2^1½	2½	2^hd	Magera C^120	Lbf	3.50	ClsrThPtrhdTrMlHrbr^1¼FvlxChrty^5	Hsl rally;just missed	8
23Apr07Beu^3	1^70 ft	:24^3	:49	1:15^4	1:47^4	3↑	102	Clm7500.6.5n3L	103	68	63/	69	-5	0	**63**	2	4^2½	4¾	4^1½	2^2	3^2½	Paucar E^117	Lbf	*1.90	FnPrc¾MntCorny^1¾ThrMlHrbrno	Bid;chased,outfinished	6
11Apr07Beu^8	5f sy^5	:22^1	:46^2		:59	3↑	101	Clm3500n3L	102		86/	67			**61**	7	8	6^2	5^3½	3^4½	3^5	Stokes LA^122	Lbf	6.50	NpolnJ^1¼GrntMuk^2¾ThrMlHrbor^2¾	Saved ground to lane	8
Previously trained by ALLEN, A. FERRIS III																												
23Mar07CT^2	7f sy^4	:24^1	:48^4	1:15^1	1:28^3	4↑	104	Clm4000n3L	102	68	60/	63	-11	-13	**48**	3	10	10^4¼	8^8	6^9½	6^18½	Acosta JD^121	Lbf	10.30	MstrsPc^4¾ClrThBss^7NbrdDys^4	Failed menace, inside	10
27Jan07CT^10	7f ft	:24	:48^4	1:15^3	1:30^1	4↑	103	Clm4000n3L	103	67	68/	73	-4	-2	**61**	4	9	10^9¼	9^7¾	5^4½	4^9	Acosta JD^121	Lbf	21.00	ShrWsdm^1ClsrTheBses^6¾Muntgmhd	Heels clipped 1/8	10
28Dec06CT^10	7f ft	:23^3	:48^2	1:14^4	1:28^4	3↑	103	Clm4000n3L	103	84	79/	53	-4	-5	**54**	2	3	3^1	3^1½	3^8	3^12¾	Stortz M^116	Lbf	15.40	ShrWsdm^10¾BluCn^7¼ThrMlHrbrhd	Lacked late response	8
07Dec06CT^2	6½ ft	:24	:47^3	1:15^3	1:23^1	3↑	105	Clm6000/5.5n3L	102	84	70/	45	-2	+6	**37**	4	4	6^2¼	9^11	10^19	9^22	Acosta JD^117	Lbf	14.40	ScndCng^1¼ShldBFn^1¼SlvtngThM^2¼	Little impact inside	10
26Aug06Tim^2	*6½ ft	:23^4	:48^3	1:15^2	1:20^4	3↑	103	Clm5000n2L	106	83	79/	66	-4	-1	**61**	1	1	1^3	1^3	1^2	1^1	Crews K^142	Lbf	7.70	ThrMlHrbr^1PinlGls^1¼CostlQulty^12	Flat;steady hand ride	8
11Aug06Cnl^9	6f ft	:22^3	:46^1	:58^3	1:11^4	3↑	104	Clm7500n2L	106	70	67/	84	-1	-4	**63**	7	6	5^8	4^8	4^7½	4^5	Fewster E^111	Lbf	13.30	SprngChck^1¾TbyThTgr¾CrolnsPrncs^2¾	Chased; empty	7
31Jly06Cnl^6	5½ ft	:23	:46^2	:58^4	1:05^1	3↑	105	Clm7500/6.5n2L	104	67	65/	65	-8	-8	**58**	1	5	6^8½	6^8¼	6^8	4^9	Fewster E^111	Lbf	12.50	MstrHbls^5¼ThAdvntg^1¾ThtBuCnRn^1¾	Inside; by faders	7

30Nov'06 Lrl 3f ft :38^1 B *3/3* 14Nov'06 Lrl 4f ft :52^1 B *2/2* ●06Nov'06 Lrl 4f ft :49 B *1/5* 31Oct'06 Lrl 4f ft :52 B *24/24* 22Jly'06 Cnl 4f ft :51^3 B *22/22* 22Jun'06 Cnl 3f ft :39 B *6/7*
16Feb'06 Lrl 4f ft :51 B *18/21* 30Oct'05 Del 4f ft :51^2 B *8/13* 29Sep'05 Lrl 4f ft :50 B *11/20* 22Sep'05 Lrl 4f ft :52 B *19/22* 05Jly'05 Del 3f ft :35^4 Bg *3/6* 29Jun'05 Del 4f ft :51^2 Bg *28/47*

tsnhorse.com

Ultimate PP's w/ Quick Play Comments **River Downs** Clm 6250NW3L 6 Furlongs. 3up Friday, May 11, 2007 **Race 5 (TDN - #5)**

E1	E2/LATE	SPD
91	90/ 78	76

Last 3 Years RACETYPE STATS:	# Races	FAVORITES Win%	Itm%	$2ROI	Average Field Size	Median $2 Win Payoff	% Winners < 5/1	% Winners >= 5/1 < 10/1	% Winners >= 10/1
TDN 3up CLM 4000 - 7500 N3L Dirt 5.5f - 6f	26	50%	85%	+0.29	7.6	$6.20	77%	15%	8%

Track Bias Stats

	* MEET Totals *					* WEEK Totals *		
DIRT 6.0f	Speed Bias: 82%		WnrAvgBL		DIRT 6.0f	Speed Bias: 67%		WnrAvgBL
# Races: 22	04/12 - 05/06		1stCall: 1.3		# Races: 6	05/03 - 05/06		1stCall: 1.6
%Wire: 36%			2ndCall: 1.1		%Wire: 50%			2ndCall: 1.7

	Early	Speed	Late	Speed		Early	Speed	Late	Speed
Runstyle:	E	E/P	P	S	Runstyle:	E	E/P	P	S
	++	+				++		+	
Impact Values	1.77	1.41	0.70	0.13	Impact Values	1.71	0.97	1.32	0.00
%Races Won	45%	36%	14%	5%	%Races Won	50%	17%	33%	0%
Post Bias:	RAIL	1-3	4-7	8+	Post Bias	RAIL	1-3	4-7	8+
		+	+			+		+	
Impact Values	0.75	1.13	1.09	0.51	Impact Values	1.43	0.48	1.79	0.00
Avg Win %	9%	14%	17%	3%	Avg Win %	17%	6%	28%	0%

Race Summary

#	HorseName	ML Odds	Med Eqp	Days Since L/R	Run Style	P T S	Avg Dist/Surf PACE-SPEED E1	E2/Late	Spd	Avg Race Rtng	Best Pace E1	E2/Late	Final Speed Sp1	Sp2	Sp3	Sp4	ACL	Rcg Spd Avg	R1	R2	R3	Mud Spd	Pedigree Stats Mud Sts	Mud %	Sire AWD	Dam Sire's AWD
3	Air Borne Etbauer	4/1	L	28	+E/P	3	87	83/ 84	* 77*	102	93	94/ 86	74.	60	48	55.	102.6	61	102	102	106	60	41	15	6.5	7.0
7	Madly Paddin Home	9/2		21	++E	6	86	88/ 73	* 71*	106	89	89/ 79	75.	67.	66.	72.	105.2	69	104	108	109		55	16	7.5	7.4
1	Sweetbaboo	6/1	L	20.	++E	5	84	77/ 79	65	104	85	86/ 79	65.	70.	68.	70.	104.2	68	104	105	103	60	130	18	7.3	7.6
5	Cardashi	5/1	L	166	P	2	80	77/ 76	(64)	107	83	79/ 79	61.	58.	61.	69.	105.7	60	105	107	107	74	213	10	6.6	7.2
6	Lootshoot Attitude	8/1	L	13	+E/P	3	83	85/ 70	* 64*	102	88	95/ 80	53	55.	58.	71.	102.0	55	104	102	102	63	557	16	6.2	7.3
2	Synhawk	12/1	L	27	++E		83	81/ 70	* 62*	103	90	88/ 76	61.	63.	48	52	104.1	57	102	103	103	58	54	9	6.9	7.1
9	Three Mile Harbor	6/1	L	9	+E/P	4	77	78/ 69	* 62*	102	86	87/ 84	62.	63	61	48	101.9	62	100	102	101	61	258	20	6.3	6.5
8	Seeking Awards	6/1	L	27..	S	2	84	78/ 71	* 61*	104	87	82/ 85	51.	71.	69.	62.	104.5	64	102	104	105	75	14	7	6.0	7.3
4	Pair Of Queens	10/1	L	24	++E	5	86	79/ 60	* 55*	105	88	84/ 72	52.	58.	50.	56.	104.0	53	106	104	104	72	257	21	6.2	5.8

Speed Last Race	Back Speed	Current Class	Average Class Last 3	Power Rating	Early Pace Last Race	Late Pace Last Race
75 Madly Paddin Home	80 Air Borne Etbauer	108.1 Madly Paddin Home	107.9 Madly Paddin Home	109.5 Madly Paddin Home	89 Madly Paddin Home	86 Air Borne Etbauer
74 Air Borne Etbauer	75 Madly Paddin Home	107.2 Air Borne Etbauer	106.1 Sweetbaboo	104.0 Air Borne Etbauer	87 Three Mile Harbor	79 Madly Paddin Home
65 Sweetbaboo	71 Lootshoot Attitude	105.7 Sweetbaboo	105.8 Cardashi	103.5 Sweetbaboo	83 Pair Of Queens	79 Sweetbaboo
62 Three Mile Harbor	71 Seeking Awards	104.7 Seeking Awards	105.4 Seeking Awards	98.3 Seeking Awards	81 Synhawk	73 Cardashi
61 Cardashi	70 Sweetbaboo	104.0 Lootshoot Attitude	104.9 Air Borne Etbauer	96.6 Cardashi	79 Air Borne Etbauer	68 Synhawk
61 Synhawk	70 Synhawk	103.8 Three Mile Harbor	102.8 Lootshoot Attitude	96.3 Three Mile Harbor	77 Sweetbaboo	68 Lootshoot Attitude
53 Lootshoot Attitude	69 Cardashi	103.0 Pair Of Queens	102.8 Three Mile Harbor	94.3 Pair Of Queens	77 Cardashi	64 Three Mile Harbor
52 Pair Of Queens	63 Three Mile Harbor	102.2 Synhawk	102.7 Pair Of Queens	92.5 Lootshoot Attitude	74 Seeking Awards	63 Seeking Awards
51 Seeking Awards	60 Pair Of Queens	NA Cardashi	101.7 Synhawk	89.8 Synhawk	65 Lootshoot Attitude	56 Pair Of Queens

tsnhorse.com

Ultimate PP's w/ Quick Play Comments **River Downs** Clm 6250NW3L 6 Furlongs 3up Friday, May 11, 2007 **Race 5 (TDN - #5)**

E1	E2/LATE	SPD
91	90/ 78	76

Last 3 Years	RACETYPE STATS:	# Races	Win%	FAVORITES Itm%	$2ROI	Average Field Size	Median $2 Win Payoff	% Winners < 5/1	% Winners >= 5/1 < 10/1	% Winners >= 10/1
TDN 3up	CLM 4000 - 7500 N3L Dirt 5.5f - 6f	26	50%	85%	+0.29	7.6	$6.20	77%	15%	8%

Track Bias Stats

	* MEET Totals *				* WEEK Totals *		
DIRT 6.0f	Speed Bias: 82%	WnrAvgBL		DIRT 6.0f	Speed Bias: 67%	WnrAvgBL	
# Races: 22	04/12 - 05/06	1stCall: 1.3		# Races: 6	05/03 - 05/06	1stCall: 1.6	
%Wire: 36%		2ndCall: 1.1		%Wire: 50%		2ndCall: 1.7	

	Early	Speed	Late	Speed		Early	Speed	Late	Speed
Runstyle:	E	E/P	P	S	Runstyle:	E	E/P	P	S
	++	+				++		+	
Impact Values	1.77	1.41	0.70	0.13	Impact Values	1.71	0.97	1.32	0.00
%Races Won	45%	36%	14%	5%	%Races Won	50%	17%	33%	0%
Post Bias:	RAIL	1-3	4-7	8+	Post Bias	RAIL	1-3	4-7	8+
		+	+			+		+	
Impact Values	0.75	1.13	1.09	0.51	Impact Values	1.43	0.48	1.79	0.00
Avg Win %	9%	14%	17%	3%	Avg Win %	17%	6%	28%	0%

Race Summary

#	HorseName	ML Odds	Med Eqp	Days Since L/R	Run Style	PT S	Avg Dist/Surf PACE-SPEED E1	E2/Late	Spd	Avg Race Rtng	Best Pace E1	E2/Late	Final Speed Sp1	Sp2	Sp3	Sp4	ACL	Rcg Spd Avg	R1	R2	R3	Mud Spd	Pedigree Stats Mud Sts	% Mud	Sire AWD	Dam Sire's AWD
3	Air Borne Etbauer	4/1	L	28	+E/P	3	87	83/ 84	* 77*	102	93	94/ 86	74.	60	48	55.	102.6	61	102	102	106	60	41	15	6.5	7.0
7	Madly Paddlin Home	9/2		21	++E	6	86	88/ 73	* 71*	106	89	89/ 79	75.	67.	66.	72.	105.2	69	104	108	109		55	16	7.5	7.4
1	Sweetbaboo	6/1	L	20.	++E	5	84	77/ 79	65	104	85	86/ 79	65.	70.	68.	70.	104.2	68	104	105	103	60	130	18	7.3	7.6
5	Cardashi	5/1	L	166	P	2	80	77/ 76	(64)	107	83	79/ 79	61.	58.	61.	69.	105.7	60	105	107	107	74	213	10	6.6	7.2
6	Lootshoot Attitude	8/1	L	13	+E/P	3	83	85/ 70	* 64*	102	88	95/ 80	53	55.	58.	71.	102.0	55	104	102	102	63	557	16	6.2	7.3
2	Synhawk	12/1	L	27	++E		83	81/ 70	* 62*	103	90	88/ 76	61.	63.	48	52	104.1	57	102	103	103	58	54	9	6.9	7.1
9	Three Mile Harbor	6/1	L	9	+E/P	4	77	78/ 69	* 62*	102	86	87/ 84	62	63	61	48	101.9	62	100	102	101	61	258	20	6.3	6.5
8	Seeking Awards	6/1	L	27..	S	2	84	78/ 71	* 61*	104	87	82/ 85	51.	71.	69.	62.	104.5	64	102	104	105	75	14	7	6.0	7.3
4	Pair Of Queens	10/1	L	24	++E	5	86	79/ 60	* 55*	105	88	84/ 72	52.	58.	50.	56.	104.0	53	106	104	104	72	257	21	6.2	5.8

Speed Last Race	Back Speed	Current Class	Average Class Last 3	Power Rating	Early Pace Last Race	Late Pace Last Race
75 Madly Paddlin Home	80 Air Borne Etbauer	106.1 Madly Paddlin Home	107.9 Madly Paddlin Home	109.5 Madly Paddlin Home	89 Madly Paddlin Home	86 Air Borne Etbauer
74 Air Borne Etbauer	75 Madly Paddlin Home	107.2 Air Borne Etbauer	106.1 Sweetbaboo	104.0 Air Borne Etbauer	87 Three Mile Harbor	79 Madly Paddlin Home
65 Sweetbaboo	71 Lootshoot Attitude	105.7 Sweetbaboo	105.8 Cardashi	103.5 Sweetbaboo	83 Pair Of Queens	79 Sweetbaboo
62 Three Mile Harbor	71 Seeking Awards	104.7 Seeking Awards	105.4 Seeking Awards	98.3 Seeking Awards	81 Synhawk	73 Cardashi
61 Cardashi	70 Sweetbaboo	104.0 Lootshoot Attitude	104.9 Air Borne Etbauer	96.6 Cardashi	79 Air Borne Etbauer	68 Synhawk
61 Synhawk	70 Synhawk	103.8 Three Mile Harbor	102.8 Lootshoot Attitude	96.3 Three Mile Harbor	77 Sweetbaboo	68 Lootshoot Attitude
53 Lootshoot Attitude	69 Cardashi	103.0 Pair Of Queens	102.8 Three Mile Harbor	94.3 Pair Of Queens	77 Cardashi	64 Three Mile Harbor
52 Pair Of Queens	63 Three Mile Harbor	102.2 Synhawk	102.7 Pair Of Queens	92.5 Lootshoot Attitude	74 Seeking Awards	63 Seeking Awards
51 Seeking Awards	60 Pair Of Queens	NA Cardashi	101.7 Synhawk	89.8 Synhawk	65 Lootshoot Attitude	56 Pair Of Queens

Ultimate PP's w/ Quick Play Comments **River Downs** Clm 4000 1 Mile. 3up Friday, May 11, 2007 **Race 6**

E1	E2/LATE	SPD
76	69/ 72	69

3 Shoo Brush (S 2)

Own: C And C Racing Stable
5/2 Green green 'c&c' on yellow diamonds
BUSH VERNON (66 11-11-10 17%)

$4,000 B. g. 7
Sire: Broad Brush (Ack Ack)
Dam: Shoo City Shoo (Lyphard's Wish (Fr))
Brdr: Marylou Whitney Stables (KY)
Trnr: Crawford Bert (33 4-8-7 12%)

Power Rating: 93.3 (6th) L 124

Life:	50 3 19 4	$62,177	77	Fst	29 1-9-5	$44,428	77
2007	8 1-5-1	$9,152	73	Off	18 0-10-1	$16,903	75
2006	11 0-4-1	$5,890	66	Dis	18 1-6-4	$16,124	75
RD	8 2-3-2	$11,553	68	Trf	3 0-0-1	$845	69
				AW	4 0-0-0	$609	66

2007	347	10%	36%	-0.44	2007	219	11%	40%	-0.47
JKYw/ S types	240	8%	33%	0.80	Down one class	76	9%	34%	+0.12
JKYw/ Trn L60	5	20%	60%	-0.80	Win last race	64	17%	45%	-0.23
JKYw/ Routes	145	12%	34%	-0.37	Claiming	527	9%	36%	-0.86

Sire Stats: AWD 7.5f 18%Mud 1207MudSts 2.83spi
Dam'sSire: AWD 7.8f 10%Mud 1087MudSts 1.36spi

★ Highest Last Race Speed Rating ★ Won last race (RD 04/28 1m70y Dirt fast Clm 5000NW3L) ● Only 3 wins in 50 career starts

DATE TRK	DIST					RR RACETYPE	CR	E1	E2/	LP	1c	2c	SPD	PP	ST	1C	2C	Str	FIN	JOCKEY		ODDS	Top Finishers	Comment	
28Apr07RD1	170 ft	:25	:51	1:16	1:47 3↑	105 Clm5000n3L	106	47	47/	92	20	-7	66	4	55	53½	56	53	1½	Bush V120	Lbf	2.00	ShoBrush½PipaChente½Lobrk	Roused sharply in time	5
15Apr07RD10	1m my	:24	:50	1:15	1:42 3↑	104 Clm5000n3L	105	53	56/	87	-12	-6	67	3	69	57	55½	35½	34½	SolomonN120	Lbf	2.40	Truth In Lending½ Lob½Shoe Brush1¼	Evenly late	6
31Mar07Beu4	1m sy	:25	:49	1:14	1:40 3↑	102 Clm5000n3L	104	66	59/	81	-9	-5	65	3	69	51¼	33½	33	24¼	Stokes LA120	Lbf	1.20	SimonPete½ShoBrsh1FinePrinc¾	Shuffled back start	6
17Mar07Beu7	1m gd	:25	:50	1:16	1:42 3↑	102 Clm4000n3L	106	55	47/	91	-13	-11	65	7	67½	57¼	42½	21	2nk	Stokes LA120	Lbf	1.30e	FrutsopOfnkShoBrsh4MnieCounty1½	Rail rally; missed	7
03Mar07Beu5	170 gd	:23	:49	1:15	1:46 3↑	103 Clm5000n3L	105	60	63/	72	-3	3	64	3	68½	66	22	28	25	Stokes LA120	Lbf	0.90	Wint5ShoBrsh5FncyFshion1½	3 wide advance 2ndturn	8
21Feb07Beu2	170 gd	:24	:48	1:15	1:47 3↑	104 Clm4000n3L	108	52	52/	80	+3	+1	63	5	68½	612	66	34	2no	Stokes LA120	Lb	1.70	FexClbGrnoShoBrsh4HrbourTd1½	Saved ground to lane	7
15Jan07Beu7	1⅛ sy	:50	1:15	1:41	1:53 4↑	106 Clm13000/S	107	71	69/	74	-5	-4	73	1	32	32½	32½	32½	2¾	CompueMA116	Lb	3.80	Warped¾Shoo Brush¾U B The Judge4½	Saved ground	6
04Jan07TP8	1⅛ ft	:23	:47	1:12	1:44 4↑	105 Clm5000n3L	105	58	52/	72	+5	+6	65	5	1112	1113	108½	78½	58½	SchaeferGA120	Lb	7.00	Mr. Shu½RoyalPayback1Truth In Lending2½	Belatedly	11
14Dec06TP2	1m ft	:23	:46	1:12	1:39 3↑	105 Clm5000n3L	107	59	64/	71	+13	+7	62	5	1010	1014	105	73½	43½	Diego I120	Lb	6.80	KanniRoy2½TrthInLndng½GypsyRvr½	Belatedly in traffic	10
11Nov06Beu8	1⅝ sy	:50	1:14	2:10	2:37 3↑	107 Clm8000/8	109	53	57/	29	+1	-3	57	7	912	89½	87	810	817½	Rojas C118	Lb	7.70	Lifemybrother3½Jordy'sPride1½GulfNws½	Showed little	11

11Sep06 TP 4f ft :50 B *12/18* 16Apr05 TP 4f ft :48 B *2/7* 06Apr05 TP 5f ft 1:03 B *9/10* 04Feb05 TP 4f ft :52 B *7/9* 06Nov04 TP 4f ft :50 B *15/23* 12Jly04 CD 4f ft :51 B *40/51*
06Jly04 CD 4f ft :49 B *23/37* 19Jun04 Tdn 6f ft 1:19 B *2/2* 04Apr04 Kee 5f ft 1:03 B *17/27* 05Jan04 GP 5f ft 1:03 B *15/17* 28Dec03 GP 5f ft 1:04 B *23/24* 20Dec03 GP 5f ft 1:04 B *28/29*

4 Divine Dancer (E/P 6)

Own: Debbie A. Zehnder
5/1 Red red 'z' on navy blue ball
OUZTS PERRY WAYNE (142 18-25-20 13%)

$4,000 Ch. g. 6
Sire: Dance Brightly (Mr. Prospector)
Dam: Royal Doris (Corporate Report)
Brdr: David Neiman (KY)
Trnr: Zehnder Charles D. (4 0-0-1 0%)

Power Rating: 93.9 (5th) L 120

Life:	38 3-6-4	$33,399	77	Fst	32 2-4-3	$22,479	77
2007	10 1-0-1	$5,971	71	Off	6 1-2-1	$10,920	77
2006	3 0-1-0	$1,414	66	Dis	14 1-3-1	$13,572	77
RD	5 0-0-2	$1,589	64	Trf	0 0-0-0	$0	
				AW	14 2-1-0	$10,825	71

2007	501	10%	34%	-0.79	2007	19	5%	26%	-1.78
JKYw/EP types	137	9%	27%	-1.10	No class chg	136	4%	26%	-1.49
JKYw/ Trn L60	2	0%	0%	-2.00	Claiming	210	5%	26%	-1.32
JKYw/ Routes	224	11%	33%	-0.60					

Sire Stats: AWD 7.0f 16%Mud 472MudSts 1.27spi
Dam'sSire: AWD 7.1f 11%Mud 731MudSts 0.81spi

● Finished far back in last start ● Poor Trainer win%

DATE TRK	DIST					RR RACETYPE	CR	E1	E2/	LP	1c	2c	SPD	PP	ST	1C	2C	Str	FIN	JOCKEY		ODDS	Top Finishers	Comment	
29Apr07RD7	1⅛ ft	:25	:50	1:15	1:49 3↑	106 Clm4000C	105	58	57/	59	-18	-10	55	6	1hd	2hd	2½	49½	511	Ouzts PW120	Lb	5.00	Eyes For Hannah2½Pavan6½Five Fives2½	Gave way	7
15Apr07RD4	6f my	:23	:46	1:00	1:14 3↑	103 Clm4000n2y+	105	74	67/	81	0	0	60	5	4	66½	57	53½	31½	Enwa A119	Lb	2.10	CricardWit½Hrdcont½DivineDncr3½	Gaining mid track	6
04Apr07TP1	6½ ft	:24	:48		1:21 3↑	106 Clm5000C	108	78	73/	86	-9	-11	71	5	1	31	32½	52	41¾	LaurentaG120	Lb	31.20	FlyingChance JarretnkMacs RobRoy1½	Moved inside	8
23Mar07TP4	6½ ft	:23	:46	1:11	1:17 3↑	106 Clm5000C	105	66	66/	90	11	10	69	2	5	67	67½	48	49½	Ouzts PW120	Lb	22.30	OnlyJo½Preston T1½NovemorsFury4½	Off rail; no threat	7
09Mar07TP4	1m ft	:24	:48	1:13	1:38 3↑	108 Clm5000C	107	61	59/	87	-14	-8	69	10	54	54	56½	68	58½	Carnejo JM120	Lb	61.20	ComndrMxms3½KngDvdsS2½Kuml1½	4 wide; nothing left	10
23Feb07TP2	6f ft	:22	:47	:59	1:13 3↑	106 Clm5000n2Y	104	82	67/	86	+4	-8	64	5	5	78½	77½	68½	47¼	Ramirez E112	Lb	24.40	DrThundrDrewsDlght½EnhncedEdition1½	6 path turn	9
09Feb07TP8	1m ft	:24	:49	1:14	1:40 3↑	108 Clm5000C	105	64	59/	63	-5	-2	54	8	59½	79½	910	819	821½	Ouzts PW120	Lb	32.10	Dytrym4½AnythingBThl1RaidThePardest	Speed for 1/2	9
01Feb07TP8	6f ft	:22	:46		1:12 3↑	106 Clm5000C	106	74	72/	85	-2	-4	67	10	1	87	86½	96½	64½	QuinonezA118	Lb	9.20	SummernkBest ProspectnkHidden Glitter1½	5 wide turn	10
17Jan07TP3	6½ ft	:23	:46	1:11	1:17 4↑	107 Clm5000n29m	107	81	80/	78	-7	-7	71	9	2	42½	43	53	67½	Ouzts PW124	Lb	11.10	Gold Sneaker3½SilverMinistr½Bobandrobnk	4 path; tired	10
05Jan07TP8	6f ft	:22	:46	:58	1:12 4↑	106 Clm5000n3L	108	78	73/	88	-1	3	71	10	5	56½	45½	2hd	12½	Ouzts PW120	Lb	1.10e	DivnDncr2½DevilishSlnoDomstcOf3½	3 wide rally, driving	10

18Nov06 TP 4f ft :50 B *43/59* 11Nov06 TP 4f ft :49 B *13/38* 04Nov06 TP 5f ft 1:04 B *20/21* 17Sep06 TP 3f ft :37 B *4/11* 03Sep06 RD 4f ft :51 B *3/6* 20Aug06 RD 3f ft :39 B *4/5*
21May06 RD 4f ft :50 B *3/11* 22Apr06 RD 4f my :52 B *5/7* 23Jly05 RD 3f ft :37 B *2/11* 09Jly05 RD 3f ft :38 B *4/9* 17Apr05 RD 4f ft :53 B *6/6* 05Dec04 Haw 3f ft :38 B *8/10*

5 Gottagetherefirst (S 3)

Own: Special K Stables
12/1 Light blue; tan stripe on sleeves
FELIX JULIO E. (88 11-16-12 13%)

$4,000 B. g. 6
Sire: Keos (Riverman)
Dam: September Splendor (Northern Supremo)
Brdr: James E. English (KY)
Trnr: Kellar Richard M. (0 0-0-0 0%)

Power Rating: 91.7 (7th) L 120

Life:	55 5-3-9	$37,621	80	Fst	40 5-3-8	$33,373	80
2007	3 0-0-0	$213	63	Off	11 0-0-3	$3,425	71
2006	17 1-0-5	$7,599	68	Dis	10 1-0-2	$5,227	80
RD	11 3-0-1	$11,427	75	Trf	4 0-0-0	$823	72
				AW	15 0-2-4	$7,075	78

2007	246	9%	37%	-0.23
JKYw/ S types	208	7%	37%	-0.41
JKYw/ Routes	96	10%	41%	+0.03

Sire Stats: AWD 7.5f 6%Mud 33MudSts 0.39spi
Dam'sSire: AWD 6.7f 13%Mud 471MudSts 0.45spi

★ Highest Speed Figure at Today's Distance (tie) ★ Drops in Class today ● Has not raced for more than 2 months

DATE TRK	DIST					RR RACETYPE	CR	E1	E2/	LP	1c	2c	SPD	PP	ST	1C	2C	Str	FIN	JOCKEY		ODDS	Top Finishers	Comment	
Previously trained by DALTON KENNETH W.																									
25Feb07TP10	1⅛ ft	:24	:47	1:13	1:46 3↑	107 Clm5000C	105	33	50/	68	-8	-10	55	2	1016	1021	1017	919	725½	Sunseri JJ120	Lb	97.80	Snow Squall7½Ship's Captain5Larry B1½	Outrun	10
17Jan07TP3	6½ ft	:23	:46	1:11	1:17 4↑	107 Clm5000n29m	105	73	74/	74	-7	7	63	7	6	99½	78	911	913	SchaeferGA120	Lb	70.10	Gold Sneaker3½SilverMinistr½Bobandrobnk	4 path turn	10
07Jan07TP7	1⅛ ft	:24	:49	1:14	1:46 4↑	107 Clm5000n26m	107	64	60/	65	8	8	59	2	42	33	52	610	712	Fortner JL120	Lb	29.10	GldCmndrOn4½PyThFxhdMchSt4½	Steadied inside early	12
23Dec06TP6	1m ft	:24	:48	1:12	1:38 3↑	106 Clm5000n2Y	108	54	57/	84	-2	+2	66	7	1111	1110	106½	69½	53½	Fortner JL120	Lb	48.70	RstyTrwk½ComndrMxms½ProdMmors½	5 wide 1/4 pl	11
07Dec06TP7	1m ft	:24	:48	1:14	1:41 3↑	106 Clm5000n2Y	105	77	62/	66	+6	+6	58	8	86½	64	77½	911	89¾	Fortner JL120	Lb	54.10	BrdsVictorynoMaywodaZ7½LittleMorenk	4 wide 1/4 pole	12
Previously trained by KELLAR RICHARD M																									
22Nov06Beu1	1m ft	:25	:50	1:16	1:43 3↑	104 Clm3500n2y+	106	56	52/	83	-8	+1	62	4	89½	84½	66½	62½	3¾	Fortner JL120	Lb	14.80	JmicnJustchdBevisDrnkGotgthrfirst1½	Angled out; rallied	10
07Nov06Beu4	170 wf	:25	:50	1:16	1:47 3↑	104 Clm3500n2y+	105	48	50/	84	-20	-10	64	10	64½	63½	53	34	31¼	Fortner JL120	Lb	11.60	PrinceLr½SpltAc1Gotgthrfirst1	Saved ground 2nd turn	10
21Oct06Beu12	6f ft	:22	:45	:58	1:11 3↑	103 Clm3500n29m	103	61	68/	83	+2	0	62	7	11	1110	1113	1011	511½	Fortner JL120	Lb	47.80	Dr.E.ClarenkFleetLine4½GrandStel1	Passed tiring rivals	11
Previously trained by LANDRY JOSEPH C.																									
05Jly06RD4	1m ft	:24	:49	1:13	1:40 3↑	104 Clm4000n2y+	99	49	46/	50	-9	-3	38	3	89½	810	813	821	830½	Sanchez C120	Lb	12.10	UBThJdg1PrncAlmdr½Shlt½	Lost ground throughout	9
Previously trained by BREHM JOEL D.																									
12Jun06Ind4	7½ fm	:23	:48	1:14	1:33 3↑	107 Clm6250	108	67	67/	79	+5	+7	67	1	6	714	713	77½	54	LaurenteG118	LBb	21.70	HazardnkIncredibl2½GenlGorgS1	Widest lane;belatedly	7

04May RD 4f ft :52 B *9/9* ●16Oct06 RD 4f ft :50 B *1/12* 26Aug05 TP 3f ft :36 B *2/3* 25Jly05 RD 3f ft :38 B *4/8* ●28Apr05 Beu 3f ft :37 B *1/10* 15Mar05 TP 4f ft :50 B *5/9*
08Mar05 TP 3f ft :36 B *1/2* 24Nov04 CD 4f sy :49 B *5/18* 29Oct04 CD 5f ft 1:00 B *4/36* 08May04 CD 5f ft 1:03 Bg *12/12* 02Apr04 CD 4f ft :50 B *22/30* 05Jan04 Crc 4f gd :51 B *33/43*

tsnhorse.com

Ultimate PP's w/ Quick Play Comments **River Downs** Clm 4000 1 Mile 3up Friday, May 11, 2007 **Race 6**

E1 76 | E2/LATE 69/72 | SPD 69

6 Ship's Captain (E/P 6)

Own: Robert A. Elkins
8/5 Red, white o in scroll horseshoe
SOLOMON NATHAN (43 10-5-4 23%)

$4,000 B. g. 6 FTKOCT 2002 $70k
Sire: Grindstone (Unbridled)
Dam: Country Casual (Royal Roberto)
Brdr: Roy Gottfeld (KY)
Trnr: Macdonald Colleen (9 1-1-2 11%)

Power Rating: 101.7 (1st) L 120

Life: 40 3-9-3	$64,033	88	Fst	31 2-8-1	$42,683 88
2007 5 0-4-0	$5,700	76	Off	1 0-0-0	$0 62
2006 14 1-3-3	$16,566	78	Dis	9 0-2-1	$6,087 75
RD 3 0-1-0	$1,197	61	Trf	8 1-1-2	$11,350 82
			AW	8 0-4-1	$8,669 78

2007	69	17%	43%	+2.78
JKYw/EP types	85	9%	25%	-0.94
+JKYw/ Trn L60	1	100%	100%	+20.60
JKYw/ Routes	22	9%	27%	0.75

2007	11	9%	36%	+0.05
2nd start w/trn	2	0%	0%	-2.00
No class chg	3	0%	0%	-2.00
Btn favorite	1	0%	100%	2.00

Sire Stats: AWD 7.2 15%Mud 332MudSts 1.69spi
Dam'sSire: AWD 6.8 12%Mud 708MudSts 1.12spi

★ Hot Jockey in last 7 days (9 3-0-1) ★ Best Dirt Speed is fastest among today's starters ● Beaten by weaker in last start
★ Switches to a high% Jockey

DATE TRK	DIST						RR	RACETYPE	CR	E1	E2/	LP	1c	2c	SPD	PP	ST	1C	2C	Str	FIN	JOCKEY		ODDS	Top Finishers	Comment	
24Apr07RD1	1 1/16 ft	:261	:51	1:15	1:504	3↑	104	Clm4000n2y+	104	54	58/	64	-12	+2	58	4	33	24	2 2½	24	2 7½	GoncalvesLR120	Lbf	10.40	Bsmalpoint7 ShipsCptn JordysPrde14	Stumbled start	4
Previously trained by LAUER MICHAEL E.																											
15Mar07TP4	◈1m ft	:251	:484	1:134	1:394	3↑	108	Clm5000C	108	62	65/	76	-11	-3	66	5	3 2½	33	2 2½	3 2½	48	LeparouxJR120	Lb	11.10	Larry B3 RaisedIchehwk Go For Aly1½	Nothing left late	7
25Feb07TP10	◈1 1/16 ft	:247	:474	1:132	1:467	3↑	107	Clm5000C	110	70	69/	85	-8	-10	76	4	5 7½	6 3½	33	24	2 7½	Diego I120	Lb	3.10	Snow Squall7 Ship's Captain Larry B1½	In tight 7/8 pl	10
24Jan07TP7	◈1 1/16 ft	:25	:497	1:142	1:47	4↑	106	Clm5000C	109	60	61/	86	-8	-5	72	4	55	5 5½	54	33	2 1½	LeparouxJR120	Lb	11.70	CaptinFish1 ShipsCptn AnythgBtTh3½	5 wide 5/16 pl	10
06Jan07TP7	◈1m ft	:241	:473	1:132	1:383	4↑	107	Clm5000C	110	70	66/	91	0	-6	75	6	6 5½	6 4½	42	3 2½	2nk	LeparouxJR120	Lb	2.50	DesertMonarch ShipsCaptn LarryB2	Waited 5/16 pl	8
10Dec06TP5	◈1 1/16 ft	:241	:473	1:113	1:44	3↑	109	Clm8000	108	62	63/	78	-4	+4	69	3	8 6½	7 7½	8 8½	11 7½	10 7½	Teator P120	Lb	14.00	PrincPrdo PruStory KnuckyTrst½	Failed to menace	12
25Oct06Kee8	◈1 1/16 ft	:51	1:154	1:403	1:583	3↑	108	Clm7500	111	71	70/	81	-4	-1	78	7	7 6½	6 3½	6 3½	1hd	2no	LeparouxJR120	Lb	9.80	ElBombo ShipsCptn HitThHdwod1½	5w bid;outgamed	10
01Oct06TP3	◈1m ft	:244	:491	1:153	1:382	3↑	106	Clm5000C	108	59	62/	86	-15	-16	70	2	5 1½	4 1½	1hd	2hd	3 1½	Coa D120	Lb	3.20	EclpOfThCt SaintDsrt1 ShpsCptn2½	Bold 4 wide move	8
16Sep06KD7	⊕7f fm	:242	:474	1:113	1:24	3↑	108	Clm10000/9	108	85	83/	85	1	-4	88	2	7	42	31	6 8½	4 9½	Mojica,Jr R118	Lb	6.20	TequlPrty FncyThret OldScudr½	Near inside,empty	11
04Sep06Elp11	⊕1m fm	:252	:49	1:121	1:362	3↑	108	Alw5000s	109	55	67/	85	-18	-4	73	3	64	6 2½	5 1½	3 2½	31	Coa D120	Lb	23.20	Chef NatisQuck ShipsCptn	7w bid;couldn't get up	11

20Apr RD 3f ft :383 B 1/2 20Apr'06 CD 4f ft :491 B 11/37 11Apr'06 CD 4f ft :49 B 16/39 27Mar'06 CD 3f ft :36 B 2/5 20Mar'06 CD 5f ft 1:021 B 2/6 10Mar'06 Cdl 5f ft 1:034 B 4/5
03Mar'06 Cdl 5f ft 1:034 B 2/3 24May'05 Kee 5f ft 1:044 B 15/17 16May'05 Kee 5f ft 1:052 B 11/11 19Apr'05 Cdl 5f ft 1:031 B 6/8 11Apr'05 Cdl 5f ft 1:034 B 11/12 03Apr'05 Cdl 4f ft :494 B 4/7

7 Proud Memories (P 4)

Own. Fairwinds Llc
5/1 Blue, yellow horseshoe: gray whip
LAURENTE GODOFREDO (18 0-2-3 0%)

$4,000 B. g. 7
Sire: Petion (Lord At War (Arg))
Dam: Waltzing Proud (Proud Truth)
Brdr: Betsy R. Kuster & Woodford R.baumgardner (KY)
Trnr: Smith Pam L. (7 0-0-1 0%)

Power Rating: 94.9 (4th) L 120

Life: 70 7-2-10	$43,416	75	Fst	54 4-2-8	$30,259 75
2007 5 0-0-1	$810	69	Off	14 3-6-2	$12,748 74
2006 16 1-1-2	$9,885	74	Dis	26 2-0-2	$12,180 74
RD 6 0-0-2	$1,250	67	Trf	2 0-0-0	$408 71
			AW	10 1-0-1	$5,689 74

2007	59	10%	29%	+1.45
JKYw/ P types	45	7%	27%	-0.77
JKYw/ Trn L60	2	0%	50%	-2.00
JKYw/ Routes	32	16%	38%	+4.07

2007	10	0%	10%	-2.00
2nd strt w/trn	3	0%	0%	-2.00
Sprnt to Rte	5	0%	20%	-2.00
No class chg	11	0%	27%	-2.00

Sire Stats: AWD 6.5 15%Mud 546MudSts 0.83spi
Dam'sSire: AWD 7.8 16%Mud 1010MudSts 1.18spi

★ May improve while returning to a route ● Beaten by weaker in last start ● Poor Trainer win%

DATE TRK	DIST						RR	RACETYPE	CR	E1	E2/	LP	1c	2c	SPD	PP	ST	1C	2C	Str	FIN	JOCKEY		ODDS	Top Finishers	Comment	
21Apr07RD8	6f ft	:224	:461	:59	1:13	3↑	104	Clm4000n19m	106	77	73/	77	-2	-3	61	4	5	35	35	46	38	Laurente G124	Lf	8.70	Mnchilo7 OBrynsLuck2 ProudMmors1½	Evenly; no rally	8
Previously trained by ROSS RAYMOND GILBERT																											
05Apr07TP10	◈1 1/16 ft	:25	:494	1:144	1:471	3↑	110	Clm5000	108	73	70/	67	-9	-2	66	3	43	4 2½	5 3½	7 8½	711	LaurenteG120	Lf	41.20	Immedyimedy SultryMod RustyTrwles½	Inside; faded	8
16Mar07TP3	◈1m ft	:241	:484	1:141	1:40	3↑	107	Clm5000n26m	106	62	62/	72	-10	-6	62	7	6 3½	6 3½	6 2½	8 5½	68	LaurenteG120	Lf	33.20	Dusnbrg PubloDSoin OndyGrime2	3 path 2nd turn	8
09Mar07TP4	◈1m ft	:244	:484	1:133	1:383	3↑	108	Clm5000C	107	63	62/	80	-14	-8	67	4	32	33	45	57	7 11½	Teator P120	Lf	41.20	CommdrMxmus KngDvdsSon2 Kuteni1½	Inside; faded	10
25Feb07TP10	◈1 1/16 ft	:247	:474	1:132	1:467	3↑	107	Clm5000C	108	58	63/	78	-8	-10	68	6	8 7½	7 9½	76	510	514	MolinaJrJF120	Lf	37.80	Snow Squall7 Ship's Captain Larry B1½	No threat	10
25Jan07TP7	◈1m ft	:241	:481	1:141	1:401	4↑	108	Clm5000n29m	106	71	70/	76	+4	-1	69	11	7 9½	58	65	89	810	Teator P120	Lf	61.80	PyThFx CommdrMxmus2 PtTheWine½	4 wide 1st turn	11
23Dec06TP9	◈1m ft	:241	:48	1:124	1:384	3↑	109	Clm5000n2Y	107	70	65/	80	-2	+3	68	1	32	4 2½	34	43	3 1½	Teator P120	Lf	47.10	RlyTrwk CmndrMxms PrdMmrs½	Near rail, mild bid	11
17Oct06Beu7	170 sy	:231	:473	1:141	1:451	3↑	104	Clm3500n29m	102	64	56/	65	-3	-3	55	7	6 8½	67	6 9½	610	6 18½	Yaranga Y120	Lf	11.50	Storm Envoy Embon Turnkey Job3½	Outrun	7
26Sep06Mnr4	1m ft	:247	:484	1:142	1:414	3↑	106	Clm5000n26m	103	58	48/	70	-7	-4	51	7	67	6 7½	711	714	7 19½	Feliz JE116	Lf	52.40	Esteemed Cafe Noir Idea Man1½	Always outrun	7
15Sep06Mnr4	1m ft	:241	:48	1:132	1:41	3↑	106	Clm5000n3Y	104	66	57/	67	-4	0	55	3	5 7½	7 3½	7 6½	68	612	Feliz JE116	Lf	30.70	RledFld BrshLghtr1 ShnonThCnon2	Proved no factor	8

●19Dec'06 Vin 4f gd :50 B 1/4 15Aug'06 Mnr 5f ft 1:024 B 5/13 ●26Jan'06 TP 4f ft :504 B 1/8 16Jan'06 TP 4f ft :51 B 4/10 ●10Jan'05 Beu (d) 4f ft :482 B 1/9 29Oct'03 Tlc 4f sy :504 B 1/3
11Oct'03 Tlc 5f ft 1:03 B 13/24 11Sep'03 Tlc 3f ft :371 B 1/3 28Jun'03 Kee 3f ft :38 B 17/26 20Jun'03 Kee 4f ft :494 B 10/17 ●10Jun'03 Kee 3f ft :36 H 1/16 17May'03 Kee 3f sy :37 B 4/13

8 Inti Raymi (E 8)

Own: Ruben Munoz
20/1 Green, green 'im' on yellow diamond
CHAVEZ CASBY R. (12 1-2-2 8%)

$4,000 Dkbbr. g. 5
Sire: Andean Chasqui (Miswaki Gold)
Dam: Final Regret (Gibouree)
Brdr: H. B. Robeson & Luz Robeson (TX)
Trnr: Drinkard Skip L. (15 1-2-2 7%)

Power Rating: 85.8 (8th) L 120

Life: 79 14-10-9	$99,169	83	Fst	60 12-9-7	$86,227 83
2007 4 0-0-0	$166	43	Off	17 2-1-2	$12,192 77
2006 17 1-0-1	$6,018	80	Dis	13 3-2-1	$22,704 77
RD 0 0-0-0	$0		Trf	2 0-0-0	$750 73
			AW	0 0-0-0	$0

2007	87	6%	25%	-0.27
JKYw/ E types	68	4%	25%	-1.36
JKYw/ Routes	34	6%	29%	-0.09

2007	65	11%	23%	-0.68
31-90daysAway	54	7%	26%	-1.70
No class chg	64	8%	25%	-0.84
Claiming	172	10%	26%	-0.85

Sire Stats: AWD 7.8 6%Mud 16MudSts 0.59spi
Dam'sSire: AWD 7.1 9%Mud 793MudSts 0.86spi

● Finished far behind weaker in last race ● Poor Speed Figures ● Outside posts have poor win%
● Poor '31-90daysAway' trainer record: 4%wins 45sts

DATE TRK	DIST						RR	RACETYPE	CR	E1	E2/	LP	1c	2c	SPD	PP	ST	1C	2C	Str	FIN	JOCKEY		ODDS	Top Finishers	Comment	
28Mar07Beu6	1m ft	:252	:49	1:141	1:394	3↑	104	Clm3500n2y+	100	67	56/	43	-10	-3	39	5	1hd	1½	7 5½	711	7 25½	HernandezL115	Lf	29.00	TwRwsOfGld4 Bghm PrivteLw3½	Checked repeatedly	8
05Mar07Beu6	1m ft	:242	:482	1:151	1:403	3↑	106	Clm4000n26m	101	79	63/	41	+1	-5	43	1	1½	1hd	52	8 9½	8 23½	HernandezL115	Lf	56.30	Despite1 Perimeur RobertoRoy	Inside duel, faltered	8
26Feb07Beu6	6f sy	:222	:464	:592	1:124	3↑	104	Clm3500n2y+	100	89	78/	47	+5	+6	41	2	6	4 2½	6 7½	10 13	10 18½	Yaranga Y120	Lf	23.50	RobrtoRy ClsicRunwy DncoLnc1½	Threw head start	11
Previously trained by MOOK; JAMES C. II																											
20Jan07Beu8	1m ft	:241	:482	1:144	1:411	3↑	104	Clm4000n16m	98	80	58/	17	+2	+1	25	1	18	1 1½	8 7½	717	838	HernandezL119	Lf	4.50	RevlesDr1 TrncolJm BghmI	Sprinted clear,stopped	9
15Dec06Beu7	6f ft	:233	:481	1:002	1:124	3↑	104	Clm3500n2Y	104	86	83/	62	-6	7	57	3	5	1 1½	21	37	5 13½	Dailey A120	Lf	6.10	CopperTrai LegendHask Mr.GarryC1	Set pace; tired	12
Previously trained by ACRES HAROLD																											
05Dec06Beu3	170 ft	:24	:474	1:14	1:462	3↑	105	Clm4000n16m	105	83	78/	55	+7	+9	63	6	1 2½	15	14	2½	4 4½	Dailey A124	Lf	12.90	RingBrr1 CptnJcb1 SlwCtyChn1½	Set pace; weakened	8
15Nov06Beu3	170 sy	:231	:47	1:134	1:463	3↑	105	Clm3500n2Y	106	84	77/	53	+8	+8	62	9	11	13	13	14	3 6½	Dailey A120	Lf	12.90	SntorDck4 FrnchShm2 IntiRymi1½	Set pace; weakened	10
Previously trained by NORTHROP, GEORGE JR																											
16Oct06Tdn2	6f ft	:223	:464	1:004	1:132	3↑	104	Clm3500n16m	104	87	83/	64	-2	-2	58	3	1	1hd	11	2½	5 5½	GonzalezLA123	Lf	1.30	DsBckyBn1 WtchPrnd2 TkThHm1	Pace; weakened	7
02Oct06Tdn8	170 gd	:23	:472	1:132	1:444	3↑	107	Clm3500n29m	106	82	77/	59	0	-2	65	1	11	1 1½	1 1½	23	712	GonzalezLA116	L	17.70	DrvgMsc7 PrcptvFrnd OlvrWdn1	Clear lead; faltered	9
17Sep06Tdn7	170 ft	:222	:463	1:141	1:481	3↑	107	Clm3500n29m	105	93	78/	45	+14	+12	57	6	14	1 5½	11	21	8 7½	Byrne J116	Lf	20.40	SpitOfMntn1 BrintSrmn ClInThCntry½	Fast pace; tired	10

27Apr RD 3f gd :37 B 1/3 03Apr Beu 4f ft :482 B 3/17 ●25May'06 LaD 5f ft 1:002 H 1/18 24Feb'06 Hou 5f ft 1:023 H 8/20 15Jan'06 Hou 4f ft :504 H 34/53 ●26Jun'05 Tdn 5f ft 1:004 B 1/6
●17Jun'05 Tdn 5f ft 1:004 B 1/9 ●29Apr'05 Tdn 5f gd 1:00 B 1/13 ●22Apr'05 Tdn 5f ft 1:003 B 1/10 ●16Apr'05 Tdn 4f ft :484 B 1/25 01Apr'05 Hou 4f ft :501 H 9/16 ●25Sep'04 Tdn 4f ft :464 B 1/11

tsnhorse.com

Ultimate PP's w/ Quick Play Comments

River Downs Clm 4000 1 Mile 3up Friday, May 11, 2007 Race 6

E1	E2/LATE	SPD
76	69/ 72	69

Last 3 Years RACETYPE STATS:	# Races	FAVORITES Win%	Itm%	$2ROI	Average Field Size	Median $2 Win Payoff	% Winners < 5/1	% Winners >= 5/1 < 10/1	% Winners >= 10/1
RD 3up CLM 4000 Dirt 8f	30	47%	80%	+0.51	8.0	$7.70	80%	17%	3%

Track Bias Stats

' MEET Totals '					' WEEK Totals '				
DIRT 8.0f	Speed Bias: 57%		WnrAvgBL		DIRT 8.0f	Speed Bias: 62%		WnrAvgBL	
# Races: 30	04/06 - 05/08		1stCall: 2.1		# Races: 8	05/03 - 05/08		1stCall: 1.8	
%Wire: 23%			2ndCall: 0.8		%Wire: 25%			2ndCall: 0.8	
	Early	Speed	Late	Speed		Early	Speed	Late	Speed
Runstyle:	E	E/P	P	S	Runstyle:	E	E/P	P	S
	++		+			++		++	
Impact Values	1.50	0.93	1.22	0.35	Impact Values	1.85	0.84	1.31	0.00
%Races Won	37%	20%	33%	10%	%Races Won	38%	25%	38%	0%
Post Bias:	RAIL	1-3	4-7	8+	Post Bias	RAIL	1-3	4-7	8+
		+				+	+		
Impact Values	0.64	1.20	0.90	0.00	Impact Values	1.40	1.40	0.57	0.00
Avg Win %	10%	19%	16%	0%	Avg Win %	25%	25%	11%	0%

Race Summary

#	HorseName	ML Odds	Med Eqp	Days Since L/R	Run Style	PT S	Avg Dist/Surf PACE-SPEED E1	E2/Late	Spd	Avg Race Rtng	Best Pace E1	E2/Late	Final Speed Sp1	Sp2	Sp3	Sp4	ACL	Rcg Spd Avg	R1	R2	R3	Mud Spd	Pedigree Stats Mud Sts	Mud % Mud	Sire AWD	Dam Sire's AWD
6	Ship's Captain	8/5	L	17	E/P	6	64	65/ 82	* 71*	108	71	70/ 91	58.	66.	76.	72.	106.6	67	104	108	107	62	332	15	7.2	6.8
7	Proud Memories	5/1	L	20	+P	4	65	65/ 75	* 67*	109	77	70/ 80	61	66.	62.	67.	105.7	63	104	110	107	62	546	15	6.5	7.8
1	Arctic Sand	6/1	L	18..	E/P	5	72	63/ 76	* 65*	105	74	70/ 88	63.	60.	66.	59.	104.2	63	103	104	106	46	372	11	7.4	8.4
3	Shoo Brush	5/2	L	13	S	2	54	52/ 85	* 65*	104	64	64/ 92	66.	67	65	65.	104.3	66	105	105	102	73	1207	18	7.5	7.8
4	Divine Dancer	5/1	L	12	E/P	6	60	58/ 73	* 62*	107	64	65/ 87	55.	60	71	69		62	106	103	106	60	472	16	7.0	7.1
2	Accordian Man	6/1	L	20	E/P	8	75	72/ 57	61	105	90	78/ 72	61.	52	42	31	105.9	52	105	106	105	72	963	14	6.3	9.1
5	Gottagetherefirst	12/1	L	75	S	3	65	60/ 72	(61)	107	77	62/ 84	55.	63	59.	66.	104.1	59	107	107	107	58	33	6	7.5	6.7
8	Inti Raymi	20/1	L	44	++E	8	73	60/ 41	* 41*	105	93	78/ 68	39.	43.	41	25.	103.7	41	104	106	104	62	16	6	7.6	7.1

Speed Last Race	Back Speed	Current Class	Average Class Last 3	Power Rating	Early Pace Last Race	Late Pace Last Race
66 Shoo Brush	76 Ship's Captain	109.1 Ship's Captain	107.7 Ship's Captain	101.7 Ship's Captain	75 Accordian Man	92 Shoo Brush
63 Arctic Sand	71 Accordian Man	107.7 Proud Memories	106.4 Proud Memories	96.8 Accordian Man	74 Arctic Sand	77 Proud Memories
61 Proud Memories	70 Arctic Sand	106.6 Shoo Brush	105.6 Divine Dancer	95.5 Arctic Sand	73 Proud Memories	69 Arctic Sand
61 Accordian Man	69 Proud Memories	106.1 Divine Dancer	105.6 Gottagetherefirst	94.9 Proud Memories	67 Inti Raymi	68 Gottagetherefirst
58 Ship's Captain	69 Divine Dancer	105.4 Arctic Sand	104.8 Shoo Brush	93.9 Divine Dancer	58 Divine Dancer	64 Ship's Captain
55 Divine Dancer	68 Shoo Brush	105.1 Gottagetherefirst	104.6 Arctic Sand	93.3 Shoo Brush	54 Ship's Captain	59 Divine Dancer
55 Gottagetherefirst	68 Inti Raymi	104.1 Accordian Man	102.5 Accordian Man	91.7 Gottagetherefirst	47 Shoo Brush	57 Accordian Man
39 Inti Raymi	66 Gottagetherefirst	100.5 Inti Raymi	100.3 Inti Raymi	85.8 Inti Raymi	33 Gottagetherefirst	41 Inti Raymi

#	Speed Last Race		#	Prime Power		#	Class Rating		#	Best Speed at Dist	
7	Time Counter	77	4	Valid Victory	113.9	8	Little Nicky Regs	110.5	8	Little Nicky Regs	101
6	Bar Time	75	8	Little Nicky Regs	112.3	7	Time Counter	109.4	7	Time Counter	86
3	Private Herb	73	6	Bar Time	110.8	4	Valid Victory	108.6	4	Valid Victory	85

7

Exacta / Trifecta / Superfecta (Ten Cent Minimum) / Pick 3 (Races 7-8-9)

Simulcast of Thistledown race number 7

	E1	E2/LATE	SPEED
PARS:	91	92/ 79	79

5½ Furlongs. Clm 6250 Purse $8,400. FOR FOUR YEAR OLDS AND UPWARD. Weight, 122 lbs. Non-winners of two races since April 11 Allowed 2 lbs. A race since then Allowed 4 lbs. Claiming Price $6,250 (Claiming races for $5,000 or less not considered in Weight Allowances) (Ohio Registered Foals Pr eferred).

Post Time: (3:05)/ 2:05/ 1:05/12:05

5 1/2 FURLONGS

---

1 **Final Endeavor (E/P 6)** $6,250 B. g. 8
6/1 Own: Merk; Ned; And David Doering
White red belt, red sleeves
CASTILLO KENDRY (22 4-4-6 18%)

Sire: Unreal Zeal (Mr. Prospector)
Dam: Dever's Endeavors (Princely Pleasure)
Brdr: Bruce Tallisman (OH)
Trnr: Doering Merk (12 2-2-1 17%)

Power Rating: 109.3 (5th) L 118

	Starts	W	P	S	Earnings	Spd		Starts	W	P	S	Earnings	Spd
Life:	62	13	12	16	$192,813	91	Fst	49	11	10	11	$160,615	91
2007	3	0	0	1	$1,260	78	Off	11	2	2	3	$28,098	83
2006	14	3	2	6	$36,704	83	Dis	7	2	0	1	$26,347	83
Tdn	35	6	9	10	$90,296	88	Trf	2	0	0	2	$4,100	82
							AW	4	1	1	2	$12,006	84

2007	32	13%	44%	-1.19	2007	25	8%	28%	+0.08	Sire Stats: AWD 6.1f 14%Mud 1779MudSts	0.38spi
JKYw/EP types	14	7%	50%	1.43	Claiming	270	9%	34%	-0.98	Dam'sSire: AWD 6.4f 12%Mud 1012MudSts	0.80spi
JKYw/ Sprints	19	11%	37%	-1.01							

★ Hot Trainer in last 14 days (4 2-2-0)

DATE TRK	DIST							RR	RACETYPE	CR	E1	E2/	LP	1c	2c	SPD	PP	ST	1C	2C	Str	FIN	JOCKEY		ODDS	Top Finishers	Comment	
22Apr07Tdn12	5f	ft	:22	:46		:583	3↑	108	[S]C6250	108		90/	70			69	4	5	21	2¼	32	49	Pilares CP118	Lbf	5.50	PremirCourt1¼Cudbrink½BarTime2¼	Chased, weakened	7
19Feb07Mnr7	5½	gd	:222	:454	:581	1:044	3↑	109	Clm10000	108	96	79/	53	-2	-1	60	4	3	5½	7¾	910	918¾	MrtinezJrLJ119	Lbf	35.10	PrrieLitesnkLacGrape5¼Tooriziforay3¼	Hustled;btw,tired	9
06Jan07Beu7	6f	sy	:224	:47	:592	1:113	3↑	108	OC11.5k/N2X	108	82	95/	76	-3	-9	79	6	1	1hd	1hd	2¼	3¾	Pilares CP122	Lbf	26.90	LordAlexndrnkFloter7¾FinlEndevornk	Dueled; weakened	8
02Dec06Mnr7	5½	ft	:222	:464	:584	1:063	3↑	111	Clm15000	107	87	82/	56	+1	+1	52	5	3	4¾	7¼	9¼	913¾	MrtinezJrLJ115	Lbf	29.80	EstmPointnoBeugrnoCplolPnc1¼	Chase,drifted,gave way	9
18Nov06Tdn12	6f	gd	:223	:463	:592	1:122	3↑	109	[S]C10000	112	85	84/	86	-3	-4	78	1	5	5¼	41	3hd	13	MrtinezJrLJ117	Lbf	4.00	FinalEndevor3SenorDSol2BarTime2¾	Rail, drew clear	7
04Nov06Tdn4	6f	ft	:222	:454	:59	1:123	3↑	109	Clm10000	109	83	82/	75	0	+3	67	6	5	3¼	33	21	3¼	MunaylaF117	Lbf	5.50	LcGrpe1MenUGone¾FinlEndevorhd	Pressed; good try	7
21Oct06Tdn7	6f	gd	:223	:463	:593	1:131	3↑	109	Clm10000	108	87	86/	73	+1	0	69	2	2	32	2¼	2¼	33	Unel-mornV117	Lbf	5.00	LacGrpe2¼IGoSo¼FinlEndevor1¼	Stalked; needed more	6
08Oct06Tdn7	6f	ft	:22	:451	:583	1:122	3↑	110	Clm10000	110	86	86/	81	+4	+7	76	7	1	6¾	56	32	3½	GonzalezLA117	Lbf	7.30	AllForLovehdLacGrpe¾FinalEndevor1	Rail; good effort	7
09Sep06Tdn2	6f	ft				1:121	3↑	110	Clm12500	110	83	85/	78	+2	+2	71	3	5	45	5¼	5¼	3¾	GonzalezLA118	Lbf	16.30	OnRoylAh2AlForLv2¼FnlEndvorhd	Mild rally; no threat	7
19Aug06Tdn8	6f	sy	:222	:463	:593	1:13	3↑	119	Clm12500	109	86	87/	65	+2	-1	63	4	5	7¾	6¾	6¾	811	Ortiz A111	Lbf	14.60	PopOnTp4OneRoyalAhhdFigimeRequst1¼	Showed little	9

10Apr Tdn 3f gd :384 B 15/16 13Apr'06 Tdn 3f ft :382 B 11/18 06Apr'06 Tdn 3f ft :39 B 15/17 27Jly'05 Kee 3f ft :37 B 3/7 06Jun'05 Tdn 4f ft :491 B 2/16 23May'05 Tdn 4f ft :484 B 2/23
●16May'05 Tdn 3f ft 1:02 B 1/7 09May'05 Tdn 4f ft :484 B 2/20 02May'05 Tdn 4f gd :522 B 17/18 18Dec'04 Tdn 3f ft :401 B 8/9 20Sep'04 Tdn 4f ft :50 B 5/27 28Jun'04 Tdn 5f ft 1:023 B 9/14

---

2 **Mr. Simon To You (E/P 0)** $6,250 B. g. 7
8/1 Own: Paul Yanos And Andrew Kopas; Jr.
Red
GONZALEZ LUIS ANTONIO (0 0-0-0 0%)

Sire: Take Me Out (Cure The Blues)
Dam: Lady Eleese (Mount Hagen (Fr))
Brdr: James Fiolieta & Carol L. Jones (KY)
Trnr: Mook; II James C. (3 1-0-1 33%)

Power Rating: 102.1 (8th) L 118

	Starts	W	P	S	Earnings	Spd		Starts	W	P	S	Earnings	Spd
Life:	44	9	4	8	$67,919	81	Fst	30	8	2	5	$51,130	81
2006	9	2	1	1	$12,077	77	Off	14	1	2	3	$16,789	78
2005	10	3	0	1	$14,829	77	Dis	7	2	1	1	$16,486	81
Tdn	24	8	2	5	$46,061	77	Trf	0	0	0	0	$0	
							AW	0	0	0	0	$0	

2007	526	15%	43%	-0.40	2007	16	6%	13%	-0.10	Sire Stats: AWD 6.6f 13%Mud 609MudSts	1.06spi
JKYw/EP types	350	17%	47%	0.36	90+ days away	1	0%	0%	-2.00	Dam'sSire: AWD 7.1f 14%Mud 652MudSts	0.81spi
JKYw/ Sprints	282	16%	45%	0.30	+1st after clm	3	33%	67%	-0.07		
					Up one class	9	11%	33%	-1.16		

★ Won last race (TDN 10/29 6f Dirt good Clm3500NW29M)

● Moves up in class from last start ● Has not raced for more than 6 months

DATE TRK	DIST							RR	RACETYPE	CR	E1	E2/	LP	1c	2c	SPD	PP	ST	1C	2C	Str	FIN	JOCKEY		ODDS	Top Finishers	Comment	
Claimed from Sipp Bridget Sipp Burton K. Trainer																												
29Oct06Tdn7	6f	gd	:23	:471	1:003	1:14	3↑	108	Clm3500n29m c	108	80	79/	84	-2	-3	72	7	3	8¾	5¼	2¼	12	SanguinettiA117	L	2.40e	MrSmonTY2SoldrsClis1ColClSm1	5 wide; drew clear	10
07Aug06Tdn3	6f	ft	:224	:461	:584	1:114	3↑	110	Clm7500	109	80	78/	86	-5	-4	73	4	2	43	4¼	5¾	5¼	Ramos HG118	L	13.60	Little NickyRegs¾Wirebender1Storm Cave1¼	No threat	6
18Jun06Tdn4	6f	ft	:22	:452	:583	1:12	3↑	110	Clm10000	106	78	69/	68	+2	+2	51	6	8	8¾	713	713	718	Ortiz A111	L	11.00e	GasshdSky Hunter1Final Endeavor1	Trailed	8
Claimed from James Mook II Mook James C. II Trainer																												
12Jun06Tdn7	5½	ft	:224	:47	:592	1:054	3↑	108	Clm5000n16m c	110	87	84/	86	-2	-6	77	2	5	31	31	11	19¾	SkerrettJ122	L	0.70	MrSmonToY9¾WreLdr¾BluBlodBut¾	Quickly; drew off	7
03Jun06Tdn13	6f	ft	:221	:454	:584	1:12	3↑	107	Clm5000n16m	108	87	87/	74	0	-1	71	3	5	22	2¼	2¼	3¾	SkerrettJ122	L	8.40	CamachonkStolenGroom3¾MrSimonToYou1	Good effort	9
Claimed from Jones Jones Carol L. Trainer																												
26May06Tdn8	6f	sy	:222	:464	:592	1:124	3↑	104	Clm2500n16m c	108	86	81/	81	-1	-6	71	4	5	42	4¼	2¼	2¾	Spieth S122	L	1.70	YoonG2¾MrSmonTY2¾MikedRiv6¾	4 wide; second best	8
07May06Tdn5	6f	ft	:224	:46	:58	1:104	3↑	108	Clm5000	107	80	76/	76	-8	-10	63	7	7	5¾	55	5¾	513	MagrellJM118	L	14.70	TruthEndures6Conte Amour2¼Fair Enough1¼	No threat	8
23Apr06Tdn11	5½	ft	:232	:472	:594	1:061	3↑	105	Clm5000n13m	106	84	80/	79	-7	-7	72	6	2	2hd	31	3¾	4¾	HanniganL122	L	3.00	MogaHinoDurngo2¾CalsGmbol1¼	Lacked late response	12
17Feb06Tam5	7f	ft	:224	:462	1:114	1:244	4↑	106	Clm6250	105	85	82/	48	-5	-8	52	2	5	3½	31	7¾	918¼	HoughtonTD118	L	8.30	RightHandMn3¾QuickAmscn4¾WrongMonrch1¼	Stopped	9
14Dec05Tdn10	6f	ft	:214	:451	:582	1:12	3↑	107	Clm3500n3Y	109	93	97/	71	+4	+7	76	9	1	31	1hd	11	12½	MartinezLJ120	L	3.00	MrSmonTY2¾DecorinkSplndidWstr1	Perfect trip; driving	9

07May Tdn 4f ft :492 B 9/20 30Apr Tdn 3f ft :382 B 10/15 05Oct'06 Tdn 4f ft :492 B 3/11 30Sep'06 Tdn 4f gd :493 B 2/11 22Mar'06 Otc 5f ft 1:052 B 2/2 24Jan'06 Cws 3f ft :40 B 1/1
02May'05 Tdn 4f gd :48 B 5/19 ●17Apr'05 Tdn 3f ft :362 B 1/16 04Aug'04 Tdn 4f ft :482 B 1/2 25Jun'04 Tdn 4f ft :52 B 6/9 02Jun'04 Tdn 3f ft :383 B 10/14 21Sep'03 TP 4f ft :493 B 6/10

Ultimate PP's w/ Quick Play Comments **River Downs** Clm 6250 5½ Furlongs 4up Friday, May 11, 2007 **Race 7 (TDN - #7)**

E1 E2/LATE SPD
91 92/ 79 79

3 Private Herb (E/P 3)

Own: Joe C. Faulkner
8/1 Lime green, white f, white lightening bolt
SKERRETT JEFFREY (79 18-3-11 23%)

$6,250 Dkbbr. g. 4 KEESEP 2004 $2k
Sire: Lucky Lionel (Mt. Livermore)
Dam: Private Eyes (Private Terms)
Brdr: Adena Springs (FL)
Trnr: Faulkner Joe C. (26 8-0-3 10%)

Power Rating: 108.5 (4th) L 120

Life:	15 4 - 3 - 0	$18,358	76	Fst	12 2 - 2 - 0	$16,238	75
2007	4 3 - 1 - 0	$13,780	75	Off	3 2 - 1 - 0	$8,120	73
2006	6 0 - 2 - 0	$2,168	70	Dis	7 2 - 3 - 0	$10,516	75
Tdn	1 1 - 0 - 0	$4,620	73	Trf	0 0 - 0 - 0	$0	
				AW	4 1 - 0 - 0	$4,572	66

2007	71	23%	42%	-0.26	2007	26	19%	38%	+4.09
JKYw/EP types	189	16%	44%	-0.79	+Wnr last race	211	24%	49%	+0.46
JKYw/ Trn L60	15	13%	33%	-1.31	No class chg	717	18%	42%	+0.30
+JKYw/ Sprints	54	22%	41%	-0.06	+Claiming	1036	19%	43%	+0.27

Sire Stats: AWD 6.2f 15%Mud 325MudSts 1.02spi
Dam'sSire: AWD 7.3f 14%Mud 1128MudSts 1.32spi

★ Hot Jockey in last 7 days (20 5-3-3) ★ Switches to a high% Jockey ★ High % Trainer
★ Won last race (TDN 04/26 5f Dirt sloppy Clm 6250NW4L)

DATE TRK	DIST						RR RACETYPE	CR	E1	E2/	LP	1c	2c	SPD	PP	ST	1C	2C	Str	FIN	JOCKEY		ODDS	Top Finishers	Comment	
26Apr07Tdn10	5f sy	:22 1	:46 2		:59 1	4↑	104 Clm6250n4L	108		99/	75			73	1	3	1hd	1hd	1hd	1 1½	MartinezJrLJ 120	L	*1.70	PrvtHrb 1½Thuntml 3¼AmITheYt hd	Dueled, clear; driving	6
30Mar07Beu4	6f ft	:22 2	:46 2	:59	1:11 3	3↑	105 Clm5000n4L	109	83	85/	79	+2	+1	73	4	6	6 4½	3 2	2 2	1no	Paucar E 120	L	*1.00	PrvteHrb no PrincOfLov 6½Frnkincns½	Up in final strides	7
05Mar07Beu2	5½ ft	:22 2	:46 2		1:04 1	3↑	104 Clm7500B.5n3L	108	74	79/	83	-2	4	75	2	4	4 7½	3 4	2 2	2hd	Paucar E 118	L	2.00	Cabrer hd PrvteHrb 4Sprt4OfPryr½	Steadied start;rallied	6
Previously trained by ROUCK MARTIN L.																										
12Jan07Beu2	5f gd	:22 4	:47 2		1:00	3↑	101 Clm3500n2L	105		94/	74			70	4	6	5 3½	4 2½	1hd	1 1½	AndersonM 120	L	*1.90	PrvteHrb 1½KingCrt 2½Lilbtolvly 2	Stalked pace; driving	11
31Dec06TP4	⊛ 1m ft	:23 2	:46 4	1:12	1:38 1	3↑	104 Clm5000n2L	104	59	52/	76	+4	+4	64	5	10 10	12 11	11 7½	6 8	5 8½	QuinonezA 112	L	7.20	TwoToMuch 1BeauCreek 2CalmipHill 2½	Lacked solid bid	12
09Dec06TP7	⊛ 6½ ft	:22 3	:45 3	1:11 3	1:18 3	3↑	102 Clm5000n2L	102	77	68/	74	-2	+2	58	12	7	7 3½	9 8½	7 6½	6 5½	Taylor P 118	L	2.60	GrdenDncr no Brnwodb 2½StrSoldr½	Evenly; no late bid	12
28Nov06Beu4	5½ ft	:22 2	:46	:58	1:04 4	3↑	103 Clm7500B.5n2L	105	85	86/	73	0	+4	70	5	2	2 2	3 2	3 2	2hd	AndersonM 118	L	2.80	SumrGlch hd PrvtHrb 1½FmsArtst 2	Finished well; gaining	8
05Nov06CD4	1m ft	:23 1	:46 2	1:11 1	1:37 1	3↑	107 Clm15000/10n2L	101	58	53/	52	-3	+2	43	7	8 5	9 9½	10 14	11 24	11 29½	Toups R 111	L	54.40	FirstComand¾WinchesterBy¾Lord Loyal 1½	Done early	11
17Oct06Beu8	5½ sy	:22 8	:47 1	1:00	1:07	3↑	103 Clm7500B.5n2L	109	86	77/	73	-1	-1	63	6	2	3½	3 1½	3 3	2¾	AndersonM 119	L	3.80	Seny¾PrvteHerb 1½ChristinsHop 6½	3 wide; came again	6
01Oct06TP4	⊛ 6f ft	:22 1	:45 3	:58 1	1:10 4	3↑	103 Clm5000n2L	103	79	75/	74	-1	-4	61	2	8	4 4½	4 4	5 4½	6 6½	Taylor P 118	L	16.10	Brockaddie hd Seney¾Colonel Mall 3	3 wide mid turn	11

28Feb Beu 3f ft :39 3 B 4/4 23Dec'06 Cdl 4f my :49 B 5/26 ●25Sep'06 Cdl 4f ft :47 2 B 1/11 08Sep'06 Cdl 4f ft :48 3 B 5/14 12Apr'06 Cdl 5f ft 1:02 4 Bg 4/4 05Apr'06 Cdl 4f ft :49 2 B 2/5
30Mar'06 Cdl 4f ft :50 1 B 4/11 15Mar'06 Cdl 4f ft :50 1 B 6/9 09Mar'06 Cdl 4f ft :50 1 B 3/6 03Mar'06 Cdl 4f ft :51 4 B 10/11 07Jan'06 Cdl 4f ft :50 3 B 8/20 04Dec'05 Cdl 4f gd :50 2 B 13/24

4 Valid Victory (E/P 7)

Own: Randy Joe Faulkner
9/2 Blue, white 'S', blue 'S' on white sleeves
MARTINEZ, JR. LUIS J. (44 7-7-7 16%)

$6,250 Dkbbr. g. 4
Sire: Valid Expectations (Valid Appeal)
Dam: Copiedell (Tejano)
Brdr: C. R. Trout (TX)
Trnr: Faulkner Randy Joe (29 5-2-6 17%)

Power Rating: 113.9 (1st) L 120

Life:	22 6 - 1 - 2	$44,385	85	Fst	17 4 - 1 - 2	$30,690	86
2007	6 2 - 0 - 1	$14,898	85	Off	5 2 - 0 - 0	$12,998	85
2006	12 3 - 1 - 0	$19,255	85	Dis	9 4 - 0 - 1	$25,115	86
Tdn	2 1 - 0 - 0	$8,090	85	Trf	2 0 - 0 - 0	$405	72
				AW	0 0 - 0 - 0	$0	

2007	111	12%	40%	0.88	+2007	53	11%	32%	-0.18
+JKYw/EP types	250	18%	41%	+0.36	+Btn favorite	33	27%	64%	-0.01
JKYw/ Trn L60	18	17%	39%	+1.00	+Claiming	312	21%	45%	+0.47
JKYw/ Sprints	79	10%	39%	-1.05					

Sire Stats: AWD 6.1f 15%Mud 527MudSts 1.27spi
Dam'sSire: AWD 7.1f 14%Mud 688MudSts 1.26spi

★ Hot Trn/Jky combo in last 14 days (10 2-0-2) ★ Drops in Class today

DATE TRK	DIST						RR RACETYPE	CR	E1	E2/	LP	1c	2c	SPD	PP	ST	1C	2C	Str	FIN	JOCKEY		ODDS	Top Finishers	Comment	
26Apr07Tdn12	5½ sy	:22 2	:46 1	:59	1:05 2	4↑	107 Alw11400n1x	107	91	89/	69	0	+1	70	5	2	2hd	2½	3 3	4 6½	SanguinettiA 122	L	*0.80	CptolPnch hd LouFlmngo 3½WhStrWh 2	Dueled, faltered	6
12Apr07Tdn4	5½ sy	:22 4	:46 4	:59 3	1:05 1	4↑	109 OC35k/N1900X	112	82	94/	85	0	-3	85	2	5	2½	1½	1 1	1 1½	SanguinettiA 118	L	15.10	VldVictory 1½Cruzble 2½WinForJoeGls hd	Rail, ridden out	6
22Mar07Hou4	5½ ft	:22 2	:45 4		1:05	4↑	107 Clm5000	107	86	83/	76	-4	-4	69	2	5	2hd	2½	3 1	5 3½	RodriguzFT 118	L	2.40	Blyldt¾BetStYet 1½StalwrtsHeir 1½	Pressed,dueled,tired	7
09Mar07Hou6	5½ ft	:22	:45		1:04 4	4↑	108 Clm15000	108	85	79/	51	0	+3	56	5	3	5 3	5 4½	6 10	6 12½	RodriguzFT 118	L	3.80	RoboSeat 3½FortBragg 4Hard ItRich 2	Heels clipped start	7
24Feb07Hou4	6f ft	:22 1	:46	:58 2	1:11 4	4↑	107 ⓢA15500n1x	108	84	81/	83	-4	-7	73	8	2	3 1½	2 1	2 1½	3 1½	RodriguzFT 116	L	*1.70	OpnPlsur 1ChrlEdw¾VldVtry¾	Chased, 3w, bid; empty	9
Claimed from Moss Aamussen Steven M. Trainer																										
26Jan07Hou8	5½ gd	:22 1	:45 4		1:04 4	4↑	105 ⓢC5000-c	110	83	86/	85	-2	-4	79	6	3	4 2½	3 2	1 1	1 4	FigueroaJ 118	L	*0.70	VldVictory 4Grugly½Faxamilion nk	Chased, 2w, driving	10
Claimed from Tbd Owners Llc Locke John G. Trainer																										
15Dec06Hou4	6f ft	:22	:45 1	:57 4	1:11 1	3↑	106 ⓢC5000-c	110	88	89/	82	-1	-3	79	7	4	3½	1hd	1 2	1 1½	RodriguzFT 119	L	*2.90	VldVctry 1½Cnons.&r nk CrCmnds½	Duel,drew off, driving	11
Claimed from Moss Blasi Scott Trainer																										
01Dec06Hou4	5½ ft	:22 3	:46 1		1:05	3↑	106 ⓢC7500n3L-c	109	81	80/	86	-7	-8	74	1	6	4 1½	4 1½	1hd	1 2½	Jacinto J 117	L	*0.50	VldVctry 2½StAlcm 1PlymtsTuel 1	Stalk, inside;drew off	6
18Nov06RP4	5½ ft	:22	:45 1	:57 1	1:03 2	3↑	107 Clm15000n3L	107	82	84/	77	-6	-4	77	9	4	6 3½	7 3½	5 4	5 6	ShepherdJ 119	L	4.30	CarnivalShow 4½SulphurWater hd Lip Gloss nk	No menace	9
Previously trained by MORSE RANDY L.																										
03Nov06RP9	ⓣ 5f fm	:21 4	:44 2		:56 3	3↑	107 Clm25000n3L	108		83/	77			72	3	6	7 5	6 7	6 8	5 10½	ShepherdJ 119	L	9.10	Bubba Fly 6½AgentHanrahy 2Carnival Show hd	No factor	9

21Jan Hou 4f sy :53 2 B 13/21 21Oct'06 RP 3f ft :35 1 H 2/11 06Aug'06 RP 5f ft 1:00 4 H 4/13 ●30Jly'06 RP 5f ft :58 4 H 1/12 15Jly'06 LS 5f ft 1:01 4 B 5/18 23Jun'06 LS 5f ft 1:01 3 H 5/20
16Jun'06 LS 5f ft 1:01 B 3/27 08May'06 LS 5f ft 1:01 3 H 5/20 30Apr'06 LS 5f ft 1:01 3 H 8/37 08Apr'06 LS 4f ft :48 3 B 9/27 01Apr'06 LS 5f ft 1:03 2 B 11/14 22Mar'06 LS 5f ft 1:04 B 1/1

5 Captain Binge (E/P 7)

Own: Burnt Clover Farm
8/1 White, green 'burnt clover farm'
URIETA-MORAN VICTOR (83 8-6-8 13%)

$6,250 Dkbbr. g. 8 KEESEP 2002 $30k
Sire: Artax (Marquetry)
Dam: Cigar Charlie (Tour D'or)
Brdr: Ernie Wells (KY)
Trnr: Marino James G. (11 1-2-1 9%)

Power Rating: 108.0 (7th) L 118

Life:	39 8 - 4 - 3	$52,710	80	Fst	28 4 - 2 - 3	$30,196	80
2007	1 1 - 0 - 0	$4,034	69	Off	11 4 - 2 - 0	$22,514	77
2006	13 4 - 2 - 0	$19,882	80	Dis	16 3 - 0 - 1	$14,098	77
Tdn	28 8 - 2 - 3	$41,009	80	Trf	0 0 - 0 - 0	$0	
				AW	0 0 - 0 - 0	$0	

2007	72	14%	44%	-1.23	2007	11	9%	36%	-1.49
JKYw/EP types	112	15%	42%	-0.26	+Up one class	8	25%	25%	+1.50
JKYw/ Trn L60	7	14%	57%	-1.20	Wnr last race	20	5%	20%	-1.20
JKYw/ Sprints	60	13%	43%	-1.36	Claiming	182	10%	29%	-0.76

Sire Stats: AWD 6.3f 16%Mud 293MudSts 1.14spi
Dam'sSire: AWD 6.8f 15%Mud 1103MudSts 1.10spi

★ Won last race (TDN 04/15 5f Dirt good Clm4000NW13M) ● Moves up in class from last start ● Poor 'Wnr last race' trainer record, 5%wins 20sts

DATE TRK	DIST						RR RACETYPE	CR	E1	E2/	LP	1c	2c	SPD	PP	ST	1C	2C	Str	FIN	JOCKEY		ODDS	Top Finishers	Comment	
15Apr07Tdn7	5f gd	:22 3	:46 2		:59 4	4↑	106 Clm4000n13m	108		84/	74			69	4	4	3 1½	1½	1 1	1 1½	Urieta-moranV 122	Lb	*1.80	CptnBing 1½RdmptnSng 1CmpChin 1½	Prevailed; driving	9
30Mar07Mnr8	6f ft	:22 4	:47 2	1:00	1:12 2	3↑	109 Clm5000	107	91	86/	65	-4	-12	62	7	3	1hd	3 1	5 7	7 17½	Marcial A 116	Lb	33.30	WtchAdWgr¾Bllybck 6½FrstWhty 2	Pressed pace; tired	8
22Jan07Mnr6	5½ gd	:23	:47 4	1:01 1	1:08 1	3↑	108 Clm5000	108	90	86/	57	+1	+1	58	8	1	2 1	3 1	6 3½	7 11½	Marcial A 118	Lb	22.20	FvrtPsn 3½LrlbNMrl¾WtAWgr 1½	Loomed to lane; spent	9
27Nov06Tdn1	6f ft	:22 2	:46 2	:59	1:12	3↑	108 Clm3500	113	89	88/	85	-1	-4	80	5	1	2 1	1hd	1 1½	1 3½	FelicianoR 116	Lb	5.10	CptnBinge 3½OrShdow 2MtchngColrs hd	Brisk hand ride	10
13Nov06Tdn8	6f gd	:22 3	:46 3	1:00	1:13 2	3↑	108 Clm3500	108	81	82/	78	-1	+1	70	10	8	7 4½	6 3½	7 2½	6 1½	FelicianoR 117	Lb	4.40	LrdthMryl nk TmCntr hd MchgCkhd	Between horses, late	12
16Oct06Tdn1	6f ft	:22 2	:46 1	:59	1:12 2	3↑	107 Clm3500	107	85	84/	78	-1	0	71	1	4	4 2	5 2½	4 3	4 2½	FelicianoR 120	Lb	*1.10	HrvestMondnc nk JohnsJo 1GnWld 1	Mild bid; no threat	6
30Sep06Tdn3	6f gd	:22 4	:46 2	:59 3	1:12 4	3↑	107 Clm3500n36m	111	86	89/	80	-3	-2	77	5	1	2 1	1hd	1 1	1½	FelicianoR 119	Lb	6.20	CptnBg¾StrvskyHr 4HyiyMthMUp 2½	Prevailed; driving	8
03Sep06Tdn7	5f sy	:22 4	:47 1		:59 3	3↑	105 Clm3500n29m	108		84/	84			77	7	3	4 1½	2 1	2 1	1½	FelicianoR 116	Lb	1.70	CptnBing¾ZelousCpo 6½PulOverPls 1	3 wide; up late	7
20Aug06Tdn10	6f gd	:22 3	:46 3	:59 3	1:13	3↑	106 Clm3500n25m	108	87	83/	73	-2	-2	66	10	2	1hd	1hd	2 2	2 1½	FelicianoR 116	Lb	*1.50	Jubalani 1½CptnBinge 1RJsGame 1½	Dueled; held place	10
07Aug06Tdn5	5f ft	:22 2	:46 1	:58 4	1:11 4	3↑	108 Clm3500n29m	109	87	84/	86	-7	-5	78	1	5	2 1	2 1½	2 2½	2¾	FelicianoR 116	Lb	5.70	HyiyMthMUp¾CptnBing 2½GmblngT 1½	Rallied, gaining	9

01May Tdn 3f ft :38 2 B 3/5 ●11Mar Mnr 3f gd :37 H 1/10 23Feb Mnr 4f ft :53 1 B 8/10 18Jan Mnr 3f ft :36 1 H 2/13 28Apr'06 Tdn 5f ft 1:04 B 9/11 18Apr'06 Tdn 4f ft :50 1 B 4/12
09Apr'06 Tdn 3f ft :35 2 B 2/23 02Apr'06 Tdn 3f ft :38 2 B 3/9 02May'05 Tdn 4f gd :50 B 10/18 16Apr'05 Tdn 4f ft :49 4 B 6/25 ●07Apr'05 Tdn 3f ft :35 4 B 1/26 14Sep'04 Mth 3f ft :37 4 B 7/11

tsnhorse.com

Ultimate PP's w/ Quick Play Comments **River Downs** Clm 6250 5½ Furlongs 4up Friday, May 11, 2007 **Race 7 (TDN - #7)** E1 91 E2/LATE 92/79 SPD 79

6 Bar Time (E/P 5)

4/1 Own. Crestview Racing Stable, Inc. Fluorescent orange
SPIETH SCOTT (64 11-10-7 17%)

$6,250 B. g. 4
Sire: Snowdon Heart (Two Punch)
Dam: Livid Lass (Blue Ensign)
Brdr: Perry Bayley (OH)
Trnr: Radosevich Jeffrey A. (52 16-12-6 29%)

Power Rating: 110.8 (3rd) L 118

Life:	18 4 2 5	$44,560	86	Fst	14 3 2 4	$36,755	86
2007	1 0 0 1	$920	75	Off	4 1 0 1	$7,827	73
2006	13 3 2 3	$34,710	86	Dis	3 0 1 1	$2,615	75
Tdn	16 4 1 5	$41,706	79	Trf	0 0 0 0	$0	
				AW	0 0 0 0	$0	

+2007	270	16%	43%	-0.87	+2007	168	20%	52%	-0.32
+JKYw/EP types	421	22%	53%	-0.33	+Claiming	1654	22%	51%	-0.28
JKYw/ Trn L60	89	17%	48%	-0.83					
JKYw/ Sprints	196	17%	45%	-0.58					

Sire Stats: AWD 6.5f 17%Mud 18MudSts 0.60spi
Dam'sSire:AWD 7.1f 15%Mud 1352MudSts 0.98spi

★ Hot Trn/Jky combo in last 14 days (18 5-4-2) ★ High % Trainer
★ Ran 3rd vs similar in last race ★ Eligible to improve in 2nd start since layoff

DATE TRK	DIST		RR	RACETYPE	CR	E1	E2/	LP	1c	2c	SPD	PP	ST	1C	2C	Str	FIN	JOCKEY	ODDS	Top Finishers	Comment	
22Apr07Tdn 12	5f ft	:22 :46 :58 3 1:05 3 4	108	Ⓢ C6250	109		86/	78			75	6	2	5 2	3 2½	2½	3 1½	Spieth S 118	L 2.40	Premier Cool 1½Cudekonk½Bar Time 1½	Saved ground	7
05Dec06Beu 8	6f ft	:22 1 :46 2 :59 1:11 4 3↑	109	Ⓢ OC16k/N4L	105	96	90/	50	+5	+5	53	2	2	2½	5 3½	5 9	5 10½	SkerrettJ 119	L 3.60	Dare HeGoes nk BlazingElement 3 Floater 10	Dropped back	5
18Nov06Tdn 12	6f gd	:22 3 :46 3 :59 2 1:12 2 3↑	108	Ⓢ C10000	109	87	85/	75	-1	-4	70	6	3	3½	3½	2hd	3 5	Spieth S 116	L *1.00	FirstEndvr 3 SnurDSol 2 BrTime 2½	Dueled; outfinished	7
29Oct06Tdn 6	6f gd	:23 :47 :58 4 1:12 3 3↑	109	Ⓢ N18000 15k	109	80	82/	82	-5	-8	73	7	3	4 4	4 2½	4 2	5 5½	Spieth S 121	L 3.00	RckStRnh 3 PgysFvrt 3 AlsNAb 1½	Wide; lacked late resp	7
24Sep06Tdn 3	6f ft	:23 2 :47 4 1:00 2 1:13 1 3↑	107	Ⓢ A15600n2x	110	83	76/	96	-7	-13	75	6	1	1½	1½	1 2	1 2½	Spieth S 117	L *0.70	BrTime 2½ RhodesiedJohnn 3 Onkn½	Nicely rated; driving	7
09Sep06Tdn 5	6f ft	:22 4 :46 3 :59 2 1:12 2 3↑	106	Alw11300n1x	111	85	87/	85	4	5	79	3	1	2 1	1 1	1 1½	1 3½	Spieth S 116	L 2.10	Bar Time 3½ Frolic Over 1½ TwiceBid 5	Drew clear; driving	6

Claimed from Inirio Olivo L. Inirio Olivo L Trainer

DATE TRK	DIST		RR	RACETYPE	CR	E1	E2/	LP	1c	2c	SPD	PP	ST	1C	2C	Str	FIN	JOCKEY	ODDS	Top Finishers	Comment	
13Aug06Tdn 6	6f ft	:22 2 :46 1 :59 2 1:12 4 3↑	104	Ⓢ C10000n3L-c	105	90	87/	64	+1	0	62	4	2	2hd	3hd	3½	4 8½	Ortiz A 111	L *0.50	SplPln 1 AlsNAbs 1 SrOfWg 3	Between horses; faded	7
01Aug06Mnr 9	6f ft	:22 2 :45 3 :58 2 1:11 4 3↑	107	Clm10000n3L	112	89	98/	81	-3	+1	86	9	2	2 1	1½	1 1	2 2	Ortiz A 108	L 5.60	LgdGlry 2 BrTim 5 BigDdyCly 7½	Led;Spath;clear 1/8;gam	10
14Jly06Tdn 6	6f ft	:22 1 :45 4 :59 1:12 3 3↑	105	Ⓢ A16200n3L	107	99	89/	71	+2	+4	70	3	2	2 1½	2 2	2 3	5 2½	Ortiz A 111	L 10.40	MetThMstr ... OnAprch 1	Stalked pace, evenly	8
19Jun06Tdn 6	6f gd	:23 :47 2 1:00 1 1:13 2 3↑	103	Clm10000n2L	108	85	79/	82	-3	-8	71	7	1	2hd	1 2½	1 4½	1 7	Ortiz A 119	L 3.20	Bar Time 7 Kadin's Cat 1½ Victory Vision 1	Ridden out	7

●31Mar Tdn 4f ft :48 1 B 1/27 14Apr06 Tdn 4f ft :49 3 Bg 4/27 08Apr06 Tdn 4f ft :51 2 B 28/35 12Nov05 Tdn 5f ft 1:04 1 B 7/8 26Oct05 Tdn 3f my :38 4 B 4/6 13Oct05 Tdn 5f ft 1:02 1 B 2/5
01Oct05 Tdn 6f ft 1:17 4 B 4/4 22Sep05 Tdn 4f ft :49 1 Bg 2/17 08Aug05 Tdn 3f ft :42 4 B 26/26 23Jly05 Tdn 3f ft :37 2 B 2/11

7 Time Counter (E/P 7)

6/1 Own: Bart Barnes And Judy Meyers Dark green, yellow and white hoops
MEYERS TOMMY (17 3-2-4 18%)

$6,250 B. g. 6 FTKDEC 2001 $1k
Sire: Count The Time (Regal Search)
Dam: British Code (Lost Code)
Brdr: Castle Rock Stud, Inc. & Robert Bestfeld& Michael Meyers (NY)
Trnr: Barnes Bart A. (9 3-0-1 33%)

Power Rating: 108.3 (6th) L 118

Life:	43 7 8 3	$69,347	88	Fst	26 2 5 1	$26,980	80
2007	1 1 0 0	$3,840	77	Off	17 5 1 2	$42,367	88
2006	14 3 3 1	$20,306	87	Dis	11 2 1 2	$17,208	86
Tdn	17 4 4 0	$25,309	77	Trf	0 0 0 0	$0	
				AW	0 0 0 0	$0	

2007	30	13%	47%	-0.53	+2007	28	21%	50%	+0.39
+JKYw/EP types	61	20%	54%	-0.04	Up one class	26	8%	42%	-1.25
+JKYw/ Trn L60	10	30%	30%	+1.66	Win last race	41	15%	54%	0.08
+JKYw/ Sprints	21	19%	38%	+0.10	Claiming	197	16%	48%	+0.07

Sire Stats: AWD 6.8f 14%Mud 437MudSts 0.99spi
Dam'sSire:AWD 6.9f 15%Mud 1528MudSts 1.37spi

★ Hot Trainer in last 14 days (7 3-0-1) ★ Hot Trn/Jky combo in last 14 days (5 3-0-0)
★ Highest Last Race Speed Rating ★ Won last race (TDN 04/28 5.5f Dirt good Clm4000N2M)
● Moves up in class from last start ● Poor 'Up one class' trainer record: 8% wins 26sts
● May regress (bounce) after big effort following layoff

DATE TRK	DIST		RR	RACETYPE	CR	E1	E2/	LP	1c	2c	SPD	PP	ST	1C	2C	Str	FIN	JOCKEY	ODDS	Top Finishers	Comment	
28Apr07Tdn 8	5½ gd	:23 :47 1 :59 4 1:06 2 4↑	107	Clm4000n2m	108	88	87/	84	-3	-4	77	4	2	2hd	1hd	1 1	1 1½	Meyers T 118	Lbl 3.80	TimCountr 1½ FrEnough 2 Peaymont nk	Confidently handled	7
27Nov06Tdn 1	6f ft	:22 2 :46 2 :59 1:12 3↑	108	Clm3500	110	87	84/	78	-1	-4	71	6	2	3 2	3 2	3 2½	4 3½	Meyers T 117	Lbl 3.60	CptnBng 2 OrShd 2 MtchgCts hd	Good position, evenly	10
13Nov06Tdn 8	6f gd	:22 3 :46 3 1:00 1:13 2 3↑	108	Clm3500	110	89	88/	74	-1	+1	72	7	3	3hd	1 1	1 1½	2nk	Meyers T 120	Lbl 6.40	LordoNMrynk TmCont hd MchgCts hd	Clear lead; caught Dead heat	12
27Oct06Tdn 8	6f sy	:22 1 :45 4 :59 1 1:13 1 3↑	107	Clm3500n39m	110	90	94/	72	+4	+9	74	8	3	4 1½	4½	2½	1 1½	Meyers T 117	Lbl 3.80	TmContr 1½ HyNRhMUp ½ AncntRk 2½	4 wide; clear late	9
02Oct06Tdn 1	6f ft	:22 3 :46 4 :59 4 1:12 4 3↑	105	Clm3500n26m	107	82	78/	79	-3	-5	68	6	2	5 2	4 1½	1hd	2 1½	Meyers T 117	Lbl 2.90	CheckStion 1½ TimeCountr 1½ GmblngGold 2½	Held place	9
15Sep06Tdn 8	1 70 ft	:23 3 :48 1 1:14 2 1:46 1 3↑	108	Clm3500n39m	105	78	73/	46	-1	-2	54	5	1½	1½	2 1	7 7	8 19	Meyers T 117	Lbl 5.10	MikeThTgr 3 StdSom ½ ProdOfPymo	Drifted out, stretch	10
31Aug06Tdn 1	1 70 ft	:23 2 :48 1:14 2 1:46 3 3↑	107	Clm3500n39m	110	77	73/	76	-2	0	73	2	1 1	1½	1 1	1 1	2no	FelicianoR 116	Lbl 2.30	RahyPyro no TimCountr 2 WrChal½	Nicely rated; missed	7
06Aug06Tdn 1	6f ft	:22 3 :46	:58 4 1:12 3↑	107	Clm3500n39m	107	87	87/	66	3	2	64	4	1	2½	2 1	2 5	4 8	Meyers T 116	Lbl 8.90	HetSein 7 LgntTgr nk StrmskysHm hd	Lacked late response	8
17Jly06Tdn 6	6f ft	:22 4 :47 :59 4 1:12 2 3↑	105	Clm3500n3y+	109	83	78/	85	-5	-7	72	7	2	2 1	2 1	2 1	1½	Meyers T 117	Lbl 12.50	TmContr ½ MuscIVson 4 ToIBndt 1½	Stalked pace; driving	9
19Jun06Tdn 6	6f gd	:22 3 :47 1:00 1 1:13 3↑	109	Clm3500n3y+	102	89	80/	62	-1	-6	55	3	7	2hd	4 1½	8 9½	8 12½	Meyers T 117	Lb 5.80	RiOutHh ½ CtchBts 2 ½ MtchgCt ½	Between horses, tired	9

21Apr Tdn 4f ft :52 2 B 17/20 14Apr Tdn 4f ft :53 2 B 17/17 06Apr Tdn 4f ft :53 2 B 10/11 ●29Mar Tdn 3f ft :36 B 1/13 17Jun06 Tdn 3f ft :38 3 B 7/11 29Aug05 Tdn 4f ft :50 3 B 10/20
17Aug05 Tdn 4f ft :50 B 4/4 10Aug05 Tdn 4f ft :50 2 B 5/8 01Jun05 Tdn 4f ft :51 2 B 7/10 23May05 Tdn 4f ft :53 1 B 23/23 30Apr05 Tdn 5f gd 1:05 4 B 1/1 20Apr05 Tdn 3f ft :37 4 B 5/9

8 Little Nicky Regs (E/P 4)

7/2 Own: Frank J. Regalbuto White, green tagge
MUNAYLLA FILMER (44 3-0-7 7%)

$6,250 B. g. 8
Sire: Carson City (Mr. Prospector)
Dam: Sister Explodent (Explodent)
Brdr: Frank Regalbuto (KY)
Trnr: Madrigal, Sr. Rodrigo (19 1-5-4 5%)

Power Rating: 112.3 (2nd) L 118

Life:	26 9 5 4	$133,340	101	Fst	18 7 5 3	$101,009	101
2007	1 0 0 1	$800	68	Off	7 2 0 1	$32,331	86
2006	10 4 1 2	$26,752	84	Dis	6 2 2 2	$40,761	101
Tdn	10 5 1 2	$28,820	85	Trf	1 0 0 0	$0	69
				AW	0 0 0 0	$0	

2007	45	7%	42%	+2.15	+2007	19	5%	53%	-0.88
+JKYw/EP types	159	18%	49%	+0.50	No class chg	212	17%	46%	-0.20
JKYw/ Trn L60	12	8%	58%	-0.23	Claiming	358	17%	48%	-0.01
JKYw/ Sprints	39	5%	44%	-0.26					

Sire Stats: AWD 8.4f 21%Mud 1329MudSts 2.19spi
Dam'sSire:AWD 7.1f 13%Mud 1340MudSts 2.21spi

★ Highest Speed Figure at Today's Distance ★ Best Dirt Speed is fastest among today's starters
★ Ran 3rd vs similar in last race ★ Eligible to improve in 2nd start since layoff
● Poor Speed Figure in only recent start ● Poor Jockey win% ● Poor Trainer win%

DATE TRK	DIST		RR	RACETYPE	CR	E1	E2/	LP	1c	2c	SPD	PP	ST	1C	2C	Str	FIN	JOCKEY	ODDS	Top Finishers	Comment	
28Apr07Tdn 2	4f gd	:22 2 :45 4 4↑	107	Clm7500	107		78/	86			68	3	6	6 8		5 8½	3 6	Munaylla F 120	Lbl 2.00	ClikSpKd 1½ AthrEtsy 4½ LilNkyRg 2	Slow early, mild rally	6
02Oct06Mnr 6	5½ ft	:21 3 :44 3 :57 2 1:04 1 3↑	110	Alw5000s	111	87	92/	71	+2	+6	79	9	2	2 4	2 4	2 8	3 2½	MunayllaF 118	Lbl 6.50	OhOfTDy 1 JmpFrJys 1½ LilNkyRg 1½	Hustled chase; hung	9
15Sep06Tdn 2	6f ft	:22 2 :45 4 :58 3 1:12 1 3↑	111	Alw3500s	114	93	96/	79	0	+2	83	7	1	2hd	1 2	1 2½	1 2½	MunayllaF 116	Lbl 5.10	LilNickyRgs 2½ StryCtBlues 1½ WolyBly ½	3 wide; driving	7
26Aug06Tdn 12	6f ft	:22 2 :45 4 :58 2 1:11 2 3↑	110	Alw3500s	108	81	77/	83	2	-1	70	4	8	7 5½	7 8½	5 8½	5 8½	GonzalezLA 119	Lbl 2.60	WolyBully ½ Stray CatBlues 6 ½ Jkort 6½	Failed to menace	8
07Aug06Tdn 3	6f ft	:22 4 :46 1 :58 4 1:11 4 3↑	110	Clm7500	111	92	85/	85	-6	-6	79	6	1	3 2	2 1	2 1	1½	MunayllaF 116	Lbl *0.60	LilNickyRgs ½ Wiretnds 1 StormCre 1½	Up in final strides	6
07Jly06Tdn 9	6f ft	:22 1 :46 :58 1 1:10 4 3↑	108	Clm5000	112	86	85/	82	-7	-10	84	2	4	1hd	1 1	1 3	1 5½	MunayllaF 116	Lbl 1.70	LilNickyRgs 5½ Hacod 2 HetSeker ½	Drew off; ridden out	7
08Jun06Tdn 2	6f ft	:22 3 :46 1 :58 4 1:11 4 3↑	107	Clm5000	109	85	84/	83	-5	-4	75	7	1	4½	3 1½	3½	3 1½	MunayllaF 118	Lbl *1.00	ARizRobn ½ SirGich 1 LilNickyRgs 4½	3 wide, bid hung	7
05May06Tdn 2	6f ft	:23 :46 3 :58 4 1:11 4 3↑	104	Clm5000n16m	109	82	84/	90	-7	-8	81	5	4	2 1½	2hd	1½	1hd	MunayllaF 122	Lbl *1.30	LilNickyRegs hd Durango 2 ½ CatsGmbo hd	Fully extended	8
14Apr06Tdn 14	5½ ft	:23 :46 4 :59 3 1:06 2 3↑	106	Clm5000n13m	109	87	89/	79	-3	0	75	10	3	1 1	1 1½	1 2	2hd	MunayllaF 122	Lbl *2.50	CniAmr hd LilNickyRg 3 ½ GblgOld ½	Clear lead just missed	11
24Mar06OP 6	6f ft	:23 :47 1 :59 4 1:12 3 4↑	106	Clm5000n13m	104	83	83/	69	8	7	63	3	1	1hd	2½	2 3½	4 8½	Burress B 113	Lbl 4.80	HColdShockUs 7 ½ FirstCoy ½ LakeCasek	Vied; weakened	9

31Mar Tdn 4f ft :49 1 B 2/37 06Feb06 OP 5f ft 1:03 B 21/36 19Jan06 OP 5f ft 1:03 3 H 9/23 08Jan06 OP 4f ft :53 3 B 41/42 02Dec05 Tdn 4f ft :49 3 B 1/2 14Nov05 Tdn 5f ft 1:04 4 B 4/5
04Nov05 Tdn 4f ft :51 2 B 13/16 10Sep05 Tlc 4f ft :51 2 B 15/26 03Sep05 Tlc 5f ft 1:02 2 B 6/27 27Aug05 Tlc 4f my :51 4 B 14/22 15Mar04 Tdn 4f ft :51 2 B 5/8 28Feb04 Tlc 4f ft :50 B 3/8

tsnhorse.com

Ultimate PP's w/ Quick Play Comments **River Downs** Clm 6250 5½ Furlongs. 4up Friday, May 11, 2007 **Race 7 (TDN - #7)**

E1	E2/LATE	SPD
91	92/ 79	79

Last 3 Years RACETYPE STATS:	# Races	FAVORITES Win%	Itm%	$2ROI	Average Field Size	Median $2 Win Payoff	% Winners < 5/1	% Winners >= 5/1 < 10/1	% Winners >= 10/1
TDN 3up CLM 4000 - 7500 Dirt 5.5f - 6f	76	46%	74%	+0.18	7.4	$6.40	76%	12%	12%

Track Bias Stats

DIRT 5.5f	* MEET Totals *		WnrAvgBL		DIRT 5.5f	* WEEK Totals *		WnrAvgBL	
# Races: 34	Speed Bias: 74%		1stCall: 1.7		# Races: 12	Speed Bias: 67%		1stCall: 1.9	
%Wire: 26%	04/12 - 05/06		2ndCall: 1.1		%Wire: 25%	05/03 - 05/06		2ndCall: 1.3	
	Early	Speed	Late	Speed		Early	Speed	Late	Speed
Runstyle:	E	E/P	P	S	Runstyle:	E	E/P	P	S
	++	+				++			
Impact Values	1.82	1.20	0.52	0.45	Impact Values	2.08	0.92	0.46	0.54
%Races Won	44%	29%	9%	18%	%Races Won	42%	25%	8%	25%
Post Bias:	RAIL	1-3	4-7	8+	Post Bias	RAIL	1-3	4-7	8+
			+			+	+		
Impact Values	0.47	0.71	1.25	0.96	Impact Values	1.49	1.24	1.11	0.39
Avg Win %	6%	9%	20%	6%	Avg Win %	17%	14%	17%	3%

Race Summary

#	HorseName	ML Odds	Med Eqp	Days Since L/R	Run Style	PTS	Avg Dist/Surf PACE-SPEED E1	E2/Late	Spd	Avg Race Rtng	Best Pace E1	E2/Late	Final Speed Sp1	Sp2	Sp3	Sp4	ACL	Rcg Spd Avg	R1	R2	R3	Mud Spd	Pedigree Stats Mud Sts	Mud % Mud	Sire AWD	Dam Sire's AWD
8	Little Nicky Regs	7/2	L	13.	+E/P	4	87	91/ 78	(80)	111	93	96/ 92	68	79.	83.	70.	109.9	77	107	110	111		1329	21	6.4	7.1
7	Time Counter	6/1	L	13.	+E/P	7	88	87/ 84	77	107	89	88/ 85	77.	71.	72.	74	107.2	73	107	108	108	74	437	14	6.8	6.9
6	Bar Time	4/1	L	19.	+E/P	5		86/ 78	75	108	96	99/ 90	75.	53.	70.	73.	107.5	66	108	109	109		18	17	6.5	7.1
2	Mr. Simon To You	8/1	L	194..	+E/P		82	80/ 85	(74)	107	87	87/ 86	72.	73.	51.	77.	106.6	65	106	110	110	71	609	13	6.6	7.1
3	Private Herb	8/1	L	15	+E/P	3	79	82/ 81	' 74'	105	85	86/ 83	73	73.	75.	70.	104.8	74	105	105	104	73	325	15	6.2	7.3
4	Valid Victory	9/2	L	15	+E/P	7	84	83/ 81	' 74'	107	88	93/ 86	70	85	69.	56.	107.5	75	107	109	107	85	527	15	6.1	7.1
5	Captain Binge	8/1	L	26..	+E/P	7	91	85/ 70	' 66'	108	91	89/ 86	69.	62.	58	80.	107.0	63	106	109	108	77	293	16	6.3	6.8
1	Final Endeavor	6/1	L	19.	+E/P	6	90	85/ 62	' 65'	109	90	91/ 86	69.	60.	79	62.	108.8	69	108	109	108	79	1779	14	6.1	6.4

Speed Last Race	Back Speed	Current Class	Average Class Last 3	Power Rating	Early Pace Last Race	Late Pace Last Race
77 Time Counter	86 Bar Time	109.4 Bar Time	110.5 Little Nicky Regs	113.9 Valid Victory	89 Valid Victory	86 Little Nicky Regs
75 Bar Time	85 Valid Victory	109.2 Time Counter	109.4 Time Counter	112.3 Little Nicky Regs	87 Time Counter	84 Time Counter
73 Private Herb	84 Little Nicky Regs	108.4 Private Herb	108.6 Valid Victory	110.8 Bar Time	79 Mr. Simon To You	84 Mr. Simon To You
72 Mr. Simon To You	80 Captain Binge	108.2 Valid Victory	108.3 Private Herb	108.5 Private Herb	NA Little Nicky Regs	78 Bar Time
70 Valid Victory	79 Final Endeavor	107.6 Captain Binge	107.9 Mr. Simon To You	108.3 Final Endeavor	NA Bar Time	75 Private Herb
69 Captain Binge	77 Time Counter	106.5 Final Endeavor	107.8 Bar Time	108.3 Time Counter	NA Private Herb	74 Captain Binge
69 Final Endeavor	77 Mr. Simon To You	NA Little Nicky Regs	107.3 Final Endeavor	108.0 Captain Binge	NA Final Endeavor	70 Final Endeavor
68 Little Nicky Regs	75 Private Herb	NA Mr. Simon To You	107.1 Captain Binge	102.1 Mr. Simon To You	NA Captain Binge	69 Valid Victory

Ultimate PP's w/ Quick Play Comments **River Downs** Clm 4000 6 Furlongs. 3up Friday, May 11, 2007 **Race 8** tsnhorse.com

#	Speed Last Race		#	Prime Power		#	Class Rating		#	Best Speed at Dist	
3	Good Humor Man	66	10	Calm Waters	103.7	2	C C Ryder	107.3	9	Elusive Indian	97
10	Calm Waters	63	3	Good Humor Man	102.8	10	Calm Waters	106.2	10	Calm Waters	93
5	Hastego	62	2	C C Ryder	101.6	6	Mighty Wind	106.2	1	Tomprado	91

8

Exacta / Trifecta / Superfecta (Ten Cent Minimum) / Pick 3 (Races 8-9-10)

	E1	E2/LATE	SPEED
PARS:	90	89/ 77	75

6 Furlongs. **Clm 4000** **Purse $5,200. SIMULCAST FROM RIVER DOWNS. FOR THREE YEAR OLDS AND UPWARD WHICH HAVE NOT WON THREE RACES IN 2006-2007 OR WHICH HAVE NEVER WON FOUR RACES. Three Year Olds, 116 lbs., Older, 124 lbs. Non-winners of a race since April 11 Allowed 2 lbs. A race since March 11 Allowed 4 lbs. Claiming Pri ce $4,000 (Ohio Registered Foals Preferred) .**

Post Time: (3:25)/ 2:25/ 1:25/12:25

Coupled : TOMPRADO - POWER FAME

1 pp 8 **Tomprado (S 0)** $4,000 B. g. 8 KEESEP 2000 $22k Power Rating: 91.1 (10th)

Own: My Way Stable — Sire: El Prado (Ire) (Sadler's Wells)

12/1 Fuchsia, blue ... — Dam: Crystal Woods (Woodman)

ENDRES JESSICA (8 1-0-0 12%) — Brdr: William A. Kelly (KY) — Trnr: Nocero Rinzy (11 0-0-3 0%)

L 120

Life:	73	9 - 8 - 6	$64,039	91	Fst	61	9 - 8 - 6	$60,650	91
2007	7	0 - 0 - 0	$1,034	67	Off	10	0 - 0 - 2	$3,381	74
2006	14	2 - 1 - 0	$7,537	78	Dis	18	3 - 3 - 4	$31,318	91
RD	4	1 - 1 - 0	$4,472	72	Trf	2	0 - 0 - 0	$0	71
					AW	1	0 - 0 - 0	$70	52

2007	173	5%	17%	-1.40	2007	138	8%	38%	-1.20
JKYw/ S types	147	4%	20%	-1.50	No class chg	621	11%	37%	-0.41
JKYw/ Trn L60	25	8%	24%	-1.34	Claiming	1143	11%	37%	-0.42
JKYw/ Sprints	132	6%	18%	1.28					

Sire Stats: AWD 7.4f 16%Mud 907MudSts 2.48spi

Dam'sSire: AWD 8.4f 12%Mud 1143MudSts 2.23spi

● Always far back in last start ● Poor Speed Figures

DATE TRK	DIST						RR RACETYPE	CR	E1	E2/	LP	1c	2c	SPD	PP	ST	1C	2C	Str	FIN	JOCKEY		ODDS	Top Finishers	Comment	
28Apr07Beu6	6f ft	:23 1	:47 3	1:00 7	1:12 2	3↑	108 Clm3500C	104	76	70/	75	-3	-4	57	3	6	6 9¾	5 7	5 10	4 11½	Endres J120	Lbf	35.90	Bi's Bad Boy3Mr. Truthful6¾Dancin Lance2	No factor	6
14Apr07RD9	6f sy5	:23	:46 1	:59 3	1:13	3↑	105 Clm4000C	103	73	73/	64	-3	-2	51	3	7	7 8¾	7 9½	6 12	4 18¾	Endres J120	Lbf	25.20	EnhncdEdtn2¾PrstonT11Hslobgod6	Passed tiring rivals	7
04Apr07Beu6	6f ft	:22 4	:47 3	:59 4	1:12 1	3↑	108 Clm3500C	104	70	71/	75	0	-4	58	1	6	6 10	6 9¼	6 7½	5 8½	Endres J120	Lbf	22.00	WintrsCom...MrTruthf?OctoberBlus3¾	No factor; inside	6
30Mar07Beu6	1m ft	:25 3	:49 2	1:14 1	1:39 1	3↑	105 Clm3500C	105	54	53/	76	-15	-5	58	5	8 9½	6 5¾	5 9	4 9	5 14¼	Endres J120	Lbf	15.10	PinnyOl...3MrTruthf7¾RdyWon?¼	Passed tiring rivals	9
20Mar07Beu4	5½ my5	:22	:44 4	:58	1:04 2	3↑	109 Clm3500C	105	76	78/	44	+4	+15	53	5	6	6 9¾	6 12	6 10	6 9	Endres J120	Lbf	23.20	MrHmingwy4MgtyWd1¾SnOfMth1¼	6 wide; lost ground	6
09Mar07Beu5	6f ft	:22 2	:46 1	:59 1	1:11 4	3↑	106 Clm3500C	106	71	73/	84	+3	+4	67	7	7	7 10	7 9¼	7 9½	4 7½	Endres J120	Lbf	29.80	R J'sGame1JadeMountain1RedneckBubba¾	Late rally	8
16Feb07Beu7	5½ ft		1:04 3	1:04 3	1:04 3	3↑	109 Clm3500C	102	69	60/	46	+2	+2	44	7	9	9 10	9 13	9 13	8 14¾	CollazoSJE120	Lbf	15.60	WhtyAlpnb2GrdsGld1¾ShesTmpt1¼	Broke in air, 4 wide	9
12Dec06Beu6	6f ft	:22 2	:46 1	:58 4	1:11 3	3↑	108 Clm4000	106	59	78/	76	+2	+7	65	7	10	10 17	10 10	10 9½	7 9½	CollazoSJE120	Lbf	39.50	CheckBouncr1¾WhzupMemn7¾Expos...	Steadied start	10
22Nov06Beu6	6f ft	:23 1	:47	:58 2	1:12 1	3↑	109 Clm3500n3Y	106	51	73/	78	3	+2	61	5	10	10 17	10 9¾	9 16	6 8	CollazoSJE124	Lbf	5.10	BlckDed2¾MgtyWldDd6UltSting¾	Passed tiring rivals	11
07Nov06Beu9	6f wf5	:22 2	:46 3	:58 2	1:12 3	3↑	109 Clm3500n3Y	108	58	62/	96	+1	0	68	2	12	11 19	9 12	6 5½	4 3	CollazoSJE124	Lbf	2.50e	Steel Rod¾Setch2Mighty Wild Dude1¾	Broke slowly	12

03Aug06 RD 3f ft :38 1 B 7/13 ●14Jun06 FE 3f ft :35 3 H 1/5 06May06 FE 4f ft :50 1 B 8/17 20Apr06 FE 3f ft :36 1 H 3/10 11Mar06 Haw 4f ft :49 H 5/57 19Feb06 Haw 3f ft :39 B 3/5
11Feb06 Haw 3f ft :39 3 B 21/21 03Feb06 Haw 3f sy :40 4 B 24/26 19Nov05 Haw 3f ft :37 4 B 11/23 28Oct05 Haw 3f ft :38 2 B 11/21 24Sep05 Haw 3f ft :37 2 B 3/20 14Sep05 AP 3f ft :36 2 B 4/14

1A pp 5 **Power Fame (E/P 5)** $4,000 B. h. 5 Power Rating: 90.8 (7th)

Own: My Way Stable — Sire: Anjiz (Nureyev)

12/1 Fuchsia, blue ... — Dam: Ponderosa Fama (Cryptoclearance)

ENDRES JESSICA (8 1-0-0 13%) — Brdr: Esece (ARG) — Trnr: Nocero Rinzy (11 0-0-3 0%)

L 122

Life:	25	3 - 4 - 3	$28,136	81	Fst	14	2 - 2 - 2	$19,536	81
2007	8	1 - 1 - 1	$4,058	76	Off	2	0 - 0 - 0	$88	56
2006	16	1 - 2 - 1	$17,348	81	Dis	5	1 - 1 - 0	$8,902	79
RD	1	0 - 0 - 0	$124	54	Trf	8	1 - 2 - 1	$8,512	80
					AW	0	0 - 0 - 0	$0	

2007	173	5%	17%	-1.40	2007	138	8%	38%	-1.20
JKYw/EP types	168	7%	27%	-1.42	1st strt w/trn	127	17%	43%	-0.07
JKYw/ Trn L60	25	8%	24%	-1.34	No class chg	621	11%	37%	-0.41
JKYw/ Sprints	132	6%	16%	-1.28	Claiming	1143	11%	37%	-0.42

Sire Stats: AWD 6.5f 11%Mud 394MudSts 0.83spi

Dam'sSire: AWD 7.5f 12%Mud 2185MudSts 1.27spi

● Others appear more likely

DATE TRK	DIST						RR RACETYPE	CR	E1	E2/	LP	1c	2c	SPD	PP	ST	1C	2C	Str	FIN	JOCKEY		ODDS	Top Finishers	Comment	
Previously trained by RANSOM PEGGIE L.																										
19Apr07RD10	5½ ft	:22 4	:46 1	:59 4	1:07	3↑	108 Clm4000	105	90	87/	56	+2	+5	54	4	2	1 1	1 1½	3 1½	6 7½	CollazoSJE120	Lb	15.80	MrPopey¾HeresLou...OnceWithAFo...½	Faltered; faded	6
30Mar07Beu1	4½ ft	:22 3	:46		:52 7	3↑	104 Clm3500n4L	105		82/	86			76	6	7	7 5		5 5½	3 4¼	Magera C124	Lb	3.40	Thestarofbe...White Devil...Power Fame...	Late rally	7
13Mar07Beu9	5f ft	:22 4	:47 1		1:00	3↑	103 Clm3500n3L	108		91/	68			67	1	2	1 1½	1 3	1 6	1 3	Magera C120	Lb	2.50	PowerFme3QuickHombr¾BoldJmyComers1¾	Driving	6
07Mar07Beu9	5½ ft	:22 2	:46 2	:58 3	1:05 3	3↑	104 Clm3500n2y↓	105	91	91/	62	+4	+8	64	7	3	3 1	3½	4 1	4 4½	CollazoSJE120	Lb	30.70	DncinLnc1MrTrthfl¾AirForbs2¾	Lugged in upper stretch	8
23Feb07Beu8	5½ gd	:22 4	:47 3	:59 4	1:05 7	3↑	104 Clm4000n16m	102	99	74/	50	+1	-3	41	7	1	1hd	1hd	6 4	7 13½	CollazoJrJE124	Lb	9.40	Humblevctor4¾CheyeneSpring¾TrueBet2	Dueled; tired	7
Previously trained by LOPEZ JOSE A.																										
03Feb07Beu8	6f ft	:22 3	:47 3	1:00 1	1:12 1	3↑	103 Clm4000n3L	99	89	77/	42	0	-8	38	6	3	1 3	1½	4 6	10 10½	CollazoJrJE120	Lb	3.70	MgicHbo6SomKndOfFrn...KingCt1¼	Set pace; faltered	10
23Jan07Beu9	5½ gd5	:22 2	:47 3	1:00 4	1:08 1	3↑	107 Clm5000n3L	100	97	90/	54	+8	+9	55	4	3	1 2	1½	2 1	9 8	CollazoJrJE120	Lb	*0.80	Ponchbrndnch¾MudCat...ClamedUp¾	Set pace; tired	10
10Jan07Beu9	6f ft	:22 2	:46 4	1:00	1:13 1	3↑	103 Clm4000n3L	104	93	91/	61	+4	+6	64	11	1	1½	1 2	1 1	2 3½	CollazoJrJE120	Lb	2.70	ToughCl3¾PowFm...ClmedUp...	Set pace; second best	12
12Dec06Mnr4	6f ft	:22 3	:47 2	1:00 4	1:15 2	3↑	103 Clm5000n3L	100	94	92/	33	+3	+3	41	4	1	2hd	2½	7 8½	7 21½	Davis JM118	Lb	*1.50	MitsuBu¾MrketApl3¾ElPrdnAct3¼	Pressed pace; wilted	8
09Oct06Mnr2	5½ ft	:21 4	:45 2	:57 4	1:04	3↑	109 Clm30000n3L	107	92	87/	66	0	-4	66	3	2	2½	2 1½	4 2½	7 11	Garcia F118	Lb	25.80	JmyJmer¾Chsbs3¾RockRdy¾	Pressed; chased; tired	9

07Dec06 Mnr 4f gd :52 2 B 4/5 17May06 Del 4f ft :47 4 Bg 2/90

Ultimate PP's w/ Quick Play Comments **River Downs** Clm 4000 6 Furlongs. 3up Friday, May 11, 2007 **Race 8** E1 E2/LATE SPD 90 89/77 75

2 PP 1 C C Ryder (E/P 5)

Own: Colleen Lawrence
4/1 White, blue and green stripes
ROSARIO, JR. HECTOR L. (3 1-0-0 33%)

$4,000 Dkbbr. g. 6
Sire: American Chance (Cure The Blues)
Dam: Rajas Secret (Storm Bird)
Brdr: John D. Gunther (KY)
Trnr: Vallance Paul (0 0-0-0 0%)

Power Rating: 101.6 (3rd) L 120

	Starts	W-P-S	Earnings	SPD		Starts	W-P-S	Earnings	SPD
Life:	16	3 - 0 - 4	$23,059	78	Fst	17	1 - 0 - 4	$20,214	78
2007	4	0 - 0 - 0	$474	77	Off	1	0 - 0 - 0	$2,845	75
2006	11	3 - 0 - 4	$19,614	78	Dis	11	1 - 0 - 3	$7,848	78
RD	4	1 - 0 - 2	$8,495	76	Trf	0	0 - 0 - 0	$0	
					AW	6	1 - 0 - 0	$5,002	78

2007	167	10%	31%	-0.74
JKYw/EP types	264	13%	36%	-0.62
JKYw/ Sprints	80	7%	25%	-1.19

Sire Stats: AWD 6.4f 15%Mud 598MudSts 1.50spi
Dam'sSire:AWD 7.7f 11%Mud 494MudSts 3.17spi

● Poor Speed Figures in last 2 starts

Previously trained by HELMBRECHT W. R

DATE TRK	DIST						RR RACETYPE	CR	E1	E2/	LP	1c	2c	SPD	PP	ST	1C	2C	Str	FIN	JOCKEY		ODDS	Top Finishers	Comment	
19Apr07RD10	5½ ft	22⁴	:46¹	:59⁴	1:07	3↑	108 Clm4000	106	86	83/	60	+2	+5	58	5	6	5²½	5⁴	5⁷	5⁸½	Felix JE120	Lb	2.30	MrPopeye½Here'sLouie¹⁰Dance WithAFool²	No factor	6
25Feb07TP4	Ⓢ 5½ ft	:22²	:46²	:58¹	1:05⁴	3↑	107 Clm5000C	106	88	77/	67	-2	-4	62	3	3	2hd	2¹	5⁶½	7⁹½	Ouzts PW120	Lb	4.80	SlapToThMusic²½Sulmn¹RstProspct¹	Between; tired	8
10Feb07TP6	Ⓢ 6f ft	:22²	:46	:58³	1:11¹	3↑	109 Clm8000	110	94	89/	80	-3	-5	77	8	3	3²½	3²½	4³	6⁸	RosrioJrHL122	Lb	21.80	GldBrck³½ThSctmnCometh¹ᵏHumblEn½	Off inside; tired	12
12Jan07TP9	Ⓢ 6f ft	:21³	:44²	:57¹	1:10¹	4↑	109 Clm16000	105	88	92/	57	+4	+8	60	2	2	2⁵	3⁸½	7¹¹	7¹⁹	RosrioJrHL120	Lbf	11.20	UnbrdldArc¹½AmbsdorJck⁶½GettnGmo	Off inside; faded	7
21Dec06TP10	Ⓢ 6f ft	:21³	:44³	:57	1:10	3↑	107 Clm7500n3L	109	92	95/	76	+4	+4	78	5	3	3¹½	2hd	1²½	1¹½	RosrioJrHL120	Lb	12.80	CCRydr¹½Ahnndr¹ᵏSlpToThMusic	3 wide; kept to task	11
08Dec06TP8	Ⓢ 6f ft	:22¹	:45⁴	:58²	1:11²	3↑	108 Clm15000n3L	106	92	92/	60	+1	+1	63	6	2	1hd	1hd	8⁶	10⁸½	RosrioJrHL122	Lb	46.90	DarrelH¹½TidyUp¹ᵏColviCowboy¹½	Shut off stretch faded	11
																								(Placed 9th through disqualification)		
24Oct06Beu7	6f ft	:22³	:47¹	1:00²	1:13¹	3↑	108 Alw8000n3L	106	91	88/	66	0	-2	65	5	2	1hd	1hd	1hd	3⁸½	RosrioJrHL124	Lb	2.60	BonsbrRd¹ᵏWhtWOz¹½KnSbBir¹½	Inside duel; held 3rd *Dead heat*	7
10Oct06Beu6	5½ ft	:22⁴	:47		1:06²	3↑	104 Alw7500n2L	110	88	92/	79	-3	+1	77	5	2	1½	1²	1⁷	1¹⁰½	RosrioJrHL122	Lb	*1.40	CCRyder¹⁰½Egsonthegnd¹½LordBcky²	Drew off; driving	6
08Sep06TP8	Ⓢ 1m ft	:23²	:47	1:13	1:39²	3↑	106 Clm15000n2L	104	93	81/	37	+12	+4	51	5	1¹½	1²½	1¹½	6⁶½	9²⁰½	RosrioJrHL120	Lb	8.20	Gorbsh¹Red Alert²½SlgoChamer¹½	Used up; stopped	11
20Aug06RD3	5½ ft	:22³	:46²	1:00	1:06⁴	3↑	102 Mdn 10k	108	95	92/	77	+4	+2	76	7	1	1hd	1hd	1³	1⁶½	RosrioJrHL124	Lb	*1.30	CCRyder⁶½ImGongWst³TimelyXprs⁴½	Drew off; driving	9

07Apr TP 4f ft :48³ B 7/22 ●31Mar TP 3f ft :36⁴ B 1/6 16Mar TP 3f ft :36² B 2/7 02Dec'06 TP 3f ft :36⁴ B 6/12 10Nov'06 TP 3f ft :38 B 4/5 22Sep'06 TP 3f ft :36² B 7/9
16Sep'06 TP 3f ft :37 B 9/20 ●11Aug'06 TP 3f ft :36⁴ B 1/4 15Jly'06 TP 4f ft :50 B 12/29 12Jun'06 TP 3f ft :37³ B 1/1 20May'06 TP 4f ft :50 B 12/23 ●09May'06 TP 3f ft :36 B 1/6

3 PP 2 Good Humor Man (P 2)

Own: Donna Brainer
3/1 Red, white 'jb'
DIEGO INOSENCIO (47 8-2-8 17%)

$4,000 Ch. g. 7 KEESEP 2001 $200k
Sire: Distorted Humor (Forty Niner)
Dam: Sweetest Gal (Honest Pleasure)
Brdr: Oisiana Farm Inc. (KY)
Trnr: Oren Jerry (10 0-1-3 0%)

Power Rating: 102.9 (2nd) L 120

	Starts	W-P-S	Earnings	SPD		Starts	W-P-S	Earnings	SPD
Life:	30	5 - 6 - 4	$81,561	82	Fst	23	4 - 5 - 3	$58,951	82
2007	5	0 - 2 - 1	$3,725	77	Off	7	1 - 1 - 1	$10,610	78
2006	10	1 - 1 - 1	$8,436	75	Dis	15	3 - 3 - 0	$23,837	78
RD	6	0 - 1 - 1	$2,026	72	Trf	0	0 - 0 - 0	$0	
					AW	5	1 - 2 - 0	$10,525	77

2007	347	11%	31%	-0.76	2007	42	2%	24%	1.55
JKYw/ P types	230	11%	32%	-0.88	No class chg	144	10%	31%	+0.09
JKYw/ Trn L60	4	0%	25%	-2.00	+Btn favorite	21	19%	38%	+0.41
JKYw/ Sprints	205	12%	32%	-0.65	Claiming	323	11%	31%	-0.10

Sire Stats: AWD 6.9f 22%Mud 388MudSts 3.16spi
Dam'sSire:AWD 7.2f 13%Mud 873MudSts 1.50spi

★ Highest Last Race Speed Rating ● Beaten by weaker in last start ● Poor Trainer win%

DATE TRK	DIST						RR RACETYPE	CR	E1	E2/	LP	1c	2c	SPD	PP	ST	1C	2C	Str	FIN	JOCKEY		ODDS	Top Finishers	Comment	
20Apr07RD7	6f ft	:23	:46³	:58⁴	1:12⁴	3↑	104 Clm4000n2y+	106	80	73/	82	-5	-8	66	7	3	7²½	6²½	2²	2²½	Zuniga E120	Lf	*1.40	BoldMov²½GodHmorMn½Hslego²½	No match for winner	8
07Apr07RD12	5½ ft	:22²	:45³	:58⁴	1:07²	3↑	104 Clm4000n2y+	106	85	91/	63	+7	+14	72	10	7	6⁶	6⁵½	4⁴½	3hd	Felix JE120	Lf	4.00	WilBlonghᴺSrAltitudeᴺᵒGodHumorMn¹½	7 wide; gaining	10
14Mar07TP7	Ⓢ 6½ ft	:23¹	:47¹	1:13³	1:20²	3↑	105 Clm5000C	109	75	78/	67	-4	-4	62	6	7	5⁵½	5²½	3⁹	4⁷½	Diego I120	Lf	2.90	Best Prospect³½Wild Sign¹½Beaulieu⁶	5 path mid turn	8
18Feb07TP3	Ⓢ 6f ft	:23	:46³	:58³	1:10³	3↑	107 Clm5000n2lfm	106	60	62/	90	-13	-15	63	1	6	5⁶½	5⁷½	4¹⁰	4¹⁰½	Diego I120	Lf	2.10	J W Dude²½Storm Tale¹ᵏEsledad²½	Stumbled start	6
12Jan07TP2	Ⓢ 6f ft	:21⁴	:45³	:58²	1:11¹	4↑	107 Clm5000n23m	110	86	89/	79	+4	+2	77	9	7	8⁵½	5²½	2½	2²½	Diego I120	Lf	21.20	ContRm²½GodHmorMn³½Cadbrnie¹ᵏ	5 wide move turn	10
29Dec06TP2	Ⓢ 6f ft	:22¹	:45²	:57⁴	1:10²	3↑	106 Clm5000n2Y	109	76	72/	83	-4	-5	65	7	7	6⁶	5⁶	5⁶	2⁶½	Diego I120	Lf	7.00	HosOfSnston³½GodHmrMn½PrspctsTr	Off inside turn	12
18Nov06Hoo1	5½ sy⁶	:22	:46³		1:05³	3↑	106 Clm4000n2Y	108	85	88/	78	-2	-3	75	4	8	5²½	2¹	3hd	3²½	Diego I120	Lf	9.70	FitToKeep¹ᵏJunkt²GodHumorMan¹½	Off rail; weakened	10
05Nov06Hoo4	6f ft	:22⁴	:46⁴	:59⁴	1:13⁴	3↑	107 Clm4000n2Y	106	87	91/	59	0	+2	61	5	4	3¹½	3hd	5³	7⁷½	Diego I120	Lf	15.30	LckyPoint¹½SyttyChrb³½ExctvStw²	Stalked 3w;faltered	10
07Oct06Hoo2	6f ft	:23	:46²	:58¹	1:11⁴	3↑	108 Clm4000n29m	106	69	67/	79	-6	-6	58	4	9	9⁷½	9⁹½	8⁷½	8¹²½	Diego I123	Lf	15.10	MnkyMrch¹½DrDbtO²½RnngRvr²	Steadied start, outrun	9
22Sep06Hoo7	6f sy⁴	:22³	:48	:59²	1:13	3↑	105 Clm4000n19m	108	85	70/	81	0	-16	71	8	7	3⁷	3hd	1½	1nk	Diego I123	Lf	14.50	GdHmrMn¹ᵏSnlorJoP¹½Swgng⁴½	3wide turn, held sway	9

28Apr'06 CD 3f ft :38¹ B 6/8 ●08Dec'05 TP 3f ft :35³ B 1/13 14Sep'05 CD 3f ft :36¹ B 3/17 15May'05 CD 5f ft 1:03 B 22/27 19Apr'05 CD 5f ft 1:04² B 10/13 31Mar'05 OP 5f ft 1:02¹ H 6/17
24Mar'05 OP 5f ft 1:01¹ H 4/17 17Jly'04 CD 5f my 1:05¹ B 16/16 07Jly'04 CD 5f ft 1:05² B 12/14 22Jun'04 CD 5f ft 1:00³ B 4/14 25May'04 CD 5f ft 1:02 B 17/27 04May'04 CD 5f ft 1:01³ B 15/36

4 PP 3 Gridwin (E/P 6)

Own: Larry A. Byer
5/1 Grape and white blocks
SOLOMON NATHAN (43 10-5-6 23%)

$4,000 B. c. 3
Sire: Winthrop (Storm Cat)
Dam: War Grid (Stalwart)
Brdr: Larry Byer (OH)
Trnr: Vazquez Ivan (15 4-1-1 27%)

Power Rating: 100.3 (5th) L 114

	Starts	W-P-S	Earnings	SPD		Starts	W-P-S	Earnings	SPD
Life:	10	3 - 0 - 1	$10,392	74	Fst	5	1 - 0 - 1	$4,296	73
2007	8	3 - 0 - 1	$9,879	74	Off	5	2 - 0 - 0	$6,096	74
2006	2	0 - 0 - 0	$513	52	Dis	5	2 - 0 - 1	$6,696	73
RD	2	0 - 0 - 0	$456	59	Trf	0	0 - 0 - 0	$0	
					AW	0	0 - 0 - 0	$0	

2007	69	17%	43%	+2.78	2007	125	16%	39%	-0.25
JKYw/EP types	85	9%	25%	0.94	Down one class	47	17%	45%	0.16
JKYw/ Trn L60	1	0%	0%	2.00	+Claiming	304	21%	44%	+0.35
+JKYw/ Sprints	47	21%	51%	+4.43					

Sire Stats: AWD 6.0f 17%Mud 72MudSts 0.47spi
Dam'sSire:AWD 6.3f 12%Mud 444MudSts 0.54spi

★ Hot Jockey in last 7 days (9 3-0-1) ★ Drops in Class today ★ High % Jockey ● Poor Speed Figures in last 2 starts

DATE TRK	DIST						RR RACETYPE	CR	E1	E2/	LP	1c	2c	SPD	PP	ST	1C	2C	Str	FIN	JOCKEY		ODDS	Top Finishers	Comment	
24Apr07RD2	5½ ft	:22¹	:45²	:58¹	1:06²	3↑	104 Clm5000n4L	104	94	84/	53	+7	+8	59	7	1	2¹½	3⁴	4⁶	4⁹	Solomon N116	Lb	9.30	Firetruck¹ᵏPreston T⁷Hidden Glitter¹½	Gave way	7
14Apr07RD8	6f sy⁴	:23	:46¹	:59³	1:13	3↑	105 Clm4000C	103	86	85/	51	-3	-2	50	4	3	4¹½	3³½	4⁸½	5¹⁰	Bracho JG120	Lb	3.20	EnhncdEdton²½PrstonT¹¹Hstnbgod⁶	Lost ground turn	7
30Mar07Beu7	6f ft	:22²	:46¹	:58³	1:11²	3↑	103 Clm4000n3L	106	87	90/	74	+1	+2	73	5	5	3²	1hd	1³	1⁴½	De LA116	Lb	3.80	Gridwin⁴½Padre¹WalrusWildOzzie½	Drew off; driving	8
14Mar07Beu8	6f sy²	:22⁴	:47²	1:00¹	1:13¹	3↑	100 Clm5000n2L	104	86	80/	70	+2	+2	61	2	5	4¹	3¹	1³	1⁵½	De LA116	Lb	*1.40	Gridwn⁵½JoshsVw½DvlsClown¹½	Saved ground; driving	8
06Mar07Beu6	6f ft	:22⁴	:46⁴	:59³	1:11²		103 Alw6200n2L	102	79	78/	59	-4	-2	51	5	2	3³½	4³½	4⁹	3¹³	De LA116	Lb	10.60	Ketchup Red⁷Sloppadylulu⁶Gridwin¹	Chased; tired	6
19Feb07Beu1	5½ gd				1:04²	3↑	100 ⓢMC5000	104	91	86/	81	+1	-3	74	9	1	1²½	1¹½	1¹	1¹	De LA118	Lb	6.80	Gridwin¹Spunky Wind⁶Kinetic Energy²½	Driving	9
23Jan07Beu1	5½ ft	:23	:48¹	1:03	1:10²		101 ⓢMdn 9.2k	101	86	68/	49	+8	+6	38	4	3	4³	3⁵	5⁵	5⁸	CollazoJrJE120	Lb	9.80	ThodrsDobl½MorGld½RsngComotn¹ᵏ	Chased; no rally	7
09Jan07Beu1	5f gd⁸	:23³	:48²		1:01¹		107 Mdn 6.7k	103		81/	60			51	7	1	2¹½	3¹½	4¹	5⁵½	Oro E120	Lb	5.70	eChstThPstr³TrlRid½DoghntMn¹½	Close up; weakened	11
19Dec06Beu1	6f ft	:22⁴	:48²	1:01⁴	1:15³		103 ⓢMdn 9.2k	104	78	75/	65	+8	+7	52	5	6	5⁸	3⁵	3²	4³	CollazoJrJE120	Lb	5.40	Spender½More Guid¹ᵏFight To Vegas²½	No late bid	9
15Nov06Beu1	4½ sy⁴	:23¹	:47³		:54¹		107 MC16000			68/					5	7	6¹¹		7²⁸	-	Luna R120	L	3.60	GoDcTexomaWildGooseCreek	Bolted, distanced	7

03Mar Beu 3f my :38¹ B 8/19 14Dec'06 Beu 3f ft :37² Bg 3/9 04Nov'06 Beu 5f sl 1:05¹ B 4/8 ●21Oct'06 Beu 5f ft 1:02³ Bg 1/8 ●13Oct'06 Beu 5f ft 1:04¹ Bg 1/5 ●04Oct'06 Beu 4f ft :49 Bg 1/8
25Sep'06 Beu 5f ft 1:05 B 1/2

tsnhorse.com

Ultimate PP's w/ Quick Play Comments **River Downs** Clm 4000 6 Furlongs. 3up Friday, May 11, 2007 **Race 8**

E1 E2/LATE SPD
90 88/ 77 75

5 pp 4 Hastego (E 7)

Own: James F. Yaegel
5/1 Green green fly on white diamond
PRESCOTT ROONEY K (66 16-20-15 19%)

$4,000 B. g. 6
Sire: Java Royal (Java Gold)
Dam: Powdrpuf Princess (Taio)
Brdr: Hutchison Farm (MD)
Trnr: Yaegel Thomas (15 0-6-2 0%)

Power Rating: 98.6 (8th)

L 124

Life:	52 5 - 7 - 7	$74,218	82	Fst	39 3 - 5 - 7	$50,814 81
2007	11 2 - 2 - 3	$8,450	71	Off	12 2 - 2 - 0	$23,375 82
2006	18 0 - 1 - 1	$4,530	68	Dis	11 2 - 1 - 1	$8,926 71
RD	1 0 - 0 - 1	$520	65	Trf	1 0 - 0 - 0	$0 70
				AW	0 0 - 0 - 0	$0

2007	486	14%	46%	-0.27
JKYw/ E types	521	17%	43%	-0.33
JKYw/ Sprints	292	14%	48%	-0.17

2007	111	11%	42%	-1.15
Wnr last race	82	10%	44%	-0.37
No class chg	440	10%	33%	0.02
Claiming	629	10%	33%	0.12

Sire Stats: AWD 7.7f 27%Mud 11MudSts 0.58spi
Dam'sSire:AWD 6.9f 12%Mud 1997MudSts 1.55spi

★ Early Speed running style helps chances
★ Won last race (BEU 04/30 6f Dirt fast Clm3500NW2Y+)

● Moves up in class from last start

DATE TRK	DIST						RR	RACETYPE	CR	E1	E2/	LP	1c	2c	SPD	PP	ST	1C	2C	Str	FIN	JOCKEY		ODDS	Top Finishers	Comment	
30Apr07Beu3	6f ft	:234	:482	1:004	1:14	3↑	103	Clm3500n2y+	107	79	75/	75	-7	-6	62	1	5	2½	1hd	11	12½	De LA122	Lbf	2.00	Hastego2½Hepnzi Bah2½Private Petition	Driving	6
26Apr07RD7	6f ft	:23	:463	:584	1:124	3↑	104	Clm4000n2y+	105	83	75/	79	-5	-8	65	8	8	3½	31½	33	33½	Feliz JE120	Lbf	3.90	BoldMove2½GodHmorMn½Hstego2½	Pressed; weakened	9
09Apr07Beu4	1 70 ft	:232	:48	1:141	1:457	3↑	103	Clm3500n2y+	103	75	71/	65	-2	+1	65	4	21	1½	2hd	31	44½	Ouzts PW124	Lbf	*1.10	PrivteLer½Hphzibh½Clymor3	Bid; dueled; weakened	7
26Mar07Beu8	1m ft	:242	:48	1:132	1:394	3↑	104	Clm3500n2y+	107	78	74/	70	+1	+4	68	4	1hd	2hd	1½	1½	31½	Stokes LA124	Lbf	2.40	RalLikeCunny½HesSoHndsom1½Hstego5½	Weakened	9
20Mar07Beu4	6f my	:222	:461	:581	1:103	3↑	103	Clm3500n1y+	107	87	85/	76	-2	-2	71	1	7	2hd	1½	12	11½	Stokes LA124	Lbf	*0.50	Hastego1½CheyenSpeng3Halover	Drew clear; driving	8
12Mar07Beu6	6f ft	:224	:464	:592	1:12	3↑	103	Clm3500n1y+	104	85	80/	74	-2	+1	65	4	4	41	52½	32	22	Stokes LA124	Lbf	4.30	CalmWters2Hstego1PrivalGold1½	3 wide; up for place	7
03Mar07Beu8	5½ gd	:223	:462	:594	1:06	3↑	102	Clm3500n1y+	103	77	77/	52	+3	+8	57	7	4	68	78	610	48½	ThorwarthO124	Lbf	11.40	HerComsBrg3AlAboutOv2WorldClsHofer2½	4 wide turn	9
19Feb07Beu8	5½ gd				1:053	3↑	102	Clm3500n1y+	104	78	76/	69	-1	-3	61	2	7	75½	65½	23	26½	ThorwarthO124	Lbf	5.60	MstyWdr5½Hstgo1½PrivtPtion1	Saved ground; 2nd best	9
24Jan07Beu5	6f gd	:23	:472	1:001	1:133	3↑	103	Clm3500n1y+	102	82	81/	71	0	+1	63	1	7	53½	54½	33½	56½	ThorwarthO124	Lbf	*1.20	StalHunter4½PrvtGold½Belondgry1½	Weakened; inside	8
19Jan07Beu8	6f ft	:23	:48	1:01	1:14	3↑	105	Clm3500n1y+	109	81	78/	75	+1	-2	64	8	5	73½	51½	32½	31	Stokes LA124	Lbf	5.80	Longstreet½Misty Wonder½Hastego1	6 wide turn	12

22Feb06 CT 3f ft :381 B 1/3 14Oct05 CT 4f my :50 B 5/9 06Jly05 CT 4f ft :504 B 11/15 03May05 Del 5f ft 1:023 B 5/22 28Apr05 Del 4f ft :511 B 11/20 18Apr05 Del 4f ft :501 B 9/14
18Apr05 Del 4f ft :501 B 7/10 26Dec04 Bow 3f ft :38 B 1/2 06Nov04 Bow 3f ft :36 B 2/16 16Oct04 Bow 3f ft :372 B 4/16 ●11May04 Bow 3f ft :36 B 1/8 08Apr04 Bow 3f ft :37 B 2/5

6 pp 7 Mighty Wind (E/P 6)

Own: Bert Crawford
6/1 Blue, blue 'BF' on gray diamond
OUZTS PERRY WAYNE (142 18-23-20 13%)

$4,000 Dkbbr. g. 12
Sire: Monde Bleu (Gb) (Last Tycoon (Ire))
Dam: Legal Breeze (Advocator)
Brdr: Jon H. Pomeroy (KY)
Trnr: Crawford Bert (33 4-6-7 12%)

Power Rating: 100.6 (4th)

L 120

Life:	84 10 - 10 - 10	$71,099	89	Fst	50 5 - 6 - 4	$34,707 89
2007	6 2 - 2 - 1	$7,083	70	Off	26 4 - 4 - 1	$28,096 77
2006	3 0 - 0 - 0	$568	60	Dis	18 2 - 2 - 2	$11,383 78
RD	17 2 - 3 - 2	$9,779	75	Trf	8 0 - 0 - 3	$8,277 77
				AW	0 0 - 0 - 0	$0

2007	581	10%	34%	-0.79
JKYw/EP types	137	9%	27%	-1.10
JKYw/ Trn L60	6	0%	67%	-2.00
JKYw/ Sprints	277	9%	34%	0.94

2007	219	11%	40%	-0.47
1st start w/trn	86	9%	33%	-1.04
No class chg	330	10%	36%	-0.96
Claiming	527	9%	36%	-0.86

Sire Stats: AWD 6.6f 21%Mud 34MudSts 0.62spi
Dam'sSire:AWD 7.3f 10%Mud 888MudSts 1.33spi

● Showed declining form & speed in last race

DATE TRK	DIST						RR	RACETYPE	CR	E1	E2/	LP	1c	2c	SPD	PP	ST	1C	2C	Str	FIN	JOCKEY		ODDS	Top Finishers	Comment	
Previously trained by OLESIAK JORDAN																											
28Apr07Beu7	5½ ft	:224	:473	1:002	1:07	3↑	106	Clm3500C	105	91	81/	57	+3	+2	52	3	1	2hd	3½	52½	57½	Rozman AA121	L	4.40	HereComesBrag½LowBolly3TrulyHonored1½	Gave way	8
14Apr07Beu13	6f sy	:22	:46	:584	1:113	3↑	106	Clm3500C	107	97	95/	63	+7	+8	68	1	1	11	11	1½	33½	SolomonN120	L	6.10	OctobrBlus1½PrRules1½MightyWd2½	Set pace; weakened	9
31Mar07Beu6	5½ sy	:214	:452	:577	1:042	3↑	106	Clm3500C	107	89	86/	61	+6	+8	66	4	3	32½	36½	25	25½	SolomonN122	L	4.50	UnwningFight5½MightyWind2½DancinLnce	Second best	6
20Mar07Beu8	5½ my	:22	:444	:58	1:043	3↑	106	Clm3500C	105	93	98/	52	+4	+15	61	4	2	2hd	21	3½	24½	MelanconP122	L	4.40	MrHngwy4½MgtyWd1½SnOfMth1½	Steadied mid stretch	6
Previously trained by PALMER PERRY																											
31Jan07Beu8	5f ft	:22	:452		:573	3↑	106	Clm3500n2y+	107		90/	88			68	6	1	1½	2hd	11	1½	HingswrthBL124	L	6.80	MightyWind½Couldbmonshine½TrulyHonored½	Gamely	10
15Jan07Beu16	5f sy	:223	:47		:593	3↑	103	Clm3500n1y+	108		91/	70			70	9	1	11½	13½	14	16	HingswrthBL124	L	52.50	Mighty Wind6A Bit Of Luck½Freke Tail½	Mild urging	10
28Jly06Mnr4	1m ft	:247	:494	1:15	1:42	3↑	106	Clm5000n18m	101	77	59/	38	5	-4	38	5	1½	1½	88	922	932½	MurphyCK121	L	55.80	ThdrStrks4OldDukPr½Brlton3½	Worked pace; wore out	10
14Jly06Mnr5	6f ft	:227	:461	:59	1:123	3↑	105	Clm5000n2Y	103	81	70/	74	-2	-2	56	1	2	53½	78½	89½	911	V8-gomezH119	L	5.00	City Boy Broke Us2½Foot Track	Early chase;faded	10
23Jun06Mnr1	5f my	:222	:454		:583	3↑	107	Clm5000n2Y	104		77/	75			60	3	4	51½	78	58	47½	V8-gomezH119	L	21.00	KngOfMt½AiyTkCh4½CrsPrpct2½	Swung wide; improved	8
Previously trained by FREEMAN DALE																											
15Nov05Beu4	1m sy	:233	:483	1:134	1:402	3↑	106	Clm3500n3Y	103	86	71/	47	+12	+3	52	9	3½	3½	52½	77½	817½	SnchezJrJA119	L	13.70	RegiTresure1½TnksLilBrothr½PrdseHights1½	Weakened	10

30Dec06 Beu 5f ft 1:054 B 8/8 22Dec06 Beu (d) 4f sy :503 B 4/11 16Dec06 Beu 4f ft :522 B 7/8 09Nov06 Beu 4f ft :534 B 11/12 31Oct06 Beu 3f sl :383 B 3/6 17Jun06 RD 4f ft :52 B 12/15
06May06 Beu 4f ft :503 B 7/15 29Apr06 Beu 4f ft :52 B 10/16 11Apr06 Beu 4f ft :523 B 11/12 01Apr06 Beu (d) 3f ft :362 B 2/13 08May05 Beu 5f ft 1:044 B 3/6 04May05 Beu 5f ft 1:06 B 3/7

7 pp 8 Not A Question (E/P 4)

Own: Jodie L. Lamb
20/1 Purple, silver stars
TOLENTINO PABLO (8 1-1-1 17%)

$4,000 Ch. g. 7 OBSJAN 2001 $2k
Sire: World Stage (Ire) (Sadler's Wells)
Dam: Shananies Question (Shananie)
Brdr: Peter Fuller (FL)
Trnr: Lamb Jodie L. (8 0-0-1 0%)

Power Rating: 94.8 (9th)

L 120

Life:	47 3 - 7 - 6	$28,356	71	Fst	38 3 - 6 - 4	$17,831 71
2007	3 0 - 0 - 0	$364	60	Off	8 0 - 1 - 2	$2,524 67
2006	12 1 - 4 - 2	$7,965	71	Dis	23 2 - 4 - 1	$10,906 70
RD	35 3 - 5 - 6	$18,125	71	Trf	0 0 - 0 - 0	$0
				AW	1 0 - 0 - 0	$45 90

2007	12	17%	50%	+3.87
JKYw/EP types	11	9%	27%	-1.20
JKYw/ Sprints	8	25%	62%	+6.80

2007	10	10%	40%	-0.62
No class chg	112	13%	38%	-0.43
Claiming	163	14%	36%	0.27

Sire Stats: AWD 6.6f 10%Mud 212MudSts 0.35spi
Dam'sSire:AWD 6.3f 20%Mud 548MudSts 1.07spi

● Finished far behind weaker in last race ● Poor Speed Figures ● Only 3 wins in 47 career starts
● Outside posts have poor win%

DATE TRK	DIST						RR	RACETYPE	CR	E1	E2/	LP	1c	2c	SPD	PP	ST	1C	2C	Str	FIN	JOCKEY		ODDS	Top Finishers	Comment	
03May07RD14	5½ ft	:23	:462	:582	1:054	3↑	105	Clm4000n2y+	103	86	75/	54	3	-4	56	3	2	57½	84	910	1018½	Paucar E120	Lb	18.00	Vacancy1½McGeever10PrayerWarrior½	Through early	10
20Apr07RD7	6f ft	:23	:463	:584	1:124	3↑	104	Clm4000n2y+	104	83	75/	73	5	-8	60	9	1	2½	21½	43	46½	Paucar E120	Lb	23.60	BoldMove2½GodHumorMn½Hastego2½	Stalked; faltered	9
07Apr07RD13	5½ ft	:222	:453	:584	1:077	3↑	104	Clm4000n2y+	102	89	86/	41	+7	+14	53	4	5	54	55½	89	1011	EnriquezJC120	Lb	24.80	Wil BelonghdSir Attitude Good Humor Man1½	Faded	10
15Nov06Beu4	5½ sy	:222	:47	:593	1:062	3↑	103	Clm3500n2y+	102	76	70/	60	-1	-2	53	10	2	88½	97½	99½	88	Paucar E120	Lb	*2.60	PrinceOfRhods3½GavotaPs1GeorgeM	Showed little	10
24Oct06Beu8	5½ ft	:23	:473	1:007	1:072	3↑	103	Clm3500n2y+	105	78	76/	74	-1	-1	68	7	8	63	64½	54½	21½	Paucar E120	Lb	*1.50	FeverLk1½NotAQustionhdGeorgM1½	Rallied; up for place	11
13Oct06Beu14	6f ft	:224	:487	1:014	1:152	3↑	103	Clm3500n2y+	109	86	85/	71	+4	0	66	7	2	33	1hd	11	21½	Paucar E120	Lb	5.80	LakeClsic1½NotAQstonMinLndnghd	Split horses turn	11
26Aug06RD15	5½ ft	:224	:467	1:01	1:08	3↑	104	Clm4000n2y+	104	87	90/	54	+5	+10	59	5	6	63½	61½	54½	66½	Paucar E120	Lb	6.80	ElegantFme3½FaxAFrdy½WilBelonghd	Stumbled start	11
17Aug06RD8	6f ft	:23	:467	:594	1:142	3↑	103	Clm4000n2y+	103	84	81/	61	0	+4	54	6	2	41½	42	41½	54½	Paucar E122	Lb	3.10	Maybe Doc Jamaican Justice½George M2½	No rally	10
05Aug06RD4	5½ ft	:23	:471	1:01	1:074	3↑	104	Clm4000n2y+	106	89	86/	71	+2	+1	67	4	4	51½	51½	31½	32½	Paucar E122	Lb	4.40	Tomprado1½George M1½Not A Question1½	Evenly late	8
28Jly06RD3	6f sy	:232	:461	:594	1:14	3↑	104	Clm4000n2y+	106	82	83/	72	-5	+3	65	7	2	3½	43	42½	32½	Paucar E122	Lb	3.90	MrJustice½NotHopering2NotAQustion2	Evenly; no rally	8

04Apr RD 3f gd :38 B 3/3 20Dec'06 TP 5f ft 1:063 B 9/9 05Oct'06 RD 5f my 1:043 B 3/3 19May'06 RD 5f my 1:05 B 4/8 30Apr'06 RD 4f ft :53 B 5/7 23Apr'06 RD 4f ft :52 B 7/9
11Sep'05 TP 4f ft :503 B 24/31 28Apr'05 RD 4f ft :511 B 16/20 20Apr'05 RD 4f ft :51 B 5/5 15Mar'05 TP 4f ft :502 B 7/9 17Apr'04 RD 5f ft 1:06 B 7/20 10Apr'04 RD 5f ft 1:054 B 7/9

tsnhorse.com

Ultimate PP's w/ Quick Play Comments

River Downs Clm 4000 6 Furlongs. 3up Friday May 11, 2007 Race 8

E1 E2/LATE SPD
90 89/ 77 75

8 pp 9 A Rizzi Rueben (NA 4)

Own: El Coqui Racing Stable
20/1 Red white statue of liberty white sleeves
CALO JOSE LUIS (64 10-8-7 16%)

$4,000 Ch. h. 8 OBSAPR 2003 $8k
Sire: Rizzi (Afleet)
Dam: Sassy Sunrise (Assert (Ire))
Brdr: D J J Racing (FL)
Trnr: Soutre Israel (13 1-2-1 8%)

Power Rating: 88.6 (11th)

L 120

Life:	51 6 - 4 - 2	$52,885	85	Fst	47 5 - 4 - 2	$47,518	85
2007	5 0 - 0 - 0	$555	45	Off	4 1 - 0 - 0	$4,567	72
2006	14 2 - 1 - 0	$13,890	81	Dis	23 3 - 2 - 1	$22,983	85
RD	2 0 - 0 - 0	$266	42	Trf	0 0 - 0 - 0	$0	
				AW	3 0 - 0 - 0	$299	45

2007	214	14%	40%	-0.52
JKYw/NA types	102	5%	15%	-1.11
JKYw/ Trn L60	2	0%	50%	2.60
JKYw/ Sprints	158	13%	38%	-0.53

2007	32	6%	22%	+0.06
No class chg	157	4%	17%	-0.15
Claiming	241	5%	17%	-0.36

Sire Stats: AWD 6.4f 14%Mud 727MudSts 1.16spi
Dam'sSire: AWD 9.4f 12%Mud 302MudSts 2.44spi

● Finished far back in last start ● Poor Speed Figures ● Outside posts have poor win%

DATE TRK	DIST						RR RACETYPE	CR	E1	E2/	LP	1c	2c	SPD	PP	ST	1C	2C	Str	FIN	JOCKEY		ODDS	Top Finishers	Comment	
27Apr07RD[8]	5½ gd[s]	:23	:46[3]	1:00[2]	1:07[4]	3↑	[104]Clm4000C	100	84	72/	36	+1	+6	34	7	4	3[2]	4[3]½	7[8]	7[13]½	Rojas C[120]	Lb	16.90	ChocLinn½ThPttyChrmn½OneEydGmblr[2]	Gave way	7
07Apr07RD[5]	5½ ft	:23	:47[1]	1:01	1:08	3↑	[106]Clm5000	102	85	79/	44	+3	+2	42	4	4	3[3]½	2[1]	5[5]½	5[15]	Moran SL[120]	Lb	34.40	Sonny's Legacy½Best Prospect[3]Zone Blue[4]	Faded	6
14Mar07TP[2] ®	6½ ft	:23[1]	:47[1]	1:13[3]	1:20[2]	3↑	[106]Clm5000C	102	81	81/	44	-4	-4	45	8	4	4[2]½	3[1]½	6[8]½	7[18]	Camejo JM[120]	Lb	86.80	BestProspect[6]½Wild Sign[1]½Beauleu[4]	4 wide; gave way	8
01Mar07TP[3] ®	6f ft	:22[1]	:45[2]	:58[1]	1:11[4]	3↑	[107]Clm5000n26m	103	74	74/	56	0	+4	43	2	6	7[8]½	7[11]	8[18]	9[22]½	Sanchez C[120]	Lb	105.60	HouseOfSensation[4]IndyEnergy[4]AskSidney½	No factor	8
18Feb07TP[3] ®	6f ft	:23	:46[3]	:58[3]	1:10[3]	3↑	[107]Clm5000n26m	102	72	66/	64	-13	-18	44	4	3	4[3]½	4[5]½	5[15]	6[21]½	Sanchez C[120]	Lb	53.20	J W Dude[2]½Storm Tale[nk]Esledad[7]½	3 wide; faded	6
20Dec06Beu[8]	6f ft	:22[3]	:46[3]	:59[2]	1:12	3↑	[107]Clm3500n3Y	104	92	93/	48	+2	+8	55	4	6	3[1]½	3[3]	8[7]½	10[17]½	CollazoJrJE[120]	Lb	76.00	SyHeyChrk[1]OutSoul[3]½DrEClre[1]½	Chased inside; tired	11
08Dec06Beu[4]	6f ft	:22[3]	:46[1]	:59	1:12[2]	3↑	[106]Clm4000n26m	104	78	77/	65	+3	+8	55	5	10	10[9]½	10[9]½	8[11]	8[11]	CamaqueC[120]	Lb	13.20	General Josh[nk]Dr. E.Claire½October Blues[no]	No factor	12
27Nov06Tdn[8]	6f ft	:22[3]	:46[1]	:59[1]	1:12	3↑	[107]Clm3500n3Y	107	84	82/	75	-4	-4	68	4	9	7[1]½	4[3]	4[7]½	4[7]½	Banda S[117]	Lb	29.30	Autbn[4]TuxdoGold[2]½DrgonThePot[1]½	Well placed; evenly	12
13Nov06Tdn[8]	6f gd	:22[3]	:46[3]	1:00	1:13[2]	3↑	[106]Clm3500	106	75	67/	78	-1	+1	56	3	9	10[7]½	12[10]	12[9]½	10[8]½	Oro E[117]	Lb	17.80	LordbchMrytou[nk]TimCount[hd]MtchngCotrs[hd]	No factor	12
09Oct06Tdn[3]	5½ ft	:22[4]	:46[3]	:59[1]	1:05[1]	3↑	[107]Clm5000	106	83	71/	66	-9	-7	64	8	4	5[2]½	6[5]½	6[10]	7[12]	MunaylaF[117]	Lb	9.10	RgimRqust[5]½VelonFun[2]½StnGrnd½	Wide early; outrun	8

26Apr RD 3f ft :39[3] B 2/2 02Oct06 Tdn 3f ft :38 B 12/26 13Aug06 Tdn 3f ft :41[1] B 8/8 25Apr06 Tdn 3f ft :40[1] B 8/8 07Feb06 Bow 3f ft :36 H 1/2 10Oct05 CT 3f ft :37[3] B 2/4
18Dec'04 Crc 4f ft :51[2] B 35/45 04Aug'04 Crc 5f ft 1:03[2] B 6/13 20Jly'04 Crc 3f gd :36[2] H 2/25 14Feb'04 Crc 4f ft :49 B 8/65 04Feb'04 Crc 4f ft :49[3] B 10/47 24Jan'04 Crc 5f ft 1:04[4] B 20/28

9 pp 10 Elusive Indian (S 0)

Own: Charles Lawson
8/1 Red, white bars on sleeves
DE LEON AZAEL (43 5-0-5 12%)

$4,000 B. g. 7 KEENOV 2000 $11k
Sire: Elusive Quality (Gone West)
Dam: Personal Lady (Personal Flag)
Brdr: Ron Wallace & Dr. Stuart Brown (KY)
Trnr: Lawson Charles (8 1-0-3 12%)

Power Rating: 98.3 (6th)

L 120

Life:	42 6 - 6 - 5	$98,911	97	Fst	29 4 - 5 - 5	$47,322	86
2007	1 0 - 0 - 0	$41	61	Off	10 2 - 0 - 0	$31,839	97
2006	15 2 - 3 - 4	$13,955	76	Dis	10 4 - 3 - 3	$54,710	97
RD	4 1 - 1 - 0	$4,264	76	Trf	3 0 - 1 - 0	$9,756	84
				AW	3 1 - 0 - 0	$4,593	71

2007	240	12%	37%	-0.73
JKYw/ S types	63	5%	27%	-1.30
JKYw/ Trn L60	7	14%	43%	-0.43
JKYw/ Sprints	156	13%	39%	0.60

2007	88	22%	53%	-0.52
+90+ days away	47	19%	43%	-0.43
No class chg	477	15%	44%	-0.58
Claiming	662	16%	45%	-0.54

Sire Stats: AWD 6.3f 17%Mud 316MudSts 3.25spi
Dam'sSire: AWD 7.6f 12%Mud 1515MudSts 1.26spi

★ Highest Speed Figure at Today's Distance

● Never threatened the leaders in last start ● Poor Speed Figures in last 2 starts
● Has not raced for more than 3 months ● Outside posts have poor win%

DATE TRK	DIST						RR RACETYPE	CR	E1	E2/	LP	1c	2c	SPD	PP	ST	1C	2C	Str	FIN	JOCKEY		ODDS	Top Finishers	Comment	
12Jan07Beu[8]	6f gd[s]	:22[2]	:46[3]	:59[3]	1:12[4]	3↑	[106]Clm3500C	104	73	78/	70	+4	+8	61	5	11	8[10]	8[7]½	7[6]	8[8]	ThorwarthO[120]	Lb	6.60	CiletComet[1]GeneralJosh[1]½SlewsTempr[2]½	Steadied start	12
28Nov06Beu[7]	6f ft	:22[1]	:46	:58	1:10[2]	3↑	[105]Clm3500C	105	78	82/	71	0	-1	64	8	7	7[8]½	5[3]½	5[6]	3[7]½	Stokes LA[120]	Lb	2.40	Smcker[1]½ImAlredyThere[4]½Elusivindn½	Split horses 1/16	9
08Nov06Beu[8]	5½ ft	:22[4]	:47	:59[2]	1:06[2]	3↑	[104]Clm3500C	107	68	75/	75	-3	-1	71	2	11	10[9]½	8[8]½	4[6]½	3[3]	Stokes LA[120]	Lb	*3.10	Brbiscuit[2]FevrLit[1]Elusivindin[2]	Steadied start; 5 wide	11
24Oct06Beu[1]	6f ft				1:12[4]	3↑	[104]Clm3500C	105	82	79/	85	-3	+1	73	1	6	5[3]	5[7]	4[3]½	2[3]½	Stokes LA[120]	Lb	2.50	Tomprdo[3]½Elusivindin[nk]Brbiscuit[1]	Saved ground to 1/4	8
07Oct06Beu[14]	5½ ft	:22[3]	:46[4]	:59[2]	1:06[2]	3↑	[104]Clm3500C	104	79	81/	74	-1	0	70	10	11	10[8]	8[3]½	6[4]½	3[1]½	Yaranga Y[120]	Lb	5.20	Luborre[1]½ElegntFme½Elusivindn½	Swung wide; rallied	11
24Sep06TP[6] ®	6½ ft	:23[1]	:46[2]	1:11[2]	1:17[3]	3↑	[107]Clm5000C	104	74	70/	75	-8	-11	60	6	5	6[4]½	7[5]	4[7]½	5[11]½	Toups R[115]	Lb	7.20	FrstNn[5]½FityBndr[5]KgOfThSin½	Off inside; no menace	8
17Aug06RD[10]	6f ft	:23[1]	:46[3]	1:00[1]	1:13[4]	3↑	[105]Clm4000C	105	82	80/	69	-4	-1	60	5	5	5[1]½	6[1]½	5[3]	6[5]½	Vitek JJ[122]	Lb	3.70	Mhoney½Tomprdo½Obvious Vision[1]½	Evenly; no rally	11
06Jly06RD[8]	1 70 ft	:25	:50[1]	1:16[1]	1:47[7]	3↑	[106]Clm4000C	103	66	52/	59	-8	-12	51	7	1hd	2½	5[7]½	9[12]	10[19]	Stokes LA[124]	Lb	*2.10	NaturesCndy[nk]WhtOfSumons[4]AskSidney[1]½	Gave way	11
22Jun06RD[13]	5½ ft	:22[4]	:46[4]	1:00[1]	1:06[3]	3↑	[103]Clm4000n2y+	108	81	85/	82	+1	-3	76	10	7	7[5]½	4[3]½	1[2]	1[5]½	Stokes LA[120]	Lb	*1.80	Elusivindn[5]½ExecutvWll[1]½SmMcGe[1]½	Drew off; driving	11
09Jun06RD[8]	6f ft	:23	:46[4]	1:00[4]	1:14[1]	3↑	[104]Clm4000n2y+	104	85	79/	71	-1	-1	61	5	5	4[1]	3[1]½	2[3]	2[2]½	Stokes LA[120]	Lb	3.50	NumbrOnShkh[2]½Elusivindn½CoprCrmnl[1]½	Evenly late	11

30Apr Beu 3f ft :38[2] B 4/13 14Mar Beu (d) 3f sy :39[1] B 9/12 04Mar'06 TP 4f ft :49 B 11/47 25Feb'06 TP 4f ft :50[2] B 6/23 10Feb'06 TP 3f ft :37[1] B 3/23 31Jan'06 TP 3f ft :37[2] B 2/7
02Jly'05 Elp 4f ft :52 B 4/14 13Mar'05 TP 4f ft :53 B 6/7 12Feb'05 TP 4f ft :48[1] B 7/23 07Nov'04 TP 4f ft :49 B 4/15 16Feb'04 Pmm 4f ft :50 B 15/25 22Dec'03 SA 5f ft 1:00[4] H 29/62

10 pp 11 Calm Waters (E/P 6)

Own: Bobby Chitress And Kelly Everett
12/1 Green, yellow diamonds
VITEK JUSTIN J. (91 13-12-11 13%)

$4,000 Gr/ro. g. 9
Sire: Wekiva Springs (Runaway Groom)
Dam: Equilibrate (Gone West)
Brdr: Pin Oak Stud (KY)
Trnr: Ratcliffe William H. (2 0-0-1 0%)

Power Rating: 103.7 (1st)

L 122

Life:	55 12 - 8 - 4	$131,578	93	Fst	45 11 - 8 - 4	$115,799	93
2007	4 2 - 0 - 0	$5,853	68	Off	6 0 - 0 - 0	$951	70
2006	8 0 - 3 - 0	$6,667	70	Dis	36 10 - 5 - 4	$97,925	93
RD	0 0 - 0 - 0	$0		Trf	4 1 - 0 - 0	$14,820	77
				AW	1 0 - 0 - 0	$78	55

2007	226	11%	36%	+0.10
JKYw/EP types	182	12%	38%	-0.34
JKYw/ Sprints	126	10%	39%	+0.30

2007	9	22%	44%	-0.71
No class chg	20	15%	45%	+0.45
Claiming	25	16%	44%	+0.17

Sire Stats: AWD 6.9f 13%Mud 540MudSts 0.86spi
Dam'sSire: AWD 7.4f 15%Mud 712MudSts 3.47spi

★ Best Dirt Speed is fastest among today's starters

● Outside posts have poor win%

DATE TRK	DIST						RR RACETYPE	CR	E1	E2/	LP	1c	2c	SPD	PP	ST	1C	2C	Str	FIN	JOCKEY		ODDS	Top Finishers	Comment	
14Apr07Beu[13]	6f sy[s]	:22	:46	:58[4]	1:11[3]	3↑	[108]Clm3500C	108	93	91/	61	+7	+6	63	7	3	3[3]	4[2]	4[4]	5[8]½	ThorwarthO[124]	Lbf	6.00	OctobrBlus[1]½PrRules[1]½MghtyWe[2]½	Chased; weakened	9
04Apr07Beu[8]	6f ft	:23[4]	:48[1]	1:00[1]	1:13	3↑	[103]Clm3500n2y+	107	80	77/	81	8	-7	67	5	3	1hd	1hd	1[1]	1[1]½	Yaranga Y[124]	Lbf	2.20	ClmWtrs[1]½BrsBdBy[1]½PastAdGrvy[2]½	Inside duel; driving	9
12Mar07Beu[8]	6f ft	:22[4]	:46[4]	:59[2]	1:12	3↑	[103]Clm3500n1y+	108	86	86/	72	-2	+1	68	7	1	2½	1[1]	1[2]	1[2]	ComqueMA[124]	Lbf	*1.60	Calm Waters[2]Hastego[1]Privat Gold[1]½	Drifted out lane	7
18Jan07TP[6] ®	6f ft	:22[3]	:46	:58[3]	1:11[2]	4↑	[107]Clm5000n19m	106	73	70/	71	4	-4	55	2	10	9[6]½	10[6]½	9[7]½	9[10]	Ouzts PW[122]	Lbf	31.70	Jarrett[2]½WildwodFirebird[nk]NovembersFury[nk]	No factor	11
26Dec06Mnr[9]	6f my	:23	:47[2]	1:00[3]	1:14[2]	3↑	[106]Clm5000n1Y	106	80	79/	75	-3	-4	64	4	5	6[4]	7[4]	6[3]½	6[7]½	WhitneyDG[121]	Lbf	4.00	DcsOpt½KngMstg[2]ActrysSn[1]	Evenly; weakened lane	10
29Oct06Mnr[5]	6f ft	:22[1]	:45[4]	:58[3]	1:11[3]	3↑	[105]Clm5000n1Y	106	83	80/	75	4	-7	66	10	3	3[1]½	3[1]	4[2]	7[5]	Parker DL[121]	Lbf	2.20	To Go½Indestructible[2]½Candler½	Stalk4w;btdlevel off	10
07Oct06Mnr[10]	6f ft	:22[2]	:46[1]	:58[4]	1:11[4]	3↑	[106]Clm5000n1Y	106	78	79/	81	-6	-8	70	9	3	3[2]½	3½	2½	2[1]½	WhitneyDG[121]	Lbf	3.50	SkyHunt[1]½CalmWtrs[3]½Candler[hd]	7 wide; turned back	10

Previously trained by GABRIEL JR LEO G

DATE TRK	DIST						RR RACETYPE	CR	E1	E2/	LP	1c	2c	SPD	PP	ST	1C	2C	Str	FIN	JOCKEY		ODDS	Top Finishers	Comment	
20Aug06AP[2]	6½ ft	:22[3]	:46[1]	1:11[2]	1:18	3↑	[107]Clm4000	106	78	74/	79	-7	-8	67	4	8	5[3]	6[4]½	7[5]	8[7]½	Emigh CA[121]	Lbf	9.00	VrgnRun[1]½JudgPrkins½WonWngWng[2]½	Bumped start	10
12Jly06AP[3]	6f ft	:22[3]	:46[1]	:58[4]	1:12[1]	3↑	[107]Clm5000	106	88	83/	63	+1	+1	58	3	4	2[1]½	5[2]½	5[4]	5[8]½	Emigh CA[121]	Lbf	3.40	Nrav[4]½Wevegotchooverd[nk]Kamp[2]½	Off rail; weakened	7
18Jun06AP[2]	6f ft	:22	:45	:57[4]	1:11[2]	3↑	[107]Clm4000	109	84	88/	72	+5	+8	70	10	4	5[3]½	4[4]	4[1]	2[2]	Emigh CA[121]	Lbf	9.00	Nav[2]CalmWters[2]OurMemnto½	4wd 1/4; second best	11

08Mar Tlc 4f ft :52[2] B 2/5 24Feb Tlc 3f ft :38[2] B 10/16 13Aug'06 AP 4f ft :50 B 34/70 06Aug'06 AP 4f ft :50[3] B 47/72 21May'06 AP 4f ft :49[3] B 5/28 24Apr'06 Haw 4f ft :50[1] B 6/21
11Apr'06 Haw 5f ft 1:01[3] B 6/40 04Apr'06 Haw 5f ft 1:03[2] B 29/40 28Mar'06 Haw 4f gd :50[2] B 10/23 21Mar'06 Haw 4f ft :52[4] B 27/37 14Mar'06 Haw 3f ft :39 B 13/26 03Nov'05 Haw 4f ft :51[7] B 19/37

Ultimate PPs w/ Quick Play Comments **River Downs** Clm 4000 6 Furlongs. 3up Friday, May 11, 2007 **Race 8**

E1	E2/LATE	SPD
90	89/ 77	75

Last 3 Years RACETYPE STATS:	# Races	Win%	FAVORITES Itm%	$2ROI	Average Field Size	Median $2 Win Payoff	% Winners < 5/1	% Winners >= 5/1 < 10/1	% Winners >= 10/1
RD 3up CLM 4000 Dirt 6f	42	24%	64%	-0.56	8.4	$8.20	71%	17%	12%

Track Bias Stats

DIRT 6.0f	* MEET Totals *			
# Races: 64	Speed Bias: 80%	WnrAvgBL		
%Wire: 47%	04/06 - 05/08	1stCall: 1.4		
		2ndCall: 1.0		
	Early	Speed	Late	Speed
Runstyle:	E	E/P	P	S
	++	+		
Impact Values	1.66	1.29	0.72	0.33
%Races Won	52%	28%	11%	9%
Post Bias:	RAIL	1-3	4-7	8+
			+	
Impact Values	0.85	0.89	1.14	0.71
Avg Win %	12%	13%	19%	4%

DIRT 6.0f	* WEEK Totals *			
# Races: 14	Speed Bias: 86%	WnrAvgBL		
%Wire: 64%	05/03 - 05/08	1stCall: 1.2		
		2ndCall: 0.8		
	Early	Speed	Late	Speed
Runstyle:	E	E/P	P	S
	++			
Impact Values	1.98	1.09	0.94	0.00
%Races Won	64%	21%	14%	0%
Post Bias	RAIL	1-3	4-7	8+
	+		+	
Impact Values	1.91	0.80	1.29	0.00
Avg Win %	29%	12%	22%	0%

Race Summary

#	HorseName	ML Odds	Med Eqp	Days Since L/R	Run Style	P T S	Avg Dist/Surf PACE-SPEED E1	E2/Late	Spd	Avg Race Rtng	Best Pace E1	E2/Late	Final Speed Sp1	Sp2	Sp3	Sp4	ACL	Rcg Spd Avg	R1	R2	R3	Mud Spd	Pedigree Stats Mud Sts	Mud % Mud	Sire AWD	Dam Sire's AWD
4	Gndwin	5/1	L	17	+E/P	6	91	87/ 69	* 69*	103	94	90/ 81	59.	50	73.	61	102.9	61	104	105	103	61	72	17	6.0	6.8
9	Elusive Indian	8/1	L	119.	S		76	79/ 77	(69)	105	85	85/ 85	61.	64.	71.	73.	104.6	65	106	105	104	66	316	17	6.3	7.6
10	Calm Waters	12/1	L	27	+E/P	6	83	82/ 77	* 68*	103	86	88/ 81	63	67.	68.	55.	104.9	66	106	103	103	64	540	13	6.9	7.4
3	Good Humor Man	3/1	L	21	P	2	75	75/ 78	* 67*	105	87	91/ 90	66.	72.	62.	63.	104.9	67	104	104	105	75	388	22	6.9	7.2
2	C C Ryder	4/1	L	22.	+E/P	5	87	86/ 68	* 66*	109	95	95/ 80	58.	62.	77.	60.	107.0	66	108	107	109		598	15	6.4	7.7
5	Hastego	5/1	L	11	++E	7	82	77/ 76	* 64*	104	85	83/ 83	62.	65.	65	68	103.6	64	103	104	103	71	11	27	7.7	6.9
1A	Power Fame	12/1	L	22	+E/P	5	91	90/ 62	* 62*	105	97	92/ 86	54.	76	67.	64.	103.8	66	108	104	103		394	11	6.5	7.5
1	Tomprado	12/1	L	13	S		72	71/ 78	* 61*	106	87	91/ 87	57.	51	58.	58	104.9	55	106	105	106	53	907	16	7.4	8.4
6	Mighty Wind	6/1	L	13	+E/P	6	91	86/ 63	* 60*	106	91	90/ 74	52.	68	66	61	105.7	62	106	106	106	70	34	21	6.6	7.3
7	Not A Question	20/1	L	8	+E/P	4	85	75/ 64	* 58*	105	90	89/ 80	56.	60.	53.	53	103.3	56	105	104	104	65	212	10	6.6	6.3
8	A Rizzi Rueben	20/1	L	14	NA	4	80	78/ 48	* 43*	106	92	93/ 83	34.	42.	45.	43.	107.9	40	104	106	105	72	727	14	6.4	9.4

Speed Last Race	Back Speed	Current Class	Average Class Last 3	Power Rating	Early Pace Last Race	Late Pace Last Race
66 Good Humor Man	81 Power Fame	107.3 C C Ryder	107.3 C C Ryder	103.7 Calm Waters	91 Calm Waters	82 Good Humor Man
63 Calm Waters	81 A Rizzi Rueben	106.5 Calm Waters	106.2 Calm Waters	102.9 Good Humor Man	87 Power Fame	75 Hastego
62 Hastego	79 Tomprado	105.9 Mighty Wind	106.2 Mighty Wind	101.6 C C Ryder	84 Gridwin	75 Tomprado
61 Elusive Indian	78 C C Ryder	105.8 Good Humor Man	105.8 Elusive Indian	100.6 Mighty Wind	83 C C Ryder	70 Elusive Indian
59 Gridwin	77 Good Humor Man	105.5 Elusive Indian	105.6 Good Humor Man	100.3 Gridwin	81 Mighty Wind	61 Calm Waters
58 C C Ryder	76 Elusive Indian	105.4 Hastego	105.3 Power Fame	98.8 Elusive Indian	79 Elusive Indian	60 C C Ryder
57 Tomprado	74 Gridwin	105.1 Power Fame	105.0 Hastego	98.8 Power Fame	75 Hastego	57 Mighty Wind
56 Not A Question	71 Not A Question	104.9 Gridwin	104.3 Gridwin	96.6 Hastego	75 Not A Question	56 Power Fame
54 Power Fame	70 Calm Waters	104.7 Tomprado	103.6 Tomprado	94.9 Not A Question	73 Good Humor Man	54 Not A Question
52 Mighty Wind	68 Mighty Wind	103.6 Not A Question	102.5 Not A Question	91.1 Tomprado	72 A Rizzi Rueben	53 Gndwin
34 A Rizzi Rueben	66 Hastego	102.3 A Rizzi Rueben	101.3 A Rizzi Rueben	88.6 A Rizzi Rueben	70 Tomprado	36 A Rizzi Rueben

#	Speed Last Race		#	Prime Power		#	Class Rating		#	Best Speed at Dist	
6	Heaven's Boy	58	7	Ready To Exchange	99.9	5	Pepper Biscuit	101.7	3	Essa's Cat	67
7	Ready To Exchange	57	3	Essa's Cat	98.5	6	Heaven's Boy	100.4	6	Heaven's Boy	61
5	Pepper Biscuit	55	6	Heaven's Boy	87.9	7	Ready To Exchange	99.8	1	Go Geta Job	60

9

Exacta / Trifecta / Superfecta (Ten Cent Minimum) / Pick 3 (Races 9-10-11)

Simulcast of Thistledown race number 9

	E1	E2/LATE	SPEED
PARS:	88	82/ 71	64

6 Furlongs. MC 4000 Purse $6,500. FOR MAIDENS, FOUR YEAR OLDS AND UPWARD. Weight, 122 lbs. Claiming Price $4,000 (Ohio Registered Foals Preferred).

Post Time: (3:45)/ 2:45/ 1:45/12:45

6 FURLONGS

---

1 **Go Geta Job (P 0)** **$4,000**
Own: Fernando Silva And Jacobo Quiroz
10/1 Gold, black ..., black diamonds
MONTERREY PEDRO (1 0-0-0 0%)

Gr/ro. g. 5 (Apr) KEESEP 2003 $4k
Sire: Wekiva Springs (Runaway Groom)
Dam: One Yum (Water Bank)
Brdr: McMillin Bros. & Billy Hay (KY)
Trnr: Silva Fernando (13 1-2-2 8%)

Power Rating: 81.1 (8th) L 122

Life:	20	0 - 0 - 3	$3,992	60	Fst	10	0 - 0 - 0	$1,549	53
2007	8	0 - 0 - 2	$1,427	60	Off	10	0 - 0 - 3	$2,443	60
2006	3	0 - 0 - 0	$129	43	Dis	9	0 - 0 - 2	$2,258	60
Tdn	2	0 - 0 - 0	$195	51	Trf	0	0 - 0 - 0	$0	
					AW	0	0 - 0 - 0	$0	

2007	2	0%	0%	-2.00
JKYw/ P types	4	0%	25%	-2.00
JKYw/ Sprints	2	0%	0%	-2.00

2007	68	14%	41%	0.58
No class chg	187	16%	47%	+0.06
+Maiden Clming	41	22%	56%	+1.15

Sire Stats: AWD 6.9f 13%Mud 540MudSts 7%1st 0.86spi
Dam'sSire: AWD 6.8f 12%Mud 822MudSts 9%1st 0.97spi
SoldAt: KEESEP 2003 $4.0k (5/7) SireAvg: $6.4k StudFee: $10,000

● Best Speed rating is well below the Avg Winning Speed

DATE TRK	DIST						RR RACETYPE	CR	E1	E2/	LP	1c	2c	SPD	PP	ST	1C	2C	Str	FIN	JOCKEY		ODDS	Top Finishers	Comment	
27Apr07Tdn3	5½ sy	:23	:48	1:02	1:08	4↑	99 MC4000	99	76	62/	68	-5	-8	51	7	7	73¼	76	75	54¾	Banda S122	Lbf	13.70	HovesOfThundr Heaven'sBoy Essa's Cat	No factor	8
12Apr07Tdn12	6f sy	:23	:48	1:01	1:14	4↑	98 MC4000	97	73	60/	66	-5	-9	41	4	7	74¾	78¾	79	913¾	Banda S122	Lbf	5.00	Shiloh'sCat Heaven'sBoy HovesOfThundr	No rally	10
31Mar07Beu2	5½ sy	:22	:46	:59	1:06	3↑	96 MC5000	99	78	71/	43	+1	+11	43	2	7	7¾	6¾	46¾	48¾	Ortiz W124	Lbf	5.00	SomstaDncr TheRiRson Ninonne	Finished mid track	7
07Mar07Beu4	6f ft	:23	:47	1:00	1:12	3↑	97 MC4000	97	77	70/	68	-7	-2	51	4	6	51¾	45	46¾	57¾	Yaranga Y124	Lbf	3.70	WinsPrpct BgShtr ThRiRsom	Between horses turn	8
28Feb07Beu8	6f gd	:22	:47		1:13	3↑	98 MC5000	99	80	76/	62	+3	+7	51	9	2	3¾	3	43	54¾	Yaranga Y124	Lb	5.20	RelyFit ImprtKstrl GodlkngGy	Between horses turn	11
20Feb07Beu4	5½ gd	:22	:48	1:00	1:07	3↑	94 MC4000	99	77	69/	65	+4	-4	51	2	5	49¾	4¾	42	39¾	Yaranga Y124	Lb	2.60	MxmmJck FslysPnt GoGtJb	Saved ground to lane	9
30Jan07Beu10	6f ft	:23	:47	:59	1:11	3↑	99 MC4000	98	79	67/	67	-7	-12	48	4	2	2hd	3½	5¾	57	Yaranga Y124	Lb	6.60	WarOfAces JoshaView RoylClae	3 wide duel, tired	11
09Jan07Beu10	6f gd	:23	:48	1:01	1:14	3↑	98 MC4000	102	68	65/	83	-2	-4	60	2	10	79¾	48	38	39¾	Oro E124	Lb	31.90	FishyReview HighlandJn GoGetJob	Saved ground	11
11Dec06Beu1	1⅛ ft	:23	:47	1:13	1:46	3↑	98 MC5000	95	64	46/	25	+2	+4	26	5	43	57	512	923	1134¾	Dailey A124	Lb	45.20	CshTown Blackan MiswkSprkle	Through after half	11

Previously trained by CLINE ROBERT C

DATE TRK	DIST						RR RACETYPE	CR	E1	E2/	LP	1c	2c	SPD	PP	ST	1C	2C	Str	FIN	JOCKEY		ODDS	Top Finishers	Comment	
22Nov06Beu8	6f ft	:22	:47	1:01	1:14	3↑	99 MC4000	97	74	68/	58	+6	+5	43	6	9	89¾	87¾	68	79¾	Erwin A119	Lb	44.30	HopelslyWld RelyFit ThatsVerie	No factor; inside	11

04Nov'06 Beu 4f sl :52 B *10/11* 14Oct'06 Beu 4f sl :51 Bg *13/20* 20Aug'05 FL 3f ft :36 B *3/12* 14Aug'05 FL 5f gd 1:02 Dg *3/6* 07Aug'05 FL 4f ft :49 B *6/14* 26Apr'05 Mnr (d) 4f my :52 B *15/20*
12Feb'05 Mnr 5f gd 1:05 Bg *14/17* 07Feb'05 Mnr 5f sl 1:06 Bg *7/11* 29Jan'05 Mnr 5f ft 1:03 B *4/9* 11Jan'05 Mnr 5f sy 1:07 Bg *9/10* 04Jan'05 Mnr 5f sl 1:07 B *8/10* 28Dec'04 Mnr 4f ft :53 B *20/25*

---

2 **Northern Cougar (NA 4)** **$4,000**
Own: Bruno Schickedanz
5/1 White, blue stripes
SPIETH SCOTT (94 11-10-7 17%)

Ch. g. 4 (May)
Sire: Northern Trend (Sunny North)
Dam: Royal Progress (Cougar's Crown)
Brdr: Bruno Schickedanz (FL)
Trnr: Radosevich Jeffrey A. (52 15-12-5 29%)

Power Rating: 83.1 (5th) L 122

Life:	4	0 - 0 - 0	$909	47	Fst	3	0 - 0 - 0	$909	47
2007	4	0 - 0 - 0	$909	47	Off	1	0 - 0 - 0	$0	28
2006	0	0 - 0 - 0	$0		Dis	2	0 - 0 - 0	$101	47
Tdn	0	0 - 0 - 0	$0		Trf	0	0 - 0 - 0	$0	
					AW	0	0 - 0 - 0	$0	

+2007	270	16%	43%	-0.67
+JKYw/NA types	77	21%	40%	+6.56
JKYw/ Trn L60	98	17%	48%	-0.83
JKYw/ Sprints	196	17%	45%	-0.58

+2007	168	20%	52%	-0.32
+Shipper	341	21%	48%	-0.46
+Down one class	231	25%	52%	-0.19
+Maiden Clming	212	20%	48%	-0.37

Sire Stats: AWD 6.0f 13%Mud 164MudSts 7%1st 0.65spi
Dam'sSire: AWD 7.0f 9%Mud 195MudSts 9%1st 0.92spi

★ Hot Trn/Jky combo in last 14 days (18 5- 4- 2) ★ Drops in Class today ★ High % Trainer ● Poor Speed Figures

DATE TRK	DIST						RR RACETYPE	CR	E1	E2/	LP	1c	2c	SPD	PP	ST	1C	2C	Str	FIN	JOCKEY		ODDS	Top Finishers	Comment	
27Apr07Mnr1	5½ ft	:22	:47	:59	1:06	3↑	96 MC5000	98	83	71/	53	4	5	45	4	3	3½	33	4¾	5¾	Pereira OM121	Lb	22.20	Lordnthuff RnsldG SpenSlnt	Chase;bumped upper (Placed 4th through disqualification)	10
09Apr07Mnr1	5f ft	:23	:48		1:02	3↑	96 MC5000	87		74/	54			39	2	6	74¾	77¾	74¾	59¾	Spieth S121	Lb	23.80	Flee The Great Biesiot Punk	Mild gain;no factor	9
24Mar07Mnr4	6f my	:23	:48	1:01	1:14	3↑	100 MC5000	97	77	64/	46	-6	-11	28	9	7	4¾	64	814	922¾	Spieth S121	L	38.80	MrcurySt HmEqty Phtto	Chased to1/4p;gave way	10
02Mar07Mnr10	6f ft	:22	:46	1:00	1:14	3↑	100 MC5000	100	74	69/	63	-1	+3	47	4	8	89¾	79	78¾	712¾	Spieth S121	L	15.50	PapasDrem Montroso OcalMrquetry	Showed little	10

07Apr Mnr 3f ft :38 Bg *7/12* 27Feb Mnr (d) 4f my :54 B *20/24* 29Dec'06 Mnr 5f ft 1:05 Bg *2/4* 23Dec'06 Mnr (d) 4f my :55 B *18/19* 15Dec'06 Mnr 4f gd :54 B *8/14* 18Oct'06 Ocl 4f ft :52 Bg *7/10*

3 Essa's Cat (P 2)

8/1 — Own: Mike Newell And Jack Wright — Purple; purple pins on white ball

BARRERA FRANCISCO (35 7-4-4 20%)

$4,000 Dkbbr. g. 4 (May)
Sire: Trajectory (Gone West)
Dam: Cat Bay (Bold Ruckus)
Brdr: Paul Bulligeeg (ONT-C)
Trnr: Newell Michael (15 4-0-2 27%)

Power Rating: 88.5 (2nd) L 117 5

Life:	18	0 - 2 - 5	$11,465	69	Fst	10	0 - 0 - 2	$4,282	62
2007	6	0 - 1 - 2	$4,479	61	Off	8	0 - 2 - 1	$7,403	69
2006	10	0 - 1 - 3	$6,528	69	Dis	6	0 - 0 - 0	$1,694	67
Tdn	3	0 - 0 - 1	$1,219	54	Trf	0	0 - 0 - 0	$0	
					AW	0	0 - 0 - 0	$0	

+2007	35	20%	43%	0.21	2007	64	19%	45%	+0.39	Sire Stats: AWD 6.6f 10%Mud 29MudSts	10% 1st 2.30spi
JKYw/ P types	6	17%	50%	-0.33	No class chg	502	10%	33%	-0.64	Dam'sSire:AWD 6.4f 19%Mud 1852MudSts	13% 1st 2.12spi
+JKYw/ Sprints	25	24%	44%	+0.35	-Btn favorite	77	23%	57%	+0.37		
					Maiden Clming	190	12%	35%	-0.66		

★ Hot Trainer in last 14 days (6 2-0-1) ★ Hot Jockey in last 7 days (11 4-0-2)
◆ Highest Speed Figure at Today's Distance ★ Best Dirt Speed is close to the Avg Winning Speed
★ Switches to a high% Jockey ★ High % Trainer ★ Ran 3rd vs similar in last race

DATE TRK	DIST						RR RACETYPE	CR	E1	E2/	LP	1c	2c	SPD	PP	ST	1C	2C	Str	FIN	JOCKEY		ODDS	Top Finishers	Comment	
27Apr07Tdn3	5½ sy	:23	:48	1:02	1:08	4↑	99 MC4000	98	79	63/	71	-3	-6	54	1	6	5	6	5	3	Stokes LA122	Lb	*2.10	HevesOfThundr HevensBoy EssasCat	Good effort	8
19Apr07Tdn1	5f ft	:22	:47		:59	3↑	101 MC10000	100		71/	71			54	1	6	6	6	6	5	Stokes LA122	Lb	4.30	PPsToFollow BgShotInTwn DhlonegGold	No threat	7
02Apr07Mnr7	5½ ft	:23	:48	1:01	1:08	3↑	99 MC5000	100	75	64/	58	0	-2	45	5	5	6	6	6	3	RamgeetAR121	Lb	4.70	WynngPwr Abronzto EsasCt	Belated gain at mid tk	10
20Mar07Mnr1	5f my	:23	:47		:59	3↑	100 MC5000	102		82/	70			61	10	6	6	5	3	2	RamgeetAR121	Lb	7.10	Hogan EsasCat SouthrnTrin	Bid5-6w;up for place	10
03Mar07Mnr1	6f ft	:22	:47	1:01	1:15	3↑	99 MC5000	99	81	77/	62	+2	+1	52	8	6	6	6	5	6	Vargas O121	Lb	13.20	Olimson Ed'sRush HolmEquity	Chased4w;no rally	10
10Feb07Mnr1	6f gd	:23	:47		1:13	3↑	100 MC10000/8	100	81	76/	60	-5	-6	50	2	6	3	3	4	5	Vargas O117	Lb	6.90	PrvlCosm Hrdwd MrlSprgs	Rail bid3/8;loomed;tired	9
03Dec06Mnr3	5½ ft	:23	:48	1:01	1:08	3↑	101 MC10000/9	101	81	71/	54	-5	-5	49	4	5	4	4	3	3	Vargas O117	Lb	12.80	BlueMonln MrcurySb EsasCt	Bumped start;chased	7
09Nov06Tdn6	6f ft	:23	:47	1:00	1:14	3↑	100 MC7500	99	80	70/	59	-2	-3	44	5	2	5	4	5	4	Hemsley D121	Lb	3.30	DonteRgsWinr GodVrsusRd MnmumJck	No rally	7
29Oct06FE7	5f my	:23	:47		1:06	3↑	102 MC5000	104		78/	78			69	1	4	4	4	3	2	David DJ120	Lb	5.35	GenerlDputy EssasCat DieTheChf	Good 3 pth trip	9
22Oct06FE8	5f sy	:22	:46		:58	3↑	102 MC5000	102		83/	64			57	1	2	3	3	3	3	Hemsley D119	Lb	7.15	GodTBAN GnrlDputy EssCt	Inside trip; held show	8

23Jan Mnr 3f gd :37 B 2/20 10Aug'06 FE 4f ft :49 H 5/7 04Aug'06 FE 3f ft :36 H 3/12 03Jun'06 WO 4f ft :49 H 32/63 20Apr'06 WO 5f ft 1:04 H 28/31 13Apr'06 WO 4f gd :52 H 28/29
06Apr'06 WO 4f ft :50 H 17/24 30Mar'06 WO 3f ft :37 H 10/27 24Mar'06 WO tr.t 3f ft :37 H 21/39 17Mar'06 WO tr.t 2f ft :26 H 12/13 03Nov'05 WO 3f ft :37 Hg 6/9 28Oct'05 WO 4f ft :50 H 14/31

4 Mr. Jupiter (NA 0)

4/1 — Own: Double D Farm Corp. — Red and blue; two horse heads

CLONINGER, JR. WELDON T. (41 15-7-2 37%)

$4,000 Ch. c. 4 (Apr)
Sire: Railway Cat (Storm Cat)
Dam: Greta's Galaxy (Fappiano)
Brdr: Double D Farm Corp. (OH)
Trnr: Crumley Jevon (28 9-5-4 32%)

Power Rating: 79.7 (7th) L 122

Life:	1	0 - 0 - 0	$139	45	Fst	0	0 - 0 - 0	$0	
2006	1	0 - 0 - 0	$139	45	Off	1	0 - 0 - 0	$139	45
2005	0	0 - 0 - 0	$0		Dis	1	0 - 0 - 0	$139	46
Tdn	1	0 - 0 - 0	$139	45	Trf	0	0 - 0 - 0	$0	
					AW	0	0 - 0 - 0	$0	

+2007	44	34%	59%	+1.03	+2007	34	26%	53%	-0.01	Sire Stats: AWD 6.5f 18%Mud 49MudSts	8% 1st 0.52spi
JKYw/NA types	25	12%	28%	-1.13	+90+ days away	41	27%	59%	+1.75	Dam'sSire:AWD 7.3f 18%Mud 624MudSts	17% 1st 5.68spi
+JKYw/ Trn L60	19	37%	58%	+0.59	+2nd career race	20	25%	55%	-0.64		
+JKYw/ Sprints	33	33%	56%	+0.79	Maiden Clming	32	16%	47%	-0.56		

★ Hot Jockey in last 7 days (20 7-4-1) ★ Hot Trn/Jky combo in last 14 days (10 3-2-0) ● Poor Speed Figure in only start ● Has not raced for more than 8 months
★ Drops in Class today ★ Switches to a high% Jockey ★ High % Trainer

DATE TRK	DIST						RR RACETYPE	CR	E1	E2/	LP	1c	2c	SPD	PP	ST	1C	2C	Str	FIN	JOCKEY		ODDS	Top Finishers	Comment	
29Aug06Tdn1	6f gd	:22	:46	1:00	1:13	3↑	100 Mdn 14k	99	71	60/	70	+2	+2	45	4	3	7	7	7	6	Feliciano R119	L	12.50	MrcRgsWnr RvsCry FnlExpss	Slow early; outrun	7

02May Tdn 4f ft :49 B 2/8 27Apr Tdn 3f gd :38 B 6/10 ●28Oct'06 Tdn 3f sy :37 B 1/4 07Sep'06 Tdn 4f ft :49 Bg 1/3 19Aug'06 Tdn 4f ft :51 Bg 15/17 14Aug'06 Tdn 4f ft :52 B 16/20
09Aug'06 Tdn 3f ft :38 Bg 7/10 13May'06 Tdn 3f my :40 B 8/13 06May'06 Tdn 3f ft :40 B 14/15 23Apr'06 Tdn 3f gd :39 B 19/22

5 Pepper Biscuit (P 1)

6/1 — Own: Michael Feriole And Mauricio Nunez — Green; blue blocks; white sleeves

CASTILLO KENDRY (32 4-4-4 13%)

$4,000 Gr/ro. h. 5 (Feb)
Sire: Suave Prospect (Fortunate Prospect)
Dam: Commodore Street (Summing)
Brdr: Michael Feriole (FL)
Trnr: Nunez Mauricio (1 0-0-0 0%)

Power Rating: 86.7 (4th) L 122

Life:	13	0 - 1 - 2	$6,717	59	Fst	13	0 - 1 - 2	$6,717	59
2006	4	0 - 0 - 2	$3,400	56	Off	0	0 - 0 - 0	$0	
2005	9	0 - 1 - 0	$3,317	59	Dis	2	0 - 0 - 0	$136	46
Tdn	0	0 - 0 - 0	$0		Trf	0	0 - 0 - 0	$0	
					AW	0	0 - 0 - 0	$0	

2007	32	13%	44%	-1.19	2007	1	0%	0%	-2.00	Sire Stats: AWD 6.8f 15%Mud 493MudSts	7% 1st 0.88spi
+JKYw/ P types	6	33%	67%	-1.00	90+ days away	4	0%	0%	-2.00	Dam'sSire:AWD 7.0f 12%Mud 832MudSts	7% 1st 1.05spi
JKYw/ Trn L60	1	0%	0%	-2.00	1st strt w/trn	9	0%	11%	-2.00		
JKYw/ Sprints	19	11%	37%	-1.01	Shipper	7	0%	14%	-2.00		

★ Drops in Class today ★ Ran 3rd vs tougher in last race ★ 60% trainer: Down one class ● Has not raced for more than 8 months

DATE TRK	DIST						RR RACETYPE	CR	E1	E2/	LP	1c	2c	SPD	PP	ST	1C	2C	Str	FIN	JOCKEY		ODDS	Top Finishers	Comment	
Previously trained by DAVID, JR. SAM B.																										
23Aug06EvD1	1m ft	:24	:49	1:15	1:43	3↑	100 MC5000	102	82	50/	73	-7	-6	55	2	4	3	3	2hd	3	LejeuneJrSP123	Lbf	*2.20	Thunderhrt Wildntwrrior PprBiscuit	No match late	10
22Jly06EvD10	1m ft	:24	:48	1:15	1:44	3↑	99 MC5000	101	66	53/	63	+10	+5	51	9	4	3	3	3	4	Fusilier C123	Lbf	2.80	Rousster SundayInSelle CarnivlyGold	No final kick	10
08Jly06EvD7	170 ft	:24	:48	1:15	1:48	3↑	100 MC5000	102	77	60/	54	+14	+8	52	11	5	4	3	2hd	3	Fusilier C123	Lbf	*2.80	Slews Cruiser Patso Pepper Biscuit	No final kick	11
02Jun06EvD10	1m ft	:24	:48	1:15	1:43	3↑	99 MC5000	100	61	55/	78	+2	+3	56	8	9	7	7	5	4	SantiagoHM122	Lb	6.30	Jvier JelsWorld WshingtonKing	Improved position	9
Previously trained by PASSLEY MARK																										
10Sep05FL8	1 1/16 ft	:23	:47	1:13	1:46	3↑	100 MC4000	99	51	44/	64	-6	-2	50	4	7	6	6	6	5	ManickrmM120	Lb	3.80	Sea Patrol Hanoi Gramps	Chkd st; lacked rally	9
30Aug05FL8	170 ft	:23	:48	1:14	1:46	3↑	100 MC4000	103	53	52/	73	-4	-8	59	1	7	5	4	2	2	ManickrmM119	Lb	5.80	Cruisin Pip Pepper Biscuit Hanoi	Finished well	8
21Aug05FL8	170 ft	:23	:48	1:15	1:49	3↑	100 MC4000	102	57	55/	59	-1	+5	53	6	8	8	4	5	4	ManickrmM119	Lb	15.90	Last Trial Hanoi Reigning Starm	With interest	11
07Aug05FL8	170 ft	:23	:47	1:14	1:46	3↑	101 MC4000	102	57	46/	71	+2	-3	54	7	11	10	7	5	4	ManickrmM119	Lb	14.80	CustomCruser LastTrial Hanoi	5-w 5/16; no solid bid	12
24Jly05FL8	170 ft	:23	:48	1:16	1:49	3↑	100 MC4000	101	62	47/	62	+3	-5	49	4	7	6	4	1hd	5	ManickrmM119	Lb	12.30	FlagTower Hnoi JosiesBoy	5-w 5/16;flattened out	12
10Jly05FL2	170 ft	:23	:48	1:13	1:45	3↑	101 MC7500	101	55	42/	75	-5	+1	53	7	8	8	7	7	7	ManickrmM119	Lb	25.75	KnowThJudg Rayalme TortSoup	Lacked response	11

04May Tdn 3f ft :38 Bg 20/23 ●22Sep'06 LaD 6f ft 1:13 H 1/5 27Aug'06 LaD 5f my 1:03 Hg 15/21 ●10Aug'06 EvD 4f my :50 B 1/5 04Aug'06 EvD 6f ft 1:19 B 1/2 29May'06 EvD 6f ft 1:18 B 3/4
11Apr'06 Tam 3f ft :38 Bg 13/20 03Jun'05 FL 4f ft :50 Bg 9/20 13May'05 FL 5f ft 1:02 D 5/18 07May'05 FL 5f ft 1:01 Dg 5/24 29Apr'05 FL 5f ft 1:03 Dg 12/20 22Apr'05 FL 3f ft :36 Dg 16/42

Ultimate PP's w/ Quick Play Comments **River Downs** MC 4000 6 Furlongs. 4up Friday, May 11, 2007 **Race 9 (TDN - #9)** E1 88 E2/LATE 82/ 71 SPD 64

6 3/1 **Heaven's Boy (E/P 5)**
Own: Drake Racing Stable
Green, white hoop, white hoop on sleeves
MAGRELL JANE M. (27 0-8-4 0%)

$4,000 B. g. 5 (Apr)
Sire: Heaven's Wish (Halo)
Dam: Attentive Nurse (Dance Furlough)
Brdr: Andy Stronach & Dean Brice (ONT-C)
Trnr: Girten Shirley K. (6 0-3-0 0%)

Power Rating: 87.9 (3rd) 122

Life:	33	0	8	5	$22,910	60	Fst	22	0	5	5	$17,822	60
2007	3	0	2	0	$2,800	58	Off	11	0	3	0	$5,088	60
2006	14	0	3	2	$9,656	65	Dis	3	0	2	1	$3,420	61
Tdn	4	0	3	1	$4,460	58	Trf	0	0	0	0	$0	
							AW	0	0	0	0	$0	

2007	30	0%	37%	-2.00
JKYw/EP types	91	8%	26%	-1.20
JKYw/ Trn L60	6	0%	50%	-2.00
JKYw/ Sprints	24	0%	38%	-2.00

2007	6	0%	50%	-2.00
+No class chg	7	29%	57%	+0.17
Maiden Clming	3	0%	100%	-2.00

Sire Stats: AWD 6.7f 6%Mud 52MudSts 5%1st 0.35spi
Dam'sSire:AWD 6.7f 18%Mud 22MudSts 6%1st 0.17spi

★ Highest Last Race Speed Rating ★ Best Dirt Speed is fastest among today's starters ● Poor Jockey win% ● Poor Trainer win%
★ Ran 2nd vs similar in last race

DATE TRK	DIST						RR	RACETYPE	CR	E1	E2/	LP	1c	2c	SPD	PP	ST	1C	2C	Str	FIN	JOCKEY	ODDS	Top Finishers	Comment
27Apr07Tdn3	5½ sy	:232	:482	1:02	1:082	4↑	97	MC4000	100	83	73/	76	-3	-6	**58**	5	1	1½	1½	11	21	MagrellJM122	2.50	HvsOfThundr1HevensBoy2½EbasCat4	Broke sharply 8
12Apr07Tdn12	6f sy	:232	:482	1:014	1:144	4↑	99	MC4000	101	83	73/	72	-5	-9	**58**	8	1	1hd	1½	2hd	22¾	MagrellJM122	6.30	ShthsCt2¾HvnsBoy1¾HvsOfThndr6	Dueled; held place 10
20Feb07Mnr2	6f my	:222	:461	:592	1:124	3↑	103	Clm5000n2L	100	75	73/	52	-2	-2	**41**	6	6	7½	6¾	810	918	HernndezAB118	22.70	Lover's Star3½FlorencohdFrostbg7	Slow early; labored 10
Previously trained by WILSON CAMPBELL																									
25Nov06Tdn1	6f ft	:23	:472	1:004	1:141	3↑	100	MC3500	101	73	70/	74	-3	-4	**56**	4	4	65	52	52	31	Madhot P122	2.20	BlondCommandoNoCrs1HvnsBoy2	Split horses; rallied 7
11Nov06Tdn8	6f sy	:234	:481	1:02	1:154	3↑	99	MC3500	104	63	61/	83	-8	-3	**56**	8	4	6¾	47	2½	2½	Unel-mornV122	4.60	eDmscusDncr½HevnsBoy3HighHalM1½	Rallied; gaining 11
Previously trained by WOODS JAMES W.																									
24Oct06FE8	170 my	:233	:48	1:134	1:451	3↑	103	MC5000/4.75	100	66	58/	53	-8	-6	**51**	3	1hd	1hd	2hd	97½	1010½	Clark C118	5.40	ImARobrnHndsIPcktsnkElGrDvd1½	Speed; duel faltered 10
09Oct06FE3	1⅛ ft	:231	:47	1:122	1:453	3↑	104	MC10000/9	104	67	60/	64	+1	0	**59**	2	711	87¼	87½	611	414	Clark C118	25.55	KngNptun¾PortoSgro13NoOneMovnk	Late mild wide try 10
18Sep06FE7	1⅛ ft	:247	:497	1:141	1:487	3↑	103	MC10000/9	102	62	65/	52	-13	-2	**55**	7	2hd	2hd	2hd	48	910	Hemsley D118	6.75	CneGrdn1¾AdmrblNsn7¾MyPrpsl1½	Vied for six faltered 9
28Aug06FE1	1⅛ my	:49	1:14	1:401	1:534	3↑	104	MC10000/9	102	59	60/	55	-13	-6	**57**	6	33	32½	32	58	612	Hemsley D118	5.40	Chfln2KngNptun3½LughngJJhd	Stalked leaders; faded 6
14Aug06FE1	170 ft	:234	:483	1:14	1:45	3↑	103	MC10000/9	109	68	71/	66	-11	-5	**65**	7	5¼	31	2½	23	2¾	Hemsley D118	12.35	VeryChrBu¾HvnsBoy1¾KngNptn3½	Bid far turn good try 7

30Mar Mnr 5f ft 1:05 B *3/4* 02Feb Mnr 5f ft 1:022 B *3/7* 16Jan Mnr 5f my 1:05 B *4/10* 27Oct06 FE 4f ft :49 Hg *3/8* ●03Jly06 FE 3f ft :354 H *1/15* 04May06 FE 3f ft :38 B *12/17*
23Apr06 FE 3f ft :38 B *18/21* 17Apr06 FE 3f ft :361 H *5/23* 02Apr06 FE 2f ft :251 B *1/3* ●26May05 FE 4f ft :48 H *1/8* 16May05 FE 4f ft :49 B *11/36* ●27Apr05 WO tr.t 3f sy :373 B *1/4*

7 5/2 **Ready To Exchange (E 5)**
Own: Bridget Sipp
Red & white quartered, red & white sleeves
SANGUINETTI ANNE (72 10-8-8 14%)

$4,000 B. g. 4 (Jan) BESNOV 2006 $5k
Sire: Ready To Order (Order)
Dam: Exchanging Glances (Silver Ghost)
Brdr: Robert Moreno (CA)
Trnr: Sipp Burton K. (58 10-8-8 18%)

Power Rating: 89.9 (1st) L 122

Life:	4	0	0	0	$1,520	62	Fst	3	0	0	0	$1,455	62
2007	4	0	0	0	$1,520	62	Off	1	0	0	0	$65	44
2006	0	0	0	0	$0		Dis	1	0	0	0	$65	44
Tdn	2	0	0	0	$455	57	Trf	0	0	0	0	$0	
							AW	0	0	0	0	$0	

2007	156	12%	37%	-1.10
JKYw/ E types	228	14%	37%	-1.04
JKYw/ Trn L60	71	17%	39%	-0.97
JKYw/ Sprints	121	12%	40%	-1.09

2007	137	13%	41%	-1.19
+Down 2+ classes	46	22%	37%	-0.10
Maiden Clming	160	11%	34%	-1.18

Sire Stats: AWD 6.8f 13%Mud 15MudSts 11%1st 1.38spi
Dam'sSire:AWD 6.9f 14%Mud 1007MudSts 14%1st 1.59spi
SoldAt: BESNOV 2006 $4.7k (1/1) SireAvg: $4.7k StudFee:$1,000

★ Best Dirt Speed is close to the Avg Winning Speed ★ Drops in Class today
★ Early Speed running style helps chances

DATE TRK	DIST						RR	RACETYPE	CR	E1	E2/	LP	1c	2c	SPD	PP	ST	1C	2C	Str	FIN	JOCKEY	ODDS	Top Finishers	Comment
19Apr07Tdn1	5f ft	:224	:47		:594	3↑	101	MC10000	101		77/	71			**57**	5	3	32	33	42½	43	SanguinettiA122	L 8.90	PPsTFlw1¾BgShtTw1¾DhingGldnk	Well placed; evenly 7
12Apr07Tdn12	6f sy	:232	:482	1:014	1:144	4↑	99	MC4000	98	83	72/	57	-5	-9	**44**	2	5	2hd	2½	3½	611½	SanguinettiA122	L 10.70	ShthsCt2¾HvnsBoy1¾HvsOfThndr6	Weakened; stretch 10
08Mar07DeD1	1m ft	:233	:492	1:154	1:44	3↑	100	MC10000	101	64	59/	71	-9	-4	**59**	4	21	2hd	1½	2hd	53	SanguinettiA123	L 9.00	WolfbnahdSilentRule1¾LoneStrFlsh½	Speed; weakened 10
17Feb07DeD10	5f ft	:23	:474		1:004	3↑	98	MC10000	98		80/	71			**62**	8	5	7½	63½	66	48½	SanguinettiA123	L 13.60	RdProspctornkFoldm3¾DixieStw2½	Moved up; no factor 10

22Mar DeD 4f ft :533 B *14/15* 06Feb DeD 4f ft :512 B *5/8* 31Jan DeD 4f wf :534 Bg *20/33* 23Jan DeD 4f ft :51 B *4/10* 16Jan DeD 3f wf :381 B *2/4* 16Jan DeD 3f ft :374 B *7/23*

tsnhorse.com

Ultimate PP's w/ Quick Play Comments **River Downs** MC 4000 6 Furlongs. 4up Friday, May 11, 2007 **Race 9 (TDN - #9)**

E1	E2/LATE	SPD
88	82/ 71	64

Last 3 Years RACETYPE STATS:	# Races	FAVORITES Win%	Itm%	$2ROI	Average Field Size	Median $2 Win Payoff	% Winners < 5/1	% Winners >= 5/1 < 10/1	% Winners >= 10/1
TDN 3up MCL 3500 - 5000 Dirt 6f	73	30%	71%	-0.55	9.7	$8.20	66%	25%	10%

Track Bias Stats

DIRT 6.0f	* MEET Totals * Speed Bias: 82%	WnrAvgBL		DIRT 6.0f	* WEEK Totals * Speed Bias: 67%	WnrAvgBL	
# Races: 22	04/12 - 05/06	1stCall: 1.3		# Races: 6	05/03 - 05/06	1stCall: 1.6	
%Wire: 36%		2ndCall: 1.1		%Wire: 50%		2ndCall: 1.7	

	Early	Speed	Late	Speed		Early	Speed	Late	Speed
Runstyle:	E	E/P	P	S	Runstyle:	E	E/P	P	S
	++	+				++		+	
Impact Values	1.77	1.41	0.70	0.13	Impact Values	1.71	0.97	1.32	0.00
%Races Won	45%	36%	14%	5%	%Races Won	50%	17%	33%	0%
Post Bias:	RAIL	1-3	4-7	8+	Post Bias	RAIL	1-3	4-7	8+
		+	+			+		+	
Impact Values	0.75	1.13	1.09	0.51	Impact Values	1.43	0.48	1.79	0.00
Avg Win %	9%	14%	17%	3%	Avg Win %	17%	6%	28%	0%

Race Summary

#	HorseName	ML Odds	Med Eqp	Days Since L/R	Run Style	P T S	Avg Dist/Surf PACE-SPEED E1	E2/Late	Spd	Avg Race Rtng	Best Pace E1	E2/Late	Final Speed Sp1	Sp2	Sp3	ACL	Rcg Spd Avg	R1	R2	R3	Pedigree Stats Mud Spd	% Mud	% 1st	SPI	DPI	Sire AWD	Dam Sire's AWD
7	Ready To Exchange	5/2	L	22	++E	5		79/ 71	* 60*	100		80/ 71	57.	44	59		53	101	98	100	44	13	11	1.38		6.8	6.9
6	Heaven's Boy	3/1		14..	+E/P	5	77	74/ 72	(58)	103	80	75/ 74	58	58	41	98.6	52	99	98	103	58	6	5	0.35		6.7	6.7
3	Essa's Cat	8/1	L	14	P	2	81	75/ 64	' 52'	100	81	61/ 74	54	54.	45.	98.8	51	99	101	99	69	10	10	2.3		6.6	6.4
1	Go Geta Job	10/1	L	14	P		78	72/ 65	' 51'	98	80	76/ 83	51	41	43	97.4	45	99	98	98	51	13	7	0.86		6.9	6.8
2	Northern Cougar	5/1	L	14	NA	4	79	70/ 58	* 46*	100	83	74/ 63	45.	39.	28		37	98	98	100	28	13	7	0.65		6.0	7.0
4	Mr. Jupiter	4/1	L	256	NA		71	60/ 70	(45)	100	71	60/ 70	45.				45	100				18	8	0.52		6.5	7.5
5	Pepper Biscuit	6/1	L	261	P	1	70	49/ 80	(44)	101			55	51	52		53	100	99	100		15	7	0.98		6.8	7.0

Speed Last Race	Back Speed	Current Class	Average Class Last 3	Power Rating	Early Pace Last Race	Late Pace Last Race
58 Heaven's Boy	62 Ready To Exchange	99.8 Essa's Cat	101.7 Pepper Biscuit	89.9 Ready To Exchange	73 Heaven's Boy	76 Heaven's Boy
57 Ready To Exchange	62 Essa's Cat	99.7 Ready To Exchange	100.4 Heaven's Boy	88.5 Essa's Cat	71 Northern Cougar	73 Pepper Biscuit
55 Pepper Biscuit	60 Go Geta Job	98.9 Northern Cougar	99.8 Ready To Exchange	87.9 Heaven's Boy	63 Essa's Cat	71 Essa's Cat
54 Essa's Cat	57 Heaven's Boy	98.2 Go Geta Job	99.6 Essa's Cat	86.7 Pepper Biscuit	62 Pepper Biscuit	71 Ready To Exchange
51 Go Geta Job	47 Northern Cougar	NA Heaven's Boy	98.2 Mr. Jupiter	83.1 Northern Cougar	62 Go Geta Job	70 Mr. Jupiter
45 Northern Cougar	45 Mr. Jupiter	NA Mr. Jupiter	97.7 Go Geta Job	81.1 Go Geta Job	60 Mr. Jupiter	68 Go Geta Job
45 Mr. Jupiter	NA Pepper Biscuit	NA Pepper Biscuit	97.6 Northern Cougar	79.7 Mr. Jupiter	NA Ready To Exchange	53 Northern Cougar

#	Speed Last Race		#	Prime Power		#	Class Rating		#	Best Speed at Dist	
1	Bri's Bad Boy	76	1	Bri's Bad Boy	110.5	7	Mr. Popeye	109.3	2	J. R.'s Town	86
2	J. R.'s Town	70	2	J. R.'s Town	107.7	8	Unwavering Flight	108.4	3	Dance With A Fool	80
7	Mr. Popeye	70	7	Mr. Popeye	105.4	3	Dance With A Fool	108.3	1	Bri's Bad Boy	80

10

Exacta / Trifecta / Superfecta (Ten Cent Minimum) / Pick 3 (Races 10-11-12)

	E1	E2/LATE	SPEED
PARS:	90	88/ 76	73

6 Furlongs. Clm 4000 Purse $7,000. SIMULCAST FROM RIVER DOWNS.
FOR REGISTERED OHIO BRED THREE YEAR OLDS AND UPWARD. Three Year Olds, 116 lbs., Older, 124 lbs. Non-winners of a race since April 11 Allowed 2 lbs. A race since March 11 Allowed 4 lbs. Claiming Price $4,000 (Races where entered for $3,500 or less not cons idered in allowances) .
Post Time: (4:05)/ 3:05/ 2:05/ 1:05

1 Bri's Bad Boy (E/P 4)

Own: Thomas M. McCann
7/2 Gold, gold gp on blue diamond, blue sleeves
LUNA RAMON (5 0-2-0 0%)

$4,000 Ch. g. 8
Sire: Chequer (Mr. Prospector)
Dam: Man Charmer (Hatchet Man)
Brdr: Thomas McCann & Judith McCann (OH)
Trnr: Cowens William D. (5 2-1-1 40%)

Power Rating: 110.5 (1st) L 122

Life:	83 15 - 16 - 6	$80,761	82	Fst	11 13 - 13 - 5	$80,708	83
2007	6 3 - 1 - 0	$8,182	76	Off	12 2 - 3 - 1	$13,053	78
2006	18 3 - 3 - 1	$5,030	78	Dis	45 12 - 11 - 5	$74,119	80
RD	12 3 - 2 - 0	$25,272	71	Trf	0 0 - 0 - 0	$0	
				AW	0 0 - 0 - 0	$0	

2007	177	18%	44%	-0.27
+JKYw/EP types	89	19%	34%	+1.05
+JKYw/ Trn L60	3	67%	100%	+0.13
JKYw/ Sprints	132	17%	48%	+0.06

+2007	58	34%	63%	+0.20
+Wnr last race	108	29%	59%	-0.01
+No class chg	136	29%	55%	+0.22
+Claiming	288	22%	49%	-0.38

Sire Stats: AWD 7.2f 10%Mud 229MudSts 0.74spi
Dam'sSire:AWD 7.5f 14%Mud 1250MudSts 1.36spi

★ Highest Last Race Speed Rating ★ Won last race (BEU 04/28 6f Dirt fast Clm 3500C)

DATE TRK	DIST						RR RACETYPE	CR	E1	E2/	LP	1c	2c	SPD	PP	ST	1C	2C	Str	FIN	JOCKEY		ODDS	Top Finishers	Comment	
28Apr07Beu8	6f ft	:23¹	:47²	1:00²	1:12²	3↑	104 Clm3500C	110	83	84/	83	-3	-6	76	2	2	2²½	1hd	1⁴	1²	Luna R124	Lb	1.10	BrisBdBoy²MrTrthful¹½DncinLnce²	Drew off; driving	6
18Apr07Beu8	6f ft	:22²	:45⁴	:58¹	1:11¹	3↑	104 Clm3500n2y+	109	86	94/	69	+1	+7	72	10	2	4²	1hd	1²	1⁴	ThorwarthO122	Lb	1.30	BrisBdBoy⁴LaLifeAvengr⁶Hphz8h½	Drew off; driving	10
04Apr07Beu8	6f ft	:23⁴	:48¹	1:00¹	1:13	3↑	103 Clm3500n2y+	106	78	71/	82	-8	-7	64	3	8	5½	3²½	3²½	2¹½	ThorwarthO124	Lb	1.00	ClmWtrs¹½BrsBdBy¹½PirstAdGrvy²½	Willingly; 2nd best	9
12Mar07Beu5	6f ft	:22⁴	:46³	:58⁴	1:11	3↑	103 C4000n1Y	106	86	86/	81	-5	-4	76	2	3	1½	1hd	1¹	1²½	Stokes LA124	Lb	*0.70	Bri's Bad Boy²½Chelsey'sDynaSea⁶StickyCal½	Driving	5
30Jan07Beu4	5½ ft	:22⁴	:46¹	:57⁴	1:04	3↑	105 Clm4000n16m	106	81	74/	76	-8	-5	64	2	5	1hd	4²½	5³½	4²½	Stokes LA124	Lb	1.00	RyndSprngs²½Frnkncre⁶⁶SlnCrk½	Angled out; no rally	7
16Jan07Beu5	5½ ft	:23	:48³	:58	1:06²	3↑	106 Clm7500	109	78	63/	88	-9	-19	70	3	3	5⁴½	5⁶	5⁸	5⁶	ConqueMA120	Lb	10.90	GeistBuster½Florida Man³½Lifes Crown¹½	Showed little	6
18Dec06Beu8	5½ ft	:22⁴	:46⁴	:59⁴	1:05²	3↑	109 Clm7500	120	82	84/	69	+2	+3	75	2	12	12⁹½	10⁷½	8⁷½	5⁶	RosarioJrHL120	Lb	15.80	DshRndr¹JimysStr¹RgtmRqust⁴	Passed tiring rivals	12
06Dec06Beu1	6f ft	:22²	:47	:59⁴	1:13¹	3↑	107 C7500	107	92	92/	62	+7	+7	65	7	3	6²½	4¹½	4³	4⁴½	Stokes LA120	Lb	*1.70	Smcker²HereComesBrag½DaFonz¹	Split horses turn	8
19Nov06Beu5	5½ ft	:22	:46¹	:58³	1:05¹	3↑	108 Clm7500	111	79	81/	78	+2	-3	72	1	9	8⁶½	5⁴½	3¹	2¹½	Stokes LA120	Lb	4.70	Pager¹½BrisBdBoy¹HereComesBrg⁶	6 wide into lane	9
27Oct06Beu10	5½ sy⁸	:21³	:45³	:57²	1:03⁴	3↑	109 Alw5000s	110	77	85/	79	0	-4	78	4	6	7⁸	6⁵½	4¹½	2⁴½	Stokes LA120	Lb	18.70	RgtmRqust⁴½BrsBdBy¹½MyErgy²½	Rallied; second best	7

05Mar Beu 4f ft :48² B 1/1 21Oct'06 Beu 5f ft 1:03¹ B 4/8 14Oct'06 Beu 4f sl :50² B 5/20 04Oct'06 Beu 5f ft 1:03¹ B 3/5 27Sep'06 Beu 5f ft 1:04 B 1/3 11Sep'06 RD 6f ft 1:17 B 2/3
02Sep'06 RD 5f ft 1:05 B 4/4 26Aug'06 RD 4f ft :51 B 2/20 19Aug'06 RD 3f ft :38 B 2/8 30Sep'05 Beu 5f ft 1:02³ B 4/6 23Sep'05 Beu 6f ft 1:15³ B 4/4 16Sep'05 Beu 5f ft 1:03² B 2/3

2 J. R.'s Town (S 3)

Own: Patricia A. Bragg
5/2 Pink, pink b on black diamond
CALO JOSE LUIS (94 10-8-7 16%)

$4,000 Ch. g. 10
Sire: Texas City (Mr. Prospector)
Dam: Just Regent (Vice Regent)
Brdr: George A. Zimmerman (OH)
Trnr: Bragg Patricia A. (2 1-1-0 50%)

Power Rating: 107.7 (2nd) L 124

Life:	97 20 - 16 - 12	$155,924	86	Fst	56 12 - 11 - 8	$100,218	86
2007	6 1 - 2 - 1	$6,936	76	Off	30 8 - 5 - 4	$55,645	86
2006	17 3 - 3 - 6	$20,786	80	Dis	61 17 - 10 - 11	$128,093	85
RD	28 8 - 5 - 5	$54,583	79	Trf	1 0 - 0 - 0	$61	60
				AW	0 0 - 0 - 0	$0	

2007	214	14%	40%	-0.52
JKYw/ S types	290	7%	30%	-0.86
+JKYw/ Trn L60	1	100%	100%	+2.80
JKYw/ Sprints	158	13%	39%	-0.53

2007	31	19%	71%	-0.41
+Wnr last race	52	19%	48%	-0.42
Claiming	203	18%	47%	-0.24

Sire Stats: AWD 6.5f 13%Mud 433MudSts 0.80spi
Dam'sSire:AWD 7.0f 16%Mud 1131MudSts 2.96spi

★ Recent Speed Ratings make him a threat ★ Highest Speed Figure at Today's Distance ● Moves up in class from last start
★ Best Dirt Speed is fastest among today's starters (tie)
★ Won last race (RD 05/01 6f Dirt fast sClm4000NW16M)

DATE TRK	DIST						RR RACETYPE	CR	E1	E2/	LP	1c	2c	SPD	PP	ST	1C	2C	Str	FIN	JOCKEY		ODDS	Top Finishers	Comment	
01May07RD7	6f ft	:22⁴	:46	:59²	1:13¹	3↑	104 C4000n16m	108	85	86/	74	-2	0	70	2	6	3¹	1¹	1½	1¹	Calo JL124	Lb	*1.40	JRsTw¹Batingspter⁴½KOfRvrCrsg²½	Drew clear; driving	7
07Apr07Beu8	5½ ft	:23	:46³	:59²	1:06	3↑	107 C4000	106	80	92/	68	-1	+8	75	2	6	5⁶	4²½	2⁴	2²	Stokes LA120	Lb	5.90	UnwvgFight²JRsTown²½DncWthAFol²½	3 wide; rallied	6
23Mar07Beu3	6f sy⁶	:22²	:46¹	:58³	1:11¹	3↑	107 C4000	106	82	79/	68	-1	+1	59	4	5	4³	4²½	4⁴	4⁶½	Stokes LA120	Lb	2.20	JonThBrnr⁴DncWthAFl⁴TrkOlTTrs⁶	Evenly; no rally	5
28Feb07Beu4	6f gd⁶	:23¹	:46	:58³	1:10³	3↑	108 Clm5000	104	71	82/	73	-9	+1	66	4	5	5⁶	4⁶½	4⁹	4⁹½	Stokes LA120	Lb	3.50	One Way Out²½CheckBouncer⁸½Lifes Crown¹	No factor	6
12Feb07Beu7	6f ft	:22²	:46		1:09³	3↑	108 Clm5000	110	72	77/	91	-3	-5	76	8	6	6⁸	6⁵	5²½	2²	Stokes LA120	Lb	*2.50	LifEsExprs²JRsTown¹Perimetr¹½	Rallied; up for place	8
30Jan07Beu8	6f ft	:23	:46⁴	:58⁴	1:10³	3↑	109 Clm7500	109	80	74/	77	-8	-10	62	1	6	1½	1hd	2½	3³	Stokes LA120	Lb	8.10	Schwhdthl¹TToGrn²JRsTw¹	Broke slow; rushed up	7
22Dec06Beu7	6f sy⁵	:22	:45⁴	:58²	1:11¹	3↑	108 Alw5000s	109	82	87/	76	+7	+7	80	5	10	9⁸½	7⁴½	4⁵	4⁴½	Stokes LA120	Lb	7.70	CoparTrl½ChckBouncr¹½HeresLou²½	9 wide into lane	11
09Dec06Beu6	1m ft	:24³	:48	1:14¹	1:41²	3↑	108 C5000	104	85	90/	60	+11	+13	72	4	4⁴½	4³½	1hd	3hd	5⁴½	Stokes LA122	Lb	4.20	SdsOK¹TkYrPck¹UBThJdg²½	4 wide bid; weakened	9
24Oct06Beu5	6f ft	:22³	:47	1:00	1:13²	3↑	107 C5000	111	72	76/	90	0	+1	74	5	8	8⁹½	4⁷	3⁷	1½	Stokes LA120	Lb	3.10	JRsTw½HrComsBrg¹½DncWthAFl²½	4 wide turn; up late	10
11Oct06Beu7	5½ sy⁵	:22	:46⁷	:59	1:05⁴	3↑	108 Clm5000	110	77	83/	70	+4	+7	73	5	6	7⁹½	5⁴½	3³	3⁵	Stokes LA120	Lb	3.70	SpdsProspct³SietRod²J.R.'sTown²½	4 wide; mild rally	8

●27Sep'06 Beu 4f ft :48² B 1/11 14Sep'05 Beu 3f ft :38³ B 8/19 19Sep'04 Beu 5f ft 1:06² B 3/8 ●11Sep'04 Beu (d) 3f ft :37 B 1/9 16Jan'03 TP 4f ft :51² Bg 4/4 19Aug'02 RD (d) 4f my :51 B 2/3
27Apr'02 RD 4f ft :50¹ B 4/19 ●01Oct'01 Tdn 4f ft :47 B 1/29 19Aug'01 Tdn 4f wf :50² B 16/34 07Jly'01 RD 4f ft :51² B 9/12 14Jun'01 RD 5f ft 1:03 B 5/10 26May'01 RD 3f ft :37 B 2/11

tsnhorse.com

Ultimate PP's w/ Quick Play Comments **River Downs** Clm 4000 6 Furlongs 3up Friday, May 11, 2007 **Race 10** E1 E2/LATE SPD 90 88/76 73

3 Dance With A Fool (E/P 6)

$4,000 B. g. 16
Own. Jodie L. Lamb
6/1 Purple silver stars
SOLOMON NATHAN (43 10-6-9 23%)

Sire: Don't Fool With Me (Tantheum)
Dam: Testy Gal (Lombard)
Brdr: Touch Of Heaven Farm (OH)
Trnr: Lamb Jodie L. (5 0-0-1 0%)

Power Rating: 102.9 (6th) L 120

Life:	116 16 17 14	$112,004	81	Fst	89 16-12-11	$79,859	80
2007	7 1-2-2	$6,665	76	Off	23 6-4-3	$30,664	81
2006	15 4-0-2	$16,214	80	Dis	76 10-14-7	$72,873	80
RD	16 3-9-5	$46,736	80	Trf	3 0-0-0	$680	68
				AW	6 0-0-0	$417	70

2007	89	17%	43%	+2.78	2007	10	10%	40%	-0.62	Sire Stats: AWD 6.1f	12%Mud	171MudSts	0.28spi
JKYw/EP types	86	9%	25%	-0.94	No class chg	112	13%	38%	0.43	Dam'sSire:AWD 6.7f	13%Mud	363MudSts	1.00spi
+JKYw/ Sprints	47	21%	51%	+4.43	Claiming	163	14%	36%	0.27				

★ Hot Jockey in last 7 days (9 3-0-1) ★ High % Jockey ★ Ran 3rd vs similar in last race

DATE TRK	DIST						RR	RACETYPE	CR	E1	E2/	LP	1c	2c	SPD	PP	ST	1C	2C	Str	FIN	JOCKEY		ODDS	Top Finishers	Comment	
19Apr07RD10	5½ ft	:22⁴	:46¹	:59⁴	1:07	3↑	108	Clm4000	109	88	85/	70	+2	+5	66	1	1	4²	4²½	4¹½	3½	Paucar E120	L	6.40	MrPpy½HrsLouvr[illegible]DncWthAFol¾	Steadied mid stretch	6
07Apr07Beu6	5½ ft	:23	:46³	:59²	1:06	3↑	107	Ⓢ C4000	107	88	93/	62	-1	+9	69	6	3	3¹	2¹	3⁴	3⁵½	Paucar E122	L	2.80	UvrgFight²JRsTwn³½DncWthAF[illegible]	3 wide, weakened	6
23Mar07Beu3	6f sys	:22²	:46¹	:58³	1:11¹	3↑	107	Ⓢ C4000	109	88	87/	73	-1	+1	69	2	2	1hd	1hd	1hd	2nk	Paucar E122	L	*1.90	JohnThBnkr[illegible]DncWthAFol[illegible]TrckOfThTrd[illegible]	Grudgingly	5
27Feb07Beu7	6f gd	:23	:46²	:58³	1:11¹	3↑	108	Ⓢ C5000	108	87	85/	81	-3	-1	79	3	5	4¹½	5⁸	5⁷½	4⁶¼	Paucar E120	L	3.20	CddBrink⁴½UnwrgFight¹JohnThBnkr¹½	Saved ground	7
09Feb07Beu1	6f ft	:22	:45⁴		1:10²	3↑	107	Ⓢ C4000n26m	110	89	91/	76	+1	+1	76	1	2	4¹½	1¹	1¹	1³	Paucar E120	L	5.90	DncWthAFol³TkYorPck⁴SlHunt½	3 wide bid; driving	7
29Jan07Beu5	5f ft	:21⁴	:45¹		:57²	3↑		Clm3500								3	7	7⁴½	5⁴½	2⁵	2⁷½	Paucar E120	L	10.00	RlsRock²½DWthAFPOEyGbl¹½	Saved ground, rallied	8
12Jan07TP7	ⓟ 6f ft	:21⁴	:45³	:58²	1:11¹	4↑	107	Clm5000n23m	109	89	84/	59	+4	+2	56	1	6	5³½	7⁶½	10⁸½	9¹⁶	Lebron V120	L	71.40	Count Rnd[illegible]½Good Humor Man[illegible]½Cuddlebrink[illegible]	Faded	10
22Dec06TP7	ⓟ 6f ft	:22¹	:45³	:58³	1:11¹	3↑	107	Clm5000	106	82	78/	71	-1	-1	59	7	9	9⁴½	8⁹½	10¹⁰	9¹⁰	Sarvis DA120	L	27.50	HonourbMur[illegible]CongWthMr³½MrPopey²½	Waited 3/8 pl	12
Previously trained by LAMB JODIE L.																											
14Nov06Beu4	5f ft	:22²	:46³		:59²	3↑	109	Clm3500	106		86/	71			67	4	2	3⁴	4⁵½	5⁸	6³	Paucar E124	L	5.50	HeyMHm½DshOff½SirmyHstg¹½	Chased; outfinished	9
24Oct06Beu5	6f ft	:22³	:47	1:00	1:13²	3↑	107	Ⓢ C5000	108	87	82/	80	0	+1	71	1	5	2¹½	2⁴	2⁷	3²	Paucar E120	L	2.30	eJRs1w½HrComsBrg¹½DncWthAFP½	Finished willingly	10

15Dec'06 TP 5f ft 1:01² B 7/14 12Apr'06 RD 3f ft :38 B 3/6 30Dec'05 TP 4f ft :50 B 6/12 13Dec'05 TP 3f ft :39² B 12/17 20Nov'05 TP 3f ft :36⁴ B 3/6 03Nov'05 TP 5f ft 1:05¹ B 5/6
11Sep'05 TP 4f ft :48⁴ B 18/31 03May'05 RD 5f ft 1:02³ B 3/4 ●13Mar'05 TP 5f ft 1:01¹ B 1/5 21Feb'05 TP 5f gd 1:02⁴ B 4/5 ●01Jan'05 TP 4f gd :48 B 1/4 22Nov'04 TP 6f ft 1:17¹ Bg 1/1

4 A Knew Beginning (E/P 5)

$4,000 Dkbr. g. 4 OHIOCT 2004 $6k
Own: C I Stables
6/1 Burgundy, white c/ white sleeves
SARVIS DEAN A. (94 23-11-17 22%)

Sire: Dayjur (Danzig)
Dam: Klassy Kris (Kris S.)
Brdr: Martha Parsons (OH)
Trnr: Grace Lori (7 2-0-3 29%)

Power Rating: 101.8 (7th) L 120

Life:	17 4-3-2	$17,876	70	Fst	11 2-0-1	$10,414	66
2007	5 2-1-1	$6,582	70	Off	6 2-1-1	$7,462	70
2006	10 1-0-1	$5,614	70	Dis	10 1-1-1	$5,497	68
RD	3 1-0-0	$4,046	70	Trf	0 0-0-0	$0	
				AW	4 0-0-0	$294	58

2007	216	16%	38%	-0.22	2007	24	17%	67%	-0.30	Sire Stats: AWD 6.4f	10%Mud	325MudSts	1.41spi
JKYw/EP types	141	11%	31%	-0.61	No class chg	51	18%	43%	-0.83	Dam'sSire:AWD 6.2f	17%Mud	1281MudSts	3.21spi
+JKYw/ Trn L60	3	33%	67%	+1.40	Claiming	132	17%	43%	0.45				
JKYw/ Sprints	114	11%	30%	-0.36									

★ Hot Trainer in last 14 days (3 2-0-0)

● Best Speed rating is well below the Avg Winning Speed

DATE TRK	DIST						RR	RACETYPE	CR	E1	E2/	LP	1c	2c	SPD	PP	ST	1C	2C	Str	FIN	JOCKEY		ODDS	Top Finishers	Comment	
19Apr07RD10	5½ ft	:22⁴	:46¹	:59⁴	1:07	3↑	104	Clm4000	107	88	86/	63	+2	+5	60	6	4	2¹	2¹½	2¹	4⁴	PrescottRA120	Lb	5.30	MrPopeye½Here'sLouvr[illegible]DanceWithAFool³½	Weakened	6
07Mar07Beu8	6f ft	:22²	:46²	:57⁴	1:11¹	3↑	108	Clm4000	108	92	87/	67	+1	0	65	2	4	3hd	5²½	4²½	3⁸	CamaqueC122	Lbf	7.50	ATee⁴½DshOfFme²½AKnwBgnng¹½	Dueled; weakened	8
26Feb07Beu7	5½ sys	:22	:45¹	:58³	1:06²	3↑	105	Clm3500C	108	88	104/	54	+8	+22	70	2	5	4⁵	3³½	2¹	1³	CamaqueC122	Lbf	4.80	AKnwBgg³[illegible]½SnOfMn[illegible]	Saved ground to lane	8
26Jan07Beu4	6f ft	:22²	:45⁴	:58²	1:10²	3↑	103	Clm4000n3L	107	83	78/	76	-5	-4	68	5	4	2hd	1¹	1¹½	1²½	CcmqueMA120	Lb	4.20	AKnwBgnng²½FrodckChrly½LdrOfThPd¹½	Driving	11
09Jan07Beu5	6f gd	:23¹	:48²	1:01²	1:14²	3↑	103	Clm4000n3L	106	87	78/	75	-1	-5	64	6	7	2hd	1hd	1¹½	2½	CcmqueMA120	Lb	4.90	RdnckBub½AKnwBgnng²½Pngs³	Dueled;clear;willingly	12
26Dec06TP2	ⓟ 6½ ft	:22⁴	:46¹	1:12	1:18²	3↑	104	Clm5000n3L	102	75	68/	66	-4	-6	52	4	8	5⁴½	5⁴½	8⁶½	8⁸	Sarvis DA118	Lb	45.80	Treal¹Divine Dancer[illegible]Paranl[illegible]	3 wide; gave way	10
14Dec06TP2	ⓟ 1m ft	:23¹	:46²	1:12¹	1:39	3↑	106	Clm5000n3L	100	84	72/	13	+13	+7	31	9	3²	3²	3¹	10¹⁴	10²⁶½	Sarvis DA118	Lb	17.40	KannRoy²½TrthInLndng½GypsyRvr½	3 wide; stopped	10
31Oct06Beu8	1m wf	:24²	:48¹	1:15²	1:42²	3↑	103	Clm4000n3L	109	82	69/	66	+9	-1	62	2	1hd	1½	1³	2½	3⁸	Stokes LA117	Lb	6.30	LcayBThN[illegible]½ShBrt²½AKnwBgg⁴½	Dueled;clear;weakened	10
19Oct06Beu6	6f sys	:22³	:47	1:00	1:13²	3↑	103	Clm5000n3L	103	80	73/	70	+1	0	56	7	6	6⁴½	6⁴½	5⁴½	5⁵½	Stokes LA117	Lb	4.10	FrstyAstr²ImperialSt[illegible]GovsAc½	Saved ground to lane	10
10Sep06TP2	ⓟ 6f ft	:22³	:46³	:59³	1:13²	3↑	102	Clm5000n3L	102	79	72/	74	-2	0	58	1	6	5³½	6⁵	6²½	6⁴	McKee J117	Lb	7.20	Doc Hodson[illegible]Gypsy Rover[illegible]Kipu¹½	No rally	9

16Apr RD 3f ft :38 B 2/3 02Oct'06 RD 3f ft :38 B 1/1 ●09Aug'06 RD 4f ft :50² B 1/6 ●15Apr'06 RD 4f my :47⁴ H 1/9 20Mar'06 TP 3f ft :36⁴ B 2/5 17Feb'06 TP 4f ft :48¹ B 7/26
10Feb'06 TP 4f ft :50 B 10/42 28Jan'06 TP 3f ft :39² B 14/16 04Nov'05 TP 4f ft :49² B 4/16 28Oct'05 TP 5f ft 1:04 B 8/12 21Oct'05 TP 5f ft 1:04⁴ B 7/12 23Sep'05 TP 5f ft 1:04¹ B 6/10

5 Nuts And Wire (P 0)

$4,000 B. g. 4
Own: Michelle L. Winter
8/1 Gray, gray 's on black star, black sleeves
ROJAS CHRISTIAN (49 7-7-3 14%)

Sire: Noble Cat (Storm Cat)
Dam: Hech (Hechizado (Arg))
Brdr: Ziba F Graham (OH)
Trnr: Houston Wayne (5 3-0-1 60%)

Power Rating: 92.6 (8th) L 120

Life:	11 3-2-2	$15,792	72	Fst	5 0-2-2	$3,922	72
2007	1 0-0-0	$52	32	Off	6 3-0-0	$11,879	66
2006	10 3-2-2	$15,740	72	Dis	7 2-1-1	$11,862	67
RD	11 3-2-2	$15,792	72	Trf	0 0-0-0	$0	
				AW	0 0-0-0	$0	

2007	163	9%	27%	+0.56	2007	11	27%	36%	+11.82	Sire Stats: AWD 6.6f	14%Mud	143MudSts	0.65spi
JKYw/ P types	99	7%	27%	+0.27	2nd after clm	6	17%	17%	+1.50	Dam'sSire:AWD 7.1f	7%Mud	285MudSts	0.44spi
+JKYw/ Trn L60	5	60%	80%	+28.40	2nd start w/trn	2	0%	0%	-2.00				
JKYw/ Sprints	83	8%	23%	+1.21	No class chg	11	9%	36%	0.53				

★ Eligible to improve in 2nd start since layoff

● Always far back vs weaker in last race ● Poor Speed Figure in only recent start

DATE TRK	DIST						RR	RACETYPE	CR	E1	E2/	LP	1c	2c	SPD	PP	ST	1C	2C	Str	FIN	JOCKEY		ODDS	Top Finishers	Comment	
17Apr07RD9	6f ft	:22⁴	:46¹	:59	1:13¹	3↑	106	Clm4000n29m	101	74	59/	55	-1	-1	32	3	7	7⁶½	7¹²	7¹⁹	7²³	Rojas C120	Lb	23.80	Series¹½LokAtThisCt²½RidThePrde¹½	Failed to menace	7
Claimed from Adams; Lena; Chady; Wiki Wilson Wallace C Trainer																											
31Aug06RD10	1m gd	:23²	:47²	1:12³	1:40³	3↑	107	Clm5000-c	106	76	76/	63	+8	+7	64	6	4⁸	4⁶½	5⁴½	5⁹½	4¹¹	Rojas C118	Lb	4.70	Jolly OlNick½U B The Judge[illegible]½Charantey[illegible]	No threat	6
Previously trained by NAPIER WILLIAM J.																											
16Aug06RD8	1⅟₁₆ ft	:25	:50	1:14²	1:46²	3↑	108	Clm6000	108	65	70/	79	-11	0	72	2	5⁴½	4⁷	4²½	4²	2²½	CcmqueMA118	Lb	8.50	BllysAc²½NtsAndWr[illegible]MnsgrRn¹	Blocked around turn	9
11Aug06RD10	1⅟₁₆ gd	:24⁴	:50	1:15	1:47⁴	3↑	104	Clm5000n3L	108	61	63/	71	7	+2	64	1	5³½	4³	3¹½	1¹½	1¹½	Paucar E117	Lb	3.70	NutsAndWr¹½WhsprRock[illegible]WnWGrn¹½	Clear, held sway	9
04Aug06RD3	6f ft	:23	:46³	:59³	1:13⁴	3↑	100	Ⓢ C5000n3L	104	85	80/	77	-2	-1	67	1	7	4¹½	2³	2²½	3³½	Stokes LA118	Lb	4.00	TrickOfTheTrde²½BlordsCt½NutsAndWr¹½	Evenly late	8
11Jly06RD1	6f my	:22⁴	:46³	1:00²	1:14³	3↑	101	Ⓢ C5000n2L	104	79	77/	77	+2	+2	65	1	8	6⁹½	4⁴	3hd	1nk	Stokes LA116	Lb	*1.80	NtsAdWr[illegible]MrcyMryMry²½PrvThs½	Bobbled; prevailed	9
27Jun06RD2	1⅟₁₆ ft	:24¹	:49	1:13⁴	1:46²	3↑	103	Clm7500n2L	106	71	70/	62	-2	+9	63	7	2hd	3hd	1hd	2hd	3¹½	Stokes LA120	Lb	12.50	WhsprRck½FrnyConchon½NutsAndWr²½	Evenly late	8
11Jun06RD2	6f sys	:23³	:47⁴	1:01³	1:14⁴	3↑	96	Ⓢ MC5000	101	76	65/	81	-6	-9	59	2	8	5⁶	3⁷	1¹½	1⁵	Stokes LA117	Lb	*0.40	NtAdWr⁵YhoItsBbL⁴Thwnsbdy[illegible]	Angled out; drew off	8
Previously trained by VAZQUEZ IVAN																											
31May06RD3	6f ft	:23¹	:46⁴	:59⁴	1:14	3↑	97	Ⓢ MC5000	103	81	76/	77	-4	-7	64	3	4	3¹½	3²½	2¹½	2hd	RosarioJrHL119	Lb	4.30	White Devil[illegible]Nuts AndWire⁷Cornered¹½	Bumped start	12
14May06RD13	6f my	:22²	:46²	1:00¹	1:14⁴	3↑	100	Ⓢ Mdn 13k	96	73	60/	34	+7	+6	15	9	5	7¹⁰	8¹⁵	11²⁹	12³¹½	RosarioJrHL119	L	13.10	IroquoisDrems³½SallyCat³½ATestToAndy¹	Steady fade	12

02Apr Ind 3f ft :42 B 2/2 22Jan Mnr 3f ft :38² B 14/16 19Nov'06 Hoo 3f my :37 B 2/12 09Nov'06 Hoo 3f ft :43⁴ B 11/11 10Oct'06 Hoo 3f ft :44 B 10/10 04Jun'06 RD 3f ft 1:04³ B 4/7
22Apr'06 RD 4f my :51² B 4/7 15Apr'06 RD 5f my 1:03 Bg 5/9 20Jly'05 Tdn 5f ft 1:02 Bg 1/2 10Jly'05 Tdn 5f ft 1:01³ Bg 4/8 02Jly'05 Tdn 5f ft 1:03 Bg 3/8 25Jun'05 Tdn 4f ft :51¹ Bg 12/16

Ultimate PP's w/ Quick Play Comments **River Downs** Clm 4000 6 Furlongs 3up Friday, May 11, 2007 **Race 10**

E1 E2/LATE SPD
90 88/ 76 73

6 Wazoo City (E 5)

20/1 — $4,000 — Dkbbr. g. 4
Own: H. And C. Brockman; T. Lenihan; R. Kerr
White, purple diamonds
OUZTS PERRY WAYNE (143 18-25-26 13%)

Sire: Slew City Slew (Seattle Slew)
Dam: Key o Colorizer (Roanoke)
Brdr: Ed Dalby; Tom Lenihan & Ray Weis (OH)
Trnr: Connelly William R. (8 1-2-1 12%)

Power Rating: 104.0 (4th) — L 124

Life:	14 3 2-0	$26,474	86	Fst	12 2-2-0	$22,127	86
2007	4 1-0-0	$4,517	64	Off	1 1-0-0	$4,080	64
2006	7 1-1-0	$12,797	82	Dis	5 2-0-0	$11,840	76
RD	1 1-0-0	$4,080	64	Trf	1 0-0-0	$267	59
				AW	4 1-1-0	$9,495	86

2007	501	10%	34%	-0.79
JKYw/ E types	154	12%	34%	-0.58
JKYw/ Trn L60	8	12%	12%	-1.58
JKYw/ Sprints	277	9%	34%	-0.94

2007	108	12%	34%	-0.89
Win last race	105	10%	46%	0.93
Claiming	318	13%	48%	-0.72

Sire Stats: AWD 7.3f 17%Mud 1272MudSts 1.37spi
Dam'sSire:AWD 7.1f 11%Mud 881MudSts 0.81spi

★ Best Dirt Speed is fastest among today's starters (tie)
★ Won last race (RD 04/27 6f Dirt good sClm5000NW3L)
● Moves up in class from last start

DATE TRK	DIST					RR	RACETYPE	CR	E1	E2/	LP	1c	2c	SPD	PP	ST	1C	2C	Str	FIN	JOCKEY		ODDS	Top Finishers	Comment	
27Apr07RD2	6f gd	:224	:461	1:00	1:14 3↑	101	sClm5000n3L	108	86	85/	68	0	+3	64	4	3	3½	1hd	12	11	Ouzts PW120	Lf	8.70	WazoCity1Augustus1½RockinEde8¼	3wide; held sway	6
25Mar07TP7	6½ ft	:224	:454	1:104	1:172 3↑	107	Clm15000n3L	105	80	75/	66	8	6	57	5	4	42	76½	812	818¾	RosarioJrHL120	Lf	5.60	Jihoke8½New Awakening2½GreatAlbert¾	Off rail; faded	8
15Mar07TP6	1m ft	:242	:48	1:13	1:391 3↑	107	Clm15000n3L	108	77	75/	63	4	+1	64	2	1hd	11	21½	52	610¾	RosarioJrHL120	Lb	3.30	Al Johnston2½Right Catagory¾Drawn¾	Faded	7
03Mar07Mnr8	5½ ft	:223	:452	:592	1:061 3↑	108	Clm30000/25n3L	109	88	73/	47	0	+7	55	1	4	3½	54½	715	717¼	WhitneyDG117	Lb	6.00	Conetsur5¼TheChoc1Cnsrvtsst1	Shell foot; gave way	7
Claimed from Moss Clark Dick R. Trainer																										
06Jun06Prm2	1m ft	:231	:462	1:113	1:372 3↑	105	Clm12500n2L-c	109	91	86/	81	+8	+4	81	3	11	11	12½	12	12½	CampbellJ117	LBb	1.40	Wazoo City2½Bobs Gray½First Whitney2	Driving	9
26May06Prm8	6f ft	:221	:453	:58	1:104 3↑	107	Clm25000n2L	109	87	81/	66	0	-2	59	5	4	42	54	58½	612	CampbellJ117	LBb	4.20	CleversHlnhdCopWthHonr4SerentyTnhd	Dropped back	8
11May06Prm1	1m ft	:232	:473	1:14	1:401 3↑	108	Clm25000n2L	109	92	85/	84	+8	+2	82	4	1½	11	11	2hd	2½	CampbellJ117	LBb	2.80	GoodOfer½WazooCity3½LodimUp½	Set pace; held well	6
Previously trained by CONTESSA GARY C																										
21Apr06Aqu1	ⓣ 1m fm	:234	:487	1:122	1:372	109	Clm40000	106	81	82/	49	0	+7	59	2	11	1hd	21½	79½	714½	Lopez CC120	Lb	5.90	PrmDmnd1½BholdThGld3½Dontlevmtc1½	Set pace; tired	8
23Feb06Aqu3	⊡ 6f ft	:222	:46	:584	1:113	112	Alw35000s	108	94	93/	56	+2	+2	60	1	4	1½	31	67½	613½	Garcia A118	Lb	4.50	Jerry Jilette1½Arborst2SirSpeedalor2½	Vied inside; tired	6
26Jan06Aqu9	⊡ 1⅙ ft	:23	:474	1:14	1:461	114	OC75k/N1X-N	110	95	90/	43	+9	3	63	8	2½	2hd	3½	814	820½	DominguezRA118	L	13.30	TrlngTwlv½Epigmic2EstrBnd3½	Chased outside;tired	9

●26Feb TP 4f ft :48 B 1/4 13Apr06 Aqu 6f ft 1:172 B 5/6 07Apr06 Aqu 5f ft 1:01 H 2/13 12Mar06 Bel tr.t 3f ft :35 H 2/32 20Jan06 Aqu ⊡ 6f ft 1:133 H 1/3 18Dec05 Aqu ⊡ 5f ft 1:03 B 11/14
●23Nov05 CD 4f ft :48 B 1/23 17Nov05 CD ⓣ (d) 4f fm :521 B 3/6 23Oct05 CD 4f gd :504 B 24/54 28Sep05 TP 5f ft 1:031 Bg 8/15 07Sep05 TP 5f ft 1:03 Bg 3/4 31Aug05 TP 5f ft 1:033 Bg 3/5

7 Mr. Popeye (E/P 5)

5/1 — $4,000 — Ch. g. 8
Own: Richard L. Alderson
Yellow, navy blue stars
VIDAL FRANCISCO A. (17 4-2-0 24%)

Sire: Flight Forty Nine (Forty Niner)
Dam: Hard Way Seven (Queen City Lad)
Brdr: Leonard W. Cavens (OH)
Trnr: Moore Dennis T. (14 3-3-2 21%)

Power Rating: 105.4 (3rd) — L 124

Life:	64 11 6 16	$78,110	78	Fst	51 11-4 12	$67,427	78
2007	7 2-1-2	$10,925	75	Off	13 0-2-4	$8,683	78
2006	18 5-1-5	$27,571	78	Dis	42 7-4 12	$49,514	78
RD	38 6-4-9	$44,628	78	Trf	0 0-0-0	$0	
				AW	13 4-1-6	$23,746	76

2007	19	26%	42%	+1.36
JKYw/EP types	32	18%	34%	0.64
JKYw/ Trn L60	2	100%	100%	+5.36
JKYw/ Sprints	17	29%	41%	+1.75

2007	61	16%	44%	-0.37
Win last race	82	21%	52%	-0.48
No class chg	209	13%	38%	-0.42
Claiming	409	12%	36%	-0.66

Sire Stats: AWD 6.0f 9%Mud 301MudSts 0.50spi
Dam'sSire:AWD 6.8f 12%Mud 299MudSts 1.09spi

★ High % Jockey ★ Won last race (RD 05/01 6f Dirt fast Clm 4000)

DATE TRK	DIST					RR	RACETYPE	CR	E1	E2/	LP	1c	2c	SPD	PP	ST	1C	2C	Str	FIN	JOCKEY		ODDS	Top Finishers	Comment	
01May07RD6	6f ft	:223	:454	:58	1:111 3↑	108	Clm4000	111	82	81/	79	0	+2	70	5	4	43½	43½	11	1nk	Vidal FA124	Lb	3.00	Mr. PopeyenkThird Day3½Le Roi½	Just lasted; driving	6
19Apr07RD10	5½ ft	:224	:461	:584	1:07 3↑	108	Clm4000	109	88	87/	71	+2	+5	67	3	3	31	32	11	1½	Vidal FA120	Lb	2.30	MrPopy½HeresLouinoOnceWithAFol3½	Bore out stretch	6
06Apr07RD8	6f ft	:23	:461	:584	1:13 3↑	107	Clm4000	109	88	91/	76	-5	-1	75	7	1	2hd	1hd	1hd	47½	SchaeferGA122	Lb	1.30	Raid The Parade1Exposer1½Here's Lousnk	Faltered	7
25Mar07TP1	ⓐ 6½ ft	:23	:462	1:114	1:183 3↑	107	Clm5000n2/6m	106	80	78/	84	-7	-8	74	6	2	21½	29½	29½	3nk	SchaeferGA120	Lb	3.80	Pa KettienoSkorn Taernk Mr. Popeye2½	Off rail; rallied	7
15Mar07TP6	ⓐ 6f ft	:221	:453	:587	1:113 3↑	107	Clm5000n3/9m	106	79	88/	84	-1	+1	73	1	6	3h	35½	21½	31½	SchaeferGA120	Lb	6.30	StpToThMsc½FlyingChnc1½MrPopeyno	Lacked late bid	7
24Jan07TP8	ⓐ 6f ft	:23	:463	:591	1:121 4↑	108	Clm5000	107	84	78/	80	-5	-3	68	8	2	41½	64½	56	74½	SchaeferGA122	Lb	12.40	TheSdmnComth1½Lcindy½Outtakenno	Lacked late bid	9
06Jan07TP8	ⓐ 6½ ft	:231	:463	1:12	1:181 4↑	107	Clm5000	106	81	78/	79	-8	-9	70	8	2	2hd	2hd	11½	2½	SchaeferGA122	Lb	3.40	Lababa½Mr. Popeye1½Lac Indy½	Off inside; outfinishd	9
22Dec06TP7	ⓐ 6f ft	:221	:452	:583	1:111 3↑	107	Clm5000	109	82	87/	73	-1	-1	70	9	4	31½	21	21	33½	SchaeferGA124	Lbf	11.70	HonoubNnoCpgWthMs3½MrPopy2½	4 wide; weakened	12
06Dec06TP4	ⓐ 6½ ft	:23	:47	1:124	1:193 3↑	107	Clm5000	111	87	79/	75	-2	-6	68	2	5	1hd	1½	12½	11	SchaeferGA120	Lb	9.00	Mr. Popeye1Treat½Act Nice1½	Dueled; clear held	12
24Oct06Beu5	6f ft	:223	:47	1:00	1:137 3↑	107	sC5000	108	83	75/	81	0	+1	66	10	1	53½	57	48½	44½	RosarioJrHL122	Lb	1.90	JRTw½HrCmsBrg1½DcWthAF2½	3 wide;finished evenly	10

17Apr05 RD 5f ft 1:02 B 2/5 11Jan04 RD 5f ft 1:034 B 2/7 04Jun04 RD 4f ft :51 B 7/10 22Jly03 RD 4f ft :50 B 9/15 10Jun03 RD 4f ft :50 B 12/20 06May03 RD 5f ft 1:022 B 3/7
29Apr03 RD 5f ft 1:06 B 5/7 22Apr03 RD 5f ft 1:04 B 5/6 25Jun02 RD 5f ft 1:041 B 4/5 04Apr02 TP 5f ft 1:034 Bg 8/11 28Mar02 TP 5f ft 1:014 Bg 2/6 21Mar02 TP 3f my :363 Bg 2/9

8 Unwavering Flight (E 6)

4/1 — $4,000 — Dkbbr. g. 5
Own: James F. Yaegel
Green; green 'jy' on white diamond
PRESCOTT ROONEY A. (90 18-20-12 10%)

Sire: Flight Forty Nine (Forty Niner)
Dam: Thistle (Louisiana Slew)
Brdr: Joseph A Berg (OH)
Trnr: Yaegel Thomas (15 0-5-2 0%)

Power Rating: 103.7 (5th) — L 122

Life:	22 5 4 2	$22,654	79	Fst	18 4-2-1	$17,689	78
2007	8 3-3-1	$11,907	79	Off	4 1-2-1	$4,965	79
2006	13 1-1-1	$7,747	67	Dis	14 2-2-1	$11,582	79
RD	5 1-0-0	$4,732	64	Trf	0 0-0-0	$0	
				AW	1 0-0-0	$225	56

2007	466	14%	46%	-0.27
JKYw/ E types	521	17%	43%	-0.33
JKYw/ Sprints	292	14%	48%	-0.17

2007	111	11%	42%	-1.15
Claiming	629	10%	33%	-0.12

Sire Stats: AWD 6.0f 9%Mud 301MudSts 0.50spi
Dam'sSire:AWD 6.3f 7%Mud 470MudSts 0.54spi

★ Drops in Class today ★ Early Speed running style helps chances
● Showed declining form & speed in last race ● Outside posts have poor win%

DATE TRK	DIST					RR	RACETYPE	CR	E1	E2/	LP	1c	2c	SPD	PP	ST	1C	2C	Str	FIN	JOCKEY		ODDS	Top Finishers	Comment	
22Apr07Tdn12	5f ft	:22	:46		:583 3↑	108	sC6250	105		87/	59			56	7	1	42	43	59¾	611½	Stokes LA118	L	4.70	PremierCourt1½Cudlebrunk½Bar Time3¼	4 wide; no rally	7
07Apr07Beu8	5½ ft	:23	:463	:582	1:06 3↑	107	sC4000	110	96	100/	72	-1	+8	78	1	1	11	11	14	12	ThorwarthO120	L	2.70	UnwvingFlght2J.R.'sTown2½DanceWithAFol2½	Driving	6
11Mar07Beu8	5½ sy	:214	:457	:577	1:042 3↑	106	Clm3500C	110	96	97/	71	+6	+8	75	3	1	1½	14	15	15½	Stokes LA122	L	2.40	UnwvngFlght5½MgityWo2½OncnLnce6	Off rail; driving	6
19Mar07Beu4	5½ sy	:221	:45	:58	1:052 3↑	106	Clm5000n4L	107	93	103/	51	+6	+10	62	3	3	3hd	1hd	1hd	32½	Luna R122	L	2.80	Tough Cut½Cabrera2Unwavering Flight½	Evenly late	8
09Mar07Beu2	5½ ft	:221	:457	:58	1:052 3↑	105	Clm3500C	107	88	98/	61	+4	+14	69	5	2	22½	22½	2½	2½	ThorwarthO122	L	2.10	KOfTdth½UnvrgFlght1½TrtyHnrd2½	Stalked; led; caught	5
27Feb07Beu2	6f gd	:23	:463	:593	1:111 3↑	108	sC5000	109	90	94/	77	-3	-1	79	5	1	11	2½	2hd	24¼	ThorwarthO120	L	20.70	Cdtbrnk4½UnvgFlght1JhnThBle1½	Dueled turn; held 2nd	7
16Feb07Beu1	5½ ft				1:044 3↑	103	sC4000C	109	85	82/	67	+1	+1	61	5	1	22	22	21½	23½	ThorwarthO121	L	1.70	RisMOl3½UnvgFlght4½SKndOfF½	Chased; second best	6
30Jan07Beu2	5f ft	:223	:453		:57 3↑	108	Clm3500n3L	107		84/	83			75	5	1	1hd	2hd	1½	14½	ThorwarthO120	L	7.70	UnwvngFlght4½GnsMuk½Lttlsolvnv2½	Drew off; driving	6
12Dec06Beu7	6f ft	:224	:463	:591	1:12 3↑	102	sC5000n3L	102	86	86/	58	+1	+4	57	8	2	52½	52	58	611	Stokes LA120	L	1.90	JhnThBole2½MyMgcind2½CmdUp1½	Saved ground turn	10
18Nov06Beu8	6f ft	:222	:46	:587	1:113 3↑	104	sA11500n3L	103	92	91/	61	+3	+8	63	5	1	21½	58	613	611½	Yaranga Y120	L	19.20	Chief Ormond2½Act The Part2Peley G7	Dropped back	8

19Oct06 Beu (d) 4f my :504 B 5/16 14Oct06 Beu 3f sl :384 B 14/19 20May06 RD 5f ft 1:022 B 2/8 ●11May06 RD 3f ft :362 H 1/7 05May06 RD 3f ft :40 B 11/11 29Mar06 Beu (d) 3f wf :433 B 2/2
20Feb06 Beu 5f ft 1:051 B 3/7 ●10Feb06 Beu 4f ft :51 B 1/9 28Jan06 Beu 3f ft :371 B 3/13 20Jan06 Beu 3f ft :421 B 12/15 19Oct05 Beu 5f ft 1:054 Bg 1/3 14Oct05 Beu 4f ft :492 Bg 2/13

Ultimate PP's w/ Quick Play Comments **River Downs** Ⓢ Clm 4000 6 Furlongs. 3up Friday, May 11, 2007 **Race 10**

E1	E2/LATE	SPD
90	88/ 76	73

Last 3 Years

		RACETYPE STATS:	# Races	Win%	FAVORITES Itm%	$2ROI	Average Field Size	Median $2 Win Payoff	% Winners < 5/1	% Winners >= 5/1 < 10/1	% Winners >= 10/1
RD	3up	Ⓢ CLM 4000 - 5000 Dirt 6f	11	18%	64%	-1.04	7.7	$9.40	100%	0%	0%

Track Bias Stats

	' MEET Totals '					' WEEK Totals '			
DIRT 6.0f	Speed Bias: 80%		WnrAvgBL		DIRT 6.0f	Speed Bias: 86%		WnrAvgBL	
# Races: 64	04/06 - 05/08		1stCall: 1.4		# Races: 14	05/03 - 05/08		1stCall: 1.2	
%Wire: 47%			2ndCall: 1.0		%Wire: 64%			2ndCall: 0.8	
	Early	Speed	Late	Speed		Early	Speed	Late	Speed
Runstyle:	E	E/P	P	S	Runstyle:	E	E/P	P	S
	++	+				++			
Impact Values	1.66	1.29	0.72	0.33	Impact Values	1.98	1.09	0.94	0.00
%Races Won	52%	28%	11%	9%	%Races Won	64%	21%	14%	0%
Post Bias:	RAIL	1-3	4-7	8+	Post Bias	RAIL	1-3	4-7	8+
			+			+		+	
Impact Values	0.85	0.89	1.14	0.71	Impact Values	1.91	0.80	1.29	0.00
Avg Win %	12%	13%	19%	4%	Avg Win %	29%	12%	22%	0%

Race Summary

#	HorseName	ML Odds	Med Eqp	Days Since L/R	Run Style	P T S	Avg Dist/Surf PACE-SPEED E1	E2/Late	Spd	Avg Race Rtng	Best Pace E1	E2/Late	Final Speed Sp1	Sp2	Sp3	Sp4	ACL	Rcg Spd Avg	R1	R2	R3	Mud Spd	Pedigree Stats Mud Sts	Mud % Mud	Sire AWD	Dam Sire's AWD
1	Bri's Bad Boy	7/2	L	13	+E/P	4	85	88/ 78	* 75*	105	92	94/ 89	76.	72.	64.	76.	105.6	71	106	104	103	78	229	10	7.2	7.5
8	Unwavering Flight	4/1	L	19	++E	6	89	97/ 70	* 75*	107	92	100/ 83	56.	78.	75	62	106.9	70	108	107	106	75	301	9	6.0	6.3
2	J. R.'s Town	5/2	L	10	S	3	79	85/ 78	* 74*	107	85	92/ 91	70.	75.	59	66.	107.2	68	104	107	107	80	433	13	6.5	7.0
3	Dance With A Fool	6/1	L	22	+E/P	6	88	90/ 73	* 73*	108	94	96/ 81	66.	69.	69	75.	107.1	68	108	107	107	70	171	12	6.1	6.7
7	Mr. Popeye	5/1	L	10	+E/P	5	83	83/ 80	* 73*	108	91	91/ 84	70.	67.	75.	74.	107.7	71	108	108	107	46	301	9	6.0	6.6
4	A Knew Beginning	6/1	L	22	[illegible]E/P	5	88	83/ 72	* 66*	106	92	87/ 76	60.	65.	70	66.	105.5	65	108	108	105	70	325	10	6.4	8.2
6	Wazoo City	20/1	L	14	++E	5	83	80/ 67	* 61*	105	88	85/ 68	64.	57.	64	55.	103.4	62	101	107	107		1272	17	7.3	7.3
5	Nuts And Wire	8/1	L	24.	P		74	59/ 55	32	106	85	80/ 77	32.	64	72	64	103.4	56	106	107	106	65	143	14	6.6	7.1

Speed Last Race	Back Speed	Current Class	Average Class Last 3	Power Rating	Early Pace Last Race	Late Pace Last Race
76 Bri's Bad Boy	80 Dance With A Fool	109.5 Mr. Popeye	109.3 Mr. Popeye	110.5 Bri's Bad Boy	86 J. R.'s Town	83 Bri's Bad Boy
70 J. R.'s Town	79 Unwavering Flight	108.9 Dance With A Fool	108.4 Unwavering Flight	107.7 J. R.'s Town	86 A Knew Beginning	79 Mr. Popeye
70 Mr. Popeye	78 J. R.'s Town	108.8 Unwavering Flight	108.3 Dance With A Fool	105.4 Mr. Popeye	85 Wazoo City	74 J. R.'s Town
66 Dance With A Fool	78 Mr. Popeye	108.8 J. R.'s Town	107.8 Bri's Bad Boy	104.0 Wazoo City	85 Dance With A Fool	70 Dance With A Fool
64 Wazoo City	76 Bri's Bad Boy	107.9 Bri's Bad Boy	107.7 A Knew Beginning	103.7 Unwavering Flight	84 Bri's Bad Boy	68 Wazoo City
60 A Knew Beginning	67 Nuts And Wire	107.5 A Knew Beginning	107.4 J. R.'s Town	102.9 Dance With A Fool	81 Mr. Popeye	63 A Knew Beginning
56 Unwavering Flight	66 A Knew Beginning	105.1 Wazoo City	105.2 Wazoo City	101.8 A Knew Beginning	59 Nuts And Wire	59 Unwavering Flight
32 Nuts And Wire	64 Wazoo City	100.5 Nuts And Wire	105.0 Nuts And Wire	92.6 Nuts And Wire	NA Unwavering Flight	55 Nuts And Wire

#	Speed Last Race		#	Prime Power		#	Class Rating		#	Best Speed at Dist	
2	Ohio Volunteer	65	6	Maddy Bell	96.1	2	Ohio Volunteer	106.4	5	Our Last Dance	75
6	Maddy Bell	62	7	Storm Believer	96.1	5	Our Last Dance	105.6	6	Maddy Bell	72
4	Star Mais	61	1	Gone For Canada	94.9	1	Gone For Canada	105.5	1	Gone For Canada	65

11

Exacta / Trifecta / Superfecta (Ten Cent Minimum)
Pick 3 (Races 11-12-13)
Pick 4 (Races 11-12-13-14)

	E1	E2/LATE	SPEED
PARS:	89	87/ 75	71

Simulcast of Thistledown race number 11

5½ Furlongs. Ⓕ Clm 4000NW4L Purse $7,300. FOR FILLIES AND MARES THREE YEARS OLD AND UPWARD WHICH HAVE NEVER WON FOUR RACES. Three Year Olds, 120 lbs., Older, 122 lbs. Non-winners of two races since April 11 Allowed 2 lbs. A race since then Allowed 4 lbs. Claiming Price $4,000 (Ohio Registered Fo als Preferred).

Post Time: (4:25)/ 3:25/ 2:25/ 1:25

1 Gone For Canada (S 0)

Own: Brenda Ketring
4/1 Shd, yellow diamonds
SANGUINETTI ANNE (72 10-9-8 14%)

$4,000 Dkbbr. m. 5
Sire: Gone For Real (Gone West)
Dam: Tender Princess (Ten Gold Pots)
Brdr: Gary Philip Joechel (ONT-C)
Trnr: Ketring Brenda (11 0-0-2 0%)

Power Rating: 94.9 (3rd) L 118

	Starts	1st	2nd	3rd	Earnings	Spd		Starts	1st	2nd	3rd	Earnings	Spd
Life:	23	3	3	3	$29,049	86	Fst	19	2	1	3	$20,493	65
2007	2	0	1	0	$2,439	65	Off	4	1	2	0	$8,556	63
2006	17	3	2	1	$24,717	63	Dis	4	1	1	1	$9,098	66
Tdn	5	1	1	0	$5,692	63	Trf	0	0	0	0	$0	
							AW	0	0	0	0	$0	

2007	156	12%	37%	-1.10
JKYw/ S types	174	6%	41%	-1.35
JKYw/ Trn L60	1	0%	0%	2.00
JKYw/ Sprints	121	12%	40%	-1.09

2007	20	0%	35%	-2.00
No class chg	141	6%	34%	-1.48
Bin favorite	6	0%	33%	-2.00
Claiming	166	6%	34%	1.28

Sire Stats: AWD 6.9f 17%Mud 73MudSts 1.12spi
Dam'sSire: AWD 7.2f 13%Mud 645MudSts 0.78spi

★ Eligible to improve in 3rd start since layoff
● Never threatened the leaders in last start ● Poor Trainer win%

DATE TRK	DIST						RR	RACETYPE	CR	E1	E2/	LP	1c	2c	SPD	PP	ST	1C	2C	Str	FIN	JOCKEY		ODDS	Top Finishers	Comment	
15Apr07Tdn6	6f gd	:22	:48	:59	1:13	4↑	105	ⒻC4000n4L	104	76	66/	74	0	0	54	1	3	56	56	69	57	Ortiz A113	L	11.80	HyLucyLou LevlBid StormBelvr	Failed to respond	7
30Mar07Mnr3	5½ ft	:23	:48	1:01	1:08	3↑	106	ⒻC5000n4L	109	69	73/	74	-2	-2	66	6	8	89	66	23	21	Ortiz A112	L	44.00	Lchne GoneForCnd LtleTots	Rally3w,closed willing	8
28Nov06Mnr4	6f ft	:22	:46	:59	1:14	3↑	106	ⒻC5000n4L	105	74	66/	73	+1	+0	52	2	5	99	1017	917	718	PereraOM121	L	53.80	Ghost Harbor FinTwnng Its Golden	Always outrun	10
11Nov06Tdn3	6f sy	:23	:47	1:01	1:15	3↑	104	ⒻC3500n3L	107	87	78/	74	0	-3	63	3	1	1hd	1hd	11	11	Ortiz A112	L	8.40	GonForCnd MisMrn NatBird	Dueled; clear, driving	8
23Oct06Tdn5	6f sy	:23	:47	1:01	1:15	3↑	104	ⒻC3500n3L	103	81	70/	78	-1	0	59	4	1	54	53	43	21	Ortiz A112	L	11.80	MisCsey GonForCnd ShshnGrl	Rallied; gaining	8
07Oct06Tdn8	6f ft	:22	:46	:58	1:13	3↑	104	ⒻC3500n3L	103	74	60/	76	+3	0	50	5	8	97	1010	811	77	SkerrettJ117	L	25.90	HyLcyLo MrqusSton ShmesKish	Failed to menace	10
22Sep06Tdn5	6f ft	:22	:47	1:00	1:14	3↑	103	ⒻC3500n3L	103	68	69/	68	+4	0	51	10	11	1112	124	98	76	SanguinettiA116	L	8.40	Msymsymsy MrqusSton LevlBid	Mild bid, no threat	12

Previously trained by WILLS DANIEL

DATE TRK	DIST						RR	RACETYPE	CR	E1	E2/	LP	1c	2c	SPD	PP	ST	1C	2C	Str	FIN	JOCKEY		ODDS	Top Finishers	Comment	
11Sep06FE2	6½ ft	:23	:46	1:12	1:18	3↑	106	ⒻC4000n3L	108	74	73/	75	0	+1	63	7	3	77	77	59	46	DevereID113	L	8.90	SilverBlz AnsWhipr Prospctnrnr	Mild rally between	7
28Aug06FE10	6f ft	:22	:46	:58	1:12	3↑	105	ⒻC4000n3L	108	68	63/	88	-1	0	62	5	4	99	910	67	57	DevereID113	L	13.20	Windfleur Cont T Mist Silver Blaze	Late outside bid	10
21Aug06FE10	1⅛ ft	:23	:47	1:13	1:48	3↑	106	ⒻC4000n3L	103	73	48/	63	+5	+5	51	4	53	64	1052	813	719	BochinskiBT118	L	12.30	Bafaul GoldmtGrl VictorianDansk	Svd grd no bid	12

22Mar Tdn 4f ft :49 B 3/4 16Aug06 FE 3f ft :37 H 3/7 01May06 FE 5f ft 1:04 H 8/10 24Apr06 FE 5f gd 1:04 H 10/11 17Apr06 FE 5f ft 1:03 H 5/6 10Apr06 FE 4f ft :49 H 4/10
03Apr06 FE 3f ft :36 H 4/11 ●29Mar06 FE 3f ft :36 H 1/29 27Nov05 WO tr.t 4f ft :49 B 10/27 12Nov05 WO 4f ft :50 H 22/45 08Nov05 WO 3f ft :39 H 9/11 02Nov05 WO 4f ft :50 B 6/10

2 Ohio Volunteer (S 0)

Own: Daniel C. Stearns
6/1 Scarlet, gray ohio, gray sleeves
BYRNE JOHN (7 0-0-0 0%)

$4,000 B. m. 5
Sire: Neon Prospect (Mr. Prospector)
Dam: Nom De Guerre (French Legionaire)
Brdr: Daniel C. Stearns Dvm (OH)
Trnr: Cucinotta Anthony (2 0-0-0 0%)

Power Rating: 94.5 (4th) L 118

	Starts	1st	2nd	3rd	Earnings	Spd		Starts	1st	2nd	3rd	Earnings	Spd
Life:	16	3	3	3	$22,946	65	Fst	12	2	1	3	$13,924	62
2006	12	2	2	3	$15,938	66	Off	4	1	2	0	$8,122	66
2005	4	1	1	0	$7,008	55	Dis	1	0	0	0	$82	39
Tdn	16	3	3	3	$22,946	65	Trf	0	0	0	0	$0	
							AW	0	0	0	0	$0	

2007	96	2%	13%	-6.90
JKYw/ S types	109	6%	22%	1.30
JKYw/ Trn L60	1	0%	0%	-2.00
JKYw/ Sprints	60	2%	13%	-1.70

2007	2	0%	0%	2.00
90+ days away	16	6%	31%	+1.94
Win last race	19	11%	26%	+0.82
No class chg	117	6%	26%	-0.72

Sire Stats: AWD 6.3f 6%Mud 95MudSts 0.28spi
Dam'sSire: AWD 6.5f 8%Mud 901MudSts 0.38spi

★ Highest Last Race Speed Rating
★ Won last race (TDN 11/17 1m70y Dirt sloppy ⒻClm3500NW3L)
● Moves up in class from last start ● Has not raced for more than 5 months ● Switches to a Low% jockey
● Best Speed rating is well below the Avg Winning Speed

DATE TRK	DIST						RR	RACETYPE	CR	E1	E2/	LP	1c	2c	SPD	PP	ST	1C	2C	Str	FIN	JOCKEY		ODDS	Top Finishers	Comment	
17Nov06Tdn3	1m70 sy	:22	:48	1:17	1:49	3↑	103	ⒻC3500n3L	109	73	61/	75	+4	-4	65	4	38	37	11	1½	13	GonzalezLA118	L	1.70	OhioVolunt PokVixen LevelBid	Clear late; driving	8
05Nov06Tdn3	1m ft	:23	:47	1:14	1:42	3↑	103	ⒻⓈClm5000n3L	109	62	56/	78	+8	+3	62	6	69	711	67	44	24	GonzalezLA118	L	3.30	MoochGirl OhioVolnt CrclPont	Rallied; up for second	7
20Oct06Tdn14	6f sy	:22	:47	1:01	1:15	3↑	103	ⒻⓈClm5000n3L	106	78	72/	78	+2	0	61	5	7	66	65	43	22	GonzalezLA117	L	10.20	LisasDncer OhioVolunter Cat'sSign	Closed willingly	9
07Oct06Tdn8	6f ft	:22	:46	:58	1:13	3↑	104	ⒻC3500n3L	105	77	69/	75	+3	0	57	7	1	86	78	54	42	MonayRaf117	L	20.90	HyLcyLo MrqusSton ShmesKish	Mild rally; stretch	10
04Sep06Tdn7	1m ft	:24	:49	1:16	1:44	3↑	103	ⒻⓈClm5000n3L	104	63	53/	75	-3	-2	59	5	42	53	44	35	34	GonzalezLA118	L	10.60	SleGrdn LdyLeb OhioVlnt	Contended; good effort	9
14Aug06Tdn6	6f ft	:23	:48	1:01	1:15	3↑	101	ⒻⓈClm5000n2L	103	78	68/	77	-5	+	57	4	3	41	32	1hd	1½	GonzalezLA116	L	6.90	OhioVlnt CrclPont EyGtASldr	Prevailed; long drive	7
30Jly06Tdn8	6f ft	:23	:47	1:00	1:13	3↑	101	ⒻⓈClm5000n2L	101	74	62/	79	-9	-9	54	8	8	64	78	79	38	Byrne J116	L	12.10	SleGrdn CrclPont OhioVolnt	Mild rally, no threat	8
03Jly06Tdn3	6f ft	:23	:47	1:00	1:13	3↑	101	ⒻⓈClm5000n2L	101	61	56/	80	-5	-6	50	2	8	810	88	87	59	Byrne J116	L	5.40	ClsSign EyeGotASlatr SleGrden	Failed to menace	9
15Jun06Tdn8	6f ft	:22	:47	1:00	1:14	3↑	101	ⒻⓈClm5000n2L	100	77	67/	77	0	-1	56	6	7	84	76	42	47	CangrAWT118	L	11.20	Yoop Hey Lucy Lou Crucial Point	Mild bid	12
29May06Tdn3	6f ft	:22	:47	:59	1:13	3↑	101	ⒻⓈClm5000n2L	102	75	69/	78	-4	-5	59	4	7	74	54	45	33	CangrAWT118	L	9.90	Folly Me Hey LucyLou OhioVolunt	Closed willingly	9

04May Tdn 4f ft :50 B 5/11 27Apr Tdn 3f gd :39 B 10/10 03May'06 Tdn 4f ft :53 B 13/13 08Apr'06 Tdn 4f ft :50 B 24/25 01Apr'06 Tdn 3f ft :38 B 6/7 17Feb06 Beu (d) 4f my :53 B 4/6
10Feb06 Beu 4f ft :41 B 22/24 10Sep05 Tdn 5f ft 1:03 B 8/13 03Sep05 Tdn 4f ft :50 B 7/12 21Aug05 Tdn 3f ft :38 Bg 4/11 14Aug05 Tdn 3f ft :37 Bg 3/5 07Aug05 Tdn 4f ft :50 B 15/19

Ultimate PPs w/ Quick Play Comments

River Downs Clm 4000NW4L 5½ Furlongs. 3upF&M Friday, May 11, 2007 **Race 11 (TDN - #11)** E1 75 E2/LATE SPD 71

3 Zippy Ziter (E 4)

Own: Bridget Sipp
5/1 Red & white quartered; red & white sleeves
MUNAYLLA FILMER (44 3-8-7 7%)

$4,000 Dkbbr. f. 3 BEESJAN 2007 $4k
Sire: Crowning Storm (Storm Cat)
Dam: My Gal Gregory (Gregory)
Brdr: Sid Craig & Jenny Craig (CA)
Trnr: Sipp Burton K. (56 10-8-8 18%)

Power Rating: 92.7 (5th) 118

Life:	2 1 - 0 - 0	$4,341	53	Fst	2 1 - 0 - 0	$4,341	53
2007	2 1 - 0 - 0	$4,341	53	Off	0 0 - 0 - 0	$0	
2006	0 0 - 0 - 0	$0		Dis	2 1 - 0 - 0	$4,341	53
Tdn	2 1 - 0 - 0	$4,341	53	Trf	0 0 - 0 - 0	$0	
				AW	0 0 - 0 - 0	$0	

2007	45	7%	42%	+2.15
JKYw/ E types	106	14%	38%	-0.42
JKYw/ Sprints	39	5%	44%	-0.26

2007	137	13%	41%	-1.18
+Down 2+ classes	46	22%	37%	-0.10
Claiming	1278	13%	37%	-0.78

Sire Stats: AWD 6.2f 19%Mud 48MudSts 0.66spi
Dam'sSire: AWD 6.4f 13%Mud 787MudSts 1.12spi

● Poor Speed Figures earned in both career starts ● Switches to a Low% jockey

DATE TRK	DIST						RR	RACETYPE	CR	E1	E2/	LP	1c	2c	SPD	PP	ST	1C	2C	Str	FIN	JOCKEY	ODDS	Top Finishers	Comment	
29Apr07Tdn7	5½ ft	:23	:47	1:00	1:07	3	106	C15000n3x2L	102	79	63/	46	-1	-6	38	9	10	8	9	10	10	SanguinetiA118	5.00e	ShbysCrk PdonlhmndOckVdet	Off slowly, outrun	10
14Apr07Tdn4	3f ft	:23	:48		1:01		104	MC6250	107		82/	62			53	2	4	1½	1hd	1	1	SanguinetiA122	*0.70e	ZipyZtr OnNeLow WhalysDrm	Dueled, ridden out	7

●27Mar DeD 4f ft :48 B 1/8 21Mar DeD 4f ft :50 Bg 8/19 16Mar DeD 4f ft :50 B 10/41 10Mar DeD 3f ft :37 B 4/19 05Mar DeD 3f ft :38 B 8/10 26Feb DeD 3f ft :39 B 4/6

4 Star Maid (S 0)

Own: Miguel Coll
9/2 White: blue bars, yellow sun
URIETA-MORAN VICTOR (62 3-9-6 13%)

$4,000 Ch. m. 5 FTMBSP 2003 $1k
Sire: Diamond (Mr. Prospector)
Dam: Karla A Star (Star De Naskra)
Brdr: Redmond C. S. Finney (MD)
Trnr: Morales Nabo (8 0-0-1 0%)

Power Rating: 91.6 (6th) L 118

Life:	34 3 - 2 - 4	$47,323	77	Fst	28 3 - 0 - 3	$37,194	77
2007	1 0 - 0 - 0	$385	61	Off	6 0 - 2 - 1	$10,129	63
2006	19 1 - 0 - 2	$16,252	65	Dis	6 1 - 1 - 0	$12,308	65
Tdn	2 0 - 0 - 0	$449	61	Trf	0 0 - 0 - 0	$0	
				AW	0 0 - 0 - 0	$0	

2007	72	14%	44%	-1.23
JKYw/ S types	133	8%	29%	-0.68
JKYw/ Trn L60	3	0%	0%	-2.00
JKYw/ Sprints	60	13%	43%	-1.36

2007	8	0%	13%	-2.00
Down one class	17	12%	29%	-0.79
Claiming	88	9%	26%	+0.47

Sire Stats: AWD 6.0f 22%Mud 157MudSts 1.00spi
Dam'sSire: AWD 6.8f 14%Mud 1541MudSts 1.88spi

★ Best Dirt Speed is fastest among today's starters ★ Drops in Class today
★ Eligible to improve in 2nd start since layoff
● Poor Trainer win%

DATE TRK	DIST						RR	RACETYPE	CR	E1	E2/	LP	1c	2c	SPD	PP	ST	1C	2C	Str	FIN	JOCKEY	ODDS	Top Finishers	Comment	
22Apr07Tdn4	5f ft	:22	:46		:59	4	105	C6250n4L	104		75/	75			61	1	5	5	5	5	4	Urieta-moranV118	L 13.70	PuertoValent LilsMyDol MadyBell	Failed to menace	6
29Nov06Tdn7	6f ft	:22	:46	:59	1:13	3	104	C3500n2Y	103	72	60/	74	-7	-4	48	2	8	8	8	8	8	Oro E117	L 9.20	OutAtHom MiveOlZigme Thershwysstory	No factor	9
Previously trained by GUTIERREZ ANGEL																										
11Nov06Del8	5½ ft	:22	:47	:59	1:05	3	107	C5000	103	66	57/	56	-13	-15	43	2	6	6	6	6	6	Jurado EM118	L 50.30	Killing Frost Sapphire Lady Theonelove	Trailed	6
28Oct06Del3	6f sy	:22	:46	:59	1:13	3	106	C5000	101	79	73/	51	-5	-7	38	4	3	4	4	4	4	Bedia AO119	L 13.40	SapphireLady Run For Sam Broken Wish	Trailed	4
14Oct06Del8	6f ft	:22	:46	:59	1:12	3	107	C5000	103	71	74/	57	-4	-5	46	2	7	6	7	7	7	Bedia AO119	L 61.90	SweetMsEl SaphireLady Theonelov	Awkward start	7
26Sep06Del3	6f ft	:22	:46	1:00	1:15	3	107	C5000n2mts	106	78	79/	54	+8	+11	48	4	4	4	3	4	3	Bedia AO121	L 9.00	All DayAllNight Jetster Star Maid	Not forward factor	4
23Aug06Del1	1 70 ft	:26	:51	1:16	1:45	3	107	C5000n2tlm	102	29	30/	65	-31	-22	41	4	6	6	6	7	7	Umana J121	L 42.30	ChrstsMmory PointLly AunthntcAlc	Showed little	7
05Aug06Del1	5½ ft	:22	:46	:59	1:05	3	108	C5000	107	73	69/	61	-2	-7	56	5	5	6	6	5	5	Pimentel J121	L 36.60	Lil's Honor Theonelove Katie Jork	No factor	7
04Jly06Del1	5½ ft	:22	:46	1:00	1:07	3	109	C5000n3L	108	76	74/	72	-2	+2	65	6	4	4	4	3	1	Bedia AO118	L 36.80	StarMd PMgc BtfulGngr	Closed with a rush 5w	6
13Jun06Del2	1m ft	:23	:47	1:15	1:42	3	109	C5000n1tmx	104	76	60/	54	+12	-2	50	1	5	5	3	4	4	Bedia AO122	L 14.20	Dancer WayneWoWeme TrueFsixon	Bid, faltered	7

●14Apr Tdn 5f ft 1:02 Bg 1/9 01Apr Tdn 4f ft :53 B 11/11 25Mar Tdn 3f ft :42 B 14/15 29Jan'06 Tam 4f ft :56 Bg 8/29 10Dec'05 Tam 4f ft :50 B 2/40 27Nov'05 Tam 4f ft :50 B 17/22
13Sep'05 Del 4f ft :49 B 9/14 18Aug'05 Del 4f ft :50 B 1/22 20Jly'05 Del 4f ft :50 B 16/37 22Jun'05 Del 4f ft :50 B 33/46 15Jun'05 Del 3f ft :37 B 10/24 11May'05 Del 5f ft 1:01 B 4/22

5 Our Last Dance (S 0)

Own: Diamond Wood Stable
6/1 Lt blue, dk blue diamonds
BARRERA FRANCISCO (35 7-4-4 20%)

$4,000 B. m. 5
Sire: Memer Mill (Forty Niner)
Dam: Rising Light (Light Idea)
Brdr: Diamond Wood Stable (OH)
Trnr: Shuman Joseph P. (15 2-4-3 13%)

Power Rating: 91.2 (7th) L 113

Life:	24 3 - 3 - 5	$37,186	75	Fst	16 3 - 2 - 5	$33,314	75
2006	12 1 - 3 - 3	$14,558	58	Off	4 0 - 1 - 0	$2,592	63
2005	6 1 - 0 - 1	$8,076	62	Dis	3 1 - 0 - 2	$10,010	75
Tdn	15 3 - 2 - 3	$28,411	75	Trf	2 0 - 0 - 0	$1,290	58
				AW	0 0 - 0 - 0	$0	

+2007	35	20%	43%	-0.21
JKYw/ S types	8	12%	25%	-1.50
+JKYw/ Trn L60	4	50%	75%	+4.40
+JKYw/ Sprints	25	24%	44%	+0.35

2007	18	11%	56%	-0.58
90+ days away	88	7%	40%	-0.65
Shipper	82	15%	48%	+0.15
Down one class	63	18%	49%	-0.78

Sire Stats: AWD 6.2f 12%Mud 394MudSts 0.61spi
Dam'sSire: AWD 7.3f 7%Mud 196MudSts 0.54spi

★ Hot Jockey in last 7 days (11 4-0-2) ★ Highest Speed Figure at Today's Distance
★ Best Dirt Speed is faster than the Avg Winning Speed ★ Drops in Class today
★ Switches to a high% jockey
● Has not raced for more than 5 months ● Poor 90+ days away trainer record: 7%wins 88sts

DATE TRK	DIST						RR	RACETYPE	CR	E1	E2/	LP	1c	2c	SPD	PP	ST	1C	2C	Str	FIN	JOCKEY	ODDS	Top Finishers	Comment	
09Dec06Mnr2	1⅛ ft	:24	:50	1:16	1:52	3	107	C5000n4L	103	51	44/	38	+1	+8	35	9	6	9	8	8	8	Felix JE118	L 12.60	I'm A CatToo AviationDre Night Alibi	Never factored	9
25Nov06Mnr8	1m ft	:25	:50	1:17	1:45	3	108	C5000n4L	107	59	55/	84	-10	-7	65	8	7	8	5	4	3	Pilares CP119	L 13.10	UpThAct SpringDt OrLstDnc	Bid 4 wide, no match	8
03Nov06Mnr8	1m ft	:25	:50	1:18	1:48	3	108	C5000n4L	107	70	67/	66	+9	+7	60	2	7	6	6	5	6	Pilares CP119	L 11.80	Mdnght SpringDell PriceCode	Step slow, no factor	9
10Oct06Mnr8	1m ft	:24	:49	1:15	1:41	3	108	C5000n4L	107	56	57/	82	-11	-11	65	1	3	3	4	3	3	Pilares CP119	L 4.20	Nplsm Mdnght OurLstDnce	Bid extended, shortSw	9
18Sep06Mnr5	1m ft	:24	:48	1:14	1:41	3	109	C5000n4L	108	74	65/	79	-1	-4	68	5	3	4	4	3hd	2	Pilares CP119	L 17.40	StpWtTr OrLtDc HncnMl	Bid incvied1/8;game2d	10
27Aug06Tdn12	1 70 sy	:23	:49	1:14	1:47	3	106	C3500n4L	107	67	59/	74	-4	+1	63	4	4	4	2	2	2	Pilares CP119	L 6.70	Shrdobbls OrLstDnc RohofRx	No match for winner	8
10Aug06Tdn4	1 70 ft	:23	:48	1:14	1:46	3	105	C3500n4L	104	57	57/	74	-3	+1	62	3	6	5	4	4	2	MunayllaF118	L 3.60	RvrUp OurLstDnce Shrdoublois	Steady advance	6
09Jly06Tdn13	1 70 ft	:23	:48	1:15	1:48	3	105	C3500n3L	106	61	48/	76	-5	-6	58	1	4	4	4	2	1	MunayllaF118	L 3.50	OrLstDnc LdyLbet Twctchd	3 wide, well handled	9
22Jun06Tdn4	6f gd	:22	:47	1:00	1:14	3	103	SCln6000n3L	104	72	65/	78	+1	-5	56	1	7	7	6	5	4	MunayllaF118	L 2.70	FollyMe Country Fox Darby's Price	Mild bid, made	7
16Jun06Tdn12	1 70 ft	:23	:48	1:14	1:46	3	103	C3500n3L	104	55	52/	77	-7	-5	61	5	6	6	5	3	3	Pilares CP118	L 4.10	Shrdobbls RylRcgntn OrLstDnc	Mild bid, no threat	9

30Apr Tdn 5f ft 1:03 B 8/9 19Apr Tdn 5f ft 1:01 B 3/5 12Apr Tdn 4f my :49 B 3/13 30Mar Tdn 4f ft :50 B 12/15 23Mar Tdn 3f gd :39 B 4/6 15Apr'06 Tdn 5f ft 1:02 B 4/16
08Apr'06 Tdn 4f ft :49 B 11/35 31Mar'06 Tdn 4f ft :49 B 3/12 25Mar'06 Tdn 3f ft :37 B 9/16 10Dec'05 Tdn 5f ft 1:05 Bg 1/2 30Nov'05 Tdn 3f ft :38 B 3/4 04Apr'05 Tdn 4f ft :50 B 7/18

Ultimate PP's w/ Quick Play Comments **River Downs** Clm 4000NW4L 5½ Furlongs. 3upF&M Friday, May 11, 2007 **Race 11 (TDN - #11)** E1 E2/LATE SPD 75 71

6 **Maddy Bell (E/P 6)** $4,000 B. f. 4 KEEJAN 2004 $5k
Own: Thomas L. Thornton
3/1 Red black tie: black stallion
MAGRELL JANE M. (37 0-9-4 0%)

Sire: Power Storm (Storm Cat)
Dam: Telephone Belle (Phone Trick)
Brdr: Fares Farm; Inc. (KY)
Trnr: Thornton Nancy (28 3-2-6 7%)

Power Rating: 96.1 (1st) L 120

Life:	24	3 - 3 - 5	$22,480	72	Fst	19	3 - 2 - 4	$19,608	72
2007	5	2 - 0 - 1	$7,940	67	Off	5	0 - 1 - 1	$2,822	57
2006	15	1 - 1 - 3	$10,480	72	Dis	13	3 - 0 - 4	$16,465	72
Tdn	5	1 - 0 - 2	$5,991	67	Trf	0	0 - 0 - 0	$0	
					AW	0	0 - 0 - 0	$0	

2007	30	0%	37%	-2.00
JKYw/EP types	91	8%	26%	-1.26
JKYw/ Trn L60	2	0%	50%	-2.00
JKYw/ Sprints	24	0%	38%	-2.00

2007	71	6%	38%	-1.37
Down one class	36	14%	39%	+0.61
Claiming	266	10%	37%	0.02

Sire Stats: AWD 6.1f 0%Mud 12MudSts 0.49spi
Dam'sSire: AWD 6.5f 16%Mud 1510MudSts 1.87spi

★ Best Dirt Speed is faster than the Avg Winning Speed ★ Drops in Class today
★ Ran 3rd vs tougher in last race
● Switches to a Low% jockey ● Poor Trainer win%

DATE TRK	DIST					RR	RACETYPE	CR	E1	E2/	LP	1c	2c	SPD	PP	ST	1C	2C	Str	FIN	JOCKEY		ODDS	Top Finishers	Comment	
22Apr07Tdn4	5f ft	:22^4	:46^4		:59^1 4↑	103	ⒻC6250n4L	109		79/	74			62	6	2	4^{1½}	4^4	4^2	3^{3½}	Yaranga Y^{120}	U	2.90	PuertoValair^{2}½MsMyDol^{2}½MadyBel¾	3 wide, mild bid	6
13Apr07Tdn11	5f ft	:22^4	:47^3		1:00^4 4↑	103	ⒻC4000n3L	107		82/	76			67	9	2	3^2	2^2	2^2	1^{1¾}	Yaranga Y^{118}	L	10.80	MaddyBel^{1}¾PyriteLis^{1}MrquisSlon^1	Drew clear; driving	10
07Feb07Beu7	5f ft	:22^4	:46^4		:59 3↑	101	ⒻC3500n2L	104		83/	70			62	7	2	2^1	2^{hd}	1½	1^{1½}	Yaranga Y^{120}	L	3.50	MaddyBel^{1}½QuiteUnqur^{nk}PrivteTrcks^{1}¾	Dueled; driving	7
27Jan07Beu7	6f ft	:22^3	:47^2	:59^4	1:12^2 3↑	105	ⒻA7500n2L	101	85	73/	42	-1	-6	33	6	1	2^{hd}	2^{hd}	7^{5½}	7^{17}	Yaranga Y^{120}	L	36.50	StrySdy^{2}½swtMssr^{nk}ChrkDrmr^{2}¾	Inside duel; faltered	7
09Jan07Beu7	5½ gd	:23	:47^1	:59	1:05^1 3↑	102	ⒻA7500n2L	105	84	74/	32	-5	-6	37	4	1	2^{2½}	3^{4½}	4^{11}	4^{29}	Phares CP^{120}	L	38.00	QualityLabel^{1}¾HapyBeper½Morgnese^{4}¾	Chased; tired	6
16Oct06Tdn8	5f ft	:22^1	:47^1		1:00^4 3↑	101	ⒻC3500n2L	102		90/	55			55	5	3	2^{hd}	1^1	1^1	3^2	SanguinettiA^{115}	L	13.60	ChristnBln^{2}¾ExcsvWtch^{nk}MdyBel^{hd}	Faltered; late stretch	9
Previously trained by RADOSEVICH JEFFREY A.																										
01Oct06Tdn8	5f gd	:22^3	:47^2		1:01^1 3↑	102	ⒻC3500n2L	103		88/	53			50	6	2	3½	1^{hd}	2^{hd}	4^{4½}	Spieth S^{116}	L	6.90	ShoshnGd^{2}¾StrmBlvr½DwntwEvl^{1}¼	Weakened; slightly	11
10Sep06Tdn6	5f ft	:22^2	:47^1		1:00^4 3↑	102	ⒻC3500n2L	99		76/	51			35	11	3	9^{3½}	11^{16}	11^{12}	8^{13}	Spieth S^{116}	L	12.30	Whiverun^{nk}StormBlvr^{2}DwntwnEvl^3	Wide trip; outrun	11
Previously trained by KUNES KAREN M.																										
04Sep06Tam2	4f ft	:22^4			:47^2 3↑	102	ⒻC5000/4 n2L	101		70/	76			46	3	6	6^8		6^{9¾}	7^8	Russell C^{118}	U	4.90	RNicole^{1}¾ClscVictory^{2}¾MgVictory^{nk}	Brk in,bumped;3wd	7
27Jly06Pen5	5f ft	:22^4	:46^4		1:00 3↑	102	ⒻC4000n2L	103		83/	64			56	5	2	1^{1½}	1^1	1^{1½}	4^{3½}	RodriguezE^{118}	U	8.20	TheBigAm^{hd}Kepilncy^{1}¾CDenied^{1}¼	Off rail; weakened	9

05Apr Tdn 3f ft :38^4 B 2/3 ●04Jan Beu 3f ft :36 B 1/11 13Oct06 Tdn 3f ft :39^1 B 8/12 15Jly06 Pen 4f ft :51^4 B 27/32 18Mar06 Pen 3f ft :38^2 B 32/38 16Dec05 Hou 4f my :51 B 24/44
10Dec05 Hou 4f ft :56^1 B 64/64 18Nov05 Hou 4f ft :55^1 B 42/42 29Oct05 Hou 4f ft :53 B 53/65 29Sep05 LaD 4f ft :49 B 4/14 10Sep05 LaD 4f ft :48^4 B 8/82 25Aug05 LaD 5f ft 1:02^2 B 17/24

7 **Storm Believer (E/P 7)** $4,000 Dkbbr. m. 6
Own: Josh Faulkner
7/2 Black; white 'f'; white lightening bolt
MARTINEZ, JR. LUIS J. (44 7-7-7 16%)

Sire: I Can't Believe (Our Native)
Dam: Storm Spirit (Future Storm)
Brdr: Colebrook Farms (ONT-C)
Trnr: Faulkner Joe C. (28 5-2-3 18%)

Power Rating: 96.1 (2nd) L 118

Life:	40	3 - 8 - 3	$27,184	65	Fst	33	2 - 6 - 2	$21,081	65
2007	5	1 - 1 - 1	$4,248	61	Off	7	1 - 2 - 1	$6,103	63
2006	16	1 - 4 - 0	$10,250	63	Dis	26	2 - 6 - 1	$17,363	61
Tdn	27	2 - 5 - 2	$17,923	65	Trf	0	0 - 0 - 0	$0	
					AW	0	0 - 0 - 0	$0	

2007	111	12%	40%	-0.68
+JKYw/EP types	250	18%	41%	+0.36
+JKYw/ Trn L60	4	25%	50%	-0.65
JKYw/ Sprints	79	10%	39%	-1.05

2007	26	19%	38%	+4.09
+Down one class	131	28%	50%	+0.77
+Claiming	1036	19%	43%	+0.27

Sire Stats: AWD 6.2f 14%Mud 234MudSts 1.03spi
Dam'sSire: AWD 6.9f 11%Mud 678MudSts 0.78spi

★ Drops in Class today ★ High % Trainer

DATE TRK	DIST					RR	RACETYPE	CR	E1	E2/	LP	1c	2c	SPD	PP	ST	1C	2C	Str	FIN	JOCKEY		ODDS	Top Finishers	Comment	
22Apr07Tdn4	5f ft	:22^4	:46^4		:59^1 4↑	103	ⒻC6250n4L	104		84/	68			61	4	3	1^1	1^1	2^{1½}	5^6	Stokes LA^{118}	Lb	3.30	PuertoValr^{2}¾MsMyDol^{2}½MdyBel¾	Faded; mid stretch	6
15Apr07Tdn5	6f gd	:22^3	:46^3	:59^3	1:13^2 4↑	104	ⒻC4000n4L	106	88	83/	66	0	0	61	6	2	1^1	2^{hd}	2^1	3^3	MrtinezJrLJ^{118}	Lb	6.20	HyLucyLou^{2}LevelBid^{1}StormBeliever^1	Pace; held well	7
27Feb07Beu8	5f gd	:22^4	:46^2		1:00^4 3↑	107	ⒻC3500n3L	106		90/	61			61	2	1	2^1	2½	1^{2½}	1^{nk}	Pautaz E^{120}	Lb	3.30	StormBlvr^{nk}PnnyGhst¾DatsMLot^2	Just lasted; driving	8
16Feb07Beu4	5f ft				:58^1 3↑	103	ⒻC3500n3L	101		98/	52			51	7	2	2^1	1^1	2^2	6^8	Pautaz E^{120}	Lb	5.90	AlFrNdy^{3}¾UpFrntAnn^{nk}NtvDughtr^{hd}	Bid; clear; weakened	8
20Jan07Beu7	5½ ft	:22^3	:47^2	1:00	1:06^3 3↑	103	ⒻC5000n3L	106	90	83/	64	+2	0	57	4	2	1^1	1^2	1^1	2^{5¾}	CcmqueMA^{120}	Lb	24.90	UGotBKidn^{4}¼StrmBlvr¾ClySrpr^3	Set pace; held 2nd	11
16Dec06Beu7	5f ft	:22^3	:48		1:01^3 3↑	102	ⒻC3500n3L	102		90/	51			50	1	1	1^{hd}	2^{hd}	3½	8^4	HernandezL^{118}	Lb	7.00	WDy^{nk}ImprlPrncs^{nk}DlsMLot^{nk}	Inside duel; weakened	11
25Nov06Tdn6	5f ft	:22^3	:47		:59^3 3↑	103	ⒻC3500n3L	103		84/	66			58	1	2	2^{hd}	5^{1½}	5^{4½}	6^7	MrtinezJrLJ^{120}	Lb	20.30	PuertoVlr^{4}½ShoshnGd^{hd}ChristnBln^{2}½	Inside; weakened	8
09Nov06Tdn1	5f ft	:22^1	:46^1		:59^1 3↑	103	ⒻC3500n3L	100		81/	51			38	2	4	2^2	7^{11}	7^{17}	7^{21½}	Feliz JE^{120}	Lb	6.70	GhostHrbor^{10}¾ShoshonGd^{hd}DrkRnbow¾	Checked; turn	7
02Nov06Tdn8	5f ft	:23	:48		1:00^3 3↑	100	ⒻC3500n2L	102		81/	71			61	1	1	1^2	1^{2½}	1^2	2^{hd}	MrtinezJrLJ^{117}	Lb	2.10	JgurAve^{hd}StormBlvr^{hd}ExcsvWtch^4	Pace; just missed (Placed 1st through disqualification)	7
16Oct06Tdn8	5f ft	:22^1	:47^1		1:00^4 3↑	101	ⒻC3500n2L	96		89/	35			33	8	1	3^{hd}	4^2	7^{5½}	7^{14½}	MrtinezJrLJ^{117}	Lb	2.20	ChristinaBln^{2}¾ExcesivWtch^{nk}MadyBel^{hd}	Chased; tired	9

22Apr06 Tdn 4f ft :52 B 6/6 13Apr06 Tdn 3f ft :38^4 B 13/18 28Mar06 Tdn 3f ft :38^2 B 23/31 28Oct05 Haw 5f ft 1:02^3 B 8/44 ●22Oct05 Haw 3f ft :37 B 1/11 17Jun05 FE 3f ft :36 B 2/9
19Apr05 FE 3f ft :36^4 H 7/25 14Apr05 FE 3f ft :40^3 H 31/31 12Nov04 Tdn 3f ft :37^2 Bg 4/8 ●07Nov04 Tdn 3f ft :35^3 B 1/16 ●01Oct04 WO tr.t 3f ft :35^3 H 1/5 13Sep04 WO 6f ft 1:16^4 H 2/2

Ultimate PP's w/ Quick Play Comments **River Downs** ⑪ Clm 4000NW4L 5½ Furlongs 3upF&M Friday, May 11, 2007 **Race 11 (TDN - #11)** E1 E2/LATE SPD 75 71

Last 3 Years RACETYPE STATS:	# Races	FAVORITES Win%	Itm%	$2ROI	Average Field Size	Median $2 Win Payoff	% Winners < 5/1	% Winners >= 5/1 < 10/1	% Winners >= 10/1
TDN 3up CLM 3500 - 5000 Dirt 5.5f	21	29%	67%	0.66	7.8	$6.80	90%	5%	5%

Track Bias Stats

DIRT 5.5f	* MEET Totals *				DIRT 5.5f	* WEEK Totals *			
# Races: 34	Speed Bias: 74%		WnrAvgBL		# Races: 12	Speed Bias: 67%		WnrAvgBL	
%Wire: 26%	04/12 - 05/06		1stCall: 1.7		%Wire: 25%	05/03 - 05/06		1stCall: 1.9	
			2ndCall: 1.1					2ndCall: 1.3	
	Early	Speed	Late	Speed		Early	Speed	Late	Speed
Runstyle:	E	E/P	P	S	Runstyle:	E	E/P	P	S
	++	+				++			
Impact Values	1.82	1.20	0.52	0.45	Impact Values	2.08	0.92	0.46	0.54
%Races Won	44%	29%	9%	18%	%Races Won	42%	25%	8%	25%
Post Bias:	RAIL	1-3	4-7	8+	Post Bias	RAIL	1-3	4-7	8+
			+			+	+		
Impact Values	0.47	0.71	1.25	0.96	Impact Values	1.49	1.24	1.11	0.39
Avg Win %	6%	9%	20%	6%	Avg Win %	17%	14%	17%	3%

Race Summary

#	HorseName	ML Odds	Med Eqp	Days Since L/R	Run Style	PTS	Avg Dist/Surf PACE-SPEED E1	E2/Late	Spd	Avg Race Rtng	Best Pace E1	E2/Late	Final Speed Sp1	Sp2	Sp3	Sp4	ACL	Rcg Spd Avg	R1	R2	R3	Mud Spd	Pedigree Stats Mud Sts	Mud %	Sire AWD	Dam Sire's AWD
6	Maddy Bell	3/1	L	19..	+E/P	6	85	81/ 73	* 64*	104	85	90/ 76	62.	67.	62.	33.	102.6	64	105	103	101	55	12	0	6.1	6.5
4	Star Maid	9/2	L	19.	S			75/ 75	61	105	78	79/ 77	61.	48.	43.	38	105.6	51	105	104	107	57	157	22	6.0	6.8
7	Storm Believer	7/2	L	19..	+E/P	7	88	86/ 65	* 61*	105	90	90/ 71	61.	61.	61.	51.	102.9	61	105	105	102	63	234	14	6.2	6.9
1	Gone For Canada	4/1	L	26..	S		73	70/ 74	* 60*	106	76	79/ 88	54.	65.	52	63	104.9	57	105	106	106	63	75	17	6.9	7.2
5	Our Last Dance	6/1	L	153	S		78	70/ 74	(57)	103	72	65/ 78	35	65	60	65		53	107	106	106	63	394	12	6.2	7.3
2	Ohio Volunteer	6/1	L	175	S		76	66/ 77	(56)	103	78	69/ 80	65	62	61	57.	102.8	63	103	103	103	65	95	6	6.3	6.5
3	Zippy Ziter	5/1		12	++E	4	79	73/ 54	* 46*	105	79	82/ 62	38.	53.			104.5	46	106	104			48	19	6.2	6.4

Speed Last Race	Back Speed	Current Class	Average Class Last 3	Power Rating	Early Pace Last Race	Late Pace Last Race
65 Ohio Volunteer	67 Maddy Bell	105.8 Gone For Canada	106.4 Ohio Volunteer	96.1 Storm Believer	73 Ohio Volunteer	75 Ohio Volunteer
62 Maddy Bell	65 Star Maid	105.3 Storm Believer	105.6 Our Last Dance	96.1 Maddy Bell	66 Gone For Canada	75 Star Maid
61 Star Maid	65 Gone For Canada	104.9 Maddy Bell	105.5 Gone For Canada	94.9 Gone For Canada	63 Zippy Ziter	74 Gone For Canada
61 Storm Believer	61 Storm Believer	104.7 Zippy Ziter	105.3 Storm Believer	94.5 Ohio Volunteer	51 Our Last Dance	74 Maddy Bell
54 Gone For Canada	59 Ohio Volunteer	104.2 Star Maid	104.9 Maddy Bell	92.7 Zippy Ziter	NA Storm Believer	68 Storm Believer
38 Zippy Ziter	56 Our Last Dance	NA Ohio Volunteer	104.7 Zippy Ziter	91.6 Star Maid	NA Maddy Bell	46 Zippy Ziter
35 Our Last Dance	53 Zippy Ziter	NA Our Last Dance	103.3 Star Maid	91.2 Our Last Dance	NA Star Maid	39 Our Last Dance

#	Speed Last Race		#	Prime Power		#	Class Rating		#	Best Speed at Dist	
2	Flirtini	57	3	Motormouth Sue	104.8	3	Motormouth Sue	104.7	3	Motormouth Sue	72
3	Motormouth Sue	56	2	Flirtini	98.7	2	Flirtini	103.4	7	Classy Forest	61
4	Tombeau De Femmes	54	7	Classy Forest	91.8	1	Gonnagetchagood	102.6	8	Rachel In Transit	61

12

Exacta / Trifecta / Superfecta (Ten Cent Minimum) / Pick 3 (Races 12-13-14)

	E1	E2/LATE	SPEED
PARS:	89	87/ 75	71

6 Furlongs. ⒻⓈAlw 13600 Purse $13,600. SIMULCAST FROM RIVER DOWNS. FOR ACCREDITED OHIO BRED FILLIES AND MARES THREE YEARS OLD AND UPWARD WHICH HAVE NEVER WON TWO RACES. Three Year Olds, 116 lbs., Older, 124 lbs. Non-winners of a race since April 11 Allowed 2 lbs. A race since March 11 Allowed 4 lbs. (Races whereenteredf or $15,000 or less not considered in allowances).

Post Time: (4:45)/ 3:45/ 2:45/ 1:45

1 Gonnagetchagood (E 3)

Own: Monica A. Wells
10/1 White, green diamond belt
ROSARIO JR. HECTOR L (3 1-0-0 33%)

B. m. 5
Sire: Cool Quaker (It's Freezing)
Dam: De Belle Rose (Wind And Wuthering)
Brdr: T. L. Shaffer (OH)
Trnr: Wells Darrell (5 0-0-1 0%)

Power Rating: 89.5 (6th) L 120

Life:	27 1 - 3 - 2	$11,341	59	Fst	20 0 - 2 - 2	$6,976	59
2007	5 0 1 - 1	$3,267	59	Off	7 1 - 1 - 0	$4,865	49
2006	12 0 - 1 - 1	$3,127	55	Dis	24 1 - 3 - 2	$10,851	59
RD	14 0 - 1 - 2	$4,741	57	Trf	0 0 - 0 - 0	$0	
				AW	0 0 - 0 - 0	$0	

2007	187	10%	31%	-0.74
JKYw/ E types	185	19%	41%	+0.13
JKYw/ Sprints	83	7%	25%	-1.19

2007	8	0%	25%	-2.00
Allowance	4	0%	25%	-2.00

Sire Stats: AWD 6.0f 13%Mud 46MudSts 0.19spi
Dam'sSire: AWD 7.1f 12%Mud 338MudSts 0.78spi

- Finished far back in last start ● Only 1 win in 27 career starts ● Poor Trainer win%
- Best Speed rating is well below the Avg Winning Speed ● Poor record at this track
- Poor record at this distance

DATE TRK	DIST					RR	RACETYPE	CR	E1	E2/	LP	1c	2c	SPD	PP	ST	1C	2C	Str	FIN	JOCKEY		ODDS	Top Finishers	Comment	
28Apr07RD11	6f ft	:22^4	:46^1	:59^2	1:13^1 3↑	107	ⒻⓈA13600n2L	101	82	78/	58	-2	-1	50	5	7	4^2	4^4	4^8	5^{13}	PrescottRA120	Lb	7.00	DrySd/MrmthS/TombrDFms	Lacked late response	8
17Apr07RD7	6f ft	:23^1	:46^4	1:00	1:13^2 3↑	105	ⒻⓈA14700n3L	109	82	66/	78	-5	-8	57	4	4	4	6^4	3^7	3^6	Diego I120	Lb	26.10	Isurissa/Bringwthy/Gngtchgd	Failed to sustain bid	6
09Apr07Beu1	6f ft	:22^4	:47^3	1:00^4	1:13^3 3↑	103	ⒻⓈClm5000n3L	102	87	76/	62	+4	+1	52	1	6	4^1	5^2	5^2	5^6	Paucar E120	Lb	3.30	BdpslSk/ErByo/UpmyVcky	Bumped 3/16, no rally	6
23Jan07Beu7	6f gd	:22^4	:48^7	1:01^4	1:15^2 3↑	103	ⒻⓈA10500n2L	101	76	70/	59	+5	+4	44	1	7	5^8	6^7	6^7	5^{10}	ComqueMA120	Lb	4.60	Era Nayou/Leah Grape/Shari's Gift	Showed little	7
17Jan07Beu1	6f ft	:22^4	:46^4	:59^4	1:12^4 3↑	101	ⒻⓈClm4000n2L	103	85	81/	66	-2	-1	59	2	6	1^1	1^5	1^7	2^1	Paucar E120	Lb	4.50	KtyRb/Gongtchgd/PhicEny	Broke slow, rushed up	7

Previously trained by ADAMS WILLIAM E.

DATE TRK	DIST					RR	RACETYPE	CR	E1	E2/	LP	1c	2c	SPD	PP	ST	1C	2C	Str	FIN	JOCKEY		ODDS	Top Finishers	Comment	
25Nov06Beu4	6f ft	:23	:47^3	1:00^3	1:14 3↑	101	ⒻⓈClm5000n2L	100	88	80/	70	-7	-3	45	1	8	7^8	7^8	7^{10}	6^{10}	DeonauthKP120	Lb	18.50	HegisBgGirl/Mymymk/MrcysHop	Ducked into gap	9

Previously trained by WELLS DARRELL

DATE TRK	DIST					RR	RACETYPE	CR	E1	E2/	LP	1c	2c	SPD	PP	ST	1C	2C	Str	FIN	JOCKEY		ODDS	Top Finishers	Comment	
31Oct06Beu6	6f wf	:22^4	:47^4	1:01	1:14^1 3↑	100	ⒻⓈClm5000n2L	99	84	72/	55	-1	-4	42	8	4	3^1	3^4	6^6	7^{11}	ComqueMA120	Lb	4.40	ShmnSctr/RglBgGirl/AlchMdm	Chased 3 wide, tired	10
06Oct06Beu13	6f ft				1:13^4 3↑	99	ⒻⓈClm5000n2L	101	88	81/	61	+8	+9	55	3	6	2^2	2^2	2^1	4^3	CamaqueC120	Lb	6.40	BustOfApls/KtyRb/BlefyRb	Chased, weakened	11
22Sep06Hoo8	5½ sy	:22	:46^2		1:07^1 3↑	102	ⒻC5000n2L	102	70	74/	52	+3	+8	49	6	9	9^9	9^7	7^5	6^4	ComqueMA118	Lb	26.80	ThSwtstRcs/CscWr/DrlnJmi	3wide turn, no rally	9
03Sep06RD8	6f ft	:23	:46^1	1:00^2	1:14^2 3↑	99	ⒻⓈClm4000n2L	101	85	82/	56	-1	+4	52	10	3	4^6	4^1	3^2	2^5	Wiek JJ120	Lb	15.50	BdptSk/Gongtchgd/BrstOfApls	Gamely, held place	12

11Mar Beu (d) 3f my :38^2 B 2/3 13Nov06 Beu 3f ft :39^1 B 5/5 21Oct'06 Hoo 4f wf :50^3 B 6/17 19Aug06 Hoo (d) 3f ft :37 Bg 5/25 08Apr'06 RD 4f my :53 B 3/4 23Aug'05 Hoo 3f ft :36^3 B 7/12
14Jun'05 RD 3f ft :38 Bg 9/13 11Jun'05 RD 4f gd :49 Hg 3/12 10Jun'05 RD 4f ft :50 Bg 4/4 07Jun'05 RD 2f ft :25 Bg 1/2 04Jun'05 RD 3f ft :38 Bg 5/13 16Oct'04 Hoo (d) 3f my :41^3 B 5/6

2 Flirtini (E/P 7)

Own: Sherry Napier
10/1 Maroon, white 'F', white sleeves
OUZTS PERRY WAYNE (142 16-25-20 13%)

B. f. 3
Sire: Devious (Danzig)
Dam: Granny's Honey (Honey Jay)
Brdr: Fair Winds Farm (OH)
Trnr: Napier William J. (36 4-3-2 15%)

Power Rating: 98.7 (2nd) L 112

Life:	9 0 - 2 - 4	$8,705	62	Fst	6 0 - 2 - 2	$4,940	62
2007	2 0 - 1 - 1	$3,420	57	Off	3 0 - 0 - 2	$1,715	57
2006	7 0 - 1 - 3	$5,285	62	Dis	4 0 - 1 - 2	$4,215	57
RD	5 0 - 2 - 0	$5,225	62	Trf	0 0 - 0 - 0	$0	
				AW	1 0 - 0 - 1	$970	56

2007	501	18%	34%	-0.78
JKYw/EP types	137	9%	27%	-1.10
JKYw/ Trn L60	3	0%	0%	-2.00
JKYw/ Sprints	277	9%	34%	0.94

2007	31	13%	35%	+6.59
8th favorite	31	16%	52%	0.35
+Allowance	66	20%	43%	+0.02

Sire Stats: AWD 5.2f 20%Mud 5MudSts
Dam'sSire: AWD 6.7f 10%Mud 1544MudSts 1.08spi

★ Highest Last Race Speed Rating ★ Eligible to improve in 3rd start since layoff
● Beaten by weaker in last start

DATE TRK	DIST					RR	RACETYPE	CR	E1	E2/	LP	1c	2c	SPD	PP	ST	1C	2C	Str	FIN	JOCKEY		ODDS	Top Finishers	Comment	
28Apr07Beu8	5½ ft	:23^4	:48^4	1:01^1	1:07^4 3↑	100	ⒻⓈMdn 9.2k	102	86	72/	75	-3	-4	57	7	2	3^1	2^1	2^{hd}	3^1	Paucar E116	Lb	9.50	Chucks Legacy/Meluvsrasins/Flirtini	Evenly late	7
07Apr07RD1	6f ft	:23^1	:48^4	1:00^1	1:14^2 3↑	100	ⒻⓈMdn 13k	101	85	84/	60	-1	+1	57	5	3	3^1	2^1	2^4	2^8	SchaeferGA118	Lb	2.30	DustySkirt/Flirtini/Royal Caper	No match for winner	5
27Oct06Beu4	6f sy	:22^3	:46^4	:58^1	1:12	105	ⒻⓈMdn 9.2k	107	84	75/	64	-4	-8	53	4	5	3	3^2	2^1	3^{11}	Adam MG119	Lb	2.40	HollyTheDud/Spirit OfFire/Flirtini	Weakened, inside	8
18Oct06Beu2	6f sy	:22^3	:46^3	:59^3	1:13	106	Mdn 6.7k	107	86	77/	67	-1	0	57	5	1	3^1	5^4	4^4	3^7	GonzalezIR118	Lb	3.80	Malcher/Dakota's Choice/Flirtini	Finished evenly	7
14Sep06TP7	⊗1m ft	:24^4	:49	1:14^3	1:41^1	107	ⒻMC15000/10	107	84	57/	67	-5	+4	56	1	2	2^1	2^1	2^{hd}	3^1	Troilo WD118	Lb	5.20	Striking Jean/Fancy Gal/Flirtini	Weakened	5
29Aug06RD1	6f my	:22^3	:46^2	:59^3	1:13^3	104	ⒻⓈMdn 13k	104	83	74/	49	+2	-1	39	5	1	4^3	4^4	5^8	6^{18}	RosarioJrHL118	Lb	1.60	AplePandowdy/HolFoodToGo/SpiritOfFire	No rally	7
13Aug06RD8	5½ ft	:23^1	:46^2	1:00^2	1:07^7	106	ⒻⓈMdn 13k	110	79	83/	68	-2	+3	62	4	4	4^3	3^3	2^2	2no	Troilo WD118	Lb	9.80	Gin's Encore/Flirtini/Idreamkingwithyou	Just missed	8
30Jly06RD11	5½ ft	:23	:47	1:00	1:07	104	ⒻⓈTakBak 40k	106	86	74/	54	0	3	48	7	4	3^1	4^6	6^4	7^{12}	Stokes LA116	Lb	30.50	Lilebitteing/LoksThePart/Repingtherwrds	Gave way	9
16Jly06RD1	5½ ft	:23^2	:46^2	1:00	1:06^4	107	ⒻMdn 10k	107	75	67/	56	-7	-1	48	7	7	7^7	5^4	6^8	6^{10}	Stokes LA117	L	5.20	Weichaprize/Mini Mom/Spirit Of Fire	Bobbled start	9

30Mar RD 4f ft :48^2 H 1/3 17Mar Npx 3f gd 1:03 B 6/15 09Mar Npx 5f gd 1:04 B 5/7 24Feb Npx 5f ft 1:05 B 5/6 ●18Feb Npx 4f ft :51 B 1/4 16Oct'06 TP 5f ft 1:01^3 B 4/7
07Oct'06 TP 5f ft 1:00^3 B 10/25 24Sep'06 TP 5f ft 1:00^2 B 5/20 05Aug'06 RD 5f ft 1:03 B 2/15 ●22Jly'06 RD 4f my :48 Bg 1/8 08Jly'06 RD 4f ft :51 Hg 8/15 ●01Jly'06 RD 4f ft :47^4 B 1/8

Ultimate PP's w/ Quick Play Comments

River Downs

Alw 13600 6 Furlongs 3upF&M Friday, May 11, 2007 **Race 12**

E1 89 | E2/LATE 87/ 75 | SPD 71

3 Motormouth Sue (E/P 7)

7/5 Own: M. V. Stables, Inc.
Yellow, green, my
VITEK JUSTIN J (91 13-19-11 13%)

Ch. f. 4
Sire: Mahogany Hall (Woodman)
Dam: R M Peggy Lulu (Houston)
Brdr: South River Ranch Inc. (OH)
Trnr: Nance Michael W. (7 1-2-1 14%)

Power Rating: 104.8 (1st) L 120

Life:	19 1 - 8 - 3	$26,515	72	Fst 15 1 - 7 - 1 $22,100 64
2007	2 0 - 2 - 0	$4,840	72	Off 4 0 - 1 - 2 $4,415 72
2006	12 1 - 4 - 2	$17,638	64	Dis 11 1 - 5 - 0 $18,963 72
RD	6 1 - 3 - 1	$16,435	72	Trf 0 0 - 0 - 0 $0
				AW 9 0 - 4 - 1 $7,073 62

2007	226	11%	36%	+0.10
JKYw/EP types	182	12%	38%	-0.34
JKYw/ Trn L60	3	0%	100%	-2.00
JKYw/ Sprints	126	10%	39%	+0.30

+2007	105	23%	61%	-0.60
+8th favorite	166	28%	64%	-0.32
+Allowance	298	27%	59%	0.34

Sire Stats: AWD 7.0f 10%Mud 233MudSts 0.63spi
Dam'sSire:AWD 6.6f 11%Mud 951MudSts 0.77spi

★ Highest Speed Figure at Today's Distance ★ Best Dirt Speed is fastest among today's starters ● Only 1 win in 18 career starts
★ Ran 2nd vs similar in last race ★ Eligible to improve in 3rd start since layoff

DATE TRK	DIST		RR	RACETYPE	CR	E1	E2/	LP	1c	2c	SPD	PP	ST	1C	2C	Str	FIN	JOCKEY		ODDS	Top Finishers	Comment	
28Apr07RD11	6f ft	:22⁴ :48¹ :59² 1:13¹ 3↑	107	ⓕA13600n2L	107	84	83/	60	-2	-1	56	6	3	3²	2¹½	2⁴	2¹⁰	Vitek JJ120	Lb	0.90	DlySrl¹⁰MtrmthS½TombrDFms²½	No match; held place	6
14Apr07RD8	6f sy	:22⁴ :46¹ :59⁴ 1:13³ 3↑	105	ⓕA10600n2L	108	91	91/	72	0	+1	72	4	1	2hd	2½	2¹	2²½	Vitek JJ120	Lb	6.10	Parwnd²½MotormouthS⁶½LdyLakesThres⁴½	Drifted late	7
22Dec06TP8	6½ ft	:22⁴ :45⁴ 1:11¹ 1:17³ 3↑	105	ⓕC15000n2L	104	84	83/	64	-5	-4	62	5	3	2¹	2¹½	7⁵½	9⁸½	PrescottRA119	Lb	16.70	JSsPrsl¹½LilOrphLcy⁴QunBts²	3 wide; steadied 1/16	12
19Nov06Beu7	6f ft	:22⁴ :47¹ :59⁴ 1:13 3↑	107	ⓕA10500n2L	104	79	71/	78	-2	-6	60	5	4	4²½	4²	2⁴	2¹½	CamaqueC118	Lb	4.10	LdySprt¹½MotormothS⁶½ErRyou½	Stalked; second best	8
03Nov06Beu8	6f ft	:22³ :47² 1:00³ 1:13³ 3↑	104	ⓕA10500n2L	107	71	68/	75	0	-3	48	3	7	7⁶	8¹²	8¹¹	8¹³½	CamaqueC118	Lb	9.80	PerfectCondition²½SunshineonselP½Bebs²	Showed little	10
16Jun06RD11	6f ft	:22⁴ :46 :58² 1:13⁴ 3↑	101	ⓕA13300n2L	104	82	73/	74	1	+3	58	8	6	5²½	3⁴	2⁵	2²½	Paucar E117	Lb	3.10	SAkBonita²½MotormouthS½MsPatch⁵	Best stride late	9
08Jun06RD5	6f ft	:23 :46⁴ 1:00¹ 1:15 3↑	101	ⓕMdn 13k	105	86	84/	68	+1	+1	64	4	3	3¹	2hd	1¹	1¹½	Paucar E117	Lb	9.10	MotormthS¹½DonnmcRchlnTrmt¹½	Draw clear; driving	11
12May06RD13	6f my	:23¹ :47² 1:00⁴ 1:15¹ 3↑	101	ⓕMdn 13k	102	81	63/	75	0	-2	51	9	11	11³½	9⁸½	6⁸½	5⁸½	Paucar E116	Lb	3.90	Imswhtsnm⁴½ClsyFrst¹⁰OrFicty³½	Lost ground; mid track	12
14Apr06RD3	5½ my	:23² :47² 1:00¹ 1:07¹ 3↑	101	ⓕMdn 13k	102	83	76/	68	-3	-5	60	6	3	3¹½	3³½	3⁷½	3⁷½	Zuniga E116	Lb	4.10	IrshVsn⁶½BcksInThWds½MotormthS²½	Lost ground turn	9
30Mar06TP8	6½ ft	:23¹ :47² 1:13² 1:20¹	102	ⓕMC7500	104	76	71/	71	-8	8	58	7	1	5²	4²½	3⁹½	2⁷	Diego I122	Lb	7.30	Arsi⁷MotormouthS¹½SkyBride³½	4w; mild bid for place	8

31Mar TP 5f ft 1:01³ B 9/28 02Feb TP 5f ft 1:02² B 8/72 15Dec'06 TP 5f ft 1:01³ B 9/74 26Oct'06 TP 5f ft 1:00¹ B 4/8 13Oct'06 TP 4f ft :51³ B 4/5 09Nov'05 TP 4f ft :50² B 8/13
19Oct'05 TP 5f ft 1:04⁴ B 6/7 24Sep'05 TP 5f ft 1:04⁴ Bg 9/10 17Sep'05 TP 4f ft :51 Bg 24/26 09Aug'05 RD 5f ft 1:03² Bg 4/8 02Aug'05 RD 4f ft :52 B 11/14

4 Tombeur De Femmes (P 2)

5/2 Own: Gene N. Stewart
Yellow, multi colored emblem
ROJAS CHRISTIAN (46 7-7-5 14%)

Ch. f. 4
Sire: French Legionaire (Gray Legion)
Dam: Kachina Doll (Man's Book)
Brdr: Gene N. Stewart (OH)
Trnr: Stewart Gene N. (2 0-0-1 0%)

Power Rating: 85.7 (8th) 120

Life:	23 1 - 2 - 2	$13,448	56	Fst 19 1 - 2 - 2 $12,198 54
2007	8 0 - 1 - 1	$4,924	56	Off 4 0 - 0 - 0 $1,250 56
2006	12 1 - 1 - 1	$7,756	51	Dis 12 1 - 2 - 2 $10,882 54
RD	5 0 - 0 - 1	$2,360	54	Trf 0 0 - 0 - 0 $0
				AW 1 0 - 0 - 0 $45 43

2007	153	9%	27%	+0.56
JKYw/ P types	99	7%	27%	+0.27
JKYw/ Trn L60	1	0%	100%	-2.00
JKYw/ Sprints	83	8%	23%	+1.21

2007	18	6%	17%	-0.71
Allowance	29	3%	21%	-1.58

Sire Stats: AWD 6.4f 8%Mud 901MudSts 0.38spi
Dam'sSire:AWD 6.8f 14%Mud 1038MudSts 1.42spi

★ Ran 3rd vs similar in last race
● Poor Speed Figures in each recent start ● Only 1 win in 23 career starts ● Poor Trainer win%
● Best Speed rating is well below the Avg Winning Speed ● Poor record at this track

DATE TRK	DIST		RR	RACETYPE	CR	E1	E2/	LP	1c	2c	SPD	PP	ST	1C	2C	Str	FIN	JOCKEY		ODDS	Top Finishers	Comment	
28Apr07RD11	6f ft	:22⁴ :46¹ :59² 1:13¹ 3↑	107	ⓕA13600n2L	102	73	70/	71	-2	-1	54	4	6	7⁷½	7⁸	3⁷½	3¹⁰½	Rojas C120		18.80	DlySrl¹⁰MtrmthS½TombrDFms²½	Improved stretch run	8
16Apr07Beu8	6f ft	:23³ :49 1:01⁴ 1:14³ 3↑	100	ⓕA10500n2L	101	79	67/	68	-3	-6	50	3	5	5³½	3¹	2¹½	2³½	Magera C120		59.30	BbyBRb³½TmbrDFms¹½FrchBb²½	Chased; second best	6
04Apr07Beu1	1m ft	:25 :50¹ 1:17 1:43 3↑	101	ⓕC4000n2L	88	47	36/	55	-7	-7	35	5	6⁸½	6⁹½	6⁹	7¹⁵	7²¹	CollazoSJE114		7.90e	Grand Note²½Candytime²½McFrench¹⁰	Outrun	7
17Mar07Beu7	6f ft	:23¹ :47² :59¹ 1:11² 3↑	103	ⓕA10500n2L	100	73	58/	58	-7	-8	34	7	5	6⁸½	5¹²	5¹⁶	7²⁸	Dailey A120		22.70	MagsChoce⁶½Guidmyder²½Cryptonite²½	3 wide; outrun	8
06Mar07Beu7	1m ft	:24⁴ :48⁴ 1:14 1:39 3↑	103	ⓕA9200n2L	101	47	42/	57	-9	-3	40	7	8¹³	7¹⁷	8¹⁶	8²⁰	8³¹½	Magera C120	f	76.90	What The Devil¹¹½Brother Thomas²½Smarmy²½	Outrun	10
20Feb07Beu7	5½ gd	:23¹ :48² 1:00² 1:07 3↑	102	ⓕA10500n2L	102	79	71/	72	-2	-6	56	6	2	4³	4¹½	4²½	4³½	Magera C120	f	53.30	Imswhtsasnm½PublcEnmy¹½LehGrpe½	4 wide; no rally	6
17Jan07Beu1	6f ft	:22⁴ :48⁴ :59² 1:12⁴ 3↑	101	ⓕOCIm5000n2L	100	76	70/	62	-2	+1	47	4	4	3⁴½	3⁶½	4⁶	5⁶½	Magera C122	f	7.70	KtlysRb¹½Gongtchgod²½PhicEny²½	Chased; weakened	7
08Jan07Beu1	5½ gd	:23¹ :47¹ :59⁴ 1:06³ 3↑	103	ⓕA10500n2L	100	72	71/	41	-3	+2	44	5	5	5⁷½	5⁹½	5¹¹	4¹⁸	Dailey A120		40.30	Cita Dita²½Era Bayou⁶½Imswhatsisnme⁸	Showed little	6
19Dec06Beu7	6f ft	:23⁴ :48³ 1:01³ 1:14⁴ 3↑	102	ⓕA10500n2L	99	79	72/	55	-1	-1	42	1	6	6⁷½	6⁹½	6⁹	6¹¹½	Dailey A119	Lf	19.20	GrecinAmor¹½Imiswhtsisnme½CitaDta½	Broke slowly	6
26Nov06Tdn3	6f ft	:23² :48⁴ 1:02 1:15² 3↑	97	ⓕMC5000	101	69	53/	81	-5	-13	48	3	6	9⁹½	5³½	3³	1¹½	Dailey A121	Lf	2.60	TmbrDFms²½MrgstrGl³½MgldMno	Circled field; drew off	9

●28Feb Beu 3f ft :35⁴ B 1/4 24Jan Beu 3f gd :36 B 2/4 04Jan Beu 3f ft :42⁴ B 9/71 27Dec'06 Beu 3f ft :40⁴ B 1/3 23Sep'06 TP 3f ft :36² B 7/12 20Jun'06 RD 3f gd :38 B 3/10
08Jun'06 RD 3f ft :38 B 5/8 18May'06 RD 3f sy :40 B 3/4 18Mar'06 Beu 3f ft :44 B 19/19 07Mar'06 Beu 4f ft :54¹ B 5/6 01Mar'06 Beu 3f ft :39 B 7/13 31Oct'05 Beu 3f ft :37¹ B 4/10

5 Bucks In The Woods (E/P 3)

20/1 Own: George A. Zimmerman
White, blue 'TS', blue sash
DE LEON AZAEL (43 5-0-4 12%)

B. f. 4
Sire: Forest Gazelle (Green Forest)
Dam: Bucks Talk (Buckfinder)
Brdr: George A. Zimmerman (OH)
Trnr: Acres Harold (8 1-1-1 13%)

Power Rating: 90.3 (6th) L 120

Life:	13 1 - 1 - 0	$7,672	61	Fst 9 1 - 0 - 0 $4,704 60
2007	2 0 - 0 - 0	$262	43	Off 4 0 - 1 - 0 $2,968 61
2006	7 1 - 1 - 0	$6,097	61	Dis 6 1 - 0 - 0 $4,516 60
RD	7 1 - 1 - 0	$7,123	61	Trf 0 0 - 0 - 0 $0
				AW 3 0 - 0 - 0 $181 42

2007	240	12%	37%	-0.73
JKYw/EP types	70	23%	46%	+0.71
JKYw/ Trn L60	1	0%	0%	-2.00
JKYw/ Sprints	156	13%	39%	-0.60

2007	13	8%	31%	-1.51
+Allowance	24	25%	58%	+6.66

Sire Stats: AWD 6.4f 14%Mud 104MudSts 0.57spi
Dam'sSire:AWD 6.9f 13%Mud 1591MudSts 1.40spi

★ Eligible to improve in 3rd start since layoff
● Finished far back in last start ● Poor Speed Figures in each recent start
● Best Speed rating is well below the Avg Winning Speed

DATE TRK	DIST		RR	RACETYPE	CR	E1	E2/	LP	1c	2c	SPD	PP	ST	1C	2C	Str	FIN	JOCKEY		ODDS	Top Finishers	Comment	
28Apr07RD11	6f ft	:22⁴ :46¹ :59² 1:13¹ 3↑	107	ⓕA13600n2L	100	86	82/	46	-2	-1	43	3	5	2¹	3²	5⁸½	8¹⁷½	De LA120	L	33.50	DlySrl¹⁰MtrmthS½TmbrDFms²½	Rail; could not keep up	8
12Apr07RD8	5½ gd	:23¹ :46 :59² 1:06³ 3↑	103	ⓕC7500n2L	98	67	78/	23	-3	+6	32	6	4	5¹⁰	5⁹½	5⁹	6²⁴	Vidal FA122	L	21.30	SlewCityQuest⁶Enduring¹½Rubysfrontstock¹½	Outrun	6

Previously trained by WILLIAMS JEFFREY M.

DATE TRK	DIST		RR	RACETYPE	CR	E1	E2/	LP	1c	2c	SPD	PP	ST	1C	2C	Str	FIN	JOCKEY		ODDS	Top Finishers	Comment	
22Aug06RD7	170 ft	:24⁷ :49³ 1:15³ 1:49⁷ 3↑	104	ⓕA13600n2L		55	66/		+4	-7		6	6⁸½	9¹²	7⁹½		-	SchaeferGA118	L	19.10	Irish VisionImswhatsisnameAloha Maiden	Eased	9
14Jly06RD1	6f ft	:23 :46⁴ 1:00⁴ 1:15¹ 3↑	98	ⓕMC5000	104	88	83/	65	+2	+3	60	5	1	1³½	1⁷½	1⁷½	1⁴½	SchaeferGA118	L	0.60	BcksInThWd⁴½MnngM³BllFyRb⁴	Led every call driving	8
12May06RD13	6f my	:23¹ :47² 1:00⁴ 1:15¹ 3↑	101	ⓕMdn 13k	102	82	70/	68	0	-2	51	12	12	8⁸½	7⁹½	5⁷½	4⁸½	Minnock B119	L	5.40	Imswhtsasnm⁴½ClsyForest⁶OurFlcty³½	Evenly; no rally	12
28Apr06RD3	6f ft	:23³ :47³ 1:01¹ 1:15² 3↑	100	ⓕMdn 13k	101	76	68/	74	-1	-2	55	4	9	8⁴	4³	3⁴	4⁴½	Minnock B117	L	3.30	RunnJoy⁴ClassyForest⁶RachelnTrnst½	Broke in air	11
14Apr06RD3	5½ my	:23² :47² 1:00¹ 1:07¹ 3↑	101	ⓕMdn 13k	102	83	73/	70	-3	-6	61	3	6	4¹½	4⁴	2⁵½	2⁶½	Minnock B119	L	21.60	IrshVsn⁶½BcksInThWds½MotrmthS²½	Gamely held place	9
05Apr06TP1	6f ft	:23⁴ :48¹ 1:01 1:14³ 3↑	98	ⓕMC5000	98	78	66/	60	-9	-10	42	8	1	1½	3⁹	6¹⁰	6¹³½	MartinezW117	L	48.10	TooCaloTutu⁴½WeShnWin⁵SingDrm³½	3 wide; gave way	12
06Jan06TP1	5½ ft	:23² :49 1:02 1:09	103	ⓕMC7500	101	84	66/	48	2	5	36	7	1	2½	4¹½	6⁴½	9¹⁵	PrescottRA122		68.60	Brbtn⁴½MotrmthS½CrshngSdsts½	Off inside; gave way	10
21Dec05TP1	6½ ft	:23⁴ :49 1:17² 1:25	105	ⓕMC7500	98	80	63/		+1	+1	-8	1	4	5³½	5⁹½	10²³	10³⁸½	PrescottRA122		29.20	SonjaSue⁶½Apelngtmpting½ReadyOk¹½	Inside; stopped	10

24Apr RD 3f ft :38³ B 7/8 06Apr RD 3f ft :36² B 2/9 30Mar RD 3f ft :37 B 1/2 21Oct'06 Beu 3f ft :37⁴ B 7/20 11Sep'06 RD 4f ft :52 B 12/17 27Sep'05 Tdn 4f my :50³ B 4/8
17Sep'05 Tdn 3f ft :38 Bg 5/12 08Aug'05 Tdn 4f ft :52 Bg 6/9

tsnhorse.com

Ultimate PP's w/ Quick Play Comments **River Downs** Alw 13600 6 Furlongs. 3upF&M Friday, May 11, 2007 **Race 12**

E1 E2/LATE SPD
89 87/75 71

6 Mercy Honey (P 2)

Own: Anna York
6/1 Red, white stripes, blue sleeves
BUSH VERNON (89 11-11-16 12%)

B. f. 4
Sire: Mercer Mill (Forty Niner)
Dam: Granny's Honey (Honey Jay)
Brdr: Four Winds Farm (OH)
Trnr: York Michael (0 0-0-0 0%)

Power Rating: 86.4 (7th) L 120

Life:	24	1-3-6	$17,537	66	Fst	21	1-3-5	$16,687	56
2006	18	1-3-5	$15,222	56	Off	1	0-0-1	$850	52
2005	6	0-0-1	$2,315	55	Dis	14	1-3-3	$13,807	52
RD	11	0-1-2	$4,764	55	Trf	0	0-0-0	$0	
					AW	3	0-0-0	$485	54

2007	347	10%	36%	0.44
JKYw/ P types	173	14%	31%	0.27
JKYw/ Sprints	202	9%	37%	-0.48

Sire Stats: AWD 6.2f 12%Mud 394MudSts 0.61spi
Dam'sSire: AWD 6.7f 10%Mud 1544MudSts 1.08spi

★ Won last race (BEU 12/20 6f Dirt fast fsMd Sp Wt)

● Moves up in class from last start ● Poor Speed Figures in each recent start ● Poor record at this track
● Has not raced for more than 4 months ● Only 1 win in 24 career starts
● Best Speed rating is well below the Avg Winning Speed

DATE TRK	DIST		RR	RACETYPE	CR	E1	E2/	LP	1c	2c	SPD	PP	ST	1C	2C	Str	FIN	JOCKEY	ODDS	Top Finishers	Comment	
20Dec06Beu[10]	6f ft	:23[4] :48[3] 1:02[4] 1:16[1] 3↑	98	Ⓕ$Mdn 9.2k	101	79	68/	69	-1	-3	50	5	2	4[2]	2[1]	1[1/2]	1[1 1/2]	Stokes LA[120]	9.70	Mercy Honey[1] Fillyforrent[nk] Mystare[4]	Driving	9
05Dec06Beu[1]	6f ft	:23[2] :48[2] 1:01[2] 1:14[4] 3↑	99	Ⓕ$Mdn 9.2k	101	79	71/	67	+1	0	52	6	3	4[3 1/2]	4[2 1/2]	4[3]	3[2]	Stokes LA[120]	3.40	Shar'sGlitter[nk] RosieK[2] MercyHony[1 1/2]	Within range; evenly	8
24Nov06Beu[3]	1m ft	:25[1] :49[2] 1:15[4] 1:43[3] 3↑	99	Ⓕ Mdn 6.7k	103	46	48/	76	-2	+1	56	3	6[7 1/2]	6[11]	3[6 1/2]	3[2]	3[2 1/2]	Paucar E[122]	1.80	RshDoson FunyHalf MercyHony[18 1/2]	Mild rally; inside	8
08Nov06Beu[6]	6f ft	:23 :47[4] 1:00[4] 1:14[4] 3↑	98	Ⓕ$Mdn 9.2k	102	68	61/	76	0	0	51	11	1	5[6]	4[6]	2[10]	3[8]	Paucar E[122]	7.70	HedMstrs[4 1/2] Dodng MrcyHny[4 1/2]	3 wide; finished evenly	12
25Oct06Beu[9]	6f ft	1:14 3↑	99	Ⓕ$Mdn 9.2k	100	71	58/	62	-3	-8	37	2	7	7[7]	5[7 1/2]	4[10]	2[10 1/2]	Paucar E[121]	6.70	Donamour[16] MercyHoney[1] HeadMistres	Second best	11
11Oct06Beu[9]	5½ sy	:22[5] :47[1] 1:00[1] 1:07[2] 3↑	99	Ⓕ Mdn 6.7k	109	62	65/	55	+3	+3	52	2	6	7[14]	6[14]	5[9 1/2]	3[8 1/2]	CamaqueC[121]	10.70	Southnwi CantCrisst MrcyHny[4 1/2]	Passed tiring rivals	8
27Sep06TP[10]	⊗ 1m ft	:24[1] :48[3] 1:13[2] 1:40[1] 3↑	101	ⒻMC5000	100	48	54/	68	-8	0	54	6	9[8]	10[8 1/2]	8[5 1/2]	6[9]	6[8 1/2]	RosarioJtHL[121]	20.20	Sonnet[2] Big Drawers[1] Pocket Medusa[1]	No menace	10
16Sep06TP[1]	⊗ 6f ft	:22[4] :46[4] 1:14 3↑	98	ⒻMC5000	99	71	65/	73	+1	+2	52	5	7	9[4 1/2]	8[8]	6[4]	5[4]	RosarioJtHL[121]	7.10	Deluce SummstHony[2] ArcticJustic	Lacked needed bid	10
Previously trained by LESHER MICHAEL D.																						
01Sep06RD[14]	5½ ft	:23[3] :48 1:01[2] 1:08[3] 3↑	99	ⒻMC5000	99	71	58/	61	-3	-6	40	10	5	8[4 1/2]	7[4 1/2]	6[5 1/2]	5[8 1/2]	RosarioJtHL[120]	6.80	VictoriG ArtAndMsc MiveOughts	Improved position	10
26Aug06RD[1]	6f ft	:23[3] :47[3] 1:02 1:15[3] 3↑	100	ⒻMC7500	101	79	73/	64	-3	-1	50	4	4	8[7 1/2]	6[5 1/2]	4[3 1/2]	4[7 1/2]	RosarioJtHL[119]	11.40	FtAKOU SrtWd MsLuisNt[1 1/2]	Bumped start, weakened	8

●29Apr RD 3f ft :36 B 1/5 17Apr RD 3f ft :37[3] B 4/8 14Apr06 RD 5f my 1:04 B 2/2 28Mar06 Npx 5f gd 1:05 Bg 6/6 12Mar06 Npx 5f gd 1:06 Bg 13/13 05Mar06 Npx 5f gd :10[2] B 8/12
03Sep05 RD 4f ft :50 B 3/6 11Jun05 RD 5f gd 1:02[3] B 3/9 07May05 RD 4f ft :50 Bg 2/11 05May05 RD 4f ft :50 Bg 7/11 ●28Apr05 RD 4f ft :49[2] B 1/20 16Apr05 RD 3f ft :37[2] B 5/19

7 Classy Forest (E/P 6)

Own: Joseph B. Keyes
15/1 Blue, white jk, white sleeves
CALO JOSE LUIS (94 10-8-7 16%)

Ch. m. 5
Sire: Forest Gazelle (Green Forest)
Dam: Dance Class (Machiavellian)
Brdr: G. A. Smith, Austin Smith &Dr. W. E. Johnson (OH)
Trnr: Keyes Joseph S. (0 0-0-0 0%)

Power Rating: 91.8 (3rd) L 120

Life:	11	1-3-1	$16,542	61	Fst	9	1-2-1	$13,917	61
2006	9	1-3-1	$15,992	58	Off	2	0-1-0	$2,625	58
2005	2	0-0-0	$550	61	Dis	8	1-3-1	$15,751	61
RD	8	1-2-0	$13,966	61	Trf	0	0-0-0	$0	
					AW	0	0-0-0	$0	

2007	214	14%	40%	-0.52
JKYw/E/P types	277	13%	40%	-0.72
JKYw/ Sprints	158	13%	39%	-0.53

Sire Stats: AWD 6.4f 14%Mud 104MudSts 0.57spi
Dam'sSire: AWD 6.5f 21%Mud 80MudSts 6.16spi

★ Sharp 4f workout (May05) ★ May improve while returning to a sprint

● Finished far back in last start ● Has not raced for more than 8 months

DATE TRK	DIST		RR	RACETYPE	CR	E1	E2/	LP	1c	2c	SPD	PP	ST	1C	2C	Str	FIN	JOCKEY	ODDS	Top Finishers	Comment	
22Aug06RD[7]	170 ft	:24[2] :49[3] 1:15[3] 1:49[2] 3↑	104	ⒻA13600n2L	102	78	70/	40	+4	+7	49	2	2hd	3[1/2]	6[1 1/2]	6[8]	6[14]	Zuniga E[122]	Lf 20.80	IrishVson[1] Imsewhatsisnme AlohaMaiden[1 1/2]	Faltered; faded	9
08Aug06RD[6]	5½ ft	:23[1] :46[3] 1:00[3] 1:07[2] 3↑	104	ⒻA10600n2L	104	87	79/	60	-2	+2	57	1	1	3hd	4[3 1/2]	6[4 1/2]	4[8]	Zuniga E[124]	Lf 18.10	Fax Ekza[4] Imsewhatsisnme AlohaMaiden[1 1/2]	Weakened	8
15Jly06RD[3]	6f ft	:22[4] :46[3] 1:00 1:14[3] 3↑	100	Ⓕ$Mdn 13k	102	86	77/	61	+1	+1	52	6	4	3hd	2hd	2hd	2[1 1/2]	Zuniga E[124]	Lf 3.70	Slybec[1] ClsyForst[hd] RchelnTrnst[1]	Steadied late stretch *(Placed 1st through disqualification)*	10
08Jun06RD[5]	6f ft	:23 :46[4] 1:00[1] 1:15 3↑	101	Ⓕ$Mdn 13k	101	86	81/	54	+1	+3	50	7	10	4[1 1/2]	3[1 1/2]	5[6]	7[9 1/2]	Perez I[119]	Lf 10.70	MotormouthS[1] Donmor[nk] RchelnTrnst[1 1/2]	Faltered; faded	11
12May06RD[13]	6f my	:23[1] :47[2] 1:00[4] 1:15[1] 3↑	101	Ⓕ$Mdn 13k	104	84	70/	76	0	-2	58	6	5	7[1 1/2]	6[6 1/2]	2[4]	2[4 1/2]	Perez I[119]	Lf 2.60	Imsewhtssnm[4] ClsyForst[nk] OrFksty[3 1/2]	Gamely held place	12
23Apr06RD[3]	6f ft	:23[3] :47[3] 1:01[1] 1:15[2] 3↑	100	Ⓕ$Mdn 13k	102	83	79/	65	-3	-2	56	10	4	4nk	1hd	2[1 1/2]	2[4]	Calo JL[124]	Lf 3.80	RnnJoy[4] ClsyForest[nk] RchelnTrnst	Gamely held place	11
14Apr06RD[3]	5½ my	:23[2] :47[2] 1:00[1] 1:07[1] 3↑	101	Ⓕ$Mdn 13k	101	86	71/	61	-3	-5	53	2	2	2hd	2[2]	4[8]	5[11]	Calo JL[124]	Lf 2.20	IrishVson[6] BcksInThWods MotormouthS[2]	Weakened	9
15Mar06Beu[4]	6f ft	:23[4] :49[3] 1:03 1:16[3] 3↑	99	Ⓕ$Mdn 9.2k	104	82	71/	72	-3	-5	55	7	2	1hd	1[1]	1[1/2]	2[1/2]	Calo JL[124]	Lf 2.30	BcpstStr ClsyFrst CorMeHot[12]	Dueled; second best	8
15Feb06Beu[4]	6f ft	:23[1] :48[3] 1:02 1:15[3] 3↑	100	Ⓕ$Mdn 9.2k	101	86	76/	58	-1	-2	49	6	4	1[4]	1[2]	2[1]	3[8]	Calo JL[124]	Lf 3.80	MchaSun[3] CorMHot[2] ClsyForst[1]	Set pace; weakened	11
31Jly05RD[4]	6f ft	:22[2] :46 :58[3] 1:11[2] 3↑	101	Ⓕ$Mdn 11k	100	85	78/	71	-4	-10	61	6	6	4[1 1/2]	3[1/2]	4[6]	4[10 1/2]	Calo JL[117]	Lf 31.80	Celesti Whatevershize RunnJoy	Failed to sustain bid	10

●06May RD 4f ft :49[1] B 1/4 22Apr RD 3f ft :36[4] B 1/3 10Mar06 Beu (d) 3f sy :38[1] B 3/6 09Feb06 Beu 4f ft :49 B 1/3 ●01Feb06 Beu 3f ft :37[2] B 1/7 ●14Jly05 RD 4f sy :51 Bg 1/4
●08Jly05 RD 3f ft :36 Hg 1/4 02Jly05 RD 4f ft :51 Bg 11/18

8 Rachel In Transit (E/P 4)

Own: Harold Acres
5/1 Red, red 's, on white ball
GARVIS DEAN A. (96 23-11-17 33%)

B. f. 4
Sire: Mercer Mill (Forty Niner)
Dam: Deposit In Transit (Deposit Ticket)
Brdr: Syble M. Acres & Rachel Cox (OH)
Trnr: Acres Harold (8 1-1-1 13%)

Power Rating: 90.8 (4th) L 120

Life:	15	1-3-5	$20,745	61	Fst	10	1-2-4	$15,745	61
2007	1	0-0-0	$680	51	Off	4	0-1-1	$4,000	54
2006	14	1-3-5	$20,065	61	Dis	11	1-3-5	$19,620	61
RD	10	0-2-5	$12,180	61	Trf	1	0-0-0	$1,000	39
					AW	0	0-0-0	$0	

2007	216	16%	38%	-0.22
JKYw/E/P types	141	11%	31%	-0.61
JKYw/ Sprints	114	11%	30%	-0.36

2007	13	8%	31%	-1.51
+Allowance	24	25%	58%	+0.06

Sire Stats: AWD 6.2f 12%Mud 394MudSts 0.61spi
Dam'sSire: AWD 6.5f 13%Mud 645MudSts 0.84spi

★ Eligible to improve in 2nd start since layoff

● Finished far back in last start ● Poor Speed Figures in each recent start ● Only 1 win in 15 career starts
● Outside posts have poor win%

DATE TRK	DIST		RR	RACETYPE	CR	E1	E2/	LP	1c	2c	SPD	PP	ST	1C	2C	Str	FIN	JOCKEY	ODDS	Top Finishers	Comment	
28Apr07RD[11]	6f ft	:22[5] :46[1] :59[2] 1:13[1] 3↑	102	ⒻA13600n2L	101	79	73/	64	-2	-1	51	8	2	6[4 1/2]	6[6 1/2]	6[10]	4[13]	Vidal FA[120]	Lb 6.90	DlySlat[10] MotmthS TombuDFms[2 1/2]	Wide trip; no rally	8
18Nov06Beu[7]	6f ft	:22[4] :47[1] :59[4] 1:13 3↑	102	ⒻA10500n2L	101	79	71/	63	-3	-6	48	8	1	3[2]	3[2]	4[8]	8[8 1/2]	Calo JL[120]	Lb 4.60	LdySpirt[1] MotormouthS[6] ErByou	Chased; gave way *Dead heat*	8
03Nov06Beu[8]	6f ft	:22[3] :47[2] 1:00[3] 1:13[3] 3↑	104	ⒻA10500n2L	103	82	69/	70	0	-3	52	4	3	3[3 1/2]	4[7 1/2]	6[9]	7[11 1/2]	Rojas C[122]	Lb 25.20	PrfctCondtion[2] Sunshineinsdr[2] Bbs[2]	3 wide; gave way	10
07Oct06Beu[8]	6f ft	:23[1] :48 1:01[3] 1:15[2] 3↑	98	Ⓕ$Mdn 9.2k	102	83	78/	66	-2	0	55	6	2	1[1/2]	1[2]	1[3 1/2]	1[4]	CamaqueC[121]	Lb 1.00	RchelnTrst[4] MrnngMn[1] TombuDFms[3]	Dueled, drew off	8
Previously trained by WILSON ARIANE B.																						
15Sep06Tdn[1]	6f ft	:23[2] :48[1] 1:01[4] 1:15[2] 3↑	98	ⒻMC10000	100	79	72/	68	-2	-4	53	2	4	3[2]	2[1/2]	2hd	2[2 1/2]	Wilson RG[120]	L 0.90	Donlsqthsn[2] RchelnTrnst[2] RosieK[1 1/2]	Bid, outfinished	7
Previously trained by ACRES HAROLD																						
24Aug06RD[13]	6f ft	:22[4] :46[2] 1:00[4] 1:15[2] 3↑	98	Ⓕ$Mdn 13k	101	79	73/	67	+9	+10	53	3	6	8[6 1/2]	8[10]	4[7 1/2]	3[7 1/2]	Mnnock B[117]	L 3.90	ErByou[3] HedMstrs[2] RchelnTrnst[1 1/2]	Improved position	12
11Aug06RD[4]	6f gd	:23[3] :47[1] 1:00[2] 1:14[2] 3↑	100	Ⓕ$Mdn 13k	102	78	68/	70	-2	-5	52	6	6	6[1 1/2]	4[4]	4[8]	3[7]	CamaqueC[119]	L 2.70	MissPatch[4] Slybeca[1] RachelnTrnst[nk]	Evenly, no rally	11
29Jly06RD[7]	6f my	:22[4] :46[3] 1:01 1:14[3] 3↑	100	Ⓕ$Mdn 13k	103	77	73/	68	+1	+2	54	7	8	9[5 1/2]	5[3 1/2]	3[1 1/2]	2[2 1/2]	Calo JL[118]	L 3.90	MisSouthernSnd[2] RchelnTrnst[2] Kingren	Evenly late	11
16Jly06RD[3]	6f ft	:22[4] :46[3] 1:00 1:14[3] 3↑	100	Ⓕ$Mdn 13k	102	75	85/	73	+1	+1	51	9	10	7[3 1/2]	5[6]	4[3 1/2]	3[7]	CamaqueC[118]	L 1.10	Slybeca[1] ClasyForest[nk] RchelnTrnst[1]	Stumbled start	10
02Jly06RD[11]	⊗ 1⅛ fm	:24[1] :50 1:13[3] 1:43[3]	106	ⒻDStarter	101	48	38/	51	-20	-17	39	4	2hd	5[1 1/2]	6[7]	8[15]	6[7 1/2]	CamaqueC[118]	L 24.60	Tomeyesqo Missy SyblesAngel	Through after half	6

●21Apr RD 4f ft :49 Bg 1/17 06Apr RD 3f ft :39 B 8/9 11Sep06 RD 3f ft :36[4] B 2/6 31May06 RD 5f ft 1:03 B 1/3 09May06 RD 3f ft :37[4] Bg 3/10 10Apr06 RD 3f ft :38[1] Bg 4/7
25Mar06 Beu 4f ft :53[4] Bg 12/15 18Mar06 Beu 3f ft :42 Bg 18/19 11Mar06 Beu (d) 3f my :40[3] B 19/24 ●03Sep05 RD 3f ft :35[4] Hg 1/4 18Aug05 RD 3f ft :37 B 2/3

tsnhorse.com

Ultimate PP's w/ Quick Play Comments **River Downs** Alw 13600 6 Furlongs. 3upF&M Friday, May 11, 2007 **Race 12**

E1	E2/LATE	SPD
89	87/ 75	71

Last 3 Years RACETYPE STATS:	# Races	FAVORITES Win%	Itm%	$2ROI	Average Field Size	Median $2 Win Payoff	% Winners < 5/1	% Winners >= 5/1 < 10/1	% Winners >= 10/1
RD 3up ALW: 12300 - 13600 N1X Dirt 6f	33	27%	79%	0.88	7.8	$9.80	52%	30%	18%

Track Bias Stats

	* MEET Totals *				* WEEK Totals *		
DIRT 6.0f	Speed Bias: 80%	WnrAvgBL		DIRT 6.0f	Speed Bias: 96%	WnrAvgBL	
# Races: 64	04/06 - 05/08	1stCall: 1.4		# Races: 14	05/03 - 05/08	1stCall: 1.2	
%Wire: 47%		2ndCall: 1.0		%Wire: 64%		2ndCall: 0.8	

	Early	Speed	Late	Speed		Early	Speed	Late	Speed
Runstyle:	E	E/P	P	S	Runstyle:	E	E/P	P	S
	++	+				++			
Impact Values	1.66	1.29	0.72	0.33	Impact Values	1.98	1.09	0.94	0.00
%Races Won	52%	28%	11%	9%	%Races Won	64%	21%	14%	0%
Post Bias:	RAIL	1-3	4-7	8+	Post Bias:	RAIL	1-3	4-7	8+
			+			+		+	
Impact Values	0.85	0.89	1.14	0.71	Impact Values	1.91	0.80	1.29	0.00
Avg Win %	12%	13%	19%	4%	Avg Win %	29%	12%	22%	0%

Race Summary

#	HorseName	ML Odds	Med Eqp	Days Since L/R	Run Style	PT S	Avg Dist/Surf PACE-SPEED E1	E2/Late	Spd	Avg Race Rtng	Best Pace E1	E2/Late	Final Speed Sp1	Sp2	Sp3	Sp4	ACL	Rcg Spd Avg	R1	R2	R3	Mud Spd	Pedigree Stats Mud Sts	Mud % Mud	Sire AWD	Dam Sire's AWD
2	Flirtini	10/1	L	13..	+E/P	7	83	78/ 68	* 57*	101	86	84/ 75	57.	57.	53	57	100.0	56	100	100	106	57	5	20	5.2	6.7
3	Motormouth Sue	7/5	L	13..	+E/P	7	84	83/ 60	56	102	86	84/ 78	56.	72	62.	60.	103.6	63	102	105	105	72	233	10	7.0	6.6
7	Classy Forest	15/1	L	262	+E/P	6	85	78/ 62	(55)	102	87	81/ 61	49	57.	52.	50.	101.1	53	104	104	100	58	104	14	6.4	8.5
1	Gonnagetchagood	10/1	L	13	++E	3	84	73/ 66	* 53*	104	88	82/ 78	50.	57.	52.	44.	103.0	53	102	105	103	49	46	13	6.0	7.1
4	Tombeur De Femmes	5/2		13	P	2	77	69/ 70	* 53*	102	79	72/ 81	54.	50.	35	34.	100.7	46	102	100	101	37	901	8	6.4	6.6
6	Mercy Honey	6/1	L	142	P	2	75	67/ 71	(51)	99	79	73/ 77	50.	52	56	51.	98.3	53	98	99	99	52	394	12	6.2	6.7
8	Rachel In Transit	5/1	L	13.	+E/P	4	79	73/ 64	51	102	83	76/ 75	51.	48.	52.	55.	99.5	50	102	102	104	54	394	12	6.2	6.5
5	Bucks in The Woods	20/1	L	13..	+E/P	3	77	80/ 35	* 38*	103	88	83/ 65	43.	32.		60.	99.7	36	102	103	104	51	104	14	6.4	6.9

Speed Last Race	Back Speed	Current Class	Average Class Last 3	Power Rating	Early Pace Last Race	Late Pace Last Race
57 Flirtini	64 Motormouth Sue	102.6 Gonnagetchagood	104.7 Motormouth Sue	104.8 Motormouth Sue	83 Motormouth Sue	75 Flirtini
56 Motormouth Sue	62 Flirtini	102.3 Motormouth Sue	103.4 Flirtini	98.7 Flirtini	82 Bucks In The Woods	71 Tombeur De Femmes
54 Tombeur De Femmes	61 Rachel In Transit	101.8 Flirtini	102.6 Gonnagetchagood	91.8 Classy Forest	78 Classy Forest	69 Mercy Honey
51 Rachel In Transit	60 Bucks In The Woods	101.7 Tombeur De Femmes	102.5 Classy Forest	90.8 Rachel In Transit	78 Gonnagetchagood	64 Rachel In Transit
50 Gonnagetchagood	59 Gonnagetchagood	101.2 Rachel In Transit	101.6 Mercy Honey	90.3 Bucks In The Woods	73 Rachel In Transit	60 Motormouth Sue
50 Mercy Honey	57 Classy Forest	99.6 Bucks In The Woods	101.5 Rachel In Transit	89.5 Gonnagetchagood	72 Flirtini	58 Gonnagetchagood
49 Classy Forest	56 Tombeur De Femmes	NA Classy Forest	101.0 Bucks In The Woods	86.4 Mercy Honey	70 Tombeur De Femmes	46 Bucks In The Woods
43 Bucks In The Woods	52 Mercy Honey	NA Mercy Honey	100.3 Tombeur De Femmes	85.7 Tombeur De Femmes	68 Mercy Honey	40 Classy Forest

#	Speed Last Race		#	Prime Power		#	Class Rating		#	Best Speed at Dist	
8	Kinkcachu	65	8	Kinkcachu	96.6	1A	Double Cross	103.5	4	Big Shot In Town	72
4	Big Shot In Town	64	4	Big Shot In Town	95.7	3	Ready To Fight	103.4	8	Kinkcachu	61
3	Ready To Fight	55	3	Ready To Fight	94.5	8	Kinkcachu	102.2	1	Shane The Man	61

13

Exacta / Trifecta / Superfecta (Ten Cent Minimum) / Daily Double

Simulcast of Thistledown race number 13

	E1	E2/LATE	SPEED
PARS:	88	84/ 73	67

6 Furlongs. Mdn 13.5k Purse $13,500. FOR REGISTERED OHIO FOALS MAIDENS, THREE YEAR OLDS AND UPWARD. Three Year Olds, 120 lbs., Older, 122 lbs .

Post Time: (5:05)/ 4:05/ 3:05/ 2:05

Coupled : SHANE THE MAN - DOUBLE CROSS

1 pp 3 Shane The Man (E/P 2)

Own: Blazing Meadows Farm Llc
12/1 Gold, gold bell on black chevron
URIETA-MORAN VICTOR (83 8-9-9 13%)

Dkbbr. c. 3 (Apr)
Sire: Parents' Reward (Mr. Prospector)
Dam: Wiseary Proof (Proof)
Brdr: Destiny Farm Llc (OH)
Trnr: Hamm Timothy E. (21 3-2-2 14%)

Power Rating: 87.3 (6th) L 120

			$					
Life:	5 0 - 0 - 2	$1,638	61	Fst	4 0 - 0 - 2	$1,521	61
2007	5 0 - 0 - 1	$1,068	61	Off	2 0 - 0 - 0	$117	49
2006	1 0 - 0 - 1	$570	67	Dis	1 0 - 0 - 1	$420	61
Tdn	1 0 - 0 - 0	$330	44	Trf	0 0 - 0 - 0	$0	
				AW	0 0 - 0 - 0	$0	

2007	72	14%	44%	-1.23
JKYw/EP types	112	15%	42%	0.26
JKYw/ Trn L60	21	14%	43%	-1.33
JKYw/ Sprints	66	13%	43%	-1.36

+2007	87	17%	55%	0.79
Maiden Sp Wt	245	18%	48%	-0.45

Sire Stats: AWD 7.1f 18%Mud 11MudSts 0.76spi
Dam'sSire:AWD 6.9f 10%Mud 452MudSts 7%1st 0.66spi

● Always far back in last start ● Poor Speed Figures

DATE TRK	DIST					RR RACETYPE	CR E1 E2/ LP	1c 2c	SPD	PP	ST	1C	2C	Str	FIN	JOCKEY	ODDS	Top Finishers	Comment	
21Apr07Tdn7	5f ft	:22³	:46³		:58³ 3↑	100 Mdn 11k	98 78/ 55		44	2	6	5⁶½	4⁸½	4⁸	5¹⁷½	Urieta-moranV120	Lb 11.10	First Nation⁶½Tescone½NorthernSemoran³½	Weakened	7
19Feb07Beu1	5½ gd				1:04⁴ 3↑	100 MC5000	97 83 69/ 47	+1 -3	44	5	4	5⁴	5⁶	7⁹½	8¹⁷	CamaqueC118	L 3.70	Gridwin¹Spunky Wind³Kinetic Energy³½	4 wide turn	9
07Feb07Beu1	5½ ft	:23	:47²	:59³	1:06⁴	100 Mdn 6.7k	100 79 62/ 55	-2 -5	41	5	2	4²	4⁵½	5⁷	5¹¹	CamaqueC120	L 4.60	LtlJoBrdy¹DrcyBy¹nStyJke⁴½	Within range; gave way	5
20Jan07Beu1	6f ft	:22²	:46³	:59³	1:12³	100 MC5000	101 87 84/ 65	+2 +2	61	3	3	3¹	1hd	2¹	3²	CamaqueC120	L 3.10	Tony½Candylin¹½ShneTheMn¹	Rail bid turn;weakened	6
09Jan07Beu1	5f gd	:23³	:48²		1:01¹	102 Mdn 6.7k	102 72/ 58		49	1	6	6⁵½	6⁷½	7⁸	6⁸	CamaqueC120	L 3.20	ChsaThPst³TnRid½Doghntn¹½	Angled out, no rally	11
16Dec06Beu3	5½ ft	:22²	:47¹	1:00⁴	1:08¹	104 MC25000/20	106 74 75/ 62	+5 +9	57	3	6	7⁸½	6⁸½	5⁵½	3⅞	CamaqueC118	5.30	RmotControl⁴RoylTr¹ShnThMn½	Angled out; rallied	7

14Apr Tdn 5f ft 1:01² Bg 8/9 21Mar Tdn 4f ft :50³ B 4/4 ●04Dec'06 Beu 4f ft :49⁴ H 1/5 23Nov'06 Tdn 4f ft :50 Bg 2/5 16Nov'06 Tdn 5f sy 1:18³ Bg 2/7 10Nov'06 Tdn 5f ft 1:19² Bg 4/4
04Nov'06 Tdn 5f ft 1:04 Bg 4/6 25Oct'06 Tdn 5f sl 1:04³ B 4/4 18Oct'06 Tdn 5f my 1:04³ B 1/2 12Oct'06 Tdn 4f ft :50⁴ B 4/7 06Oct'06 Tdn 4f ft :49⁴ B 4/11 25Sep'06 Tdn 3f ft :37 B 6/14

1A pp 5 Double Cross (S 1)

Own: Bruce Ryan & Blazing Meadows Farm, Llc
12/1 Yellow, green diamonds
SKERRETT JEFFREY (70 16-3-11 23%)

Dkbbr. c. 3 (Apr)
Sire: Parents' Reward (Mr. Prospector)
Dam: Cross Me Not (Naverone)
Brdr: Bruce Ryan (OH)
Trnr: Hamm Timothy E. (21 3-2-2 14%)

Power Rating: 91.0 (4th) Blnkr On 120

Life:	3 0 - 0 - 1	$1,192	50	Fst	2 0 - 0 - 1	$1,102	50
2007	1 0 - 0 - 0	$90	44	Off	1 0 - 0 - 0	$90	44
2006	2 0 - 0 - 1	$1,102	50	Dis	2 0 - 0 - 1	$1,102	50
Tdn	3 0 - 0 - 1	$1,192	50	Trf	0 0 - 0 - 0	$0	
				AW	0 0 - 0 - 0	$0	

2007	71	23%	42%	0.26
JKYw/ S types	121	7%	24%	-1.63
JKYw/ Trn L60	2	0%	50%	-2.00
+JKYw/ Sprints	54	22%	41%	-0.06

+2007	87	17%	55%	0.79
1stTimeBlinkers	24	12%	38%	+1.03
Blls favorite	95	18%	45%	-1.12
Maiden Sp Wt	245	18%	48%	-0.45

Sire Stats: AWD 7.1f 18%Mud 11MudSts 0.76spi
Dam'sSire:AWD 6.8f 7%Mud 144MudSts 5%1st 0.73spi

★ Hot Jockey in last 7 days (20 5-3-3) ★ May improve with blinkers added today
★ Switches to a high% Jockey ★ Eligible to improve in 2nd start since layoff

● Always far back vs weaker in last race ● Poor Speed Figures ● Outside posts have poor win%

DATE TRK	DIST					RR RACETYPE	CR E1 E2/ LP	1c 2c	SPD	PP	ST	1C	2C	Str	FIN	JOCKEY	ODDS	Top Finishers	Comment	
28Apr07Tdn6	5½ gd	:23³	:48¹	1:00⁴	1:07² 3↑	107 MC10000	100 72 57/ 58	-6 -10	44	4	8	6⁵½	6⁶½	6¹⁰	6¹³½	Urieta-moranV120	*1.30	eMrBuckey¹½Kinkch½SoubrettePnch⁶	Failed to menace	8
11Sep06Tdn4	6f ft	:23	:47³	1:00³	1:13⁴	106 MC25000	100 70 66/ 70	-3 -6	50	5	6	6⁷½	5⁵½	5⁷	3¹⁰	SarmientoR119	3.50	eCyMyM³½CSayWthM⁶½GtOwPyt¹½	Mild rally; no threat *Dead heat*	10
24Aug06Tdn7	6f ft	:23³	:48²	1:01²	1:14¹	107 Mdn 11k	105 72 57/ 63	-10 -14	37	6	4	4³	5⁵	6⁸½	5¹⁴½	Ramos HG118	18.20	Yes Or Not⁵½CindyMyMn²Pure Vision²½	Brief foot; tired	7

03May Tdn 4f ft :50 Bg 2/5 21Apr Tdn 5f ft 1:02⁴ B 4/8 10Apr Tdn 5f gd 1:03² Bg 3/5 30Mar Spc 3f ft :42¹ Bg 2/5 16Aug'06 Tdn 5f ft 1:04 Bg 3/6 07Aug'06 Tdn 5f ft 1:03 B 3/8
26Jly'06 Tdn 5f ft 1:02³ Bg 3/4 17Jly'06 Tdn 5f ft 1:03³ Bg 6/8 01Jly'06 Tdn 5f ft 1:03⁴ Bg 4/7 26Jun'06 Tdn 4f ft :50¹ Bg 10/22 17Jun'06 Tdn 4f ft :51¹ B 8/10 12Jun'06 Tdn 3f ft :36¹ B 3/7

2 pp 1 Lucky He's Perfect (NA 0)

Own. Sharon Hunter
4/1 Hot pink; lime green yoke
MARTINEZ, JR. LUIS J. (44 7-7-7 16%)

B. c. 3 (Apr)
Sire: Best Of Luck (Broad Brush)
Dam: P For Perfect (Turkoman)
Brdr: Elisabeth Alexander (OH)
Trnr: Radosevich Jeffrey A. (52 16-13-6 29%)

120

Life:	0 0 - 0 - 0	$0	Fst	0 0 - 0 - 0	$0
2007	0 0 - 0 - 0	$0	Off	0 0 - 0 - 0	$0
2006	0 0 - 0 - 0	$0	Dis	0 0 - 0 - 0	$0
Tdn	0 0 - 0 - 0	$0	Trf	0 0 - 0 - 0	$0
			AW	0 0 - 0 - 0	$0

2007	111	12%	40%	0.68
JKYw/NA types	39	10%	28%	-1.08
JKYw/ Sprints	79	10%	39%	-1.05

+2007	168	20%	52%	0.32
1st time str	53	17%	34%	-0.08
+Debut MdnSpWt	32	19%	34%	+6.18
Maiden Sp Wt	117	15%	40%	-0.38

Sire Stats: AWD 7.1f 13%Mud 109MudSts 7%1st 0.63spi
Dam'sSire:AWD 8.1f 14%Mud 1325MudSts 4%1st 1.16spi

★ High % Trainer

● First time starter ● Only 7% Sire win rate with 1st-Time starters

16May Tdn 4f ft :50¹ Bg 7/35 02May Tdn 4f ft :49⁴ B 4/8 20Apr Tdn 4f ft :49⁴ Bg 8/29 16Aug'06 Tdn 4f ft :51 B 4/9 07Aug'06 Tdn 4f ft :51¹ B 16/25 24Jly'06 Tdn 5f ft 1:04³ B 20/20
09Jly'06 Tdn 4f ft :54¹ Bg 9/10

tsnhorse.com

Ultimate PP's w/ Quick Play Comments **River Downs** Mdn 13.5k 6 Furlongs 3up Friday, May 11, 2007 **Race 13 (TDN - #13)** E1 88 E2/LATE 84/73 SPD 67

3 (pp 2) Ready To Fight (E 1)

Own: Pyrite Stables
5/1 Light blue
HERNANDEZ LUCIANO (11 1-0-0 9%)

Ch. g. 3 (Apr)
Sire: Fit To Fight (Chieftain)
Dam: Jet Ready (Northjet (Ire))
Brdr: Dr. D. W. Frazier (OH)
Trnr: Feliciano Miguel A. (17 4-4-2 24%)

Power Rating: 94.5 (3rd) L 115⁵

Life:	14 0 - 0 - 4	$7,446	70	Fst	9 0 - 0 - 1	$5,640	70
2007	5 0 - 0 - 1	$2,730	70	Off	5 0 - 0 - 1	$1,806	64
2006	9 0 - 0 - 3	$4,716	64	Dis	7 0 - 0 - 2	$3,271	58
Tdn	8 0 - 0 - 3	$4,891	64	Trf	0 0 - 0 - 0		58
				AW	0 0 - 0 - 0		58

2007	222	9%	28%	-0.65	2007	80	11%	43%	0.41
JKYw/ E types	102	8%	30%	1.36	+Maiden Sp Wt	117	19%	54%	-0.68
JKYw/ Sprints	158	11%	32%	-0.46					

Sire Stats: AWD 7.0f 15%Mud 2284MudSts 17%1st 1.26spi
Dam'sSire: AWD 8.1f 9%Mud 388MudSts 4%1st 1.18spi

★ Best Dirt Speed is faster than the Avg Winning Speed ● Poor Speed Figures in last 2 starts

DATE TRK	DIST					RR RACETYPE	CR E1 E2/ LP 1c 2c	SPD PP ST 1C 2C Str FIN	JOCKEY	ODDS	Top Finishers	Comment	
19Apr07Tdn⁶	5½ ft	:22³	:46²	:59³	1:06² 3↑	102 Mdn 14k	101 82 75/ 58 +1 +2	55 3 5 43½ 55 56½ 57½	MartinezJrLJ¹²⁰	Lb 3.60	DazisChoice¹ Chrsn³ NormndyMls¹	Failed to menace	7
16Mar07Tam⁸	1 1/16 gd	:23²	:48¹	1:15	1:50	107 MC50000/45	103 82 66/ 21 +8 +3	38 10 3³ 3² 2⁴ 9¹⁰ 9²⁹	GonzalezLA¹¹⁶	Lb 14.30	Taxcab³ AlphaLucky² LaterGaiter	Stopped after half	10
18Feb07Tam¹¹	1 1/16 ft	:23²	:48	1:14²	1:48⁴	109 MC25000	106 82 71/ 72 +9 0	70 3 4⁴ 4³ 6²½ 5⁵ 4⁵½	Martin G¹¹³	Lb 8.90	PpsSpcl¹ CrtQrt³ GoRnAtDym	Well placed; gave way	9
03Feb07Tam⁴	7f gd	:22⁴	:46²	1:13²	1:27⁴	108 MC25000	105 88 75/ 66 +1 +3	60 7 2 5³ 6⁷½ 6⁴½ 8⁷½	Martin G¹¹³	Lb 23.20	MsPotn¹ FstrDrm¹ MrtcsThGrl¹½	Gradually weakened	11
14Jan07Tam⁵	1 1/16 ft	:24²	:49²	1:15	1:46²	108 MC25000	106 82 54/ 85 -18 -21	68 7 1hd 1½ 1¹½ 3⁴ 3⁶½	Martin G¹¹³	Lb 10.30	LaVrdd PopsSpcl³ RdyTFght⁴½	Slow pace, gave way	9
26Dec06Tam¹⁰	6f wf	:22³	:46³	:59	1:13⁴	108 MC25000	105 73 73/ 73 +1 +2	57 2 6 8⁸½ 8⁷½ 6⁷½ 6⁸½	GonzalezP¹²⁰	Lb 60.50	Bonzi Mo'sPoccino³ FutureDrama	Failed to menace	9
09Dec06Tam¹¹	7f ft	:22¹	:46²	1:13	1:26²	106 MC25000	105 77 71/ 59 +3 -2	53 4 8 9⁷½ 9⁸ 7⁹ 7¹⁵½	ClementeA¹²⁰	Lb 8.00	Family Biz³ Maui Escapade Bonzi	Evenly	12
18Nov06Tdn³	1m sy	:24³	:49²	1:16	1:44²	105 Mdn 13k	107 77 70/ 68 +2 +3	64 6 1² 1¹½ 1¹ 1hd 3²½	Spieth S¹¹⁸	Lb 3.10	BobiesDevil¹ Smmy RedyToFight³½	Pace, held well	7
27Oct06Tdn¹¹	6f sy	:22⁴	:47¹	1:00⁴	1:14³	106 Mdn 11k	106 89 78/ 81 +2 0	53 3 2 2hd 3¹½ 3² 7⁶	FelicianoR¹¹⁹	Lb 9.00	PolishSixBl¹ Dargh BobiesDvl½	Pressed; weakened	10
09Oct06Tdn⁷	6f ft	:23	:47	:59⁴	1:13²	104 Mdn 13k	104 82 70/ 68 -5 -5	51 4 2 6¹½ 6⁴½ 6⁹½ 7⁹½	FelicianoR¹¹⁹	Lb *2.00	Sthisdnct¹ PlshSxBl⁴ NrdyMls²	Never far back; evenly	12

03Apr Tam 3f ft :40² H 15/15 07Mar Tam 4f ft :50² B 13/26 27Jan Tam 4f ft :51 B 34/57 02Dec'06 Tam 4f ft :54³ B 64/64 03Aug'06 Tdn 5f ft 1:04² B 6/6 24Jly'06 Tdn 5f ft 1:04¹ B 16/20
14Jly'06 Tdn 4f ft :50⁴ B 15/21 26Jun'06 Tdn 4f ft :51 Bg 14/22 12Jun'06 Tdn 3f ft :37 B 9/17

4 Big Shot In Town (P 3)

Own: Dianne M. Cooper
2/1 Blue, white flying 'd'
GONZALEZ LUIS ANTONIO (0 0-0-0 0%)

Ch. g. 5 (Mar)
Sire: Saratoga Six (Alydar)
Dam: Castle Quest (Fit To Fight)
Brdr: Dominic Giglio Jr. (OH)
Trnr: Schuster Robin (29 1-3-0 3%)

Power Rating: 96.7 (2nd) L 122

Life:	19 0 - 2 - 1	$8,455	72	Fst	8 0 - 1 - 1	$5,185	72
2007	3 0 - 1 - 0	$1,685	60	Off	2 0 - 1 - 0	$1,290	64
2006	4 0 - 0 - 0	$900	60	Dis	4 0 - 1 - 1	$5,330	72
Tdn	1 0 - 1 - 0	$1,560	60	Trf	0 0 - 0 - 0		58
				AW	0 0 - 0 - 0		58

2007	526	15%	43%	-0.40	2007	33	3%	21%	0.82
JKYw/ P types	168	11%	42%	-1.05	2nd strt w/trn	42	2%	17%	-1.63
JKYw/ Sprints	282	16%	45%	0.30	Maiden Sp Wt	10	10%	50%	-1.32

Sire Stats: AWD 6.7f 18%Mud 1171MudSts 13%1st 1.66spi
Dam'sSire: AWD 7.0f 15%Mud 2284MudSts 11%1st 1.26spi

★ Highest Speed Figure at Today's Distance ★ Best Dirt Speed is fastest among today's starters ● Beaten by weaker in last start ● Poor Trainer win%

DATE TRK	DIST					RR RACETYPE	CR E1 E2/ LP 1c 2c	SPD PP ST 1C 2C Str FIN	JOCKEY	ODDS	Top Finishers	Comment	
19Apr07Tdn¹	5f ft	:22⁴	:47		:59⁴ 3↑	101 MC10000	102 75/ 74	60 4 4 5³½ 4³½ 3²½ 2¹½	Munayfa F¹²²	Lb 2.50	PPsToFlw¹ BgShtInTw¹ DhlongGld⁴	4 wide; gaining	7
Previously trained by GIGLIO JR. DOMINIC													
07Feb07Aqu⁴	6f ft	:23	:47¹	1:00¹	1:14 3↑	103 MC20000/18	107 87 85/ 55 +2 +3	53 4 3 2² 3¹½ 3⁶ 6⁹	EspinozaJL¹²⁰	Lb 35.75	LostCpy MyByJJ SouthrnCrk²	Chased outside; tired	9
27Jan07Aqu⁴	1m ft	:24¹	:47³	1:13¹	1:40¹ 4↑	104 MC20000	101 82 77/ 19 +3 +8	38 3 1hd 1½ 3¹½ 5⁸½ 9²⁴	MartinJrEM¹²²	Lb 21.20	DoubAgnt ProngTheWy² MdowLoch³	Set pace; tired	9
17Dec06Aqu⁵	1 1/16 ft	:24¹	:47³	1:12⁴	1:46³ 3↑	103 MC20000	99 77 77/	+3 +6 20 2 4²½ 3³ 2²½ 8¹⁷ 11⁴⁴	MartinJrEM¹²²	Lb 40.75	DividendYld¹ MdowLoch² Wodend	Steadied first turn	11
29Nov06Aqu⁶	1 70y ft	:24⁴	:48⁴	1:13²	1:43 3↑	104 MC20000	102 87 70/ 57 -14 -7	60 1 1hd 1hd 1hd 4⁸ 4¹⁴½	MartinJrEM¹²²	Lb 26.90	MisterZee² McClmont² GreatAlbert½	Vied inside; tired	7
05Oct06Bel²	6½ ft	:22⁴	:46³	1:11²	1:18¹ 3↑	103 MC35000	100 74 68/ 66 -2 -6	51 1 4 8⁴½ 6⁹½ 6¹¹ 7¹⁶	EspinozaJL¹²²	Lb 6.80	ReadyRead MyBird'sWird¹ BlckAndAmber½	Outrun	8
14Sep06Bel⁹	6f sy	:22³	:46¹	:59	1:12² 3↑	103 MC35000	101 94 83/ 55 +3 +8	52 8 3 3¹ 5⁴½ 5¹⁴ 8¹⁸½	EspinozaJL¹²²	Lb 6.90	GloryAIS¹⁰ MyBrdWrd Rvsnndrrs½	Brief speed; tired	9
29May05Mth¹¹	6f ft	:22¹	:45⁴	:58³	1:11² 3↑	109 MC35000	110 87 86/ 76 +3 -1	72 4 8 7³½ 4³½ 4¹½ 3⁶½	Garcia A¹¹⁶	Lb 6.10	ComphrSois⁴ Seczone² BigShotInTown	In close start	8
Previously trained by PECORARO ANTHONY													
28Apr05Aqu³	6f gd	:22⁴	:47²	1:00²	1:13⁴	107 MC35000	110 84 79/ 74 +2 -2	64 2 4 3²½ 2¹ 1¹½ 2¹	Garcia A¹²⁰	Lb 2.75	ItsAlLy¹ BgShtInTw⁴ PcAmbsdor⁴½	Bumped after start	5
30Mar05Aqu¹	6½ ft	:22³	:45²	1:11	1:17³	109 MC50000	106 82 79/ 71 -9 +1	65 5 3 5² 5⁶ 5⁶ 5⁸½	Garcia A¹²⁰	L 2.75	LAug FinshMv¹ PcAmbsdor	Between foes; no rally	8

11Apr Tdn 4f ft :51² B 20/25 01Apr Tdn 4f ft :49³ B 2/11 26Mar Tdn 3f ft :38⁴ B 6/13 25Jan Bel tr.t 4f ft :50 B 37/51 01Nov'06 Bel 4f ft :49⁴ B 13/50 25Oct'06 Bel 4f ft :53³ B 23/23
01Oct'06 Bel 4f ft :49¹ B 7/39 08Sep'06 Bel 5f ft 1:01¹ H 18/51 24Aug'06 Bel tr.t 5f ft 1:02 B 3/13 19Aug'06 Bel tr.t 3f ft :37² B 4/12 16May'05 Mth 4f ft :48³ H 3/36 ●21Apr'05 Bel 4f ft :47¹ H 1/15

5 Auburn Boy (E 1)

Own: Mary L. Hurley
8/1 Blue & white sleeves
MEYERS TOMMY (17 3-2-4 18%)

Ch. g. 4 (Mar)
Sire: Political Folly (Deputy Minister)
Dam: Jacine's Will (Tour D'or)
Brdr: Mary Hurley (OH)
Trnr: Hurley Mary L. (6 0-0-2 0%)

Power Rating: 89.8 (5th) L 122

Life:	8 0 - 1 - 0	$4,066	60	Fst	5 0 - 1 - 0	$2,822	60
2007	2 0 - 0 - 0	$1,125	57	Off	3 0 - 0 - 0	$1,244	57
2006	6 0 - 1 - 0	$2,941	60	Dis	6 0 - 1 - 0	$2,541	60
Tdn	8 0 - 1 - 0	$4,066	60	Trf	0 0 - 0 - 0		58
				AW	0 0 - 0 - 0		58

2007	30	13%	47%	-0.53	2007	12	0%	33%	-2.00
JKYw/ E types	30	13%	53%	-0.85	+Maiden Sp Wt	11	18%	36%	-0.53
+JKYw/ Sprints	21	19%	38%	+0.10					

Sire Stats: AWD 6.0f 6%Mud 32MudSts 0.30spi
Dam'sSire: AWD 6.8f 15%Mud 1103MudSts 14%1st 1.10spi

★ Eligible to improve in 3rd start since layoff ● Beaten by weaker in last start ● Best Speed rating is well below the Avg Winning Speed ● Poor Trainer win%

DATE TRK	DIST					RR RACETYPE	CR E1 E2/ LP 1c 2c	SPD PP ST 1C 2C Str FIN	JOCKEY	ODDS	Top Finishers	Comment	
28Apr07Tdn⁴	5½ gd	:23³	:48¹	1:00⁴	1:07⁷ 3↑	102 MC10000	107 76 69/ 70 -6 -10	54 6 7 4²½ 3hd 4⁴½ 4⁷½	SanguinettiA¹²²	Lb 10.60	MrBucky¹ Khochi SoubrtPnch⁴	Loomed boldly; faded	8
19Apr07Tdn⁶	5½ ft	:22³	:46²	:59³	1:06² 3↑	102 Mdn 14k	107 81 76/ 60 +1 +2	57 1 7 5⁴ 4⁵ 4³½ 4⁶½	SanguinettiA¹²²	Lb 5.90	Dakota's Choice¹ Chfton³ Normandy Mils¹½	No threat	7
19Nov06Tdn⁴	6f sy	:23	:48⁴	:59²	1:12 3↑	102 Mdn 13k	106 80 80/ 65 -4 -8	57 2 6 4³½ 4³½ 4⁸ 4¹⁰½	Feliz JE¹²¹	Lb 19.50	Intwldthdy BttyThms FWBaLgcy⁴½	Failed to menace	6
01Nov06Tdn⁴	6f ft	:22⁴	:46³	1:00	1:13³ 3↑	99 MC5000	107 82 78/ 70 -2 0	60 2 5 2¹½ 2¹ 2hd 2½	Feliz JE¹²¹	Lb 4.40	Hrcntmn AbrnBy⁴ BlysCnl½	Drew even; outfinished	9
06Oct06Tdn²	6f ft	:22⁴	:46⁴	:59³	1:13 3↑	101 Mdn 13k	98 78 71/ 62 -2 -4	48 3 8 7⁴½ 6⁴½ 7⁶½ 7¹¹½	SnchezJrJA¹²¹	Lb 66.50	RoyNemsis¹ RedGeorg² Knkcchu½	Failed to menace	8
23Sep06Tdn¹	6f ft	:22⁷	:46³	1:00¹	1:14² 3↑	100 Mdn 14k	98 84 72/ 55 +4 +6	42 4 6 4³ 5⁷ 7¹¹ 7¹⁷½	SnchezJrJA¹²⁰	Lb 37.20	FirstExpenses¹ Koinsky¹ RavensCry²	Contended; tired	8
10Sep06Tdn⁵	6f ft	:22¹	:46²	:59⁴	1:13³ 3↑	100 Mdn 14k	98 91 83/ 50 +4 +4	47 6 4 3½ 3² 4⁵ 5¹¹½	SnchezJrJA¹²⁰	Lb 24.60	El Ciesto⁵ Augustus² RavensCry⁴	Good position, tired	7
28Aug06Tdn¹	6f gd	:22²	:46³	1:00¹	1:13⁴ 3↑	100 Mdn 14k	97 86 82/ 38 +2 +2	37 6 7 3² 2¹ 5⁷ 7¹⁸½	SnchezJrJA¹¹⁹	Lb 41.10	MrcoRgsWnr⁵ RvsCry¹ FrstExpns¹	Through after half	7

09May Tdn 3f ft :38² B 4/5 13Apr Tdn 3f ft :36³ B 5/17 29Mar Tdn 3f ft :37² B 5/13 04Oct'06 Tdn 3f ft :39¹ B 2/2 21Sep'06 Tdn 3f ft :39³ B 11/11 26Aug'06 Tdn 3f ft :40¹ B 17/17
14Aug'06 Tdn 5f ft 1:03⁴ Bg 5/9 07Aug'06 Tdn 4f ft :51¹ Bg 16/25 30Jly'06 Tdn 4f ft :51⁴ Bg 12/12 14Jly'06 Tdn 4f ft :50⁷ B 14/21 30Jun'06 Tdn 3f ft :38 B 7/13 12Jun'06 Tdn 3f ft :37⁴ B 14/17

Ultimate PP's w/ Quick Play Comments

River Downs — Mdn 13.5k 6 Furlongs 3up Friday May 11, 2007 — Race 13 (TDN - #13)

E1	E2/LATE	SPD
88	84/73	67

6 Explicit Jet (NA 0)

8/1
Own: Jean Tait
Wht: green emblem; gold sleeves
CLONINGER JR. WELDON T (41 15-7-9 37%)

Dkbbr. g. 3 (Mar)
Sire: Explicit (Distant View)
Dam: Jet A Hi (High Counsel)
Brdr: Jean M. Tait (OH)
Trnr: Crumley Javon (26 9-4-4 22%)

120

Life:	0 0 - 0 0	$0	Fst	0 0 - 0 0	$0
2007	0 0 0 0	$0	Off	0 0 - 0 0	$0
2006	0 0 0 0	$0	Dis	0 0 - 0 0	$0
Tdn	0 0 0 0	$0	Trf	0 0 - 0 0	$0
			AW	0 0 0 0	$0

+2007	44	34%	59%	+1.03
JKYw/NA types	25	12%	28%	-1.13
+JKYw/ Trn L60	19	37%	58%	+0.59
+JKYw/ Sprints	33	33%	55%	+0.79

+2007	34	26%	53%	-0.01
1st time str	21	14%	52%	+0.70
Debut MdnSpWt	18	17%	56%	+1.14
+Maiden Sp Wt	64	22%	55%	+0.22

Sire Stats: AWD 6.2f 100%Mud 1MudSts 15%1st 0.56spi
Dam'sSire: AWD 6.4f 11%Mud 446MudSts 13%1st 0.70spi

★ Hot Jockey in last 7 days (20 7-4-1) ★ Hot Trn/Jky combo in last 14 days (10 3-2-0) ● First time starter
★ High % Jockey ★ High % Trainer ★ 15% Sire wins with 1st-Time starters

07May Tdn 4f ft :50 B 12/20 28Apr Tdn 4f ft :53[2] B 15/16 23Apr Tdn 3f ft :39[2] Bg 20/22 16Apr Tdn 4f ft :50[1] B 7/11 ●11Apr Tdn 3f ft :36 Bg 1/14 28Mar Tdn 4f ft :51[2] B 3/6
20Mar Tdn 3f ft :38[4] B 6/2

7 Remember Jim (NA 0)

12/1
Own: Donna Foor
Tea; pink 'H' pink horseshoe
MAILHOT PIERRE (21 0-0-2 0%)

Dkbbr. c. 3 (May)
Sire: Colony Key (Keycolony)
Dam: Ima Angie (French Legionaire)
Brdr: Donna Foor (OH)
Trnr: White Alan D. (2 0-0-0 0%)

120

Life:	0 0 0 0	$0	Fst	0 0 - 0 0	$0
2007	0 0 - 0 0	$0	Off	0 0 - 0 0	$0
2006	0 0 - 0 0	$0	Dis	0 0 - 0 0	$0
Tdn	0 0 - 0 0	$0	Trf	0 0 - 0 0	$0
			AW	0 0 - 0 0	$0

2007	21	0%	10%	-2.00
JKYw/NA types	51	8%	20%	+1.63
JKYw/ Sprints	17	0%	12%	2.00

2007	28	4%	21%	-1.81
1st time str	19	0%	16%	-2.00
Debut MdnSpWt	14	0%	21%	2.00
Maiden Sp Wt	78	9%	23%	1.19

Sire Stats:
Dam'sSire: AWD 6.5f 8%Mud 901MudSts 4%1st 0.38spi

● First time starter ● Poor Jockey win% ● Poor Trainer win%

02May Beu 5f ft 1:05[3] B 1/7 06Apr Beu 5f ft 1:04[4] Bg 1/2 30Mar Beu 4f ft :50[2] Bg 9/14 09Mar Beu 4f ft :51 B 10/14 27Jan Beu 4f ft :52 B 20/22 20Jan Beu 3f ft :38[3] B 8/13
11Dec'06 Beu 3f ft :40 B 3/4

8 Kinkcachu (E 6)

7/2
Own: Mark Vegour; Inc.
Black; red 'my' red braces
ORO ERNESTO (53 4-4-10 8%)

B. g. 4 (Apr)
Sire: Railway Cat (Storm Cat)
Dam: Lady Whirlwind (Native Royalty)
Brdr: Hedy Hammon (OH)
Trnr: Schuster Robin (29 1-3-5 3%)

Power Rating: 98.0 (1st)

L 122

Life:	3 0 - 1 - 1	$3,249	65	Fst	2 0 - 0 - 1	$1,449	61
2007	1 0 1 0	$1,800	65	Off	1 0 - 1 - 0	$1,800	65
2006	2 0 - 0 - 1	$1,449	61	Dis	2 0 - 0 - 1	$1,449	61
Tdn	3 0 - 1 - 1	$3,249	65	Trf	0 0 - 0 - 0	$0	
				AW	0 0 0 0	$0	

2007	216	8%	30%	+0.41
JKYw/ E types	170	11%	31%	-0.28
JKYw/ Trn L60	6	0%	17%	-2.00
JKYw/ Sprints	134	8%	28%	+0.19

2007	33	3%	21%	-1.82
Maiden Sp Wt	10	10%	50%	1.32

Sire Stats: AWD 6.3f 18%Mud 49MudSts 8%1st 0.52spi
Dam'sSire: AWD 7.1f 12%Mud 1210MudSts 8%1st 1.20spi

★ Highest Last Race Speed Rating ★ Early Speed running style helps chances ● Beaten by weaker in last start ● Poor Trainer win% ● Outside posts have poor win%
★ Eligible to improve in 2nd start since layoff

DATE TRK	DIST						RR	RACETYPE	CR	E1	E2/	LP	1c	2c	SPD	PP	ST	1C	2C	Str	FIN	JOCKEY		ODDS	Top Finishers	Comment	
28Apr07Tdn[6]	5½ gd	:23[3]	:48[1]	1:00[4]	1:07[2]	3↑	107	MC10000	105	83	75/	81	6	10	65	1	4	1½	1hd	2hd	2½	Oro E[122]	L	3.70	McRocky[1]Kinkcch[1]SoubretPnch[4]	Dueled; held place	8
06Oct06Tdn[2]	6f ft	:22[4]	:46[4]	:59[3]	1:13	3↑	101	Mdn 13k	102	86	81/	66	3	-4	61	1	2	1[1]	1hd	2[1]	3¾	Oro E[121]	L	10.10	RoyNemsis[1]RetGeorg[2]Kinkcch	Weakened, slightly	8
23Sep06Tdn[1]	6f ft	:22[2]	:46[3]	1:00[1]	1:14[2]	3↑	100	Mdn 14k	100	85	74/	65	+4	+5	52	8	5	3[3]	4[5]	5[4]	6[4]	Oro E[120]		64.40	FirstExpense[1]Kolnsky[1]RvensCry[1]	Wide early; evenly	8

19Apr Tdn 4f ft :49[1] B 8/13 12Apr Tdn 4f my :50[3] B 10/19 06Apr Tdn 3f ft :38[4] B 4/6 28Mar Tdn 3f ft :41[3] B 2/2 17Sep'06 Tdn 5f ft 1:02[4] B 3/4 08Sep'06 Tdn 4f ft :50[4] Bg 7/11
01Sep'06 Tdn 4f ft :50 B 4/11

Ultimate PP's w/ Quick Play Comments **River Downs** Ⓢ Mdn 13.5k 6 Furlongs. 3up Friday May 11, 2007 **Race 13 (TDN - #13)**

E1	E2/LATE	SPD
88	84/ 73	67

Last 3 Years RACETYPE STATS:	# Races	Win%	FAVORITES Itm%	$2ROI	Average Field Size	Median $2 Win Payoff	% Winners < 5/1	% Winners >= 5/1 < 10/1	% Winners >= 10/1
TDN 3up Ⓢ MSW 12000 - 14500 Dirt 6f	38	34%	74%	-0.72	8.0	$6.60	82%	13%	5%

Track Bias Stats

	' MEET Totals '				' WEEK Totals '	
DIRT 6.0f	Speed Bias: 82%	WnrAvgBL	DIRT 6.0f		Speed Bias: 67%	WnrAvgBL
# Races: 22	04/12 - 05/06	1stCall: 1.3	# Races: 6		05/03 - 05/06	1stCall: 1.6
%Wire: 36%		2ndCall: 1.1	%Wire: 50%			2ndCall: 1.7

	Early	Speed	Late	Speed		Early	Speed	Late	Speed
Runstyle:	E	E/P	P	S	Runstyle:	E	E/P	P	S
	++	+				++		+	
Impact Values	1.77	1.41	0.70	0.13	Impact Values	1.71	0.97	1.32	0.00
%Races Won	45%	36%	14%	5%	%Races Won	50%	17%	33%	0%
Post Bias:	RAIL	1-3	4-7	8+	Post Bias	RAIL	1-3	4-7	8+
		+	+			+		+	
Impact Values	0.75	1.13	1.09	0.51	Impact Values	1.43	0.48	1.79	0.00
Avg Win %	9%	14%	17%	3%	Avg Win %	17%	6%	28%	0%

Race Summary

#	HorseName	ML Odds	Med Eqp	Days Since L/R	Run Style	P T S	Avg Dist/Surf PACE-SPEED E1	E2/Late	Spd	Avg Race Rtng	Best Pace E1	E2/Late	Final Speed Sp1	Sp2	Sp3	ACL	Rcg Spd Avg	R1	R2	R3	Mud Spd	Pedigree Stats % Mud	% 1st	SPI	DPI	Sire AWD	Dam Sire's AWD
8	Kinkcachu	7/2	L	13.	++E	6	83	75/ 81	65	103	86	81/ 81	65.	61.	52	101.9	59	102	101	100		18	8	0.52		6.5	7.1
3	Ready To Fight	5/1	L	22	++E	1	81	75/ 63	* 58*	105	85	78/ 68	55.	38	70		54	102	107	105	64	15	11	1.26		7.0	8.1
4	Big Shot In Town	2/1	L	22.	P	3	87	80/ 65	* 57*	103	87	85/ 74	60.	53.	38	100.3	50	101	103	104	52	16	13	1.65		6.7	7.0
5	Auburn Boy	8/1	L	13.	++E	1	79	73/ 65	* 56*	103	91	83/ 70	54.	57.	57	99.4	56	102	102	102	57	6	0	0.3		6.0	6.8
1	Shane The Man	12/1	L	20.	+E/P	2	85	77/ 56	* 50*	100	87	84/ 66	44.	44.	41.	100.7	43	100	100	103		18	0	0.76		7.1	6.9
1A	Double Cross	12/1	b	13.	S	1	72	57/ 58	44	103	72	66/ 70	44.	50.	37.	104.7	44	102	106	107		18	0	0.76		7.1	6.9
2	Lucky He's Perfect	4/1		.	NA		No Starts Available															13	7	0.63		7.1	8.1
6	Explicit Jet	8/1		..	NA		No Starts Available															100	15	0.56		6.2	6.4
7	Remember Jim	12/1		..	NA		No Starts Available																				6.5

Speed Last Race	Back Speed	Current Class	Average Class Last 3	Power Rating	Early Pace Last Race	Late Pace Last Race
65 Kinkcachu	65 Kinkcachu	105.2 Kinkcachu	103.5 Double Cross	96.0 Kinkcachu	75 Kinkcachu	81 Kinkcachu
60 Big Shot In Town	61 Shane The Man	103.1 Ready To Fight	103.4 Ready To Fight	95.7 Big Shot In Town	75 Ready To Fight	74 Big Shot In Town
55 Ready To Fight	60 Big Shot In Town	102.2 Big Shot In Town	102.2 Kinkcachu	94.5 Ready To Fight	69 Auburn Boy	70 Auburn Boy
54 Auburn Boy	60 Ready To Fight	101.9 Auburn Boy	101.6 Big Shot In Town	91.0 Double Cross	57 Double Cross	59 Ready To Fight
44 Shane The Man	60 Auburn Boy	100.1 Double Cross	101.1 Auburn Boy	89.6 Auburn Boy	NA Big Shot In Town	58 Double Cross
44 Double Cross	50 Double Cross	99.8 Shane The Man	98.3 Shane The Man	87.3 Shane The Man	NA Shane The Man	55 Shane The Man
NA Lucky He's Perfect	NA Lucky He's Perfect	NA Lucky He's Perfect	NA Lucky He's Perfect	NA Lucky He's Perfect	NA Lucky He's Perfect	NA Lucky He's Perfect
NA Explicit Jet	NA Explicit Jet	NA Explicit Jet	NA Explicit Jet	NA Explicit Jet	NA Explicit Jet	NA Explicit Jet
NA Remember Jim	NA Remember Jim	NA Remember Jim	NA Remember Jim	NA Remember Jim	NA Remember Jim	NA Remember Jim

#	Speed Last Race		#	Prime Power		#	Class Rating		#	Best Speed at Dist	
10	Laterornever	60	10	Laterornever	98.8	10	Laterornever	102.5	10	Laterornever	67
9	Grand Sand	53	1	H D's Affair	91.4	9	Grand Sand	101.7	1	H D's Affair	64
5	Cryptoless	50	9	Grand Sand	90.0	1	H D's Affair	100.9	9	Grand Sand	63

14

Exacta / Trifecta / Superfecta (Ten Cent Minimum)

	E1	E2/LATE	SPEED
PARS:	71	59/ 64	59

1 Mile. MC 5000 Purse $5,200. SIMULCAST FROM RIVER DOWNS. FOR MAIDENS, THREE YEAR OLDS AND UPWARD. Three Year Olds, 116 lbs., Older, 124 lbs. Claiming Price $5,000 (Ohio Registered Foals Preferred) .

Post Time: (5:25)/ 4:25/ 3:25/ 2:25

1 H D's Affair (S 2)

8/1 Own: Sano Park: Llc
Yellow, black sp, red bars on sleeves
HILL ROBERT R. (12 2-3-1 17%)

$5,000 Dkbbr. g. 3 (Apr)
Sire: Rod And Staff (Marsayas)
Dam: Sassafter (Colonial Affair)
Brdr: Harold Coyle (KY)
Trnr: Burton Tim (1 0-0-0 0%)

Power Rating: 91.4 (2nd) L 116

Life:	6	0	1	0	$2,305	64	Fst	6	0	1	0	$2,305	64
2007	6	0	1	0	$2,305	64	Off	0	0	0	0	$0	
2006	0	0	0	0	$0		Dis	4	0	1	0	$2,203	64
RD	1	0	0	0	$61	46	Trf	0	0	0	0	$0	
							AW	4	0	1	0	$2,244	64

2007	21	14%	38%	+2.48
JKYw/ S types	24	8%	25%	+2.15
+JKYw/ Routes	14	21%	50%	+4.73

2007	11	9%	18%	-0.87
Maiden Clming	7	14%	29%	+1.14

Sire Stats: AWD 7.2 8%Mud 12MudSts 6%1st 0.48spi
Dam'sSire:AWD 7.2 13%Mud 456MudSts 7%1st 1.36spi

★ Best Dirt Speed is faster than the Avg Winning Speed ★ Drops in Class today

DATE TRK	DIST					RR	RACETYPE	CR	E1	E2/	LP	1c	2c	SPD	PP	ST	1C	2C	Str	FIN	JOCKEY	ODDS	Top Finishers	Comment	
13Apr07RD14	1m ft	:24	:49	1:14	1:41 3↑	107	MC7500	99	69	60/	49	-5	-6	46	4	3	5	7	9	9	Zuniga E116	Lbf 8.30	R. Harold Honey Of ADevil Laterornever	Off slowly	9
25Mar07TP	1m ft	:24	:48	1:14	1:40 3↑	103	MC7500	103	56	59/	76		-5	62	5	3		5	5	5	Lebron V117	Lb 14.20	Triton Faith InAction Cellars Grange	Hesitated start	9
01Mar07TP	1⅛ ft	:24	:49	1:13	1:47 3↑	104	MC15000	101	15	14/	70	-12	-8	35	2	9	8	8	9	7	Lebron V117	Lb 9.20	Rove Guilty Man Unbridled Devil	Outrun	8
18Feb07TP	1m ft	:23	:47	1:14	1:40	108	MC30000	104	63	53/	54	0	-5	45	10	7	7	7	8	8	Diego I122	Lb 12.00	MocinaMn Gentlemenm WitHorn	Carried 5w early	10
27Jan07Mnr	170 ft	:23	:47	1:12	1:42	108	Mdn 24k	101	62	52/	20	-13	-12	27	5	6	6	8	10	10	Parker DL117	Lb 3.10	Mgvol ProphiMn ToldSupris	Walked after a 1/2mile	10
06Jan07TP	1m ft	:23	:48	1:14	1:39	105	MC15000	107	29	43/	95	4	-7	64	3	11	11	11	5	2	Lebron V122	Lb 42.30	Hacker Craft H D's Affair D' Springs	5 wide 1/4 pl	11

19Jan TP 5f ft 1:02 Bg 9/15 22Dec'06 TP 5f ft 1:02 Bg 6/8 12Dec'06 TP 4f ft :49 Bg 6/16 01Dec'06 TP 4f ft :53 B 16/17

2 Ky Ridge Runner (S 0)

20/1 Own: Jamie Biddle
White, red 'kssdy', red bars on sleeves
SOLOMON NATHAN (43 10-5-9 23%)

$5,000 Dkbbr. g. 5 (Apr)
Sire: England (Sir Ivor)
Dam: Royal Faith (Native Royalty)
Brdr: Jerry F Straw & Michelle L Straw (KY)
Trnr: Womack Hulon Leslie (7 0-1-1 0%)

Power Rating: 78.0 (8th) L 124

Life:	32	0	3	2	$5,597	57	Fst	23	0	3	2	$4,662	57
2007	3	0	0	0	$372	47	Off	7	0	0	0	$935	50
2006	19	0	3	2	$4,460	57	Dis	11	0	1	1	$2,254	53
RD	10	0	0	0	$1,027	56	Trf	0	0	0	0	$0	
							AW	7	0	0	0	$499	57

2007	68	17%	43%	+2.78
JKYw/ S types	76	9%	39%	-0.54
JKYw/ Routes	22	9%	27%	-0.75

+2007	18	6%	39%	-1.07
No class chg	51	16%	35%	0.45
Maiden Clming	60	8%	27%	-1.15

Sire Stats: AWD 8.2 0%Mud 16MudSts 0%1st 0.13spi
Dam'sSire:AWD 7.1 12%Mud 1210MudSts 8%1st 1.20spi

★ Hot Jockey in last 7 days (9 3- 0- 1) ★ High % Jockey
★ Eligible to improve in 3rd start since layoff

● Always far back in last start ● Poor Speed Figures in each recent start ● Poor Trainer win%

DATE TRK	DIST					RR	RACETYPE	CR	E1	E2/	LP	1c	2c	SPD	PP	ST	1C	2C	Str	FIN	JOCKEY	ODDS	Top Finishers	Comment	
27Apr07RD	170 gd	:23	:48	1:14	1:47 3↑	100	MC5000	99	62	49/	33	+7	+8	47	6	6	7	6	7	6	Parker E124	Lb 20.30	GuilyMan CountyRoscomon ThirdSeason	No rally	10
14Apr07RD	1m sy	:25	:50	1:16	1:43 3↑	99	MC5000	97	36	28/	67	8	-8	38	5	7	7	6	5	4	Servis DA124	Lb 10.90	Admrce WickdE Spll CodysFirst	Passed tired foes	7

Previously trained by LANDRY JOSEPH C.

DATE TRK	DIST					RR	RACETYPE	CR	E1	E2/	LP	1c	2c	SPD	PP	ST	1C	2C	Str	FIN	JOCKEY	ODDS	Top Finishers	Comment	
06Jan07TP	1⅛ ft	:24	:48	1:14	1:47 4↑	100	MC5000	98	57	43/	55	3	-7	44	1	7	7	6	6	7	Sanchez C124	Lbf 38.40	CntThEgg RmboRnr Bsnipns	3 wide middle move	8
22Dec06TP	1m ft	:23	:47	1:13	1:41 3↑	99	MC5000	99	59	51/	68	+16	+11	53	5	10	10	10	7	5	Sanchez C124	Lb 57.20	PrizeHuntr StoleMyThundr GrandSnd	4 wide 1/4 pl	12
06Dec06TP	1⅛ ft	:23	:48	1:14	1:48 3↑	99	MC5000	99	50	41/	80	+9	+8	57	10	12	12	12	9	8	Sanchez C124	Lb 112.20	Prizewd GrndSnd PadyMcNaly	Improved position	12
29Nov06Beu	170 ft	:23	:47	1:13	1:44 3↑	99	MC4000	97	41	34/	67	+2	0	44	10	10	9	7	7	6	Endres J124	Lb 3.40	Lost Deputy Blacken Seattle Pass	Outrun	10
14Nov06Beu	170 ft	:24	:48	1:16	1:49 3↑	99	MC5000	99	33	27/	70	+2	+8	42	3	10	10	8	6	4	Endres J124	Lb 15.30	PbonsShdow LostDputy BestMiners	Broke slowly	10
07Nov06Beu	1m wf	:25	:49	1:15	1:42 3↑	99	Mdn 6.7k	96	38	27/	63	-10	0	35	1	7	7	6	6	6	Endres J124	Lb 4.20	King Khan Mugal Ruler Fine With Me	Outrun	7
07Oct06Beu	170 ft	:24	:49	1:17	1:51 3↑	99	MC5000	101	37	26/	74	-1	0	44	5	6	6	4	2	2	Endres J124	Lb 11.50	Omnton KyRdgRunr MyFrndPp	Rail rally; 2nd best	6
22Sep06TP	1m ft	:24	:47	1:13	1:40 3↑	100	MC5000	100	68	57/	59	+6	+4	50	2	7	7	6	6	6	Endres J124	Lb 47.80	UnbridledCird Crucifixion Lindens	4 path 2nd turn	8

06Apr RD 4f ft :52 B 3/3 16Aug'06 RD 3f ft :38 B 2/3 07Feb'06 TP 5f ft 1:05 B 8/8 30Jan'06 TP 4f ft :51 B 2/5 11Jan'06 TP 4f ft :52 Bg 9/10 05Jan'06 TP 3f ft :37 B 4/8
22Dec'05 TP 4f ft :53 B 21/28 14Dec'05 TP 3f ft :38 B 12/12 27May'05 RD 4f ft :51 B 4/10 07Feb'05 TP 3f ft :38 B 4/8 29Dec'04 TP 5f ft 1:03 B 8/9 17Dec'04 TP 5f ft 1:05 B 16/18

tsnhorse.com

Ultimate PP's w/ Quick Play Comments **River Downs** MC 5000 : Mile 3up Friday, May 11, 2007 **Race 14**

E1 71 | E2/LATE 59/64 | SPD 58

3 Seattle Pass (P 5)

20/1 Own: Carl Keith
Gray red a red sleeves
TOLENTINO PABLO (9 1-1-1 17%)

$5,000 B. g. 5 (May)
Sire: Seattle High (Seattle Dancer)
Dam: Pass The Poker (Leonard's Lad)
Brdr: Sharon Sanders (KY)
Trnr: Allen Billy D. (8 0-0-0 0%)

Power Rating: 79.5 (6th) L 124

Life:	20 0 - 0 - 1	$1,463	56	Fst 16 0 - 0 - 1 $1,323 58
2007	4 0 - 0 - 0	$247	49	Off 1 0 - 0 - 0 $40 41
2006	12 0 - 0 - 1	$1,116	56	Dis 1 0 - 0 - 0 $220 49
RD	2 0 - 0 - 0	$183	47	Trf 3 0 - 0 - 0 $100 48
				AW 12 0 - 0 - 0 $688 49

2007	12	17%	50%	+3.87
JKYw/ P types	13	15%	31%	+3.11
JKYw/ Routes	4	0%	25%	2.00

2007	12	8%	25%	-1.20
31-90daysAway	15	7%	13%	-1.36
Shipper	5	0%	0%	2.00
+No class chg	10	20%	50%	-0.58

Sire Stats:
Dam'sSire:AWD 8.2f 22%Mud 37MudSts 9%1st 0.48spi

● Finished far back in last start ● Has not raced in 56 days

DATE TRK	DIST		RR RACETYPE	CR E1 E2/ LP 1c 2c	SPD	PP	ST	1C	2C	Str	FIN	JOCKEY	ODDS	Top Finishers	Comment
16Mar07TP6	1 1/16 ft	:244 :492 1:157 1:474 3↑	100 MC5000	99 67 49/ 54 -1 -3	47	2	1hd	32	67 1/2	612	617	Zuniga E124	L 21.30	GgisAdLghshdRmbRnr2ThrdSsn4 1/2	Speed for 1/2 inside 8
25Feb07TP7	1m ft	:244 :494 1:161 1:417 3↑	100 MC5000	97 61 48/ 60 -14 -15	45	11	47 1/2	31	43 1/2	916	970 1/4	Diego I124	L106.50	TwiceThPlsur6GrenBoyhdStolMyThndr7 1/2	4-5 wide top 11
24Jan07TP1	1m ft	:243 :49 1:15 1:413 4↑	100 MC5000	99 65 53/ 56 1 -1	49	5	76	74 1/2	96 1/2	1115	1115	Endres J124	L103.20	Cosmic StarhdIsamutepoint1 1/2Trion1	Speed for 1/2 12
07Jan07TP1	6 1/2 ft	:223 :454 1:114 1:184 4↑	101 MC7500	95 72 59/ 45 0 +3	29	8	5	58 1/2	714	827	876 1/4	Endres J124	L102.30	FormlTestimony16MjorTom2Dr.Furlow1 1/2	Through early 8
11Dec06Beu1	1 70 ft	:232 :473 1:134 1:463 3↑	96 MC5000	96 48 33/ 48 +3 +4	32	11	64 1/2	715	916	1125	829 1/4	Sanchez J124	L 14.70	CahTown2Blacken16 1/2MiswicSpride1	5 wide first turn 11
29Nov06Beu1	1 70 ft	:231 :471 1:131 1:447 3↑	96 MC4000	99 64 60/ 61 +2 0	56	3	57 1/2	47	44	49 1/2	310	Sanchez J124	L 38.40	Lost Deputy8 1/2Blacken3 1/2Seattle Pass3 1/2	3 wide 2nd turn 10
17Nov06Beu4	5f sy	:224 :472	1:003 3↑	96 MC3500	97 62/ 59	41	5	11	1114	1113	1012	79 1/2	Endres J124	L 67.60	Go John GohdDr. Specht1 1/2Robey1 1/2	No factor 11
01Oct06TP1	6f ft	:23 :463 :587 1:113 3↑	100 MC5000	99 69 41/ 59 -9 -6	21	11	4	87 1/2	1117	1123	1126 1/2	Endres J124	L148.70	Blackenberry2 1/2Priorwood2 1/2Crucifixion1 1/2	5 wide turn 11
14Sep06TP1	6f ft	:23 :464	1:131 3↑	100 MC5000	99 76 59/ 53 -4 -2	30	12	4	72 1/2	108 1/2	1113	1116 1/2	Fortner JL124	L 51.20	EscpTdcsnoNrthrnAlnc1 1/2Cornrd hd	Bumped start; 5wide 12
03Sep06RD14	1 70 ft	:24 :492 1:14 1:462 3↑	101 MC7500	100 56 55/ 51 -9 +3	47	6	99 1/2	97 1/2	88 1/2	915	818 1/2	Rojas C124	L 20.60	DelightfulyRd7 1/2RoylBel4PrwghJohd	Failed to menace 10

09Nov06 CD 3f sy :38 B 4/4 13Oct06 CD 5f ft 1:053 B 22/34 26Aug06 TP 3f ft :364 B 1/2 18Aug06 RD 4f ft :514 B 2/4 14Apr06 CD 4f ft :494 B 12/25 24Mar06 CD 3f ft :364 B 2/4
06Jan06 Cd 4f ft :522 B 9/9 25Jun05 Cd 5f ft 1:033 B 7/14 09Jun05 Cd 4f ft :503 B 7/8 21May05 Cd 4f ft :503 B 15/16 10May05 Cd 3f ft :373 Bg 3/6 04May05 Cd 5f ft 1:051 Bg 5/6

4 Northern Alliance (E/P 5)

7/2 Own: Ripplewood Farm
Blue red and white hoops, white star
OUZTS PERRY WAYNE (142 19-25-20 13%)

$5,000 Ch. g. 4 (May)
Sire: Mutakddim (Seeking The Gold)
Dam: Northern Wool (Northern Baby)
Brdr: Ripplewood Farm (KY)
Trnr: Jones Sr. Herbert W. (2 1-0-0 50%)

Power Rating: 89.9 (4th) L 124

Life:	9 0 - 2 - 0	$3,568	64	Fst 8 0 - 2 - 0 $3,404 64
2007	5 0 - 0 - 0	$768	63	Off 1 0 - 0 - 0 $156 34
2006	4 0 - 2 - 0	$2,792	64	Dis 3 0 - 0 - 0 $644 57
RD	1 0 - 0 - 0	$156	34	Trf 0 0 - 0 - 0 $0
				AW 7 0 - 2 - 0 $3,362 64

2007	501	10%	34%	-0.79
JKYw/EP types	137	9%	27%	-1.10
JKYw/ Trn L60	1	0%	0%	-2.00
JKYw/ Routes	224	11%	33%	-0.60

+2007	19	16%	42%	-0.32
No class chg	11	9%	55%	-1.64
+Btn favorite	10	30%	80%	-0.66
+Maiden Clming	29	21%	34%	+1.85

Sire Stats: AWD 6.5f 18%Mud 505MudSts 17%1st 1.63spi
Dam'sSire:AWD 8.1f 15%Mud 841MudSts 10%1st 2.06spi

★ Best Dirt Speed is faster than the Avg Winning Speed ● Finished far back in last start

DATE TRK	DIST		RR RACETYPE	CR E1 E2/ LP 1c 2c	SPD	PP	ST	1C	2C	Str	FIN	JOCKEY	ODDS	Top Finishers	Comment
14Apr07RD2	1m sy	:25 :507 1:161 1:434 3↑	99 MC5000	87 65 54/ 35 -9 -9	34	3	34	31	28	411	527 1/4	Ouzts PW124	Lb *0.60	Advnce17WickdESpl3 1/2CodysFirst3 1/2	Carried out 1st turn 7
01Apr07TP9	1m ft	:241 :474 1:147 1:421 3↑	101 MC5000	101 61 60/ 56 +7 +5	51	6	77	58 1/2	57 1/2	56	57	PrescottRA124	Lb 8.40	GreenBoyhdHoneyOfADvl1 1/2RusnSnow6	In tight early 8
23Mar07TP11	6 1/2 ft	:233 :471 1:123 1:191 3↑	100 MC5000	102 74 71/ 77 -13 -13	63	7	3	31	2 1/2	31 1/2	43 1/4	PrescottRA124	Lb 7.20	Rez1Honey Of A Devil1 1/2Tricks 1/2	3 wide; weakened 11
07Mar07TP1	6f ft	:231 :471 1:001 1:134 3↑	102 MC5000	98 78 65/ 58 -8 -4	40	2	7	52	68 1/2	611	614 1/2	Sarvis DA124	Lb 3.20	NotoriousNick2Jericho Road1 1/2Miguel1 1/2	Inside; faded 8
14Jan07TP1	6 1/2 ft	:224 :461 1:113 1:181 4↑	99 MC5000	100 76 61/ 76 -8 -6	56	4	6	63	97 1/2	96	57 1/2	Sarvis DA124	b 2.70	Wilderness Trail1 1/2RezhdStrong Beau 1/2	No threat 12
14Dec06TP1	6 1/2 ft	:224 :46 1:113 1:18 3↑	100 MC5000	103 80 79/ 70 -5 -4	64	12	1	31 1/2	1hd	11 1/2	21 1/2	Sarvis DA123	b 5.90	LuckyLo1 1/2NorthrnAlnc1 1/2FlMgnonhk	3 wide; outfinished 12
21Oct06Beu2	6f ft	:232 :48 1:01 1:142 3↑	100 MC5000	98 77 68/ 55 -3 -5	39	9	9	63 1/2	72 1/2	75 1/2	912	Pascas E121	b *1.50	MonrchsRst1 1/2Cichon3 1/2Gzznhk	Checked start; 5 wide 11
04Oct06TP1	1m ft	:24 :473 1:132 1:402 3↑	102 MC7500	103 79 68/ 58 +9 +4	57	11	2 1/2	32	31 1/2	44 1/2	47 1/2	Lebron V117	b 7.20	Content Cat7 1/2Itsmutepoint1 1/2Free Trade4 1/2	7 wide early 12
14Sep06TP1	6f ft	:23 :464	1:131 3↑	100 MC5000	104 76 70/ 75 -4 -2	68	6	12	62 1/2	62 1/2	31	2no	HrnndzJrBJ121	b 3.70	EscpTdcsnoNrthrnAlnc1 1/2Cornrdhk	Sluggish st; bumped 12

02Mar Tlc 4f my :53 B 3/9 27Jan Tlc 4f ft :52 B 15/17 06Jan Tlc 4f sy :521 B 10/11 09Dec'06 Tlc 4f ft :52 B 10/11 17Nov'06 Tlc 5f my 1:033 B 2/8 08Sep'06 Tlc 5f ft 1:031 Bg 4/10
02Sep'06 Tlc 4f gd :491 B 10/31 19Aug'06 Tlc 5f ft 1:051 Bg 9/12 11Aug'06 Tlc 4f ft :512 B 6/8 21Jly'06 Tlc 4f ft :51 B 3/8 17Jun'06 Tlc 4f ft :57 B 23/23 02Jun'06 Tlc 4f ft :534 B 11/13

5 Cryptoless (S 0)

20/1 Own: L. D. Anglin
Red black dots white sleeves
SUNSERI JAMES JOSEPH (18 1-1-1 7%)

$5,000 B. c. 4 (Jun)
Sire: Cryptoclearance (Fappiano)
Dam: Quileese (Fulmar)
Brdr: Dr. James Wright (KY)
Trnr: Anglin L. D. (4 0-1-0 0%)

Power Rating: 76.0 (10th) L 124

Life:	21 0 - 0 - 0	$1,277	56	Fst 18 0 - 0 - 0 $1,017 56
2007	7 0 - 0 - 0	$559	56	Off 5 0 - 0 - 0 $260 50
2006	14 0 - 0 - 0	$718	53	Dis 4 0 - 0 - 0 $295 44
RD	10 0 - 0 - 0	$529	50	Trf 0 0 - 0 - 0 $0
				AW 9 0 - 0 - 0 $665 56

2007	33	9%	24%	+0.58
JKYw/ S types	34	6%	12%	-1.71
JKYw/ Trn L60	4	0%	75%	-2.00
JKYw/ Routes	17	6%	24%	-1.66

2007	13	0%	8%	-2.00
No class chg	22	0%	5%	-2.00
Maiden Clming	48	2%	10%	-1.91

Sire Stats: AWD 7.5f 12%Mud 2185MudSts 6%1st 1.27spi
Dam'sSire:AWD 7.0f 12%Mud 388MudSts 6%1st 0.46spi

● Finished far back in last start ● Never in-the-money in 21 career starts ● Poor Trainer win%

DATE TRK	DIST		RR RACETYPE	CR E1 E2/ LP 1c 2c	SPD	PP	ST	1C	2C	Str	FIN	JOCKEY	ODDS	Top Finishers	Comment
27Apr07RD14	1 70 gd	:234 :487 1:14 1:471 3↑	100 MC5000	99 55 47/ 63 +7 +9	50	3	101	1013	913	68	514	Sunseri JJ124	L 60.40	GityMn1 1/2ConflyRoszmn1ThrdSsn4	Improved position 10
20Apr07RD13	6f ft	:223 :464 1:003 1:142 3↑	99 MC5000	98 58 54/ 72 +3 -1	41	1	12	1210	1211	1010	910 1/2	Sunseri JJ124	L148.30	Honey Of A Devil1 1/2Virgil H.hdTricks1 1/2	Outrun 12
16Mar07TP6	1 1/16 ft	:244 :492 1:152 1:474 3↑	100 MC5000	98 52 41/ 47 -3 -3	38	1	88 1/2	89 1/2	811	818	825	Sunseri JJ124	L 67.20	GgiesAndLaughshdRmboRuner6ThrdSeson4 1/2	Outrun 8
17Feb07TP5	6 1/2 ft	:237 :484 1:124 1:192 3↑	100 MC5000	94 63 51/ 34 -10 -6	14	6	5	68	514	619	625 1/2	Rojas C124	L 14.30	ScotchRite1JoyeauxDinosur2KensonsCourt7	Outrun 6
09Feb07TP4	1 1/16 ft	:244 :50 1:162 1:501 3↑	100 MC5000	98 50 38/ 28 -3 -3	25	1	812	910	912	921	934	Rojas C124	L 62.10	Make A Way1 1/2Green Boy4Polish Cat4 1/2	Well back 9
18Jan07TP3	1m ft	:243 :493 1:14 1:381 4↑	101 MC7500	98 60 52/ 54 -9 -7	44	4	48 1/2	34 1/2	45 1/2	612	620 1/2	Rojas C124	L 50.30	MaintysGiant2 1/2FlthInAction7TapMjesty4	Inside; faded 6
06Jan07TP3	1 1/16 ft	:243 :494 1:152 1:474 4↑	100 MC5000	100 53 41/ 78 -15 -14	56	1	85 1/2	72 1/2	73 1/2	62 1/2	53 1/2	Rojas C124	L115.60	CseyWest1 1/2GreenBoyhdStolMyThundr1	Lacked late bid 10
23Dec06TP7	6f ft	:224 :461 :587 1:111 3↑	102 MC7500	99 64 55/ 74 -7 -6	44	6	10	119	1112	1117	1116 1/2	Rojas C123	L158.70	Deputy Banker1 1/2Chipinga1 1/2Camp Carsona2 1/2	Outrun 12
07Dec06TP8	6 1/2 ft	:231 :473 1:133 1:202 3↑	100 MC7500	99 69 58/ 64 -1 -7	43	3	12	128 1/2	89 1/2	813	815 1/2	Duarte S116	L 80.60	Galestone1 1/2Wicked WalthdDeputy Banker2 1/2	No factor 12
Previously trained by CARLISLE KRISTINA															
22Aug06RD1	1m ft	:241 :484 1:144 1:451 3↑	100 MC7500	87 41 37/ 54 +13 +16	35	4	918	922	921	916	922 1/2	Bracho JA119	L105.00	Rhysnhzon4 1/2ChefulColo1 1/2ForAcrs1 1/2	Never threatened 10

04Dec'06 TP 3f ft :364 B 1/2 ●14Nov'06 TP 3f ft :352 B 1/9 28Jun'06 RD 5f ft 1:034 B 2/3 04Mar'06 TP 5f ft 1:04 Bg 15/24 25Feb'06 TP 4f ft :512 B 12/23 18Feb'06 TP 4f ft :504 Bg 2/15
04Feb'06 TP 4f ft :522 Bg 22/26 28Jan'06 TP 4f ft :523 Bg 25/29 14Jan'06 TP 4f ft :53 B 19/21 03Jan'06 TP 3f ft :373 B 3/7 24Dec'05 TP 3f ft :401 B 7/12

tsnhorse.com

Ultimate PP's w/ Quick Play Comments **River Downs** MC 5000 1 Mile 3up Friday, May 11 2007 **Race 14**

E1 71 | E2/LATE 59/ 64 | SPD 59

6 Helio Wave (NA 0)
5/1 — Own: Harry D. Burns — Red, white, w
CASTANEDA BONNIE (8 3-4-1 25%)

$5,000 Ch. g. 4 (Apr) — Sire: Hypnothal (Rare Performer) — Dam: Tiffany Place (Naverone) — Brdr: Harry D. Burns (KY) — Trnr: Burns Kenneth H. (0 0-0-0 0%)

Power Rating: 77.8 (9th) — 124

Life: 4 0-0-0 $303 52 Fst 4 0-0-0 $303 52
2007 1 0-0-0 $120 49 Off 0 0-0-0 $0
2006 3 0-0-0 $183 52 Dis 0 0-0-0 $0
RD 2 0-0-0 $113 52 Trf 0 0-0-0 $0
AW 2 0-0-0 $190 51

2007 23 9% 39% -0.30 | 2007 1 0% 0% -2.00 | Sire Stats: AWD 7.1f 20%Mud 5MudSts 14%1st 0.17spi
JKYw/NA types 30 7% 17% -0.13 | 90+ days away 1 0% 0% -2.00 | Dam'sSire:AWD 6.9f 7%Mud 144MudSts 5%1st 0.73spi
JKYw/ Routes 4 0% 0% -2.00 | Maiden Clming 4 0% 0% -2.00

● Never threatened the leaders in last start ● Has not raced for more than 4 months

DATE TRK DIST RR RACETYPE CR E1 E2/ LP 1c 2c SPD PP ST 1C 2C Str FIN JOCKEY ODDS Top Finishers Comment
06Jan07TP[1] 1 1/16 ft :24[1] :48[4] 1:14[4] 1:47[4] 4↑ 100 MC5000 99 53 37/ 68 3 7 49 4 8 8 7 7 5 CastanedaB[124] 20.80 CountTheEgle RamboRuner Bismutepoint No threat 8
15Dec06TP[1] 1 1/16 ft :24 :48 1:13[1] 1:45[1] 3↑ 101 MC7500 99 51 41/ 69 6 9 51 7 11 11 12 10 9 CastanedaB[124] 73.20 Sea Of Victory Prospectable Jones Way No threat 12
03Sep06RD[14] 1 70 ft :24 :49 1:14 1:46 3↑ 101 MC7500 101 46 49/ 66 6 12 52 3 10 10 9 7 5 Adam MG[124] 50.60 DeighttayRd RoyBert ProughJo Improved position 10
17Aug06RD[14] 6f ft :23 :46 :59 1:13 3↑ 99 MC5000 99 57 53/ 83 50 2 12 12 12 9 8 Adam MG[124] 52.00 Unexcused MrMarquetMaker Wetchmo No factor 12

01May Tdc 5f ft 1:06[1] Bg 7/8 17Apr Tdc 5f ft 1:05[3] B 5/10 10Apr Tdc 4f ft :52 B 5/15 29Dec'06 Tdc 5f ft 1:05[4] Bg 7/7 07Dec'06 Tdc 5f ft 1:07[2] B 13/13 30Nov'06 Tdc 5f ft 1:09[4] B 4/4
11Aug'06 Tdc 4f ft :50[4] B 4/8 03Aug'06 Tdc 5f ft 1:04[4] Bg 4/8 27Jly'06 Tdc 5f ft 1:05[2] Bg 4/4

7 Fire Glenn (NA 4)
5/1 — Own: Jani L. Purtee — Green, orange stripes
CALO JOSE LUIS (64 10-8-7 16%)

$5,000 Dkbbr. g. 3 (Jan) — Sire: Deputy Commander (Deputy Minister) — Dam: Cypress Groves (Conquistador Cielo) — Brdr: James T. Hines Jr. (KY) — Trnr: Asbury David W. (6 1-1-0 17%)

Power Rating: 86.3 (5th) — L 116

Life: 3 0-0-0 $351 32 Fst 2 0-0-0 $253 32
2007 3 0-0-0 $353 32 Off 1 0-0-0 $100 14
2006 0 0-0-0 $0 Dis 0 0-0-0 $0
RD 2 0-0-0 $200 32 Trf 0 0-0-0 $0
AW 1 0-0-0 $153 32

2007 214 14% 40% -0.52 | 2007 31 10% 35% +1.65 | Sire Stats: AWD 7.6f 13%Mud 395MudSts 4%1st 1.48spi
JKYw/NA types 102 5% 15% -1.11 | 1st at route 11 0% 0% -2.00 | Dam'sSire:AWD 7.2f 16%Mud 1924MudSts 9%1st 2.09spi
JKYw/ Trn L60 5 0% 40% -2.00 | Sprnt-Sprnt-Rte 29 3% 24% +1.11
+JKYw/ Routes 56 18% 45% -0.50 | Sprnt to Rte 48 4% 25% +0.03

★ Drops in Class today ★ May improve at the longer distance
● Poor Speed Figures ● Has never raced at a route distance
● Poor '1st at route' trainer record: 0%wins 11sts

DATE TRK DIST RR RACETYPE CR E1 E2/ LP 1c 2c SPD PP ST 1C 2C Str FIN JOCKEY ODDS Top Finishers Comment
29Apr07RD[4] 6f ft :22[2] :45[1] :58[2] 1:12[2] 103 Mdn 10k 98 81 73/ 41 +1 +4 32 8 7 9 6 6 7 Paucar E[121] Lb 14.30 PrivateVendor ToughChoice DnceWorld No threat 8
12Apr07RD[13] 6f gd :22[3] :46 :58[4] 1:11[3] 3↑ 104 Mdn 10k 99 93 92/ 1 +1 +2 14 1 3 1 4 9 9 Calo JL[115] Lb 32.00 ProrBen KoimoCrek SultryPisu Through after half 10
24Mar07TP[6] 5f ft :22[2] :46 :58[7] 1:11 108 Mdn 26k 104 75 67/ 48 4 7 32 2 4 8 8 9 9 Lebron V[122] L 54.20 Malebar Knights Cross Fantastic Bud No menace 9

26Apr RD 3f my :38[2] B 3/4 03Apr RD 4f ft :52 Bg 2/2 17Mar TP 6f ft 1:17[2] B 3/4 11Mar TP 5f ft 1:02[4] Bg 7/10 02Mar TP 4f ft :54[4] Bg 10/10 24Feb TP 5f ft 1:04[2] Bg 8/16
03Feb TP 4f ft :51[1] B 10/12

8 Vin's Buster (NA 4)
12/1 — Own: Tim Glyshaw — Black, gold circled g, gold sleeves
ADAM MATHEU G. (17 2-4-2 12%)

$5,000 Dkbbr. g. 3 (May) — Sire: Saratoga Six (Alydar) — Dam: Vincetta (Lion D'or) — Brdr: Kenneth R. Gravett (KY) — Trnr: Glyshaw Tim (4 2-1-0 50%)

Power Rating: 78.1 (7th) — L 116

Life: 2 0-0-0 $179 39 Fst 2 0-0-0 $179 39
2007 2 0-0-0 $179 39 Off 0 0-0-0 $0
2006 0 0-0-0 $0 Dis 0 0-0-0 $0
RD 0 0-0-0 $0 Trf 0 0-0-0 $0
AW 2 0-0-0 $179 39

2007 88 10% 33% -0.77 | 2007 34 15% 53% -0.58 | Sire Stats: AWD 6.7f 18%Mud 1171MudSts 13%1st 1.65spi
JKYw/NA types 108 3% 12% -1.51 | 1st strt w/trn 18 6% 22% -1.18 | Dam'sSire:AWD 6.7f 10%Mud 517MudSts 6%1st 0.60spi
+JKYw/ Trn L60 5 40% 60% +2.60 | 31-90daysAway 33 6% 33% -1.20
JKYw/ Routes 39 8% 33% -0.99 | 1st at route 7 0% 14% -2.00

★ Drops in Class today ★ May improve at the longer distance
● Poor Speed Figures earned in both career starts ● Outside posts have poor win%
● Has never raced at a route distance ● Poor '1st strt w/trn' trainer record: 6%wins 18sts

DATE TRK DIST RR RACETYPE CR E1 E2/ LP 1c 2c SPD PP ST 1C 2C Str FIN JOCKEY ODDS Top Finishers Comment
Previously trained by COLEBROOK JOHN T.
04Apr07TP[9] 6f ft :23[3] :48[1] 1:01 1:13[2] 3↑ 101 MC7500 99 69 55/ 49 8 15 24 5 11 9 10 11 13 Laurente G[117] Lb 12.20 DeltaSlam KensonsCount City OfStars No menace 11
16Mar07TP[2] 6½ ft :23[4] :47[2] 1:13 1:20[1] 104 MC30000/20 100 66 56/ 61 -12 -7 39 2 6 6 6 7 7 LaurenteG[118] 7.20 Silver Zephyr Jus' Beautiful Deaver No menace 7

04May TP 5f ft 1:02 B 3/4 26Apr TP 5f ft 1:04 B 1/1 27Mar Kee 4f ft :49[4] B 24/36 09Mar Kee 4f ft :47 Hg 2/36 02Mar Kee 4f ft :47[3] B 7/13 23Feb Kee 4f ft :50[4] B 4/6
31Jan Kee 4f ft :51[4] B 4/9 26Jly'06 Tdc 3f ft :40[1] B 8/9

9 Grand Sand (P 2)
10/1 — Own: Thomas E. Nugent — Green, yellow 'ton', yellow sleeves
VITEK JUSTIN J. (81 12-12-11 12%)

$5,000 B. g. 4 (Mar) FTKDEC 2003 $5k — Sire: Sandpit (Brz) (Baynoun (Ire)) — Dam: Torne Ann (Blushing Groom (Fr)) — Brdr: Darry D. Hayes (IN) — Trnr: Nugent Thomas E. (8 2-2-0 25%)

Power Rating: 90.0 (3rd) — L 124

Life: 17 0-2-1 $6,188 64 Fst 11 0-2-1 $4,385 63
2007 6 0-0-0 $707 54 Off 5 0-0-0 $1,671 64
2006 11 0-2-1 $5,481 63 Dis 9 0-1-1 $3,853 63
RD 4 0-0-0 $408 64 Trf 1 0-0-0 $138 53
AW 9 0-1-1 $2,525 63

2007 226 11% 36% +0.10 | 2007 27 19% 44% +3.73 | Sire Stats: AWD 7.4f 11%Mud 372MudSts 2%1st 0.71spi
JKYw/ P types 103 13% 34% 0.68 | No class chg 27 15% 33% -0.88 | Dam'sSire:AWD 8.2f 22%Mud 202MudSts 14%1st 6.41spi
JKYw/ Trn L60 3 0% 33% -2.00 | Maiden Clming 21 5% 38% -1.58 | SoldAt: FTKDEC 2003 $4.5k (1/1) SireAvg: $4.5k StudFee:$7,500
JKYw/ Routes 100 13% 33% -0.14

★ Best Dirt Speed is faster than the Avg Winning Speed
● Outside posts have poor win%

DATE TRK DIST RR RACETYPE CR E1 E2/ LP 1c 2c SPD PP ST 1C 2C Str FIN JOCKEY ODDS Top Finishers Comment
04May07RD[13] 1m ft :24[2] :48 1:14[4] 1:42[4] 3↑ 103 Clm5000n2L 102 49 57/ 63 +1 0 53 5 8 7 4 4 5 Rojas C[120] Lb 12.30 WhifThght LhsRckstr CsyWst Lost ground 2nd turn 9
26Apr07RD[12] 1 1/16 my :24[2] :49[1] 1:13[4] 1:48 3↑ 101 MC7500 103 72 69/ 64 -2 -1 64 2 4 3 3 3 4 Rojas C[124] Lb 17.80 Timefortony Apache Chief Tejano Rick No rally 10
25Feb07TP[7] 1m ft :24[4] :48[4] 1:16[1] 1:41[7] 3↑ 100 MC5000 100 56 53/ 76 -14 -15 58 10 9 7 2 3 5 SchaeferGA[125] Lb 60.30 TwceThPlsur GrenBoy SlotMyThndr 5 wide 3/8 pl 11
09Feb07TP[4] 1 1/16 ft :24[4] :50 1:18[2] 1:50[1] 3↑ 100 MC5000 98 56 50/ 24 -3 -5 30 5 9 8 6 8 8 Vitek JJ[124] Lb 12.50 Make A Way Green Boy Polish Car Outrun 9
02Feb07TP[1] 1m ft :24[4] :49[3] 1:16[2] 1:44[2] 3↑ 101 MC7500 99 62 48/ 31 0 +1 28 5 6 7 7 7 7 Mojica O[124] Lb 24.10 Prospectable Deputy Grant Major Tom Stopped 7
18Jan07TP[4] 1m ft :24[3] :48[3] 1:14 1:39[1] 4↑ 101 MC7500 99 58 51/ 64 -8 -7 50 6 5 5 5 5 5 MojicaJr R[124] Lb 4.30 Mainly'sGrant FaithinAction TapMyesty No menace 6
22Dec06TP[1] 1m ft :23[4] :47[1] 1:13[4] 1:41[2] 3↑ 98 MC5000 101 82 68/ 56 +16 +11 56 8 3 3 2 2nd 3 MojicaJr R[123] Lb 3.40 PrzHuntr SlotMyThndr GrndSnd 3 wide, bid, tired 12
06Dec06TP[9] 1 1/16 ft :23[3] :48 1:14 1:48[2] 3↑ 99 MC5000 101 78 66/ 63 +8 +6 63 2 4 4 3 2nd 2 MojicaJr R[123] Lb 7.50 Prorwd GrndSd PadyMcNly Boxed inside: missed 12
08Nov06Hoo[11] 1m my :24[1] :48[3] 1:15 1:43[2] 3↑ 99 Mdn 17k 99 54 48/ 73 -2 +4 54 5 7 7 6 5 4 MojicaJr R[118] Lb 3.10 Swiss Ice RunawayJake X Appeal Mild gain off rail 7
20Oct06Hoo[1] 1 1/16 gd :23[3] :48[1] 1:14[4] 1:49[3] 3↑ 102 C10000n2L 102 59 55/ 57 -1 -3 52 3 7 7 6 6 4 MojicaJr R[117] Lb 5.20 RsclyRbr MyAdct HsrRenck Saved ground: no rally 8

04Nov'06 Tdc 4f ft :52[3] B 29/37 19Jly'06 Tdc 5f ft 1:04[3] Bg 5/9 08Jly'06 Tdc 4f ft :53 B 24/30 29Jun'06 Tdc 5f ft 1:06 B 9/11 14Jun'06 Tdc 4f ft :51[3] B 6/9 12Apr'06 Tdc 3f ft :37[4] B 4/12
24Feb'06 Tdc 4f ft :52[3] B 7/9 02Feb'06 Tdc 4f ft :50[4] B 3/4 23Dec'05 Tdc 5f ft 1:04[4] B 6/6 07Dec'05 Tdc 4f ft :49[3] Bg 5/7 01Dec'05 Tdc 4f ft :53 B 7/8 25Nov'05 Tdc 3f ft :37[2] Bg 6/3

tsnhorse.com

Ultimate PP's w/ Quick Play Comments **River Downs** MC 5000 1 Mile 3up Friday May 11, 2007 **Race 14**

E1	E2/LATE	SPD
71	59/ 64	59

10 **Laterornever (E 8)** $5,000
Own: C I Stables
5/2 Burgundy, white cr, white sleeves
SARVIS DEAN A (99 23-11-17 23%)

B. g. 3 (Mar)
Sire: Honour And Glory (Relaunch)
Dam: Here And Now (Fr) (Exit To Nowhere)
Brdr: Fab Oak Stable (KY)
Trnr: Grace Lon (7 2-0-2 29%)

Power Rating: 98.8 (1st) L 116

Life:	7	0 - 1 - 2	$3,211	67	Fst	6	0 - 1 - 2	$3,003	67
2007	7	0 - 1 - 2	$3,211	67	Off	1	0 - 0 - 0	$208	60
2006	0	0 - 0 - 0	$0		Dis	4	0 - 1 - 2	$2,870	67
RD	2	0 - 0 - 1	$813	67	Trf	0	0 - 0 - 0	$0	
					AW	5	0 - 1 - 1	$2,393	61

2007	216	16%	38%	-0.22
JKYw/ E types	110	16%	35%	-0.56
JKYw/ Trn L60	3	33%	67%	-1.40
JKYw/ Routes	102	22%	46%	-0.06

2007	24	17%	67%	-0.50
No class chg	51	18%	43%	-0.83
Btn favorite	16	12%	56%	1.14
Maiden Clmng	9	22%	67%	+0.56

Sire Stats: AWD 6.8 17%Mud 735MudSts 13%1st 1.42spi
Dam'sSire: AWD 9.5 18%Mud 17MudSts 8%1st 2.40spi

★ Hot Trainer in last 14 days (3 2-0-0) ★ Highest Last Race Speed Rating
★ Highest Speed Figure at Today's Distance ★ Best Dirt Speed is fastest among today's starters
● Outside posts have poor win%

DATE TRK	DIST						RR RACETYPE	CR	E1	E2/	LP	1c	2c	SPD	PP	ST	1C	2C	Str	FIN	JOCKEY		ODDS	Top Finishers	Comment
27Apr07RD[14]	170 gd	:23[4]	:48[2]	1:14	1:47[1]	3↑	[100]MC5000	[102]	82	74/	53	+7	+8	60	1	2hd	2hd	2hd	1[1]	4[9]½	Diego I[118]	Lb	*1.70	GuityMn½ContyRoscomon[1]ThirdSeson[4]	Weakened 10
13Apr07RD[14]	1m ft	:24[2]	:49[1]	1:14[3]	1:41[3]	3↑	[102]MC7500	[103]	73	68/	75	-5	-6	67	7	2½	2½	2hd	3[2]½	3[6]	PrescottRA[115]	Lb	6.00	R. Harold[hd]Honey Of ADevil[6]½Laterornever[3]	Weakened 9
01Apr07TP[1]	◈ 1m ft	:24[3]	:48[4]	1:15[1]	1:41	3↑	[101]MC5000	[102]	68	55/	75	-7	-11	59	4	1½	1½	1hd	2[1]	2[5]	Felix JE[117]	Lb	4.50	Bsmtpont[5]Ltrornvr[1]½SttMyThndr½	inside, held place 9
22Mar07TP[2]	◈ 1m ft	:24[2]	:48[3]	1:14[3]	1:40[4]		[103]MC7500	[102]	60	46/	62	-5	-5	46	6	5½	6[8]½	8[10]	7[18]	6[21]	Sarvis DA[122]	Lb	5.20	SlfMdMn[12]½Lkndwthbrt[1]¾MlsTwPts[3]½	4 wide; gave way 9
08Mar07TP[1]	◈ 1m ft	:24[4]	:49[1]	1:14[4]	1:42	3↑	[103]MC7500	[104]	67	64/	69	-6	+1	61	6	1[1]	1[1]½	1[1]½	1½	3[1]½	Sarvis DA[117]	Lb	50.20	Juliska[1]½Timelorlony½Laterornever[1]	3 wide early 9
01Mar07TP[3]	◈ 5½ ft	:23[2]	:48	1:01	1:07[4]	3↑	[100]MC5000	[99]	70	47/	53	0	4	40	3	7	9[7]½	9[12]	9[16]	7[11]½	Sarvis DA[117]	Lb	3.80	WickedWit½AnotherFineOn[2]½JoyeuxDenoue½	Outrun 10

Claimed from Fab Oak Stable Biancone Patrick L. Trainer

DATE TRK	DIST						RR RACETYPE	CR	E1	E2/	LP	1c	2c	SPD	PP	ST	1C	2C	Str	FIN	JOCKEY		ODDS	Top Finishers	Comment
27Jan07TP[7]	◈ 6½ ft	:23	:47[1]	1:13[3]	1:20[2]		[104]MC7500-c	[103]	80	69/	62	-4	-8	50	8	4	4[1]½	5[2]½	4[6]½	5[7]	LeparouxJR[122]	b	2.70	Tahlequah[no]Twenty Amp[1]Tribal Spirit[4]	3 wide; tired 10

22Feb TP 4f ft :52[1] Bg 15/25 23Jan TP 4f ft :50[2] B 14/20 14Jan TP 4f ft :48[4] Bg 8/12 ●07Jan TP 4f ft :47[2] Bg 1/15 31Dec06 TP 4f ft :48[2] B 8/25 20Dec06 Kee 4f ft :49 B 6/11

Last 3 Years RACETYPE STATS:	# Races	Win%	FAVORITES Itm%	$2ROI	Average Field Size	Median $2 Win Payoff	% Winners < 5/1	% Winners >= 5/1 < 10/1	% Winners >= 10/1
RD 3up MCL 5000 Dirt 8f	26	23%	73%	-0.82	8.8	$8.10	62%	15%	23%

Track Bias Stats

DIRT 8.0f	* MEET Totals *		WnrAvgBL	
# Races: 30	Speed Bias: 57%		1stCall: 2.1	
%Wire: 23%	04/06 - 05/08		2ndCall: 0.8	
	Early	Speed	Late	Speed
Runstyle:	E	E/P	P	S
	++		+	
Impact Values	1.50	0.93	1.22	0.35
%Races Won	37%	20%	33%	10%
Post Bias:	RAIL	1-3	4-7	8+
		+		
Impact Values	0.64	1.20	0.90	0.00
Avg Win %	10%	19%	16%	0%

DIRT 8.0f	* WEEK Totals *		WnrAvgBL	
# Races: 8	Speed Bias: 62%		1stCall: 1.8	
%Wire: 25%	05/03 - 05/08		2ndCall: 0.8	
	Early	Speed	Late	Speed
Runstyle:	E	E/P	P	S
	++		++	
Impact Values	1.85	0.84	1.31	0.00
%Races Won	38%	25%	38%	0%
Post Bias	RAIL	1-3	4-7	8+
	+	+		
Impact Values	1.40	1.40	0.57	0.00
Avg Win %	25%	25%	11%	0%

Race Summary

#	HorseName	ML Odds	Med Eqp	Days Since L/R	Run Style	PTS	Avg Dist/Surf PACE-SPEED E1	E2/Late	Spd	Avg Race Rtng	Best Pace E1	E2/Late	Final Speed Sp1	Sp2	Sp3	ACL	Rcg Spd Avg	R1	R2	R3	Pedigree Stats Mud Spd	% Mud	% 1st	SPI	DPI	Sire AWD	Dam Sire's AWD
10	Laterornever	5/2	L	14	++E	8	74	66/ 68	* 62*	101	82	74/ 75	60.	67.	59.	101.1	62	100	102	101		17	13	1.42		6.8	9.5
6	Helio Wave	5/1		125..	NA		49	45/ 68	(52)	101	53	49/ 69	49.	51.	52.		51	100	101	101		20	14	0.17		7.1	6.9
1	H D's Affair	8/1	L	28	S	2	63	57/ 60	* 51*	104	69	60/ 95	46.	62.	35.	104.6	48	102	103	104		8	6	0.48		7.2	7.2
4	Northern Alliance	7/2	L	27	E/P	5	61	60/ 56	51	102	79	68/ 58	34	51.	63		49	99	101	100	34	18	17	1.63		6.5	9.1
3	Seattle Pass	20/1	L	56	+P	5	66	51/ 57	* 48*	101	67	60/ 61	47.	45.	49.	97.5	47	100	100	100	41	0	0	0.09		0.0	8.2
2	Ky Ridge Runner	20/1	L	14..	S		62	49/ 55	47	101	68	57/ 80	47.	38	44.	99.1	43	100	99	100	47	0	0	0.13		8.2	7.1
9	Grand Sand	10/1	L	7..	+P	2	54	53/ 54	* 47*	101	82	69/ 83	53.	64	58.	98.8	58	103	101	100	64	11	2	0.71		7.4	8.2
5	Cryptoless	20/1	L	14	S		56	47/ 55	* 44*	101	76	66/ 78	50.	41	38.		43	100	99	100		12	6	1.27		7.5	7.0
7	Fire Glenn	5/1	L	12	NA	4	78	70/	(32)	106			32	14	32		26	103	104	108		13	4	1.48		7.6	7.2
8	Vin's Buster	12/1	L	37	NA	4	69	56/	(32)	103			24	39			32	101	104			18	13	1.65		6.7	6.7

tsnhorse.com

Ultimate PP's w/ Quick Play Comments **River Downs** MC 5000 1 Mile. 3up Friday, May 11, 2007 **Race 14**

E1	E2/LATE	SPD
71	59/ 64	59

Speed Last Race	Back Speed	Current Class	Average Class Last 3	Power Rating	Early Pace Last Race	Late Pace Last Race
60 Laterornever	67 Laterornever	102.7 H D's Affair	102.5 Laterornever	98.8 Laterornever	82 Laterornever	68 Helio Wave
53 Grand Sand	64 H D's Affair	102.6 Laterornever	101.7 Grand Sand	91.4 H D's Affair	73 Fire Glenn	63 Cryptoless
50 Cryptoless	63 Grand Sand	100.9 Northern Alliance	100.9 H D's Affair	90.0 Grand Sand	69 H D's Affair	63 Grand Sand
49 Helio Wave	57 Ky Ridge Runner	99.6 Grand Sand	100.0 Fire Glenn	89.9 Northern Alliance	67 Seattle Pass	55 Ky Ridge Runner
47 Seattle Pass	57 Northern Alliance	98.6 Ky Ridge Runner	99.8 Northern Alliance	85.3 Fire Glenn	65 Northern Alliance	54 Seattle Pass
47 Ky Ridge Runner	56 Cryptoless	97.7 Cryptoless	99.8 Helio Wave	79.5 Seattle Pass	62 Ky Ridge Runner	53 Laterornever
45 H D's Affair	56 Seattle Pass	97.6 Seattle Pass	98.1 Vin's Buster	78.1 Vin's Buster	55 Vin's Buster	49 H D's Affair
34 Northern Alliance	52 Helio Wave	NA Helio Wave	98.0 Ky Ridge Runner	78.0 Ky Ridge Runner	55 Cryptoless	49 Vin's Buster
32 Fire Glenn	NA Fire Glenn	NA Fire Glenn	97.6 Cryptoless	77.8 Helio Wave	53 Helio Wave	41 Fire Glenn
24 Vin's Buster	NA Vin's Buster	NA Vin's Buster	97.5 Seattle Pass	76.0 Cryptoless	49 Grand Sand	35 Northern Alliance

FIRST RACE
Thistledown
May 11th, 2007

1 MILE. (1.35^{3}) CLAIMING. Purse $6,600 FOR FOUR YEAR OLDS AND UPWARD WHICH HAVE NOT WON A RACE IN 2006-2007. Weight, 120 lbs. Claiming Price $4,000 (Ohio Registered Foals Preferred). (Clear 79)

Value of Race: $6,600 Winner $3,960; second $1,320; third $660; fourth $330; fifth $132; sixth $66; seventh $66; eighth $66. Mutuel Pool $25,845 Exacta Pool $22,329 Superfecta Pool $14,559 Trifecta Pool $20,327

Last Raced	#	Horse	M/Eqt.	A/S	Wt	PP	St	¼	½	¾	Str	Fin	Jockey	Cl'g Pr	Odds $1
29Apr07 ^{13}TDN^{6}	8	Mountain Top (GB)	L bf	6G	120	8	5	$7^{1\frac{1}{2}}$	7^{2}	5^{2}	$1^{2\frac{1}{2}}$	1^{3}	Urieta-Moran V	4000	3.30
12Jun06 ^{2}DEL^{5}	5	Slews Resurrection	L f	8G	120	5	7	$6^{\frac{1}{2}}$	6^{hd}	6^{hd}	2^{2}	$2^{2\frac{1}{2}}$	Gonzalez L A	4000	3.90
03May07 ^{9}TDN^{2}	6	Proud American	L	7M	116	6	4	3^{2}	3^{3}	3^{hd}	3^{hd}	3^{hd}	Pilares C P	4000	2.70
17Nov06 ^{10}MNR^{10}	7	Bandana	L b	10G	120	7	8	$5^{\frac{1}{2}}$	4^{1}	$4^{\frac{1}{2}}$	$4^{1\frac{1}{2}}$	$4^{3\frac{1}{2}}$	Magrell J M	4000	20.20
20Apr07 ^{10}TDN^{5}	1	European Defense	L b	10G	120	1	1	2^{3}	$2^{1\frac{1}{2}}$	2^{hd}	$5^{1\frac{1}{2}}$	$5^{3\frac{3}{4}}$	Munaylla F	4000	22.10
28Apr07 ^{4}TDN^{5}	4	Cinematic	L f	6G	120	4	3	1^{hd}	$1^{1\frac{1}{2}}$	$1^{\frac{1}{2}}$	$6^{\frac{1}{2}}$	6^{2}	Sanguinetti A	4000	1.50
28Apr07 ^{12}TDN^{5}	2	Sober Moment	L f	7M	116	2	6	8	8	8	8	$7^{2\frac{3}{4}}$	Dailey A	4000	44.00
23Feb07 ^{7}BEU^{8}	3	Perfect Call	L	6G	118	3	2	4^{2}	$5^{\frac{1}{2}}$	7^{3}	7^{hd}	8	Hernandez L	4000	58.50

OFF AT 1:06 Start Good. Ridden out. Track Fast.

TIME :23^{4}, :48^{2}, 1:14^{4}, 1:41^{3} (:23.90, :48.40, 1:14.82, 1:41.66)

$2 Mutuel Prices:				
	8- MOUNTAIN TOP (GB)	8.60	6.00	3.00
	5- SLEWS RESURRECTION		5.00	3.20
	6- PROUD AMERICAN			2.60

$2 EXACTA 8-5 PAID $37.20 $1 SUPERFECTA 8-5-6-7 PAID $224.30
$2 TRIFECTA 8-5-6 PAID $102.60

Bay Gelding, (Apr), by Zafonic - Monroe by Sir Ivor. Trainer Morales Nabu. Bred by Juddmonte Farms(GB).

MOUNTAIN TOP (GB) unhurried early, rallied at the quarter pole five wide, drew off through the lane while being ridden out. SLEWS RESURRECTION allowed to settle, rallied in the upper stretch, split horses and was second best. PROUD AMERICAN well placed, lacked a late response and went evenly late. BANDANA never far back, needed more in late stretch. EUROPEAN DEFENSE vied for the lead, then weakened in the upper stretch. CINEMATIC set the pace and dueled for the lead, stumbled badly in the upper stretch and dropped back. SOBER MOMENT showed little. PERFECT CALL well placed, was through after a half. The stewards posted the inquiry sign but took no action.

Owners- 8, Coll Miguel ; 5, Gary M. King Racing Stable, Inc. ; 6, Cowan Elmer C.; 7, Bookman Racing Stable LLC ; 1, Mark Yagour, Inc. ; 4, Sipp Bridget ; 2, Newman Tracy L.; 3, Pizzurro Antonio N.

Trainers- 8, Morales Nabu ; 5, King Gary M.; 6, Cowan Gary ; 7, Huffman Candace M.; 1, Schuster Robin ; 4, Sipp Burton K.; 2, Newman Tracy L.; 3, Pizzurro Antonio N.

Breeders- 8, Juddmonte Farms (GB); 5, Johnny Long (FL); 6, Donald R. Dizney (FL); 7, R. K. Lucas (KY); 1, Mark Yagour Inc. (OH); 4, Coal Creek Farm (KY); 2, Upson Downs Farm (KY); 3, Westwind Farm (KY)

THIRD RACE
Thistledown
May 11th, 2007

5½ FURLONGS. (1.03^{1}) CLAIMING. Purse $6,900 FOR THREE YEAR OLDS AND UPWARD WHICH HAVE NEVER WON TWO RACES. Three Year Olds, 120 lbs.; Older, 122 lbs. Non-winners of a race since April 11 Allowed 2 lbs. A race since March 11 Allowed 4 lbs. Claiming Price $4,000 (Ohio Registered Foals Preferred). (Clear 79)

Value of Race: $6,900 Winner $4,140; second $1,380; third $690; fourth $345; fifth $69; sixth $69; seventh $69; eighth $69; ninth $69. Mutuel Pool $46,136 Pick 3 Pool $2,762 Exacta Pool $55,842 Superfecta Pool $25,228 Trifecta Pool $48,350

Last Raced	#	Horse	M/Eqt.	A/S	Wt	PP	St	¼	⅜	Str	Fin	Jockey	Cl'g Pr	Odds $1
25Mar07 ^{1}HOU^{6}	6	Hunterpunter	L b	3G	116	6	1	1^{1}	1^{1}	1^{3}	1^{4}	Spieth S	4000	1.50
27Apr07 ^{11}TDN^{9}	7	What Now Wynn	L b	5G	118	7	8	7^{hd}	$4^{\frac{1}{2}}$	3^{hd}	$2^{2\frac{1}{2}}$	Cloninger, Jr. W T	4000	15.70
20Apr07 ^{12}TDN^{6}	4	Windcauseruckus	L b	4G	118	4	4	2^{hd}	2^{2}	2^{3}	$3^{1\frac{1}{2}}$	Martinez, Jr. L J	4000	6.10
27Apr07 ^{3}TDN^{1}	1	Hooves of Thunder	L	5G	122	1	5	4^{1}	5^{2}	5^{3}	$4^{1\frac{3}{4}}$	Skerrett J	4000	4.90
21Apr07 ^{4}BEU^{3}	5	Erotick Mountain	L f	5G	118	5	2	3^{3}	3^{5}	$4^{1\frac{1}{2}}$	$5^{\frac{1}{2}}$	Gonzalez L A	4000	9.90
06May07 ^{12}TDN^{8}	9	Go Ryan Go	L b	4G	118	9	7	9	8^{2}	6^{hd}	$6^{\frac{1}{2}}$	Oro E	4000	10.90
27Apr07 ^{11}TDN^{6}	2	Command the Best	L b	7H	118	2	6	5^{1}	7^{1}	$8^{2\frac{1}{2}}$	$7^{1\frac{1}{2}}$	Urieta-Moran V	4000	37.90
27Apr07 ^{11}TDN^{10}	3	Great Charisma	L b	6G	118	3	9	8^{1}	$6^{\frac{1}{2}}$	7^{hd}	8^{3}	Hernandez L	4000	3.50
20Nov06 ^{6}TDN^{8}	8	Society Fox	L b	4G	118	8	3	6^{1}	9	9	9	Mailhot P	4000	29.70

OFF AT 1:49 Start Good. Won driving. Track Fast.

TIME :22^{4}, :46^{3}, :59^{2}, 1:06 (:22.80, :46.64, :59.44, 1:06.18)

$2 Mutuel Prices:				
	6- HUNTERPUNTER	5.00	3.40	3.00
	7- WHAT NOW WYNN		12.20	6.60
	4- WINDCAUSERUCKUS			4.60

$2 EXACTA 6-7 PAID $46.40 $1 SUPERFECTA 6-7-4-1 PAID $662.70
$2 TRIFECTA 6-7-4 PAID $316.20

Bay Gelding, (Feb), by Albert the Great - Expect Anna by Valid Expectations. Trainer Radosevich A. Jeffrey. Bred by Kevin Halter(KY).

HUNTERPUNTER was away alertly and sprinted out to set the pace, widended and drew off through the lane, driving. WHAT NOW WYNN allowed to settle, rallied in the upper stretch while four wide and closed willing. WINDCAUSERUCKUS stalked the winner, lacked a late response and went evenly late. HOOVES OF THUNDER well placed, saved ground and went evenly. EROTICK MOUNTAIN good position, then tired. GO RYAN GO wide early, was not a threat. COMMAND THE BEST had brief foot and was through early. GREAT CHARISMA failed to menace. SOCIETY FOX was no factor.

Owners- 6, Halter Pamela ; 7, R and P Racing Stables, Inc. ; 4, Faulkner Josh ; 1, Schickedanz Bruno ; 5, Lehman Eleanor B.; 9, Peruvian Glass and More, Inc. ; 2, Rapp, Dave and Burnt Clover Farm ; 3, Behrens, Ashley and Ronald ; 8, Eafford James

Trainers- 6, Radosevich Jeffrey A.; 7, Faulkner Rodney C.; 4, Faulkner Joe C.; 1, Radosevich Jeffrey A.; 5, Lehman Thomas D.; 9, Morales Ricardo ; 2, Marino James G.; 3, Behrens Ronald P.; 8, Eafford James

Breeders- 6, Kevin Halter (KY); 7, T. Wynn Jolley & Harry Hoglander (FL); 4, James T. Sabiston (ON); 1, Box Arrow Farm, Kimberly Conn & RandyConn (ON); 5, Michelle Severson (FL); 9, David Ranney (NY); 2, Dr. J. Fred Miller III (KY); 3, Farnsworth Farms (KY); 8, Andy Stronach & Dean Brice (ON)

$2 Pick Three (8-5-6) Paid $133.60; Pick Three Pool $2,762.

FIFTH RACE
Thistledown
May 11th, 2007

6 FURLONGS. (1.08^{2}) CLAIMING. Purse $7,500 FOR THREE YEAR OLDS AND UPWARD WHICH HAVE NEVER WON THREE RACES. Three Year Olds, 120 lbs.; Older, 122 lbs. Non-winners Of Two Races Since April 11 Allowed 2 lbs. A Race Since Then Allowed 4 lbs. Claiming Price $6,250 (Ohio Registered Foals Preferred). (Clear 79)

Value of Race: $7,500 Winner $4,500; second $1,500; third $750; fourth $375; fifth $75; sixth $75; seventh $75; eighth $75; ninth $75. Mutuel Pool $26,963 Pick 3 Pool $3,301 Exacta Pool $28,218 Superfecta Pool $15,934 Trifecta Pool $26,037

Last Raced	#	Horse	M/Eqt.	A/S	Wt	PP	St	¼	½	Str	Fin	Jockey	Cl'g Pr	Odds $1
20Apr07 ^{12}TDN^{1}	7	Madly Paddlin Home		3G	118	7	1	2^{2}	2^{4}	$2^{4\frac{1}{2}}$	$1^{2\frac{1}{2}}$	Sanguinetti A	6250	1.60
13Apr07 ^{13}TDN^{1}	3	Air Borne Etbauer	L b	4G	120	3	6	$1\frac{1}{2}$	$1\frac{1}{2}$	1^{hd}	$2^{2\frac{1}{4}}$	Spieth S	6250	2.30
17Apr07 ^{3}RD ^{6}	4	Pair of Queens	L b	4G	118	4	2	$4^{1\frac{1}{2}}$	4^{3}	$3^{1\frac{1}{2}}$	$3^{1\frac{1}{2}}$	Cloninger, Jr. W T	6250	14.40
26Nov06 ^{2}TDN^{6}	5	Cardashi	L b	5G	114	5	4	3^{hd}	3^{2}	4^{3}	$4^{2\frac{1}{2}}$	Barrera F	6250	5.40
21Apr07 ^{13}TDN^{3}	1	Sweetbaboo	L b	5G	118	1	7	6^{2}	5^{2}	5^{4}	5^{4}	Skerrett J	6250	4.20
02May07 ^{6}BEU^{2}	9	Three Mile Harbor	L bf	5G	118	9	8	7^{hd}	7^{3}	6^{1}	$6\frac{1}{2}$	Urieta-Moran V	6250	19.90
28Apr07 ^{14}TDN^{9}	6	Lootshoot Attitude	L f	6G	118	6	5	8^{2}	9	8^{hd}	7^{hd}	Pilares C P	6250	40.70
14Apr07 ^{7}BEU^{6}	2	Synhawk	L b	6G	118	2	9	9	8^{hd}	7^{hd}	8^{3}	Martinez, Jr. L J	6250	49.80
14Apr07 ^{14}TDN^{5}	8	Seeking Awards	L b	4G	118	8	3	5^{hd}	6^{1}	9	9	Gonzalez L A	6250	18.80

OFF AT 2:26 Start Good. Won driving. Track Fast.

TIME :22^{2}, :45^{3}, :58^{1}, 1:11^{2} (:22.52, :45.60, :58.34, 1:11.46)

$2 Mutuel Prices:				
	7- MADLY PADDLIN HOME	5.20	3.00	2.60
	3- AIR BORNE ETBAUER		3.00	3.00
	4- PAIR OF QUEENS			5.60

$2 EXACTA 7-3 PAID $17.00 $1 SUPERFECTA 7-3-4-5 PAID $202.70

$2 TRIFECTA 7-3-4 PAID $118.60

Bay Gelding, (Apr), by Robannier - Ooomiak by Peteski. Trainer Sipp K. Burton. Bred by Robert H Walter Family Trust(CA).

MADLY PADDLIN HOME vied for the lead the entire way, gained command in late stretch, driving. AIR BORNE ETBAUER dueled for the lead, was outfinished late but was second best. PAIR OF QUEENS well placed, went evenly through the stretch. CARDASHI well placed, lacked a late response and had an even effort. SWEETBABOO never far back, saved ground but was not a threat. THREE MILE HARBOR failed to menace. LOOTSHOOT ATTITUDE was no factor. SYNHAWK allowed to settle, showed little. SEEKING AWARDS had brief foot and was through early.

Owners- 7, Sipp Bridget ; 3, Boggs Jack L.; 4, Crumley Racing Stable LLC ; 5, Yellow Bird Stable ; 1, Zielinski, Richard and Garrison, Nancy ; 9, Morgan Kenneth A.; 6, O'Leary Katie ; 2, Faulkner Randy Joe; 8, Hamilton, Debbie and Skipper

Trainers- 7, Sipp Burton K.; 3, Radosevich Jeffrey A.; 4, Crumley Jevon ; 5, Shuman Joseph P.; 1, Zielinski Richard ; 9, Morgan Kenneth A.; 6, O'Leary Aaron A.; 2, Faulkner Randy Joe; 8, Faulkner Rodney C.

Breeders- 7, Robert H Walter Family Trust (CA); 3, Kaaren Biggs & Hays Biggs (AR); 4, David Miller (MD); 5, Audre Cappuccitti (ON); 1, Four Horsemen's Ranch & Thomas J. Cooper (FL); 9, McKathan Farms (IN); 6, Adena Springs (ON); 2, Jack D. Fisher (KY); 8, Rolling Oaks Farm (TX)

$2 Pick Three (6-7-7) Paid $165.00; Pick Three Pool $3,301.

SEVENTH RACE
Thistledown
May 11th, 2007

5½ FURLONGS. (1.03^{1}) CLAIMING. Purse $8,400 FOR FOUR YEAR OLDS AND UPWARD. Weight, 122 lbs. Non-winners of two races since April 11 Allowed 2 lbs. A race since then Allowed 4 lbs. Claiming Price $6,250 (Claiming races for $5,000 or less not considered in Weight Allowances) (Ohio Registered Foals Pr eferred). (Clear 79)

Value of Race: $8,400 Winner $5,040; second $1,680; third $840; fourth $420; fifth $252; sixth $84; seventh $84. Mutuel Pool $15,005 Pick 3 Pool $1,819 Exacta Pool $14,827 Superfecta Pool $10,603 Trifecta Pool $15,137

Last Raced	#	Horse	M/Eqt.	A/S	Wt	PP	St	¼	⅜	Str	Fin	Jockey	Cl'g Pr	Odds $1
22Apr07 ^{12}TDN^{3}	6	Bar Time	L	4G	118	6	1	$3^{1\frac{1}{2}}$	1^{1}	$1\frac{1}{2}$	1^{nk}	Spieth S	6250	1.70
26Apr07 ^{12}TDN^{4}	4	Valid Victory	L	4G	120	4	3	2^{hd}	2^{1}	$2^{1\frac{1}{2}}$	2^{1}	Martinez, Jr. L J	6250	2.50
28Apr07 ^{8}TDN^{1}	7	Time Counter	L bf	6G	118	7	2	6^{3}	6^{2}	5^{1}	$3\frac{3}{4}$	Meyers T	6250	6.90
29Oct06 ^{7}TDN^{1}	2	Mr. Simon to You	L	7G	118	2	7	7	7	7	$4\frac{3}{4}$	Gonzalez L A	6250	12.30
26Apr07 ^{10}TDN^{1}	3	Private Herb	L	4G	120	3	6	$5\frac{1}{2}$	5^{1}	3^{hd}	5^{nk}	Skerrett J	6250	4.20
15Apr07 ^{7}TDN^{1}	5	Captain Binge	L b	6G	118	5	5	4^{hd}	3^{hd}	4^{hd}	$6^{1\frac{1}{2}}$	Urieta-Moran V	6250	10.70
22Apr07 ^{12}TDN^{4}	1	Final Endeavor	L bf	8G	118	1	4	1^{hd}	4^{hd}	$6^{2\frac{1}{2}}$	7	Castillo K	6250	8.60

OFF AT 3:07 Start Good. Won driving. Track Fast.

TIME :22^{4}, :46^{3}, :59^{1}, 1:05^{4} (:22.92, :46.68, :59.34, 1:05.88)

$2 Mutuel Prices:				
	6- BAR TIME	5.40	3.60	2.60
	4- VALID VICTORY		3.20	3.60
	7- TIME COUNTER			4.40

$2 EXACTA 6-4 PAID $14.80 $1 SUPERFECTA 6-4-7-2 PAID $153.60

$2 TRIFECTA 6-4-7 PAID $71.60

Bay Gelding, (Jan), by Smolderin Heart - Livid Lass by Blue Ensign. Trainer Radosevich A. Jeffrey. Bred by Perry Bayley(OH).

BAR TIME dueled down the backside while three wide, gained a clear lead at the quarter pole, then prevailed in a long stretch drive, gamely. VALID VICTORY dueled for the lead while between horses early, saved ground through the stretch and just missed in a good effort. TIME COUNTER allowed to settle, rallied in the upper the stretch while three wide and closed willing. MR. SIMON TO YOU slow early, closed a gap late and was gaining. PRIVATE HERB contended, but needed more late. CAPTAIN BINGE well placed, went evenly in the stretch. FINAL ENDEAVOR dueled for the lead from the rail, was in tight at the three eight's pole, then weakened.

Owners- 6, Crestview Racing Stable, Inc. ; 4, Faulkner Randy Joe; 7, Barnes, Bart and Meyers, Judy ; 2, Kopas, Jr., Andrew and Yanos, Paul ; 3, Faulkner Joe C.; 5, Burnt Clover Farm ; 1, Doering, David, Ned and Mark

Trainers- 6, Radosevich Jeffrey A.; 4, Faulkner Randy Joe; 7, Barnes Bart A.; 2, Mook, II James C.; 3, Faulkner Joe C.; 5, Marino James G.; 1, Doering Mark

Breeders- 6, Perry Bayley (OH); 4, C. R. Trout (TX); 7, Castle Rock Stud, Inc. & Robert Seefeld& Michael Mayro (KY); 2, James Pullella & Carol L. Jones (KY); 3, Adena Springs (FL); 5, Ernie Wells (KY); 1, Bruce Tallisman (OH)

Scratched- Little Nicky Regs(28Apr07 ^{2}Tdn^{3})

$2 Pick Three (7-4-6/8) Paid $156.60; Pick Three Pool $1,819.

NINTH RACE

Thistledown

May 11th, 2007

6 FURLONGS. (1.08²) MAIDEN CLAIMING. Purse $6,500 FOR MAIDENS, FOUR YEAR OLDS AND UPWARD. Weight, 122 lbs. Claiming Price $4,000 (Ohio Registered Foals Preferred). (Clear 79)

Value of Race: $6,500 Winner $3,860; second $1,320; third $660; fourth $330; fifth $198; sixth $66; seventh $66. Mutuel Pool $20,837 Pick 3 Pool $1,314 Exacta Pool $22,143 Superfecta Pool $12,445 Trifecta Pool $19,198

Last Raced	#	Horse	M/Eqt.	A/S	Wt	PP	St	¼	½	Str	Fin	Jockey	Cl'g Pr	Odds $1
19Apr07 ¹TDN⁴	7	Ready to Exchange	L	4G	122	7	1	1hd	1½	1¹	12¾	Sanguinetti A	4000	1.40
27Apr07 ³TDN²	6	Heaven's Boy		5G	122	6	3	3hd	2½	2½	2½	Magrell J M	4000	4.10
28Aug06 ¹TDN⁶	4	Mr. Jupiter	L	4G	122	4	4	2hd	3¹	3¹	3¾	Cloninger, Jr. W T	4000	3.30
27Apr07 ³TDN³	3	Essa's Cat	L b	4G	117	3	2	4²	5³	5⁴	42¼	Barrera F	4000	3.80
27Apr07 ¹MNR⁴	2	Northern Cougar	L b	5G	122	2	7	5³	4¹	4hd	51¾	Spieth S	4000	17.80
23Aug06 ¹EVD³	5	Pepper Biscuit	L b	5G	122	5	5	7	7	7	6²	Castillo K	4000	9.80
27Apr07 ³TDN⁵	1	Go Geta Job	L bf	5G	122	1	6	6hd	6¹	6hd	7	Monterrey P	4000	23.00

OFF AT 3:46 Start Good. Ridden out. Track Fast.

TIME :23¹, :47², 1:00¹, 1:13¹ (:23.30, :47.40, 1:00.34, 1:13.28)

$2 Mutuel Prices:				
	7- READY TO EXCHANGE	4.80	3.00	2.10
	6- HEAVEN'S BOY		4.40	2.80
	4- MR. JUPITER			2.80

$2 EXACTA 7-6 PAID $16.60 $1 SUPERFECTA 7-6-4 PAID $83.00

$2 TRIFECTA 7-6-4 PAID $67.40

Bay Gelding, (Jan), by Ready to Order - Exchanging Glances by Silver Ghost. Trainer Sipp K. Burton. Bred by Robert Moreno(CA).

READY TO EXCHANGE dueled for the lead down the backside while four wide, drew clear through the stretch while being ridden out. HEAVEN'S BOY well placed while between horses, could not match strides late with the winner but held place. MR. JUPITER pressed the pace and saved ground, had no excuse and went evenly, late. ESSA'S CAT vied for the lead, weakened slightly in the lane. NORTHERN COUGAR had good position, but lacked a late response. PEPPER BISCUIT failed to menace. GO GETA JOB was no factor.

Owners- 7, Sipp Bridget ; 6, Drake Racing Stable ; 4, Double D Farm Corp. ; 3, Newell, Mike and Wright, Jack ; 2, Schickedanz Bruno ; 5, Feriole, Michael and Nunez, Mauricio ; 1, Silva, Fernando and Quiros, Jacobo

Trainers- 7, Sipp Burton K.; 6, Girten Shirley K.; 4, Crumley Jevon ; 3, Newell Michael ; 2, Radosevich Jeffrey A.; 5, Nunez Mauricio ; 1, Silva Fernando

Breeders- 7, Robert Moreno (CA); 6, Andy Stronach & Dean Brice (ON); 4, Double D Farm Corp. (OH); 3, Paul Buttigieg (ON); 2, Bruno Schickedanz (FL); 5, Michael Feriole (FL); 1, McMillin Bros. & Billy Hay (KY)

Ready to Exchange was claimed by Miller Gary M.; trainer, Miller Gary M.

$2 Pick Three (6/8-2-7) Paid $78.20; Pick Three Pool $1,314.

ELEVENTH RACE

Thistledown

May 11th, 2007

5½ FURLONGS. (1.03¹) CLAIMING. Purse $7,300 FOR FILLIES AND MARES THREE YEARS OLD AND UPWARD WHICH HAVE NEVER WON FOUR RACES. Three Year Olds, 120 lbs.; Older, 122 lbs. Non-winners of two races since April 11 Allowed 2 lbs. A race since then Allowed 4 lbs. Claiming Price $4,000 (Ohio Registered Fo als Preferred). (Clear 79)

Value of Race: $7,300 Winner $4,380; second $1,460; third $730; fourth $365; fifth $219; sixth $146. Mutuel Pool $19,856 Pick 3 Pool $1,329 Exacta Pool $16,806 Superfecta Pool $9,985 Trifecta Pool $16,294

Last Raced	#	Horse	M/Eqt.	A/S	Wt	PP	St	¼	⅜	Str	Fin	Jockey	Cl'g Pr	Odds $1
22Apr07 ⁴TDN⁴	4	Star Maid	L	5M	118	3	5	5³	3hd	3¹	1¹	Urieta-Moran V	4000	3.60
09Dec06 ³MNR⁸	5	Our Last Dance	L	5M	114	4	3	3¹	4³	42½	2½	Barrera F	4000	10.00
22Apr07 ⁴TDN³	6	Maddy Bell	L	4F	120	5	2	2⁵	1hd	1¹	3³	Magrell J M	4000	2.70
15Apr07 ⁵TDN⁵	1	Gone for Canada	L	5M	118	1	4	4hd	5¹	5⁴	4¾	Sanguinetti A	4000	8.60
22Apr07 ⁴TDN⁵	7	Storm Believer	L b	6M	118	6	1	1hd	2⁴	2hd	55½	Martinez, Jr. L J	4000	1.10
17Nov06 ³TDN¹	2	Ohio Volunteer	L	5M	118	2	6	6	6	6	6	Byrne J	4000	11.40

OFF AT 4:25 Start Good. Won driving. Track Fast.

TIME :22⁴, :47, 1:00, 1:06³ (:22.86, :47.06, 1:00.06, 1:06.78)

$2 Mutuel Prices:				
	4- STAR MAID	9.20	5.60	2.80
	5- OUR LAST DANCE		11.20	5.60
	6- MADDY BELL			2.40

$2 EXACTA 4-5 PAID $70.80 $1 SUPERFECTA 4-5-6-1 PAID $279.30

$2 TRIFECTA 4-5-6 PAID $212.20

Chestnut Mare, (Mar), by Diamond - Karle a Star by Star de Naskra. Trainer Morales Nabu. Bred by Redmond C. S. Finney(MD).

STAR MAID allowed to settle, rallied at the top of the stretch while three wide, and was up late, driving. OUR LAST DANCE never far back, rallied through the stretch on the rail, and was up for second. MADDY BELL dueled for the lead until the top of the stretch, shook clear in mid stretch then, faltered slightly in late stretch. GONE FOR CANADA never far back, saved ground but was not a threat. STORM BELIEVER dueled for the lead until the quarter pole, then faltered in the stretch. OHIO VOLUNTEER showed little and trailed.

Owners- 4, Coll Miguel ; 5, Diamond Wood Stable ; 6, Thornton Thomas L.; 1, Ketring Brenda ; 7, Faulkner Josh ; 2, Stearns Daniel C.

Trainers- 4, Morales Nabu ; 5, Shuman Joseph P.; 6, Thornton Nancy ; 1, Ketring Brenda ; 7, Faulkner Joe C.; 2, Cucinotta Anthony

Breeders- 4, Redmond C. S. Finney (MD); 5, Diamond Wood Stable (OH); 6, Fares Farm, Inc. (KY); 1, Gary Philip Jaeckel (ON); 7, Colebrook Farms (ON); 2, Daniel C. Stearns DVM (OH)

Scratched- Zippy Ziter(29Apr07 ⁷Tdn¹⁰)

$2 Pick Three (7-6-4) Paid $412.00; Pick Three Pool $1,329.

THIRTEENTH RACE **6 FURLONGS. (1.08^{2}) MAIDEN SPECIAL WEIGHT. Purse $13,500 (Includes $2,500 OTF - Ohio Thoroughbred Fund) FOR REGISTERED OHIO FOALS MAIDENS. THREE YEAR OLDS AND UPWARD. Three Year Olds, 120 lbs.; Older, 122 lbs. (Clear 79)**

Thistledown

May 11th, 2007

Value of Race: $13,500 Winner $8,100; second $2,700; third $1,350; fourth $675; fifth $270; sixth $135; seventh $135; eighth $135. Mutuel Pool $21,565 Pick 3 Pool $1,391 Exacta Pool $18,343 Superfecta Pool $11,593 Trifecta Pool $16,720

Last Raced	#	Horse	M/Eqt.	A/S	Wt	PP	St	¼	½	Str	Fin	Jockey	Odds $1
19Apr07 ^{1}TDN^{2}	4	Big Shot in Town	L b	5G	122	3	7	4^{1}	1^{hd}	1^{1}	1^{1}	Gonzalez L A	2.30
28Apr07 ^{6}TDN^{4}	5	Auburn Boy	L bf	4G	122	4	4	5^{hd}	$4^{1\frac{1}{2}}$	3^{2}	2^{nk}	Meyers T	17.70
28Apr07 ^{6}TDN^{2}	8	Kinkcachu	L	4G	122	7	2	2^{hd}	2^{1}	$2^{1\frac{1}{2}}$	3^{3}	Oro E	2.50
19Apr07 ^{5}TDN^{5}	3	Ready to Fight	L b	3G	118	1	6	6^{2}	6^{3}	$5^{2\frac{1}{2}}$	$4^{3\frac{1}{4}}$	Hernandez L	4.80
	6	Explicit Jet	L	3G	120	5	1	$1^{\frac{1}{2}}$	$3^{\frac{1}{2}}$	$4^{1\frac{1}{2}}$	5^{5}	Cloninger, Jr. W T	2.30
21Apr07 ^{7}TDN^{5}	1	Shane the Man	L b	3C	120	2	3	$3^{1\frac{1}{2}}$	$5^{\frac{1}{2}}$	6^{5}	6^{7}	Urieta-Moran V	a - 13.60
	7	Remember Jim	f	3C	120	6	8	8	$7^{\frac{1}{2}}$	$7^{1\frac{1}{2}}$	$7^{4\frac{1}{4}}$	Mailhot P	23.10
21Apr07 ^{7}TDN^{5}	1A	Double Cross	b	3C	120	8	5	$7^{\frac{1}{2}}$	8	8	8	Skerrett J	a - 13.60

a - Coupled: Shane the Man and Double Cross

OFF AT 5:07 Start Good. Won driving. Track Fast.

TIME :22^{4}, :46^{4}, :59^{4}, 1:13^{2} (:22.80, :46.96, :59.98, 1:13.56)

$2 Mutuel Prices:

4- BIG SHOT IN TOWN	**6.60**	**4.00**	**2.40**
5- AUBURN BOY		**16.00**	**4.80**
8- KINKCACHU			**2.20**

$2 EXACTA 4-5 PAID $88.40 $1 SUPERFECTA 4-5-8-3 PAID $322.00

$2 TRIFECTA 4-5-8 PAID $261.60

Chestnut Gelding, (Mar), by Saratoga Six - Castle Quick by Fit to Fight. Trainer Schuster Robin. Bred by Dominic Giglio Jr.(OH).

BIG SHOT IN TOWN well placed early, rallied at the quarter pole while three wide, and prevailed late, driving. AUBURN BOY never far back, rallied in mid stretch and was up for second. KINKCACHU pressed the pace and dueled for the lead, weakened only slightly in late stretch. READY TO FIGHT never far back, put in an even effort. EXPLICIT JET had good early speed, then tired. SHANE THE MAN chased until the top of the stretch, then tired. REMEMBER JIM was no factor. DOUBLE CROSS was outrun.

Owners- 4, Cooper Dianne M.; 5, Hurley Mary L.; 8, Mark Yagour, Inc. ; 3, Pyrite Stables ; 6, Tait Jean ; 1, Blazing Meadows Farm LLC ; 7, Foor Donna ; 1A, Ryan, Bruce and Blazing Meadows Farm

Trainers- 4, Schuster Robin ; 5, Hurley Mary L.; 8, Schuster Robin ; 3, Feliciano Miguel A.; 6, Crumley Jevon ; 1, Hamm Timothy E.; 7, White Alan D.; 1A, Hamm Timothy E.

Breeders- 4, Dominic Giglio Jr. (OH); 5, Mary Hurley (OH); 8, Hedy Hammon (OH); 3, Dr. D. W. Frazier (OH); 6, Jean M. Tait (OH); 1, Destiny Farm LLC (OH); 7, Donna Foor (OH); 1A, Bruce Ryan (OH)

Scratched- Lucky He's Perfect

$2 Pick Three (4-3-4/2) Paid $102.60; Pick Three Pool $1,391.

Thistledown Attendance: Unavailable Mutuel Pool: $0.00

SECOND RACE
River Downs
May 11th, 2007

6 FURLONGS. (1.08^{3}) CLAIMING. Purse $6,800 (Includes $800 OTF - Ohio Thoroughbred Fund) FOR REGISTERED OHIO BRED FILLIES AND MARES THREE YEARS OLD AND UPWARD WHICH HAVE NEVER WON TWO RACES. Three Year Olds, 116 lbs.; Older, 124 lbs. Non-winners of a race since April 11 Allowed 2 lbs. A race since March 11 Allowed 4 lbs. Claiming Price $5,00 0. (Clear 80)

Value of Race: $6,800 Winner $4,080; second $1,360; third $680; fourth $340; fifth $204; sixth $136. Mutuel Pool $25,848 Daily Double Pool $6,964 Exacta Pool $22,021 Superfecta Pool $13,131 Trifecta Pool $19,455

Last Raced	#	Horse	M/Eqt.	A/S	Wt	PP	St	¼	½	Str	Fin	Jockey	Cl'g Pr	Odds $1
26Nov06 ^{4}TP ^{7}	5	Slybecca	L	4F	120	5	2	2^{hd}	2^{1}	$2^{1/2}$	$1^{1\,1/2}$	Felix J E	5000	1.20
16Apr07 ^{8}BEU^{3}	6	French Babe	b	6M	122	6	4	$3^{1\,1/2}$	1^{hd}	1^{2}	$2^{3\,1/4}$	Rojas C	5000	7.80
04May07 ^{1}RD ^{1}	3	Chestnut Anna		6M	124	3	3	1^{hd}	$3^{1/2}$	$4^{1\,1/2}$	3^{hd}	Endres J	5000	19.90
28Apr07 ^{11}RD ^{7}	4	Morning Moon	L b	4F	120	4	1	4^{2}	$4^{1\,1/2}$	3^{1}	4^{2}	Calo J L	5000	6.30
21Apr07 ^{2}BEU^{2}	2	Julie's Rib	L b	6M	120	2	5	5^{5}	6	5^{1}	$5^{5\,1/4}$	Ouzts P W	5000	1.40
24Mar07 ^{4}BEU^{1}	1	Careful Carol	b	3F	114	1	6	6	$5^{1/2}$	6	6	Adam M G	5000	11.40

OFF AT 1:31 Start Good For All But JULIE'S RIB. Won driving. Track Fast.
TIME :23^{2}, :47^{4}, 1:01, 1:16^{3} (:23.40, :47.80, 1:01.00, 1:16.60)

$2 Mutuel Prices:

5- SLYBECCA	4.40	2.80	2.80
6- FRENCH BABE		5.20	4.20
3- CHESTNUT ANNA			4.80

$2 EXACTA 5-6 PAID $30.40 $2 SUPERFECTA 5-6-3-4 PAID $798.00
$2 TRIFECTA 5-6-3 PAID $239.20

Dark Bay or Brown Filly, (Apr), by Flight Forty Nine - Sly Spitfire by Pleasant Tap. Trainer Moore T. Dennis. Bred by Dick Alderson(OH).

SLYBECCA dueled for the lead and pressed the pace from the outside,, rallied into the stretch on the inside, drew clear late under heavy pressure. FRENCH BABE pressed the pace and dueled for the lead from the outside, was six wide on the turn and lost ground, drew clear in upper stretch, weakened and ran evenly late. CHESTNUT ANNA dueled for the lead and set the pace from the inside, faltered in the stretch and faded. MORNING MOON was well placed on the outside early, rallied into the stretch, failed to sustain the bid and dropped back. JULIE'S RIB bobbled at the start, was never a factor. CAREFUL CAROL was no factor while six wide and lost ground.

Owners- 5, Alderson Richard L.; 6, Richards Stanley ; 3, Verderber Greg ; 4, Hoover Greg ; 2, Thomas Mary Ann; 1, M. Y. Stables, Inc.

Trainers- 5, Moore Dennis T.; 6, Richards Stanley ; 3, Verderber Greg ; 4, Hoover Greg ; 2, Thomas Mary Ann; 1, Nance Michael W.

Breeders- 5, Dick Alderson (OH); 6, Daniel C. Stearns DVM. (OH); 3, Dr. Greg R. Verderber (OH); 4, Pine Ridge Farm (OH); 2, Win Row Farm, Ltd. & Ronald F. Bates (OH); 1, South River Ranch Inc. (OH)

$2 Daily Double (8-5) Paid $25.00; Daily Double Pool $6,964.

FOURTH RACE
River Downs
May 11th, 2007

5½ FURLONGS. (1.03) STARTER ALLOWANCE. Purse $8,300 FOR THREE YEAR OLDS AND UPWARD WHICH HAVE STARTED FOR A CLAIMING PRICE OF $5,000 OR LESS IN 2006-2007. Three Year Olds, 116 lbs.; Older, 124 lbs. Non-winners Of A Race Since April 11 Allowed 2 lbs. A Race Since March 11 Allowed 4 lbs. (Races Where Entered For $4,000 Or Less Not Considered In Allowances). (Clear 80)

Value of Race: $8,300 Winner $4,980; second $1,660; third $830; fourth $415; fifth $249; sixth $83; seventh $83. Mutuel Pool $27,087 Pick 3 Pool $3,226 Exacta Pool $24,056 Superfecta Pool $15,177 Trifecta Pool $21,656

Last Raced	#	Horse	M/Eqt.	A/S	Wt	PP	St	¼	⅜	Str	Fin	Jockey	Odds $1
27Oct06 ^{10}BEU^{4}	7	City Rapid	L	8H	120	6	1	2^{5}	2^{3}	1^{hd}	$1^{3/4}$	Rosario, Jr. H L	4.80
28Apr07 ^{9}RD ^{1}	8	Swissle Stick	L bf	5H	124	7	2	$1^{1/2}$	1^{2}	2^{5}	$2^{5\,1/4}$	Prescott R A	1.90
27Apr07 ^{8}IND^{2}	2	Steelyeyed	L b	7G	120	1	5	6^{6}	5^{2}	5^{4}	$3^{1/2}$	Felix J E	2.30
26Apr07 ^{5}RD ^{1}	3	Warner Jazz Man	L b	7G	124	2	3	3^{1}	4^{3}	3^{1}	$4^{4\,3/4}$	Bush V	15.50
22Apr07 ^{1}KEE^{3}	5	Step to the Music	L bf	4G	122	4	6	$4^{1\,1/2}$	3^{1}	4^{1}	5^{2}	Ouzts P W	2.80
27Apr07 ^{8}RD ^{1}	4	Choice Union	L	6H	120	3	7	7	7	7	$6^{1/2}$	Sarvis D A	26.20
26Apr07 ^{11}RD ^{3}	6	Look At This Cat	L bf	4C	120	5	4	5^{hd}	6^{4}	6^{2}	7	Solomon N	17.20

OFF AT 2:08 Start Good. Won driving. Track Fast.
TIME :22^{4}, :46, :59^{2}, 1:07 (:22.80, :46.00, :59.40, 1:07.00)

$2 Mutuel Prices:

7- CITY RAPID	11.60	5.00	3.20
8- SWISSLE STICK		4.20	2.60
2- STEELYEYED			2.60

$2 EXACTA 7-8 PAID $34.40 $2 SUPERFECTA 7-8-2-3 PAID $573.40
$2 TRIFECTA 7-8-2 PAID $99.60

Chestnut Horse, (Apr), by Carson City - Zili by Zilzal. Trainer Lawson Charles. Bred by Cranford Stud(KY).

CITY RAPID pressed the pace early from the inside, was allowed to settle on the turn, came again after being angled out on the turn, was fully extended to hold the margin late. SWISSLE STICK set the pace while off the rail, drew clear on the turn and was taken to the inside, could not go with the winner and ran evenly late. STEELYEYED was void of early speed, improved position in the stretch but was no threat. WARNER JAZZ MAN was in a good stalking position on the inside, ran evenly and had no rally. STEP TO THE MUSIC was well placed in mid pack, had no rally. CHOICE UNION was no factor. LOOK AT THIS CAT failed to menace.

Owners- 7, Lawson Charles ; 8, Nash Robert D.; 2, McGee Rebecca K.; 3, Davis Boys Stable ; 5, Tilley Jennifer B.; 4, Boone, Hilary J. and Nugent, Thomas E. ; 6, Womack Hulon L.

Trainers- 7, Lawson Charles ; 8, Flint Bernard S.; 2, McGee Rebecca K.; 3, Davis Melvin E.; 5, Murphy Carolyn S.; 4, Nugent Thomas E.; 6, Womack Hulon Leslie

Breeders- 7, Cranford Stud (KY); 8, Mary H. Caldwell (CA); 2, Liberation Farm & Oratis Thoroughbreds (KY); 3, Charles M. Massey (KY); 5, Kenneth L Ramsey & Sarah K Ramsey (KY); 4, John Franks (FL); 6, Jeffrey L. Whitesell (OH)

Scratched- Rarify(22Apr07 ^{1}Kee^{8})

$2 Pick Three (5-6-7) Paid $104.00; Pick Three Pool $3,226.

SIXTH RACE
River Downs
May 11th, 2007

1 MILE. (1.36^{1}) CLAIMING. Purse $5,200 FOR THREE YEAR OLDS AND UPWARD WHICH HAVE NOT WON TWO RACES IN 2006-2007. Three Year Olds, 116 lbs.; Older, 124 lbs. Non-winners of a race since April 11 Allowed 2 lbs. A race since March 11 Allowed 4 lbs. Claiming Price $4,000 (Ohio Registered Foals Pref erred). (Clear 80)

Value of Race: $5,200 Winner $3,120; second $1,040; third $520; fourth $260; fifth $104; sixth $52; seventh $52; eighth $52. Mutuel Pool $41,793 Pick 3 Pool $2,030 Exacta Pool $38,423 Superfecta Pool $22,401 Trifecta Pool $24,656

Last Raced	#	Horse	M/Eqt.	A/S	Wt	PP	St	¼	½	¾	Str	Fin	Jockey	Cl'g Pr	Odds $1
29Apr07 ^{2}RD ^{5}	4	Divine Dancer	L b	6G	120	4	3	4$\frac{1}{2}$	4hd	2^{1}	1hd	1^{4}	Ouzts P W	4000	10.50
21Apr07 ^{3}RD ^{5}	2	Accordian Man	L b	6G	120	2	2	2^{6}	2^{10}	1^{3}	2^{4}	2^{2}	Vidal F A	4000	3.90
28Apr07 ^{1}RD ^{1}	3	Shoo Brush	L bf	7G	124	3	7	6^{1}	6^{3}	6^{5}	3^{1}	3$^{1\frac{1}{2}}$	Bush V	4000	2.60
24Apr07 ^{1}RD ^{2}	6	Ship's Captain	L bl	6G	120	6	6	7$^{2\frac{1}{2}}$	7^{3}	7^{3}	5$\frac{1}{2}$	4^{1}	Solomon N	4000	2.00
23Apr07 ^{1}BEU^{3}	1	Arctic Sand	L b	8G	120	1	1	3$^{2\frac{1}{2}}$	3^{1}	4$^{2\frac{1}{2}}$	4^{6}	5$^{4\frac{3}{4}}$	Calo J L	4000	6.60
21Apr07 ^{6}RD ^{3}	7	Proud Memories	L f	7G	120	7	5	5^{2}	5^{3}	5hd	6^{10}	6$^{10\frac{1}{4}}$	Laurente G	4000	8.20
25Feb07 ^{10}TP ^{7}	5	Gottagetherefirst	L b	6G	120	5	8	8	8	8	7^{3}	7^{15}	Sunseri J J	4000	13.40
28Mar07 ^{8}BEU^{7}	8	Inti Raymi	L f	9G	120	8	4	1hd	1hd	3$^{1\frac{1}{2}}$	8	8	Chavez C R	4000	36.80

OFF AT 2:48 Start Good. Won driving. Track Fast.
TIME :24, :48^{4}, 1:14^{3}, 1:29^{2}, 1:44^{2} (:24.00, :48.80, 1:14.60, 1:29.40, 1:44.40)

$2 Mutuel Prices:				
	4- DIVINE DANCER	23.00	10.00	3.80
	2- ACCORDIAN MAN		5.80	3.60
	3- SHOO BRUSH			3.00

$2 EXACTA 4-2 PAID $160.40 $2 SUPERFECTA 4-2-3-6 PAID $1,509.60
$2 TRIFECTA 4-2-3 PAID $714.40

Chestnut Gelding, (May), by Dance Brightly - Royal Doris by Corporate Report. Trainer Zehnder D. Charles. Bred by David Neiman(KY).

DIVINE DANCER was in a good stalking position on the inside in mid pack, rallied on the far turn and dueled for the lead in upper stretch, drew off under firm handling. ACCORDIAN MAN pressed the pace and dueled for the lead on the inside, drew off on the second turn, could not go with the winner but was second best. SHOO BRUSH was void of early speed, rallied into the stretch and loomed boldly, flattened out and ran evenly late. SHIP'S CAPTAIN was void of early speed while six and seven wide and lost ground, improved position but was not a factor. ARCTIC SAND was well placed on the inside, had no rally. PROUD MEMORIES was in a good stalking position in mid pack, had no rally. GOTTAGETHEREFIRST failed to menace. INTI RAYMI dueled for the lead and set the pace from the outside, faltered in the stretch and faded.

Owners- 4, Zehnder Debbie A.; 2, Kobman Randy ; 3, C and C Racing Stable ; 6, Elkins Robert A.; 1, Eyerman Lee J.; 7, Fairwinds LLC ; 5, Special K Stables ; 8, Munoz Rudy I.

Trainers- 4, Zehnder Charles D.; 2, Crawford Bert ; 3, Crawford Bert ; 6, MacDonald Colleen ; 1, Eyerman Lee J.; 7, Smith Pam L.; 5, Kellar Richard M.; 8, Drinkard Skip L.

Breeders- 4, David Neiman (KY); 2, Richard Lake (KY); 3, Marylou Whitney Stables (KY); 6, Roy Gottlieb (KY); 1, Runnymede Farm Inc. (KY); 7, Betsy R. Kuster & Woodford R.Baumgardner (KY); 5, James E. English (KY); 8, H. B. Robeson & Luz Robeson (TX)

$2 Pick Three (7-7-4) Paid $1,048.80; Pick Three Pool $2,030.

EIGHTH RACE
River Downs
May 11th, 2007

6 FURLONGS. (1.08^{3}) CLAIMING. Purse $5,200 FOR THREE YEAR OLDS AND UPWARD WHICH HAVE NOT WON THREE RACES IN 2006-2007 OR WHICH HAVE NEVER WON FOUR RACES. Three Year Olds, 116 lbs.; Older, 124 lbs. Non-winners of a race since April 11 Allowed 2 lbs. A race since March 11 Allowed 4 lbs. Claiming Pri ce $4,000 (Ohio Registered Foals Preferred). (Clear 80)

Value of Race: $5,200 Winner $3,120; second $1,040; third $520; fourth $260; fifth $52; sixt $52; seventh $52; eighth $52; ninth $52. Mutuel Pool $32,559 Pick 3 Pool $1,880 Exacta Pool $29,544 Superfecta Pool $16,140 Trifecta Pool $24,305

Last Raced	#	Horse	M/Eqt.	A/S	Wt	PP	St	¼	½	Str	Fin	Jockey	Cl'g Pr	Odds $1
19Apr07 ^{10}RD ^{5}	2	C C Ryder	L b	5G	120	1	6	3hd	2$^{2\frac{1}{2}}$	1^{2}	1$^{7\frac{1}{2}}$	Rosario, Jr. H L	4000	3.10
28Apr07 ^{7}BEU^{5}	6	Mighty Wind	L	12G	120	6	1	2^{3}	1$^{2\frac{1}{2}}$	2^{5}	2$^{2\frac{1}{2}}$	Ouzts P W	4000	13.10
24Apr07 ^{2}RD ^{4}	4	Gridwin	L b	3C	114	3	2	4$\frac{1}{2}$	5^{1}	3$^{2\frac{1}{2}}$	3nk	Solomon N	4000	5.10
12Jan07 ^{8}BEU^{8}	9	Elusive Indian	L b	7G	120	8	9	9	9	6^{1}	4$^{3\frac{1}{4}}$	De Leon A	4000	8.80
30Apr07 ^{3}BEU^{1}	5	Hastego	L bf	6G	124	4	7	6hd	6hd	5^{1}	5$^{1\frac{1}{4}}$	Prescott R A	4000	4.60
14Apr07 ^{13}BEU^{5}	10	Calm Waters	L bf	9G	122	9	5	5^{1}	4hd	4^{1}	6$^{1\frac{1}{2}}$	Vitek J J	4000	6.60
20Apr07 ^{7}RD ^{2}	3	Good Humor Man	L f	7G	120	2	8	8$^{2\frac{1}{2}}$	7$\frac{1}{2}$	7$\frac{1}{2}$	7^{8}	Diego I	4000	2.50
27Apr07 ^{8}RD ^{7}	8	A Rizzi Rueben	L b	6H	120	7	4	7hd	8^{1}	8^{3}	8$^{2\frac{1}{2}}$	Calo J L	4000	67.30
	1A	Power Fame (ARG)	L b	5H	122	5	3	1$\frac{1}{2}$	3^{1}	9	9	Endres J	4000	24.70

OFF AT 3:27 Start Good. Won driving. Track Fast.
TIME :22^{3}, :46^{3}, 1:00, 1:15 (:22.60, :46.60, 1:00.00, 1:15.00)

$2 Mutuel Prices:				
	2- C C RYDER	8.20	4.80	4.60
	6- MIGHTY WIND		11.40	4.60
	4- GRIDWIN			4.20

$2 EXACTA 2-6 PAID $91.00 $2 SUPERFECTA 2-6-4-9 PAID $2,523.60
$2 TRIFECTA 2-6-4 PAID $508.80

Dark Bay or Brown Gelding, (May), by American Chance - Rajas Secret by Storm Bird. Trainer Vallance Paul. Bred by John D. Gunther(KY).

C C RYDER stalked the pace while never far back, was angled out on the turn and rallied into the stretch, drew off under heavy pressure. MIGHTY WIND pressed the pace and dueled for the lead, drew clear on the turn, could not go with the winner but was second best. GRIDWIN was well placed in mid pack, had no rally. ELUSIVE INDIAN was void of early speed, improved position in the stretch but was no threat. HASTEGO was in a good stalking position in mid pack, had no rally. CALM WATERS was well placed in mid pack on the outside, weakened and dropped back. GOOD HUMOR MAN failed to menace. A RIZZI RUEBEN was no threat. POWER FAME (ARG) set the pace while saving ground, faltered in the stretch and faded.

Owners- 2, Lawrence Colleen ; 6, Crawford Bert ; 4, Byer Larry A.; 9, Lawson Charles ; 5, Yaegel James F.; 10, Childress, Robert and Everett, Kelly ; 3, Brainer Donna ; 8, El Coqui Racing Stable ; 1A, My Way Stable

Trainers- 2, Vallance Paul ; 6, Crawford Bert ; 4, Vazquez Ivan ; 9, Lawson Charles ; 5, Yaegel Thomas ; 10, Ratcliffe William H.; 3, Orm Jerry ; 8, Sostre Israel ; 1A, Nocero Rinzy

Breeders- 2, John D. Gunther (KY); 6, Jim H. Plemmons (KY); 4, Larry Byer (OH); 9, Ron Wallace & Dr. Stuart Brown (KY); 5, Hutchison Farm (MD); 10, Pin Oak Stud (KY); 3, Dixiana Farm Inc. (KY); 8, D J J Racing (FL); 1A, Esece (ARG)

Scratched- Not a Question(03May07 ^{14}RD^{10}), Tomprado(28Apr07 ^{6}Beu^{4})

$2 Pick Three (4-6/8-2) Paid $208.00; Pick Three Pool $1,880.

TENTH RACE
River Downs
May 11th, 2007

6 FURLONGS. (1.08^{3}) CLAIMING. Purse $7,000 (Includes $800 OTF - Ohio Thoroughbred Fund) FOR REGISTERED OHIO BRED THREE YEAR OLDS AND UPWARD. Three Year Olds, 116 lbs.; Older, 124 lbs. Non-winners of a race since April 11 Allowed 2 lbs. A race since March 11 Allowed 4 lbs. Claiming Price $4,000 (Races where entered for $3,500 or less not cons idered in allowances). (Clear 80)

Value of Race: $7,000 Winner $4,200; second $1,400; third $700; fourth $350; fifth $210; sixth $70; seventh $70. Mutuel Pool $26,041 Pick 3 Pool $1,589 Exacta Pool $25,361 Superfecta Pool $14,953 Trifecta Pool $22,943

Last Raced	#	Horse	M/Eqt.	A/S	Wt	PP	St	¼	½	Str	Fin	Jockey	Cl'g Pr	Odds $1
27Apr07 ^{2}RD ^{1}	6	Wazoo City	L f	4G	124	5	4	5^{3}	4^{hd}	1^{hd}	$1^{1\frac{3}{4}}$	Ouzts P W	4000	4.90
01May07 ^{5}RD ^{1}	7	Mr. Popeye	L b	8G	124	6	2	2^{hd}	$3^{\frac{1}{2}}$	$4^{2\frac{1}{2}}$	$2^{2\frac{3}{4}}$	Vidal F A	4000	4.30
22Apr07 ^{12}TDN^{6}	8	Unwavering Flight	L	6G	122	7	1	$3^{\frac{1}{2}}$	2^{1}	2^{hd}	$3^{\frac{1}{2}}$	Prescott R A	4000	3.00
19Apr07 ^{10}RD ^{3}	3	Dance With a Fool	L	10G	120	2	5	$4^{\frac{1}{2}}$	5^{4}	5^{3}	$4^{\frac{3}{4}}$	Solomon N	4000	3.80
01May07 ^{7}RD ^{1}	2	J. R.'s Town	L b	10G	124	1	7	6^{3}	6^{5}	6^{6}	$5^{1\frac{1}{4}}$	Calo J L	4000	3.10
19Apr07 ^{10}RD ^{4}	4	A Knew Beginning	L bf	4G	120	3	3	1^{hd}	1^{hd}	3^{hd}	6^{11}	Sarvis D A	4000	7.00
17Apr07 ^{3}RD ^{7}	5	Nuts and Wire	L b	4G	120	4	6	7	7	7	7	Rojas C	4000	22.30

OFF AT 4:06 Start Good For All But UNWAVERING FLIGHT. Won driving. Track Fast.
TIME :23^{1}, :46^{2}, 1:00, 1:14^{2} (:23.20, :46.40, 1:00.00, 1:14.40)

$2 Mutuel Prices:				
	6- WAZOO CITY	11.80	6.20	3.00
	7- MR. POPEYE		5.60	2.80
	8- UNWAVERING FLIGHT			3.40

$2 EXACTA 6-7 PAID $57.20 $2 SUPERFECTA 6-7-8-3 PAID $753.40
$2 TRIFECTA 6-7-8 PAID $166.00

Dark Bay or Brown Gelding, (May), by Slew City Slew - Kay's Colonizer by Roanoke. Trainer Connelly R. William. Bred by Ed Dalby, Tom Lenihan & Ray Weis(OH).

WAZOO CITY stalked the pace while never far back, rallied into the stretch, dueled briefly and drew clear under constant pressure. MR. POPEYE bobbled at the start, was rushed up and dueled for the lead, ran evenly late and had no late closing response. UNWAVERING FLIGHT pressed the pace and dueled for the lead from the outside, weakened in the stretch and began to fade. DANCE WITH A FOOL was in a good stalking position in mid pack, ran evenly and had no rally. J. R.'S TOWN was void of early speed, was seven wide on the turn and lost ground, had no rally. A KNEW BEGINNING dueled for the lead and set the pace, faltered in the stretch and faded. NUTS AND WIRE failed to menace.

Owners- 6, Brockman, H. and C., Lenihan, T., Kerr, R. and Schaeffer, B. ; 7, Alderson Richard L.; 8, Yaegel James F.; 3, Lamb Jodie L.; 2, Bragg Patricia A.; 4, C I Stables ; 5, Winter Michelle L.

Trainers- 6, Connelly William R.; 7, Moore Dennis T.; 8, Yaegel Thomas ; 3, Lamb Jodie L.; 2, Bragg Patricia A.; 4, Grace Lori ; 5, Houston Wayne

Breeders- 6, Ed Dalby, Tom Lenihan & Ray Weis (OH); 7, Leonard W. Cavens (OH); 8, Joseph A Borg (OH); 3, Touch of Heaven Farm (OH); 2, George A. Zimmerman (OH); 4, Martha Parsons (OH); 5, Ziba F Graham (OH)

Scratched- Bri's Bad Boy(28Apr07 ^{6}Beu^{1})

$2 Pick Three (2-7-6) Paid $615.60; Pick Three Pool $1,589.

TWELVETH RACE
River Downs
May 11th, 2007

6 FURLONGS. (1.08^{3}) ALLOWANCE. Purse $13,600 (Includes $3,000 OTF - Ohio Thoroughbred Fund) FOR ACCREDITED OHIO BRED FILLIES AND MARES THREE YEARS OLD AND UPWARD WHICH HAVE NEVER WON TWO RACES. Three Year Olds, 116 lbs.; Older, 124 lbs. Non-winners of a race since April 11 Allowed 2 lbs. A race since March 11 Allowed 4 lbs. (Races whereentered for $15,000 or less not considered in allowances). (Clear 80)

Value of Race: $13,600 Winner $8,160; second $2,720; third $1,360; fourth $680; fifth $272; sixth $136; seventh $136; eighth $136. Mutuel Pool $22,889 Pick 3 Pool $1,283 Exacta Pool $27,544 Superfecta Pool $18,869 Trifecta Pool $25,261

Last Raced	#	Horse	M/Eqt.	A/S	Wt	PP	St	¼	½	Str	Fin	Jockey	Odds $1
28Apr07 ^{11}RD ^{2}	3	Motormouth Sue	L b	4F	120	3	5	$2^{\frac{1}{2}}$	1^{1}	1^{4}	$1^{6\frac{1}{4}}$	Vitek J J	0.60
28Apr07 ^{11}RD ^{8}	5	Bucks in the Woods	L	4F	120	5	6	$7^{2\frac{1}{2}}$	$7^{2\frac{1}{2}}$	2^{hd}	2^{1}	De Leon A	34.80
28Apr07 ^{8}BEU^{3}	2	Flirtini	L b	3F	112	2	2	1^{1}	$2^{1\frac{1}{2}}$	$3^{2\frac{1}{2}}$	3^{3}	Ouzts P W	6.70
22Aug06 ^{7}RD ^{6}	7	Classy Forest	L f	5M	120	7	7	5^{1}	3^{hd}	5^{2}	$4^{\frac{1}{2}}$	Calo J L	11.80
28Apr07 ^{11}RD ^{5}	1	Gonnagetchagood	L b	5M	120	1	3	$4^{\frac{1}{2}}$	4^{1}	4^{hd}	$5^{2\frac{1}{2}}$	Rosario, Jr. H L	32.40
28Apr07 ^{11}RD ^{3}	4	Tombeur de Femmes		4F	120	4	8	8	8	$6^{2\frac{1}{2}}$	$6^{5\frac{3}{4}}$	Rojas C	7.90
28Apr07 ^{11}RD ^{4}	8	Rachel in Transit	L b	4F	120	8	1	$3^{\frac{1}{2}}$	5^{2}	7^{3}	$7^{19\frac{1}{4}}$	Sarvis D A	4.80
20Dec06 ^{10}BEU^{1}	6	Mercy Honey	L	4F	120	6	4	6^{3}	$6^{\frac{1}{2}}$	8	8	Bush V	16.70

OFF AT 4:46 Start Good For All But MOTORMOUTH SUE. Won driving. Track Fast.
TIME :23^{1}, :47^{1}, 1:00^{3}, 1:15^{3} (:23.20, :47.20, 1:00.60, 1:15.60)

$2 Mutuel Prices:				
	3- MOTORMOUTH SUE	3.20	2.60	2.10
	5- BUCKS IN THE WOODS		18.20	15.60
	2- FLIRTINI			2.80

$2 EXACTA 3-5 PAID $73.60 $2 SUPERFECTA 3-5-2-7 PAID $1,435.00
$2 TRIFECTA 3-5-2 PAID $343.40

Chestnut Filly, (Apr), by Mahogany Hall - R M Peggy Lulu by Houston. Trainer Nance W. Michael. Bred by South River Ranch Inc.(OH).

MOTORMOUTH SUE bobbled at the start, stalked the pace while never far back, rallied on the turn and drew clear, drew off through the stretch under heavy pressure. BUCKS IN THE WOODS was void of early speed, rallied into the stretch, ran evenly late and was second best. FLIRTINI set the pace while saving ground, weakened on the turn and faded in the drive. CLASSY FOREST lunged at the start, stalked the pace while seven wide and lost ground, rallied on the turn and loomed boldly, flattened out in the stretch and dropped back. GONNAGETCHAGOOD was in a good stalking position on the inside, had no rally. TOMBEUR DE FEMMES failed to menace. RACHEL IN TRANSIT flashed brief speed before stopping and dropping back. MERCY HONEY was no threat, bled.

Owners- 3, M. Y. Stables, Inc. ; 5, Zimmerman George A.; 2, Napier Sherry ; 7, Keyes Joseph S.; 1, Wells Monica A.; 4, Stewart Gene N.; 8, Acres Harold ; 6, York Anna

Trainers- 3, Nance Michael W.; 5, Acres Harold ; 2, Napier William J.; 7, Keyes Joseph S.; 1, Wells Darrell ; 4, Stewart Gene N.; 8, Acres Harold ; 6, York Michael

Breeders- 3, South River Ranch Inc. (OH); 5, George A. Zimmerman (OH); 2, Fair Winds Farm (OH); 7, G. A. Smith, Austin Smith &Dr. W. E. Johnston (OH); 1, T. L. Shaffer (OH); 4, Gene N. Stewart (OH); 8, Syble M. Acres & Rachel Cox (OH); 6, Fair Winds Farm (OH)

$2 Pick Three (6-4-3) Paid $331.40; Pick Three Pool $1,283.

FOURTEENTH RACE 1 MILE. (1.36[1]) MAIDEN CLAIMING. Purse $5,200 FOR MAIDENS, THREE YEAR OLDS AND UPWARD. Three Year Olds, 116 lbs.; Older, 124 lbs. Claiming Price $5,000 (Ohio Registered Foals Preferred). (Clear 80)

River Downs

May 11th, 2007

Value of Race: $5,200 Winner $3,120; second $1,040; third $520; fourth $208; fifth $52; sixth $52; seventh $52; eighth $52; ninth $52; tenth $52. Mutuel Pool $37,398 Pick 3 Pool $2,738 Pick 4 Pool $2,221 Daily Double Pool $4,156 Exacta Pool $39,441 Superfecta Pool $24,569 Trifecta Pool $33,380

Last Raced	#	Horse	M/Eqt.	A/S	Wt	PP	St	¼	½	¾	Str	Fin	Jockey	Cl'g Pr	Odds $1
27Apr07 ^{14}RD ^{4}	10	Laterornever	L b	3G	116	10	7	$3^{2\frac{1}{2}}$	3^{3}	2^{7}	2^{10}	1^{1}	Sarvis D A	5000	1.00
14Apr07 ^{2}RD ^{5}	4	Northern Alliance	L b	4G	124	4	2	2^{7}	1^{3}	1^{5}	$1^{2\frac{1}{2}}$	$2^{12\frac{1}{2}}$	Ouzts P W	5000	2.90
06Jan07 ^{1}TP ^{5}	6	Helio Wave	b	6G	124	6	8	4^{hd}	4^{1}	$3^{\frac{1}{2}}$	3^{1}	3^{2}	Castaneda B	5000	15.70
04May07 ^{13}RD ^{5}	9	Grand Sand	L b	4G	124	9	9	10	$9^{\frac{1}{2}}$	10	$5^{\frac{1}{2}}$	$4^{2\frac{1}{2}}$	Vitek J J	5000	8.90
13Apr07 ^{14}RD ^{9}	1	H D's Affair	L bf	3G	116	1	6	8^{hd}	$6^{\frac{1}{2}}$	$5^{\frac{1}{2}}$	4^{6}	$5^{4\frac{1}{2}}$	Hill R R	5000	10.00
16Mar07 ^{6}TP ^{6}	3	Seattle Pass	L	5G	124	3	4	5^{1}	5^{3}	6^{3}	6^{1}	6^{hd}	Tolentino P	5000	32.10
27Apr07 ^{14}RD ^{6}	2	Ky Ridge Runner	L b	5G	124	2	5	$7^{1\frac{1}{2}}$	10	9^{1}	7^{7}	$7^{13\frac{1}{4}}$	Solomon N	5000	53.00
27Apr07 ^{14}RD ^{5}	5	Cryptoless	L	4C	124	5	3	6^{3}	8^{5}	8^{2}	8^{5}	8	Sunseri J J	5000	50.20
29Apr07 ^{6}RD ^{7}	7	Fire Glenn	L b	3G	116	7	1	$1^{\frac{1}{2}}$	2^{5}	4^{1}	9^{10}	9	Calo J L	5000	8.60
04Apr07 ^{9}TP ^{11}	8	Vin's Buster	L b	3G	116	8	10	9^{4}	7^{hd}	7^{1}	10	10	Adam M G	5000	17.80

OFF AT 5:26 Start Good. Won driving. Track Fast.

TIME :24[2], :49[1], 1:15, 1:29, 1:44[3] (:24.40, :49.20, 1:15.00, 1:29.00, 1:44.60)

$2 Mutuel Prices:

10- LATERORNEVER	4.00	2.80	2.40
4- NORTHERN ALLIANCE		3.00	2.80
6- HELIO WAVE			5.80

$2 EXACTA 10-4 PAID $16.40 $2 SUPERFECTA 10-4-6-9 PAID $457.60

$2 TRIFECTA 10-4-6 PAID $98.00

Bay Gelding, (Mar), by Honour and Glory - Here and Now (FR) by Exit to Nowhere. Trainer Grace Lori. Bred by Fab Oak Stable(KY).

LATERORNEVER was well placed early on the outside, rallied on the far turn and into the stretch, drew clear late constant handling. NORTHERN ALLIANCE dueled for the lead and set the pace while saving ground, drew off on the far turn, gave way grudgingly and was second best. HELIO WAVE was steadied entering the first turn, was six wide throughout and lost ground, ran evenly and had no rally. GRAND SAND was void of early speed, had a mild rally late and some late gain. H D'S AFFAIR was unhurried early, rallied on the second turn and into the stretch, failed to sustain the bid and ran evenly late. SEATTLE PASS was steadied entering the first turn was in a good stalking position in mid pack, had no rally. KY RIDGE RUNNER was no factor. CRYPTOLESS failed to menace. FIRE GLENN set the pace and dueled for the lead, gave way and dropped back, was eased in the stretch. VIN'S BUSTER was no threat, was eased.

Owners- 10, C I Stables ; 4, Ripplewood Farm ; 6, Burns Harry D.; 9, Nugent Thomas E.; 1, Sano Park, LLC ; 3, Keith Carl ; 2, Biddle Jamie ; 5, Anglin L. D.; 7, Purtee Jani L.; 8, Glyshaw Timothy D.

Trainers- 10, Grace Lori ; 4, Jones, Sr. Herbert W.; 6, Burns Kenneth H.; 9, Nugent Thomas E.; 1, Burton Tim ; 3, Allen Billy D.; 2, Womack Hulon Leslie; 5, Anglin L. D.; 7, Asbury David W.; 8, Glyshaw Tim

Breeders- 10, Fab Oak Stable (KY); 4, Ripplewood Farm (KY); 6, Harry D. Burns (KY); 9, Darry D. Hayes (IN); 1, Harold Coyle (KY); 3, Sharon Sanders (KY); 2, Jerry F Straw & Michelle L Straw (KY); 5, Dr. James Wright (KY); 7, James T. Hines Jr. (KY); 8, Kenneth R. Gravett (KY)

$2 Daily Double (4-10) Paid $15.20; Daily Double Pool $4,156.
$2 Pick Three (3-4-10) Paid $23.80; Pick Three Pool $2,738.
$2 Pick Four (4-3-4-10) Paid $118.60; Pick Four Pool $2,221.

River Downs Attendance: Unavailable Mutuel Pool: $0.00

CPSIA information can be obtained at www.ICGtesting.com
Printed in the USA
BVOW001703100713

325562BV00003B/130/A